ANNUAL EDITIONS

Marketing

Twenty-Seventh Edition

05/06

W9-BNA-146

EDITOR

John E. Richardson

Pepperdine University

Dr. John E. Richardson is a professor of marketing in The George L. Graziadio School of Business and Management at Pepperdine University. He is president of his own consulting firm and has consulted with organizations such as Bell and Howell, Dayton-Hudson, Epson, and the U.S. Navy as well as with various service, nonprofit, and franchise organizations. Dr. Richardson is a member of the American Marketing Association, the American Management Association, the Society for Business Ethics, and the Beta Gamma Sigma honorary business fraternity.

McGraw-Hill/Dushkin

2460 Kerper Blvd., Dubuque, IA 52001

Visit us on the Internet
http://www.dushkin.com

Credits

1. **Marketing in the 2000s and Beyond**
   Unit photo—© Getty Images/Ryan McVay
2. **Research, Markets, and Consumer Behavior**
   Unit photo—© Getty Images/Duncan Smith
3. **Developing and Implementing Marketing Strategies**
   Unit photo—© Getty Images/Keith Brofsky
4. **Global Marketing**
   Unit photo—© Getty Images/PhotoLink/Annie Reynolds

Copyright

Cataloging in Publication Data
Main entry under title: Annual Editions: Marketing. 2005/2006.
1. Marketing—Periodicals. I. Richardson, John E., *comp*. II. Title: Marketing.
ISBN 0–07–310200–8   658'.05   ISSN 0730–2606

Twenty-Seventh Edition

Cover image © Corbis/Royalty Free
Printed in the United States of America   1234567890QPDQPD987654   Printed on Recycled Paper

Editors/Advisory Board

Members of the Advisory Board are instrumental in the final selection of articles for each edition of ANNUAL EDITIONS. Their review of articles for content, level, currentness, and appropriateness provides critical direction to the editor and staff. We think that you will find their careful consideration well reflected in this volume.

EDITOR

John E. Richardson
Pepperdine University

ADVISORY BOARD

John L. Beisel
Pittsburg State University

Joseph L. Bonnici
Central Connecticut State University

Steve W. Brown
Arizona State University

Carol Carnevalle
Empire State College

Howard W. Combs
San Jose State University

Steve Corbin
University of Northern Iowa

Sandra L. Lueder
Southern Connecticut State University

Steven J. Lysonski
Marquette University

Bart Macchiette
Plymouth State College

Gordon H. G. McDougall
Wilfrid Laurier University

D. Terry Paul
Ohio State University

David L. Ralph
Pepperdine University

Catherine Rich-Duval
Merrimack College

Brad Sago
Whitworth College

Andy Sernovitz
Wharton School of Business

Donald Shiner
Mount Saint Vincent University

Darlene B. Smith
Loyola College

Rajendra Srivastava
Emory University

Joseph R. Stasio
Merrimack College

Paul M. Wellen
Roosevelt University

Staff

Preface

In publishing ANNUAL EDITIONS we recognize the enormous role played by the magazines, newspapers, and journals of the public press in providing current, first-rate educational information in a broad spectrum of interest areas. Many of these articles are appropriate for students, researchers, and professionals seeking accurate, current material to help bridge the gap between principles and theories and the real world. These articles, however, become more useful for study when those of lasting value are carefully collected, organized, and reproduced in a low-cost format, which provides easy and permanent access when the material is needed. That is the role played by ANNUAL EDITIONS.

The new millennium should prove to be an exciting and challenging time for the American business community. Recent dramatic social, economic, and technological changes have become an important part of the present marketplace. These changes—accompanied by increasing domestic and foreign competition—are leading a wide array of companies and industries toward the realization that better marketing must become a top priority to assure their future success.

How does the marketing manager respond to this growing challenge? How does the marketing student apply marketing theory to the real world practice? Many reach for the *Wall Street Journal, Business Week, Fortune,* and other well-known sources of business information. There, specific industry and company strategies are discussed and analyzed, marketing principles are often reaffirmed by real occurrences, and textbook theories are supported or challenged by current events.

The articles reprinted in this edition of *Annual Editions: Marketing 05/06* have been carefully chosen from numerous different public press sources to provide current information on marketing in the world today. Within these pages you will find articles that address marketing theory and application in a wide range of industries. In addition, the selections reveal how several firms interpret and utilize marketing principles in their daily operations and corporate planning.

The volume contains a number of features designed to make it useful for marketing students, researchers, and professionals. These include the *topic guide* to locate articles on specific marketing subjects; *World Wide Web* pages; the *table of contents* abstracts, which summarize each article and highlight key concepts; and a *glossary* of key marketing terms.

The articles are organized into four units. Selections that focus on similar issues are concentrated into subsections within the broader units. Each unit is preceded by a list of unit selections, as well as a list of key points to consider that focus on major themes running throughout the selections, Web links that provide extra support for the unit's data, and an overview that provides background for informed reading of the articles and emphasizes critical issues.

This is the twenty-seventh edition of *Annual Editions: Marketing.* Since its first edition in the mid-1970s, the efforts of many individuals have contributed toward its success. We think this is by far the most useful collection of material available for the marketing student. We are anxious to know what you think. What are your opinions? What are your recommendations? Please take a moment to complete and return the *article rating form* on the last page of this volume. Any book can be improved and this one will continue to be, annually.

John E. Richardson

John E. Richardson
Editor

Contents

UNIT 1
Marketing in the 2000's and Beyond

The concepts in bold italics are developed in the article. For further expansion, please refer to the Topic Guide.

UNIT 2
Research, Markets, and Consumer Behavior

The concepts in bold italics are developed in the article. For further expansion, please refer to the Topic Guide.

UNIT 3
Developing and Implementing Marketing Strategies

The concepts in bold italics are developed in the article. For further expansion, please refer to the Topic Guide.

The concepts in bold italics are developed in the article. For further expansion, please refer to the Topic Guide.

UNIT 4
Global Marketing

The concepts in bold italics are developed in the article. For further expansion, please refer to the Topic Guide.

Topic Guide

This topic guide suggests how the selections in this book relate to the subjects covered in your course. You may want to use the topics listed on these pages to search the Web more easily.

On the following pages a number of Web sites have been gathered specifically for this book. They are arranged to reflect the units of this *Annual Edition.* You can link to these sites by going to the DUSHKIN ONLINE support site at *http://www.dushkin.com/online/.*

ALL THE ARTICLES THAT RELATE TO EACH TOPIC ARE LISTED BELOW THE BOLD-FACED TERM.

Services marketing

Target marketing

World Wide Web Sites

The following World Wide Web sites have been carefully researched and selected to support the articles found in this reader. The easiest way to access these selected sites is to go to our DUSHKIN ONLINE support site at *http://www.dushkin.com/online/*.

AE: Marketing 05/06

The following sites were available at the time of publication. Visit our Web site—we update DUSHKIN ONLINE regularly to reflect any changes.

General Sources

CyberAtlas Demographics
http://cyberatlas.internet.com/big_picture/demographics/article/0,,5901_150381,00.html

The Baruch College–Harris poll commissioned by *Business Week* is used at this site to show interested businesses who are on the Net in the United States. Statistics for other countries can be found by clicking on Geographics.

General Social Survey
http://www.icpsr.umich.edu/GSS99/

The GSS (see DPLS Archive: *http://DPLS.DACC.WISC.EDU/SAF/*) is an almost annual personal interview survey of U.S. households that began in 1972. More than 35,000 respondents have answered 2,500 questions. It covers a broad range of variables, many of which relate to microeconomic issues.

Krislyn's Favorite Advertising & Marketing Sites
http://www.krislyn.com/sites/adv.htm

This is a complete list of sites that include information on marketing research, marketing on the Internet, demographic sources, and organizations and associations. The site also features current books on the subject of marketing.

Retail Learning Initiative
http://www.retailsmarts.ryerson.ca

This series of small business and retail marketing links from Canada connects to many more business links in the United States and to workshops and dialogue forums.

STAT-USA/Internet Site Economic, Trade, Business Information
http://www.stat-usa.gov

This site, from the U.S. Department of Commerce, contains Daily Economic News, Frequently Requested Statistical Releases, Information on Export and International Trade, Domestic Economic News and Statistical Series, and Databases.

U.S. Census Bureau Home Page
http://www.census.gov

This is a major source of social, demographic, and economic information, such as income/employment data and the latest indicators, income distribution, and poverty data.

UNIT 1: Marketing in the 2000's and Beyond

American Marketing Association Code of Ethics
http://www.marketingpower.com/

At this American Marketing Association site, use the search mechanism to access the organization's Code of Ethics for marketers.

Futures Research Quarterly
http://www.wfs.org/frq.htm

Published by the World Future Society, this publication describes future research that encompasses both an evolving philosophy and a range of techniques, with the aim of assisting decision-makers in all fields to understand better the potential consequences of decisions by developing images of alternative futures. From this page explore the current and back issues and What's Coming Up!

Center for Innovation in Product Development (CIPD)
http://web.mit.edu/cipd/research/prdctdevelop.htm

CIPD is one of the National Science Foundation's engineering research centers. It shares the goal of future product development with academia, industry, and government.

Marketing in the Service Sector
http://www.ext.colostate.edu/pubs/ttb/tb010424.html

At this site, Frank Leibrock discusses and recommends two books by Harry Beckwith that target marketing in the service sector. Read his reasons for thinking they make sense to owners of small businesses, then read the books themselves.

Professor Takes Business Ethics to Global Level
http://www.miami.com/mld/miamiherald/4426429.htm

This is a discussion by Professor Robert W. McGee of the challenges that the new century brings to business and its relation to ethical issues at a global level. The article by Mike Seemuth provides interesting reading about the important part that government plays in business decisions. Tariffs and protectionism are highlighted.

Remarks by Chairman Alan Greenspan
http://www.federalreserve.gov/boarddocs/speeches/2000/20000322.htm

These remarks were made by chairman Alan Greenspan on March 22, 2000, concerning the challenges that face American businesses, workers, and consumers as the U.S. economy embarked on the new century.

UNIT 2: Research, Markets, and Consumer Behavior

Canadian Innovation Centre
http://www.innovationcentre.ca/company/Default.htm

The Canadian Innovation Centre has developed a unique mix of innovation services that can help a company from idea to market launch. Their services are based on the review of 12,000 new product ideas through their technology and market assessment programs over the past 20 years.

CBA.org: Research and Develop
http://www.cba.org/CBA/National/Marketing/research.asp

This interesting article, written by Elizabeth Cordeau, president of a Calgary-based management consulting firm to law firms and legal associations (featured on the Web by CBA, the information service of the Canadian Bar Association), claims that good marketing begins with excellent market research.

Industry Analysis and Trends
http://www.bizminer.com/market_research.asp

The importance of using market research databases and pinpointing local and national trends, including details of industry and small business startups, is emphasized by this site of the Brandow Company that offers samples of market research profiles.

Marketing Intelligence
http://www.bcentral.com/articles/krotz/123.asp

This article discusses five market intelligence blunders made by the giant retailer K-Mart. "There were warning signs that Kmart management mishandled, downplayed or just plain ignored," Joanna L. Krotz says.

Maritz Marketing Research
http://www.maritzresearch.com

Maritz Marketing Research Inc. (MMRI) specializes in custom-designed research studies that link the consumer to the marketer through information. Go to Maritz Loyalty Marketing in the Maritz Companies menu to find resources to identify, retain, and grow your most valuable customers. Also visit Maritz Research for polls, stats, and archived research reports.

USADATA
http://www.usadata.com

This leading provider of marketing, company, advertising, and consumer behavior data offers national and local data covering the top 60 U.S. markets.

WWW Virtual Library: Demography & Population Studies
http://demography.anu.edu.au/VirtualLibrary/

More than 150 links can be found at this major resource to keep track of information of value to researchers in the fields of demography and population studies.

UNIT 3: Developing and Implementing Marketing Strategies

American Marketing Association Homepage
http://www.marketingpower.com

This site of the American Marketing Association is geared to managers, educators, researchers, students, and global electronic members. It contains a search mechanism, definitions of marketing and market research, and links.

Consumer Buying Behavior
http://www.courses.psu.edu/mktg/mktg220_rso3/sls_cons.htm

The Center for Academic Computing at Penn State posts this course data that includes a review of consumer buying behaviors; group, environment, and internal influences; problem-solving; and post-purchasing behavior.

Product Branding, Packaging, and Pricing
http://www.fooddude.com/branding.html

Put forward by fooddude.com, the information at this site is presented in a lively manner. It discusses positioning, branding, pricing, and packaging in the specialty food market, but it applies to many other retail products as well.

UNIT 4: Global Marketing

CIBERWeb
http://ciber.centers.purdue.edu

The Centers for International Business Education and Research were created by the U.S. Omnibus Trade and Competitiveness Act of 1988. Together, the 26 resulting CIBER sites in the United States are a powerful network focused on helping U.S. business succeed in global markets. Many marketing links can be found at this site.

International Business Resources on the WWW
http://globaledge.msu.edu/ibrd/ibrd.asp

This Web site includes a large index of international business resources. Through *http://ciber.bus.msu.edu/ginlist/* you can also access the Global Interact Network Mailing LIST (GINLIST), which brings together, electronically, business educators and practitioners with international business interests.

International Trade Administration
http://www.ita.doc.gov

The U.S. Department of Commerce is dedicated to helping U.S. businesses compete in the global marketplace, and at this site it offers assistance through many Web links under such headings as Trade Statistics, Cross-Cutting Programs, Regions and Countries, and Import Administration.

World Chambers Network
http://www.worldchambers.net

International trade at work is viewable at this site. For example, click on Global Business eXchange (GBX) for a list of active business opportunities worldwide or to submit your new business opportunity for validation.

World Trade Center Association On Line
http://iserve.wtca.org

Data on world trade is available at this site that features information, services, a virtual trade fair, an exporter's encyclopedia, trade opportunities, and a resource center.

We highly recommend that you review our Web site for expanded information and our other product lines. We are continually updating and adding links to our Web site in order to offer you the most usable and useful information that will support and expand the value of your Annual Editions. You can reach us at: *http://www.dushkin.com/annualeditions/.*

UNIT 1

Marketing in the 2000's and Beyond

Unit Selections

Key Points to Consider

- Dramatic changes are occurring in the marketing of products and services. What social and economic trends do you believe are most significant today, and how do you think these will affect marketing in the future?

- Theodore Levitt suggests that as times change the marketing concept must be reinterpreted. Given the varied perspectives of the other articles in this unit, what do you think this reinterpretation will entail?

- In the present competitive business arena, is it possible for marketers to behave ethically in the environment and both survive and prosper? What suggestions can you give that could be incorporated into the marketing strategy for firms that want to be both ethical and successful?

DUSHKIN ONLINE **Links: www.dushkin.com/online/**
These sites are annotated in the World Wide Web pages.

American Marketing Association Code of Ethics
  http://www.marketingpower.com/
Futures Research Quarterly
  http://www.wfs.org/frq.htm
Center for Innovation in Product Development (CIPD)
  http://web.mit.edu/cipd/research/prdctdevelop.htm
Marketing in the Service Sector
  http://www.ext.colostate.edu/pubs/ttb/tb010424.html
Professor Takes Business Ethics to Global Level
  http://www.miami.com/mld/miamiherald/4426429.htm
Remarks by Chairman Alan Greenspan
  http://www.federalreserve.gov/boarddocs/speeches/2000/20000322.htm

"If we want to know what a business is we must start with its purpose. . . . There is only one valid definition of business purpose: to create a customer. What business thinks it produces is not of first importance—especially not to the future of the business or to its success. What the customer thinks he is buying, what he considers 'value' is decisive—it determines what a business is, what it produces, and whether it will prosper." —Peter Drucker, *The Practice of Management*

When Peter Drucker penned these words in 1954, American industry was just awakening to the realization that marketing would play an important role in the future success of businesses. The ensuing years have seen an increasing number of firms in highly competitive areas—particularly in the consumer goods industry—adopt a more sophisticated customer orientation and an integrated marketing focus.

The dramatic economic and social changes of the last decade have stirred companies in an even broader range of industries—from banking and air travel to communications—to the realization that marketing will provide them with their cutting edge. Demographic and lifestyle changes have splintered mass, homogeneous markets into many markets, each with different needs and interests. Deregulation has made once-protected industries vulnerable to the vagaries of competition. Vast and rapid technological changes are making an increasing number of products and services obsolete. Intense international competition, rapid expansion of the Internet-based economy, and the growth of truly global markets have many firms looking well beyond their national boundaries.

Indeed, it appears that during the new millennium marketing will take on a unique significance—and not just within the industrial sector. Social institutions of all kinds, which had thought themselves exempt from the pressures of the marketplace, are also beginning to recognize the need for marketing in the management of their affairs. Colleges and universities, charities, museums, symphony orchestras, and even hospitals are beginning to give attention to the marketing concept—to provide what the consumer wants to buy.

The selections in this unit are grouped into four areas. Their purposes are to provide current perspectives on marketing, discuss differing views of the marketing concept, analyze the use of marketing by social institutions and nonprofit organizations, and examine the ethical and social responsibilities of marketing.

The articles in the first subsection provide significant clues about salient approaches and issues that marketers need to address in the future in order to create, promote, and sell their products and services in ways that meet the expectation of consumers.

The selections that address the marketing concept include Levitt's now classic "Marketing Myopia," which first appeared in the *Harvard Business Review* in 1960. This version includes the author's retrospective commentary, written in 1975, in which he discusses how shortsightedness can make management unable to recognize that there is no such thing as a growth industry. The second article describes five retail superstores' strategy for pleasing customers and keeping them coming back for more. The last article in this subsection, "What Drives Customer Equity," discloses the significance of customer equity as a significant determinant of the long-term value of a company.

In the *Services & Social Marketing* subsection, the first article reveals opportunities and risks inherent in an approach that seeks services-led growth. The second article underscores the importance of a hospital creating a brand and benefits that differentiates. The final article in this subsection describes why learning to deal with angry customers is a crucial part of today's service landscape.

In the final subsection, a careful look is taken at the strategic process and practice of incorporating ethics and social responsibility into the marketplace. "Trust in the Marketplace" discusses the importance of gaining and maintaining customers' trust. "Ethics Can Be Gauged by Three Key Rules" suggests some helpful guidelines for dealing with multi-cultural ethics.

THE NEXT 25 YEARS

Population projections calculated exclusively for *American Demographics* for the next quarter century forecast a larger, older and more diverse nation, one with many opportunities—and challenges—for businesses.

BY ALISON STEIN WELLNER

In 2025, the oldest Baby Boomers will celebrate their 79th birthday. The youngest members of Gen Y will mark their 31st birthday, and the oldest Gen Xers will be two years away from being eligible for Social Security benefits—assuming they still exist.

It's always difficult to predict the future, and crystal balls are particularly cloudy when it comes to speculation about what this country will be like politically, socially and culturally a quarter century from now. In statistician-speak, too many variables are interacting in unpredictable ways for a steady hand to paint a detailed picture of tomorrow. But there is an exception: demographics. The demographic book on 2025 is already written, as most of the people who will be alive in 22 years in this country are alive today.

So what are the fundamental demographic trends that will shape the consumer market over the next 25 years? To help answer that question, *American Demographics* teamed up with MapInfo, a Troy, N.Y.-based market research firm, to create population projections to 2025. We found that the trends likely to influence business agendas of tomorrow are already gaining momentum today—and the smartest companies have started developing strategies to suit the three largest and most likely demographic trends that will shape the marketplace of tomorrow. Even in a down economy, these companies are aware that they'll need to meet the needs of a population that's growing at a feverish pace. They're tweaking marketing plans to suit a nation that will increasingly be dominated by people over age 65. They're working to understand emerging ethnic groups now, instead of waiting another 10 years, realizing that the majority white population is on its way to becoming a minority.

But even demographic projections are fallible: Consumers have the ability to throw them off course. By def-

inition, projections make assumptions based on past behavior, and future behavior may or may not follow the same patterns. To create projections such as these, demographers analyze birth rates, death rates and immigration, and project forward three different numbers—one that indicates the highest possible number, one that indicates the lowest and one that's in between, a number known as "the middle series." The projections that follow mostly rely on the middle series—which means they assume people will continue to have children at about the same rate, deaths will continue at about the same rate and immigration will fall between the current rate and its highest number. To the extent that demographics are destiny, here's what's in the cards.

America the Crowded

On the business agenda:

- More opportunity, more niche markets
- Environmental concerns moving front and center

If your idea of America conjures up visions of unlimited wide, open spaces, or of houses on acres and acres of land, you may be in for quite a shock during the next two decades. By 2025, the U.S. population is expected to exceed 350 million people—an increase of about 70 million and a boost of 25 percent, according to projections by MapInfo.

This puts the nation on a growth trajectory that's similar to the one experienced just after World War II, when the GIs came home and helped create the Baby Boom in the 1950s and 1960s. Population growth slowed during the 1970s and 1980s but experienced a surge during the

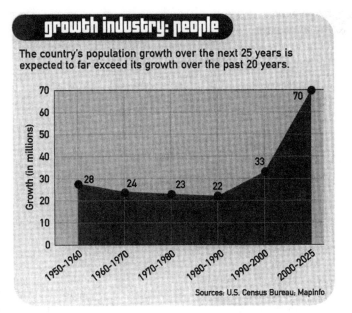

growth industry: people

The country's population growth over the next 25 years is expected to far exceed its growth over the past 20 years.

Growth (in millions)

28 — 24 — 23 — 22 — 33 — 70

1950-1960 | 1960-1970 | 1970-1980 | 1980-1990 | 1990-2000 | 2000-2025

Sources: U.S. Census Bureau; MapInfo

ing expert and author of *TrendSpotting* (Perigee, 2002). A larger U.S. population will require more water and more land to provide food; it also means that more pollution will be created, according to a 2001 report by Lori Hunter, an analyst at the Santa Monica, Calif.-based think tank RAND. Indeed, population growth means that natural resources will be stretched in the coming years, says Dan McGinn, president of the McGinn Group, a marketing communications firm in Arlington, Va. "More people means more demand for resources, which means shortages of resources. Land, water, power—there will be less to go around," he adds. Expect to see escalating conflicts at the local level over land use, in which the benefits of population growth will be pitted against the cost to the environment. Also expect products and services to be scrutinized more closely for their environmental impact.

1990s. Expect record-shattering growth to continue, as Americans live longer, birth rates hold steady and immigration continues apace. This wide expanse of growing humanity means that nearly every market segment will expand in numbers over the next 25 years, because more people means more pocketbooks.

However, this *massive* market does not herald a return to the *mass* market. "This [population] growth will combine with increasing diversity to create an ever-growing list of market segments," says Josh Calder, chief editor of the Global Lifestyles project, a research venture of Social Technologies, an Arlington, Va.-based consultancy. "I saw a professionally made bumper sticker the other day that said, 'Proud to be Sikh and American.' Such niches driven by ethnicity, attitudes and interest will proliferate," he adds.

As the population increases, niche markets may become unwieldy for businesses to target with a single marketing strategy. For example, many companies have one marketing strategy to reach Hispanic consumers. But by 2025, the Hispanic market will double, to 70 million consumers. As a result, the niche market of today will become a mass market in its own right, segmented not only by nationality (i.e., Mexican, Guatemalan) but also by spending behavior and other psychographic characteristics. Vickie Abrahamson, cofounder and executive vice president of Minneapolis-based Iconoculture, a trends consulting firm, dubs this movement "beehiving." Says Abrahamson, "Beehiving is the growth of tight-knit, alternative communities sharing common values and passions. Marketers must tap in to beehive rituals, customs and language to build trust and patronage."

Of course, population growth can present some challenges. "Don't you ever wonder how we'll have all the resources to take care of everyone on this planet? It's stunning to think about," says Richard Laermer, market-

the graying future

Those over the age of 60 will likely dominate by 2025.

	2000	2025	DIFFERENCE	PERCENT DIFFERENCE
Total	281,421,906	351,070,000	69,648,094	24.7%
Under 5 years	19,175,798	23,183,000	4,007,202	20.9%
5–9	20,549,505	22,845,000	2,295,495	11.2%
10–14	20,528,072	23,166,000	2,637,928	12.9%
15–19	20,219,890	23,449,000	3,229,110	16.0%
20–24	18,964,001	22,481,000	3,516,999	18.5%
25–29	19,381,336	21,257,000	1,875,664	9.7%
30–34	20,510,388	21,615,000	1,104,612	5.4%
35–39	22,706,664	22,728,000	21,336	0.1%
40–44	22,441,863	22,374,000	-67,863	-0.3%
45–49	20,092,404	21,031,000	938,596	4.7%
50–54	17,585,548	19,318,000	1,732,452	9.9%
55–59	13,469,237	18,452,000	4,982,763	37.0%
60–64	10,805,447	18,853,000	8,047,553	74.5%
65–69	9,533,545	19,844,000	10,310,455	108.1%
70–74	8,857,441	17,878,000	9,020,559	101.8%
75–79	7,415,813	14,029,000	6,613,187	89.2%
80–84	4,945,367	9,638,000	4,692,633	94.9%
85+	4,239,587	8,930,000	4,690,413	110.6%

Source: MapInfo and American Demographics

The Mighty Mature Market

On the business agenda:

- The senior market gaining new allure
- Creating ageless multigenerational brands

the mixed society

By 2025, white non-Hispanics will hold a mere 60 percent majority.

	WHITE, NON-HISPANIC	BLACK, NON-HISPANIC	ASIAN/PACIFIC ISLANDER, NON-HISPANIC	NATIVE AMERICAN, NON-HISPANIC	HISPANIC
Population, all ages	210,984	45,567	23,564	2,787	68,168
Percent of total population	60.1%	13.0%	6.7%	0.8%	19.4%
Population, under 5 years	11,872	3,103	1,642	196	6,370
5–9	12,034	3,065	1,583	199	5,964
10–14	12,319	3,180	1,677	221	5,769
15–19	12,495	3,359	1,652	224	5,719
20–24	11,985	3,170	1,641	213	5,472
25–29	11,418	2,907	1,703	201	5,028
30–34	11,993	2,865	1,780	187	4,790
35–39	12,938	3,198	1,771	190	4,631
40–44	13,311	3,176	1,634	202	4,051
45–49	12,834	2,836	1,524	180	3,657
50–54	11,888	2,596	1,356	148	3,330
55–59	11,664	2,419	1,263	130	2,976
60–64	12,502	2,343	1,141	114	2,753
65–69	13,838	2,413	978	107	2,508
70–74	13,071	1,978	800	93	1,936
75–79	10,531	1,429	606	72	1,391
80–84	7,471	816	400	49	902
85–89	3,950	385	217	29	496
90–94	1,859	199	118	17	264
95–99	745	90	54	10	116
100+	267	41	22	6	45
Median age	43.2 years	36.9 years	35.3 years	33.8 years	29.8 years

NOTE: Population numbers in thousands

Source: MapInfo

The biggest growth market, by far, will be the 65 and older set. In 2000, this group included 35 million people, about 12 percent of the population. By 2025, as Baby Boomers age and life expectancy continues to increase, the number of seniors will double, to more than 70 million people. To put this in perspective, the U.S. will have twice as many seniors in 2025 as it has African Americans today.

The graying of America means that companies will have to do more than pay lip service to the idea of marketing to older people. "The era of youth domination in business and marketing will be over," contends Maddy Dychtwald, the author of *Cycles: How We Will Live, Work, and Buy* (Free Press, 2003). "We've always been very youth focused because the percentage of young people has always overwhelmed the percentage of older adults. Since this domination will be balancing out, we will see more industries and companies begin to seek customers outside of the 18-to-34 demographic," she says. Dychtwald cites a recent Pepsi commercial as an indication of things to come. The ad features a teenage boy in the middle of a mosh pit at a rock concert. He turns around to discover his father rocking out nearby. "The Pepsi Generation is not just about youth anymore," she says. "In fact, it's becoming multigenerational, which is good news for business. It increases their potential target market dramatically."

Still, businesses are not going to suddenly lose all interest in the 18-to-34 demographic. "America loves

magnet markets

Metros with a high diversity quotient, or that have a large senior population are expected to grow the fastest over the next 25 years; areas with a low diversity quotient are more likely to shrink.

METROPOLITAN AREA	2000	2005	2010	2015	2020	2025	CHANGE	PERCENT CHANGE
Laredo, TX	194,636	227,570	261,073	295,656	331,176	367,815	173,179	89.0%
Punta Gorda, FL	142,297	166,531	190,665	215,186	240,104	265,542	123,245	86.6%
Las Vegas, NV-AZ	1,581,525	1,836,721	2,093,204	2,355,460	2,622,811	2,897,008	1,315,483	83.2%
Austin-San Marcos, TX	1,259,929	1,452,492	1,645,797	1,843,311	2,044,712	2,251,148	991,219	78.7%
Provo-Orem, UT	370,532	423,693	476,961	531,378	586,832	643,683	273,151	73.7%
Phoenix-Mesa, AZ	3,276,401	3,689,337	4,105,093	4,531,884	4,968,122	5,416,621	2,140,220	65.3%
Naples, FL	253,806	285,648	317,698	350,581	384,177	418,739	164,933	65.0%
Medford-Ashland, OR	181,824	203,962	226,198	248,931	272,152	295,966	114,142	62.8%
West Palm Beach-Boca Raton, FL	1,137,775	1,275,564	1,412,373	1,551,564	1,692,865	1,837,450	699,675	61.5%
Wilmington, NC	234,816	262,761	290,765	319,409	348,657	378,676	143,860	61.3%
Orlando, FL	1,654,675	1,847,142	2,042,204	2,243,626	2,450,435	2,663,763	1,009,099	61.0%
Huntington-Ashland WV-KY-OH	315,379	315,296	315,753	317,042	319,011	321,537	6,158	2.0%
Toledo, OH	618,056	617,729	618,309	620,615	623,998	628,522	10,466	1.7%
Pittsburgh, PA	2,356,378	2,354,353	2,355,811	2,363,989	2,376,583	2,393,744	37,366	1.6%
Buffalo-Niagara Falls, NY	1,168,948	1,167,651	1,168,075	1,171,903	1,177,887	1,186,172	17,224	1.5%
Jamestown, NY	139,663	139,488	139,511	139,933	140,634	141,593	1,930	1.4%
Lawton, OK	114,886	114,695	114,692	115,022	115,523	116,298	1,412	1.2%
Muncie, IN	118,722	118,689	118,752	119,037	119,485	120,099	1,377	1.2%
Parkersburg-Marietta, WV-OH	151,138	150,877	150,821	151,185	151,848	152,807	1,669	1.1%
Youngstown-Warren, OH	594,416	593,378	593,165	594,563	597,065	600,601	6,185	1.0%
Sharon, PA	120,219	119,972	119,890	120,154	120,620	121,271	1,052	0.9%
Binghamton, NY	251,897	250,751	249,948	249,860	250,236	251,055	-842	-0.3%

Source: Woods & Poole Economics; MapInfo 2003

youth—and all things associated with it," points out Ann A. Fishman, president of Generational Target Marketing Corp., in New Orleans. Adds Rob Duboff, senior vice president of Bowne Decision Quest, based in Waltham, Mass., "Even if there is no increase in the 18-and-under age segment, many marketers will continue to target it as these people start to establish their adult buying habits."

Instead, companies will have to learn to establish brands that attract older consumers without alienating younger ones, says Dychtwald. "It's becoming clear that people aren't over the hill at 50 anymore. Smart marketers will capitalize on this knowledge and create the image of an ageless society where people define themselves more by the activities they're involved in than by their age." Although grandparents can be age 45, 65 or 85, what they have in common is that they all want to buy gifts for their grandchildren, she reports. "You could have college students ages 20, 30 and 60. It's all part of a more cyclic life, where people cycle in and out of different life-stage events based on their interests rather than their age," explains Dychtwald.

The Consumer Kaleidoscope

On the business agenda:

- Devising marketing campaigns that appeal to many demographic segments
- Figuring out how to address the shrinking white majority

By 2025, the term "minority," as it's currently used, will be virtually obsolete. Non-Hispanic whites will still be the majority race in America—but just barely. According to MapInfo's projections, the share of non-Hispanic whites will fall to 60 percent by 2025, from 70 percent today. And the Hispanic population will almost double, to more than 68 million, from 35 million today, growing to 19 percent of the population from 12 percent. The number of Asians in the U.S. will also double, reaching 24 million, or 7 percent of the population, from its current 4 percent.

Companies that have not yet developed a multicultural marketing strategy will have to "wake up and smell the Thai tacos," quips Abrahamson. "If a company today is concentrating solely on a white audience, then it is living in another galaxy, far, far away," she says. Indeed, as the multicultural market becomes a multibillion-dollar market, companies that are already focusing on nonwhite consumers will find themselves at a distinct advantage, says Mark Seferian, director of business development at EchoboomX, a marketing firm based in Denver. "The companies that are currently working to understand emerging ethnic groups will have a huge advantage over the companies that wait another 10 years," he says. (This will be particularly true in fast-growing metro areas, which will tend to be more diverse. See chart, "The Mixed Society.")

Many businesses will not be able to adapt to the realities of the new marketplace, argues McGinn. "Diversity will be much more than a buzzword—diversity will be the key to economic survival," he says. Ethnic newspapers, magazines, television and radio will see phenomenal growth over the coming decades, McGinn believes, and the mainstream media will have to join forces with these ethnic specialists to stay in business. "Companies will not be able to keep swimming in the mainstream, because there is no mainstream. Instead, it's a series of parallel creeks, some constantly filling, some drying up a little," he says.

One of those "drying" creeks will be the declining majority—the white consumer market, which will experience slow growth over the next 25 years. Companies that market to white America will have to rethink their strategies, according to Rob Frankel, a branding expert based in Los Angeles. "The more cynical side of me suspects a subtle 'white market' will define itself, probably premium-positioned, probably leveraging white angst at lost population dominance," he says. If the current gap in wealth and income between white and nonwhite consumers holds for the next 25 years, businesses will find ample reason to target the nation's 210 million non-Hispanic white consumers.

Will tomorrow's multicultural marketing strategies continue to be segmented by race, with one strategy for "mainstream," one for African American consumers, another for Asians, another for Hispanics? Or will an increasingly multicultural population prefer inclusive, "fusion" strategies that attempt to encompass many different nationalities or racial identities in one campaign, such as those pioneered by clothing retailers Benetton and The Gap? The answer will depend on how Americans come to view their racial identity over the next two and a half decades. For instance, the increasing number of multiracial consumers may not necessarily lead to a consumer culture that blends racial identities, because there's growing evidence that multiracial consumers will think of themselves as a distinct racial group. Former Census Bureau director Kenneth Prewitt points to a growing number of organizations on college campuses aimed at helping multiracial students assert their group identity.

It will become a major challenge for businesses to grasp such subtle matters of cultural identity. To do this, companies will have to rely more heavily on in-depth market research techniques, such as ethnographic research, or new qualitative methods that rely on cognitive science, which promise to give markets an understanding of their consumer's culture, says Seferian. Ethnography enables marketers to understand a culture other than their own through direct observation, absorbing subtle differences in communication styles, behavior patterns and lifestyle. (For more on ethnography, see "Watch Me Now," *American Demographics*, July/August 2002, and "The New Science of Focus Groups," in the March 2003 issue.)

In a nation no longer dominated by one group, most businesses will be marketing to a consumer base that will include a patchwork of racial and ethnic identities. Understanding the differences in consumers' cultural identities will make the difference between failure and success.

High Performance Marketing

Marketing must become a leader for change across the corporation

By Jagdish N. Sheth and Rajendra S. Sisodia

EXECUTIVE briefing

Marketing productivity as we define it includes both efficiency and effectiveness to generate loyal and satisfied customers at low cost. However, many companies either create loyal customers at an unacceptably high cost or alienate customers—and employees— in their search for marketing efficiencies. We believe marketing needs to change in order to reestablish itself as a fundamental driver of business success and that the solution lies in "high performance marketing."

Two major changes have emerged in marketing practice over the past five years. The first is the use of the Internet in marketing. An era of intense experimentation with this technology has taught us several lessons. For example, applicability for business-to-consumer e-commerce turned out to be much narrower than most marketers expected. E-mail marketing appeared to be an efficient marketing channel at first, but its abuse and overuse may soon dilute its effectiveness just as direct mail became synonymous with junk mail and telemarketing degenerated from a cost-effective two-way interactive channel into sometimes intrusive customer harassment.

The Internet has empowered customers—usually to the disadvantage of marketers. Now customers can readily search for the best "deal" on every transaction and can communicate with each other to spread word— both positive and negative—about their product purchase experiences. Marketers have been at least moderately successful in the use of "mass personalization" technologies such as collaborative filtering to tailor recommendations to customers and generate some incremental sales.

The second major development has been the popularization of customer relationship management (CRM) software and the rise of 1-to-1 marketing. The CRM industry has exploded in the last few years, growing at 40% per year as more than 2,000 vendors have emerged, promising to achieve the seamless integration of sales, marketing, and customer service around the needs of individual customers. The CRM software market is expected [to] reach $10 billion in 2001 (according to AMR Research), while the worldwide CRM services business reached $34 billion in revenues in 1999, growing

at an annual 20% rate with a projected reach of $125 billion by 2004, according to IDC.

These developments, though momentous, have not brought marketing appreciably closer to our stated ideal of "effective efficiency." In many ways, the marketing function remains as troubled as ever. Major new problems have arisen, such as the ability of customers to readily organize themselves into powerful groups speaking with a unified voice, while others have subsided somewhat. For example, as media continue to get fragmented and more addressable, marketing noise levels have decreased somewhat.

The Trouble With Marketing

Marketing is still not truly customer-centric. For all the lip service that has been paid, marketers are still attempting to control and drive customers to behave in ways they want, rather than organizing their own activities around customer needs. The Internet has not altered this in any significant way.

Most CRM implementations have been expensive failures. CRM, fundamentally, is really just fine-tuned target marketing, albeit with better coordination between sales, marketing, and customer service than we have had in the past. Many companies rushed to embrace CRM as a cure-all that would make them more customer-focused and successful, ignoring the reality that no software can overcome the lack of a customer-centric culture and mindset. Even for companies already possessing a strong customer-centric orientation, there is no guarantee that grafting a CRM system on top will lead to major improvements; it can even lead to deteriorated performance if it takes away from employees' flexibility and responsiveness in dealing with customers.

Most CRM systems do little to improve the customer experience; they just enable marketers to better deploy their resources. Overall, companies have probably lost more money than they have gained through these implementations. In fact, it is estimated that 60% to 80% of CRM projects do not achieve their goals, and 30% to 50% fail outright. CRM implementations in most companies have been initiated by CEOs and led by CIOs; the marketing function has rarely taken the lead or even been actively involved in the decision making. CEOs have embraced CRM technology as a way to finally get some precision and accountability in their marketing efforts. However, the treatment has rarely matched the disease, with the unsurprising result that the marketing function remains as malaise-ridden as ever.

Marketing spending continues to yield poor returns, especially on advertising and branding. For example, many dot-coms spent the bulk of their venture funding on outrageously expensive advertising campaigns, under the delusion that having a recognizable brand would solve all of their other business problems.

The promise of radically efficient business models that leverage the uniqueness of the Internet has given way to widespread disillusionment and a seeming return to "business as usual." However, the root cause of the dot-com debacle was not poor technology or lack of capital, but companies' failure to understand customer behavior. They were left dumbfounded when the anticipated huge changes in behavior required for success didn't happen. Companies especially failed to understand the psychology of consumer resistance to innovation and failed to develop strategies to overcome such resistance.

We believe marketers have not yet fully examined how their function needs to change in order to reestablish itself as a primary driver of business success. High performance marketing (HPM) may be the solution to their problems.

High Performance Organizations

Jordan defines high performance organizations as "groups of employees who produce desired goods or services at higher quality with the same or fewer resources. Their productivity and quality improve continuously, from day to day, week to week, and year to year, leading to the achievement of their mission." (See Additional Reading)

High performance organizations share many characteristics. In addition to identifying and eliminating non-value-added activities, leveraging technology in the service of their mission, and having a strong, organization-wide customer orientation, they also have inspirational and transformational leadership that focuses their resources and energies on achieving a clearly defined mission.

Organizations that perform well empower employees to act autonomously to achieve the corporate mission and provide incentives to individual employees to align their behaviors with the achievement of better outcomes for customers. They also have organizational cultures that embody a high degree of trust—what Carnevale calls "an expression of faith and confidence that a person or an institution will be fair, reliable, ethical, competent, and non-threatening."

High performance organizations tend to use systems thinking, so all employees have a dynamic understanding of how the "living" organization functions and the interdependencies between components and subsystems. They are flexible and adaptable to changing circumstances, emphasizing continuous improvement, reinvention, and innovation.

High Performance Marketing

The operations and manufacturing functions at many leading companies today can be described as "high performance" because they have demonstrated continuous quality improvements and cost reductions. More than anything else, marketers will have to start thinking in new and creative ways about everything in their domain—markets, customers, budgets, organizational structures, information, and incentives. We propose the marketing function needs to adopt the following tenets in order to move toward true high performance.

Customer centricity. Customer-centric marketing will lead to non-intuitive consequences. First, whereas traditional marketing has been concerned with demand management, customercentric marketing will lead the marketing function toward "supply management"—the ability to rapidly respond to customer requirements rather than focusing on controlling them. Second, traditional marketing practices emphasize the acquisition of customers, while customer-centric marketing emphasizes the retention of the "right" customers along with the "outsourcing" of the rest. Third, whereas traditional firms and customers are institutionally separate with little interaction, customer-centric marketing will lead to customers and firms co-creating products, pricing, and distribution. Fourth, customer-centric marketing will be characterized by more "fixed costs" and fewer variable costs; companies will make infrastructure investments that greatly reduce transaction costs. Finally, the vocabulary, metrics, and organizations will evolve toward a customer focus rather than product focus or segment focus. For example, Procter & Gamble renamed its channel sales organization "customer business development" in early 1999.

Investment orientation. In most companies, sales and marketing expenditures are several times greater than capital expenditures. Yet capital expenditures are subject to a far greater amount of analysis and evaluation than marketing expenditures. Most marketing activities involve a substantial lag between action and effect. When marketing is treated as an expense, the causality often becomes reversed, as marketing budgets tend to be determined by sales forecasts. Treating marketing as an investment forces companies to come to grips with the temporal relationship between current marketing actions and future marketplace reactions.

Well-spent marketing resources applied to a brand in its early years can build a stock of value that can be sustained or even enhanced with very small amounts of spending. Marketing investments can pay off if they are well-timed and targeted. Investments made at the right stage of the product life cycle and directed at the most profitable customers deliver superior returns.

Systems thinking. Systems modeling is an integrative approach that combines systems thinking and the principles of cybernetics. It incorporates causal-loop diagramming to show sequences of cause-and-effect relationships as well as stock-and-flow diagrams to represent systemic effects of feedback on the accumulations and rates of flow in the system. These two system representations are coupled in order to simulate the behavior of the system. Modeling and simulating the system helps managers recognize and understand the dynamic patterns of system behavior. Systems dynamics offers a great deal of potential to marketers, but is hardly used. For example, it is a useful approach to model the customer acquisition and retention process.

Incentive alignment. The incentives provided to marketing employees are haphazard and often at odds. Most advertising agencies are still paid a commission proportional to the volume of advertising run, creating a disincentive for higher impact advertising that needs fewer exposures. Many salespeople are still compensated on short-term customer acquisition measures, with little regard for customer profitability or longevity.

The guiding principle in creating incentive systems is to use market mechanisms wherever possible. In their book, *Free to Choose* (1990, Harcourt Brace), Milton and Rose Friedman present a framework for evaluating the relative productivity of spending in different circumstances. The "Friedman Matrix" categorizes business spending along two dimensions: whose money is spent and for whose benefit the money is spent. The way to align employee and company interests is to organize every spending decision in such a manner that employees act as though they are spending their own money for their own benefit. This will ensure that they are both effective and efficient in their resource allocation.

The framework suggests that resources are spent most optimally when they are "owned" by an individual and spent by that individual for his or her own purposes. In buying a family car, for example, individuals are likely to spend what they know they can afford and get a car

that satisfies their needs. On the other hand, individuals able to spend someone else's money on themselves (e.g., buying an expense account meal) are likely to get what they want (effective), but will probably spend more than if they were paying their own money (inefficient). A third situation exists when an individual spends his or her own money (staying within a budget) to purchase a gift for someone else; while efficient, this is unlikely to optimally satisfy the recipient (ineffective). Finally, when individuals (e.g., bureaucrats) are charged with spending other people's money (e.g., taxpayers) on things that do not affect them directly (e.g., welfare), spending is neither effective nor efficient.

Incentive alignment is a guiding principle for moving toward high performance marketing. Examples include creating sales force compensation schemes to reward customer retention and profitability (as the insurance industry has done in recent years) and incentivizing new product development teams to create high quality new products in a short time without consuming inordinate resources.

Avoid incremental thinking. When it comes to changes in how the marketing function is defined, organized, and compensated, incremental thinking will not suffice. Given product parity and near-perfect information availability and matching, the quality of a firm's marketing strategy and execution will be prime drivers of market capitalization.

For too long, the marketing function has been content to focus on relatively trivial tactics and has been lackadaisical about taking a prominent role in shaping the overall fortunes of the corporation. In other words, marketing has not aspired to a higher level and has demonstrated no zeal or passion to elevate its respect and relevance within the corporation. Other functional areas have rallied around ambitious and organization-transforming initiatives, such as TQM and Six Sigma (driven by operations), Economic Value Added (driven by CFOs), and the Balanced Scorecard (driven by accounting).

Marketing needs to break out of its "doer rather than leader" role and its preoccupation with the mundane. We believe marketing needs to become a leader for change and transformation across the corporation. Marketing must take hold of the leadership levers for the corporation. The best way for it to do so is to leverage its fundamental identity as the voice of the customer within the corporation. Marketing needs to go outside the box and break many of the self-imposed rules that have relegated it to a constricted role.

Understand market growth. One of the biggest gaps remaining in marketing know-how is an understanding of what determines market growth. Marketers must attempt to grow the total market, not just try to protect and grow their market share. Several factors can contribute to market growth, such as an emphasis on emerging markets and the creative "dematuring" or revitalization of mature markets through the fusion of non-traditional technologies (as Yamaha did by incorporating digital electronics into pianos) or injecting elements of fashion and personalization (as some European manufacturers have done with small appliances). Commodity markets in developing markets such as India and China are ripe for dematuring, through the introduction of packaging, processing, and other value-adding functions.

View customers differently. Just as we have gone through significant changes in how we think about employees and shareholders, we will need to engage in some fresh thinking about customers. Customers should be viewed and managed as assets of the organization to be invested in, depreciated, and replaced. In addition to the outsourcing of customers (e.g., using business partners to serve certain customer groups), companies also need to think about trading, sharing, firing, and outright selling customers.

Harness marketing information. In *2020 Vision* (1992, Simon & Schuster), Stan Davis and Bill Davidson described the "information exhaust" that companies generate through their ongoing transactions and relationships with customers. In the past, most of this exhaust was discharged into the atmosphere and disappeared. Smart companies, however, have developed ways to "turbocharge" the core business by harnessing this information flow. Through feedback mechanisms, this allows the marketing "engine" to operate at a higher level of efficiency. Information exhaust also can generate highly profitable sidelines that in some cases may become more profitable than the core business. For example, by focusing on the lifetime value of customers, General Motors' U.S. operation sees the potential for substantial synergies across its automotive, consumer credit, mortgage, and even its communications businesses.

Firms can use this thinking to guide strategic decisions on entering new businesses. For example, entry into the credit card business is often dictated not by the economics of that business per se, but by the usable information used to improve the core business. Similar examples can be found in the magazine and software industries, as the recent merger of AOL and Time Warner demonstrates. Given their potential value, it is imperative that firms develop sound mechanisms for sharing information and managing marketing knowledge. Marketing employees need to receive incentives to share information that could be of broader value to the corporation.

Prepare for a new role. Senior management needs to reconsider how to control and integrate the marketing function for best results—to determine the proper role of the marketing function in a corporation where virtually all functions have become market-oriented. To start with, the sales-marketing-customer service separation must end, and marketers must take on the responsibility for attracting as well as retaining and growing profitable customers. Additionally, marketing has to be accorded greater say over key decision areas such as procurement, pricing, product development, and logistics, all of which have been gradually taken away from marketing departments.

In the future marketing will get wider but shallower; it will encompass a wider range of activities but will perform fewer of them in house. Many activities will be outsourced to best-in-class external suppliers, while others will be performed in various parts of the corporation. The marketing manager's job will evolve from a "doer" to a coordinator of internal and external resources pertinent to customer retention and profitable growth.

The marketing function will also, in a more deliberate way, formally incorporate upstream linkages that were once the domain of the purchasing department. Key suppliers will become an integral part of the marketing team and will be involved in strategic planning and new product development. For example, this is already happening in the automotive industry.

Employ dynamic budgeting. The budgeting process is probably one of the biggest contributors to marketing's problems. Budgeting is static, forecast-driven (based on notoriously inaccurate forecasts subject to intense and deliberate distortions and game playing), counterintuitive (e.g., mixing cause and effect in advertising), and subject to the "use it or lose it" rule. Budgets escalate year after year in prosperous times, with little consideration for changes in actual needs over time.

Static budgeting needs to be replaced with dynamic budgeting, where resources are requested and allocated based on an "as needed and justified" basis. Rather than budget by scale or in some proportion to the top line, budgeting should be driven by the size of the opportunity, the anticipated ROI, and increase in shareholder value. This requires decoupling the marketing budgeting for a brand from the current brand's revenue level and instead coupling it to the opportunity for revenue and profit growth that the brand presents. In situations where more traditional budgeting procedures persist, managers need to receive direct incentives not to fully use their budgets, just as U.S. farmers are often given incentives not to plant crops.

Consider how marketing budgets and customer-related responsibilities are typically allocated in companies. The marketing budget usually covers advertising, sales promotions, market research, and some portion of distribution costs. It may include the cost of the sales force, though in many companies it does not. It almost never includes the cost of customer service, and usually does not include product development.

It is not unusual to find situations where sales, customer service, and new product development are funded out of budgets that are not under marketing's control. Clearly, we need to create transparent incentive schemes to focus all marketing personnel on the essentials: the profitability of what they do and the maintenance of high levels of customer satisfaction and retention.

Change marketing metrics. Marketing employees for too long have been measured on market share, with little or no consideration to the profitability of that market share. Of late, there has been some movement toward thinking more about the bottom-line impact or measuring marketing based on its profit impact.

Ultimately, the measure that matters most for a business is shareholder value or market capitalization. It is a summary descriptor of all the value the business has created and is expected to create in the future. The question for the marketing function is: How can it affect the company's market capitalization? The measure of marketing's success must move from "share of market" to "share of market capitalization" within the industry. Operationalizing this will be one of the key challenges for marketing in the years to come.

Filling the Void

Reflecting the greater emphasis on shareholder value in recent years, the CFO today drives most companies. However, a preoccupation with finances can be dangerous because it can lead companies to lose sight of the true driver of business success—the long-term satisfaction and retention of profitable customers.

In our view, marketing has a great opportunity to create excitement around becoming customer-centric and in the process can satisfy both the CEO and the CFO. If, on the other hand, it continues to take a back seat within the corporation, it will be abdicating its fiscal responsibilities. High performance marketing is really "inspirational marketing" that can rally the corporation to set and achieve much higher goals than ever before. While it has a number of tenets as discussed earlier, its defining characteristic is that it is customer-centric. In order to operationalize customer-centric marketing fully, it is

essential that companies create a new senior executive role that takes an outside-in perspective rather than the inside-out perspective adopted by others. This role is that of a "chief customer officer" (CCO).

The CCO position, while currently seen mostly in small high-tech companies, is expected to become commonplace. The Meta Group projects that 25% of Global 2000 businesses will have a CCO by 2003, while Gartner expects 15% of U.S. companies to have such a position by 2003. Cisco Systems has been a pioneer in this regard; it established the position of senior vice president of customer advocacy in 1991, with Cisco's customer service, product design, and IT groups reporting to it.

There is a void at the top of most major corporations, and marketing must move quickly to fill it. If it does not, marketing will continue to become more marginalized, and all stakeholders—customers, employees, and shareholders—will suffer as a result.

Additional Reading

Carnevale, David G. (1995), *Trustworthy Government: Leadership and Management Strategies for Building Trust and High Performance*. New York: Jossey-Bass.

Jordan, Sephena A. (1999), "Innovative Cultures + Empowered Employees = High Performance Organizations," *Public Productivity & Management Review*, (23:1),109–113.

Sheth, Jagdish N., Rajendra S. Sisodia, and Arun Sharma (2000), "The Antecedents and Consequences of Customer-Centric Marketing," *Journal of the Academy of Marketing Science*, (28:1), 55–66.

About the Authors

Jagdish N. Sheth is the Charles H. Kellstadt professor of marketing at the Goizueta Business School at Emory University in Atlanta.

Rajendra S. Sisodia is trustee professor of marketing at Bentley College in Waltham, Mass. He may be reached at rsisodia@bentley.edu.

From *Marketing Management,* September/October 2001, pp. 18-23. © 2001 by the American Marketing Association. Reprinted by permission.

Marketing High Technology: Preparation, Targeting, Positioning, Execution

A range of strategies are available to the high-tech marketing manager taking a shot at launching the latest technology.

Chris Easingwood and Anthony Koustelos

Commercialization of new high-tech products is often the costliest stage of the entire product development process. Yet even when the process is well managed, the risk of failure remains high. New high-tech products usually have just one shot at the market. Get it wrong and the consequences are invariably fatal. And although the launch strategy is critical, this stage is largely neglected in the business press and academic literature on high-tech marketing, innovation, and new product development.

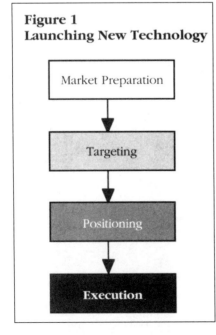

**Figure 1
Launching New Technology**

- Market Preparation
- Targeting
- Positioning
- Execution

Persuading a market to adopt a new technology is generally comprised of four stages, shown in Figure 1. The first step, market preparation, involves readying customers and other companies for the change. Typically this stage takes place while the product is still in development, though not necessarily so. The second stage in planning the marketing of the product is targeting, followed by positioning based on the expected competitive situation. The final stage involves execution and consists of the strategies that are often the most visible part of the mix, used to achieve specific results. Each of the four stages will be described in turn.

MARKET PREPARATION

Market preparation is intended to get the market ready for the new technology by building awareness and, most important, forming relationships. Figure 2 shows some examples.

Cooperation/Licensing/Alliances

In many cases, the way a marketer chooses to set up the market is crucial. Some form of cooperation is increasingly seen not as an option but as a necessity. Few companies can go it alone, at least not when the launch of major technology is concerned.

Alliances and licensing arrangements encourage the adoption of technological standards for at least two good reasons.

One is because of the expected boost to sales. Customers are reluctant to adopt when faced with competing and incompatible technologies (recall the days of the VHS and Betamax videocassette formats). They realize that markets rarely allow two competing technologies to thrive, and eventually coalesce around the preferred one, condemning the other(s) to decline.

The other reason is that companies sometimes seek to establish their own technology as the standard, to preempt those of rivals and avoid having a competing standard imposed. This was very much the reason for Psion, Motorola, Ericsson, and Nokia forming a consortium called Symbian. The four agreed to adopt Psion's computer operating system, called EPOC, in the hope that this would become the industry standard for the next generation of wireless communication devices, such as mobile phones and palm-top computers. The mobile phone is expected to become "smart," sending and receiving data, downloading from the Internet, and storing large amounts of information. The alliance is also an attempt to prevent Microsoft's Windows CE operating system in consumer electronics from becoming the standard. Ericsson, Motorola, and Nokia each had to abandon its own operating system in adopting Psion's—a sacrifice that may prove worthwhile, given *Fortune's* claim that David Potter, Psion's CEO, is the man Microsoft's Bill Gates fears the most (Wallace 1998).

Figure 2
Market Preparation: Some Examples

Form alliances	Psion, Motorola, Ericsson, and Nokia adopting Psion's computer operating system to thwart Microsoft's Windows CE operating system
Supply to OEMs	IBM licensing its hard disk drives
Provide pre-launch information	Apple providing information on the Macintosh NC

Sometimes the alliances formed can be informal or "loose," arising through mutual advantage. This is because, more and more, technological products rarely stand alone. They depend on the existence of other products and technologies. A good example is the World Wide Web, with its groupings of businesses that include browsers, on-line news, e-mail, network retailing, and financial services. Arthur (1996) calls these networks of products and services that support and enhance each other "mini-ecologies." They are increasingly the basic frameworks of knowledge-based industries, and companies have to secure themselves a place in these loose alliances built around a mini-ecology.

Supply to OEMs

Market preparation can also be tackled by sharing the new technology with original equipment manufacturers (OEMs). This increases the awareness of the product and the technology, and boosts sales via expansion to new markets. IBM developed two powerful hard disk drives, Travel-Star 8GS and 3GN, for its own ThinkPad notebooks, but decided to license them to Acer, Gateway 2000, Dell, and other OEMs as well, which plan to use the drives in their portable PCs. This market preparation tactic enables the producer to retain full ownership of its technology while at the same time expanding market potential beyond its own marketing capacity, albeit at a lower margin.

Provide Pre-Launch Information

The type of information released before launch, and the manner in which it is delivered, can be a key tactical decision in the product launch. The publicly visible demonstration of this strategy is the article in the press, detailing the time the product

will reach the market, the basis of the technology, and other information. Intel has been releasing details of its new MMX technology-based Pentium-II chip. Articles have also appeared on the Macintosh NC, Apple's forthcoming network computer, based on the company's powerful new chip, PowerPC 750. Those who typically need to be informed before the launch are the distribution network, service suppliers (such as software houses), and the media, who in turn inform potential customers.

The information to be released has to be planned carefully so as to arouse sufficient interest in the new product without losing a competitive edge in a market where imitation can materialize with lightning speed. A careful balance must be drawn that allows for the need to have influential components of the market's infrastructure informed without giving a technological lead away to competitors.

Educate the Market

A special form of providing pre-release information is an education program. This is very ambitious and more long-term than merely releasing information, and thus it is less common. It is exactly what Intel did in the early days of the microchip. Rather than marketing the product directly—there were just too many markets with too many applications for that—it set about educating the various markets on the potential of the technology, leaving them with much greater in-depth knowledge to work out how the product might be used in their particular markets.

However, education has to be managed and timed carefully. Otherwise, the company sells the vision before it has the product to deliver that vision. Not surprisingly, smaller companies shy away from trying to educate markets, leaving it to larger corpo-

rations with their greater resources and longer planning horizons.

Create Special Distribution Arrangements

Finally, technology may be launched into new markets as well as currently served markets, which would entail establishing new channels of distribution. Distribution rights may be given to competitors in these new markets. New distribution can also be gained through joint ventures, possibly involving collaborative development of the technology.

TARGETING

Adoption of a new technology is likely to be faster if the marketing strategy is compatible with the segment targeted. Easingwood and Lunn (1992) examined the diffusion of telecommunications products and found that clearly targeted products diffused more rapidly than non-targeted ones (see Figure 3 for examples).

Target Innovative Adopters

Targeting innovative adopters can take two main forms: (a) targeting both companies and innovative individuals within those companies, or (b) targeting sectors.

Innovative Companies and Individuals. Based on the familiar model, the technology adoption life cycle, this strategy identifies innovative adopters because they are prepared to buy without seeing the product up and running elsewhere. They do not insist that the technology have a "track record." Moore (1991) divides these early buyers—only a small percentage of the total potential market, but hugely influential—into technological enthusiasts, or "techies," and visionaries. Techies are intrigued by technology and will explore a

Figure 3
Targeting: Some Examples

Target innovative adopters	NTT taking its global photo transmission system to sectors, such as the insurance industry, that are likely to be early adopters
Target pragmatists	Amgen using a large sales force to promote its hepatitis C drug to *all* hospital specialists
Target conservatives	Microsoft aiming its integrated software product Works at the PC conservative market
Target current customers	IBM Software Group working with many of the Global 5000
Target competitors' customers	Xerox targeting its digital copiers at Hewlett-Packard customers

product's potential for themselves. Their endorsement is vital because it means the product does, in fact, work. Visionaries are the managers with clout, often very senior, who can see a product's potential for overturning existing ways of operating, delivering significant value and competitive advantage to those organizations prepared to grasp the new technology.

Technological enthusiasts and visionaries, although placed together in this innovative group, are very different in some regards. Techies are excited by the technology itself, whereas the visionaries try to find its greater worth—some single, compelling application that uses the full range of the new technology. A visionary is motivated by a potentially significant leap forward, not by the newness of the technology.

Visionaries are a rare breed. They not only have the ability to see the potential when no one else can, they also have the management drive and charisma to persuade the rest of an organization to back the vision. They anticipate a radical discontinuity between the old ways and the new, realizing that this rarely happens smoothly, and so they will tolerate the glitches and setbacks that inevitably occur before this is achieved.

The only way to work with visionaries, says Moore, is to use a small, high-level sales force. Constantly looking to leverage technology, visionaries typically maintain good relationships with techies, so this segment should not be neglected. And techies can be reached fairly easily through the technical and business press. It is their job to stay alert to all developments, wher-

ever their sources, not just to focus on their own industry.

Early Adopting Sectors. Innovators can sometimes be hard to identify, but they are worth searching out. They start the ball rolling. However, an alternative to identifying individuals with these special attractive characteristics is to target whole sectors that are likely to be early buyers.

USDC developed an active-matrix flat panel display screen—in effect, the first "paper-quality" screen, with each pixel linked to its own transistor—and targeted the product at some of the world's leading air forces, a sector with a pressing need for the latest technology.

In the telecommunications sector, NTT has developed Digital Photo System, a means of transmitting a photo by a digital camera over the airways via cellular phones to a laptop computer and from there to a printer. The whole process takes about 10 seconds and can be done globally. The service was aimed initially at the newspaper and insurance sectors, both of which would particularly benefit from an acceleration in the speed of the internal processing of photographs.

Target the Pragmatists

Sometimes called the "early majority," pragmatists (as Moore calls them) are the large group of adopters following behind the techies and visionaries, though Moore argues that the gap between the two groups is so large it deserves to be called a chasm. Pragmatists typically comprise large organizations with a clear need to adopt new technologies to retain or improve competi-

tiveness, but with a reluctance to do so. The dislocation would be so extensive and the size of the investment required to switch the whole firm over to the new technology so large that they are risk-averse. People in this group are reasonably comfortable about taking on new technology, but only when some well-established references exist. Their preference is for evolution, not revolution. They are looking for something that can be slotted into existing ways of doing things. "If the goal of visionaries is to take a quantum leap forward," explains Moore, "the goal of pragmatists is to make a percentage improvement—incremental, measurable, predictable progress."

Marketing to pragmatists is a matter of:

- attending the industry conferences and trade shows;
- getting frequent mentions in the industry magazines;
- being installed in other companies in the same industry;
- developing industry-specific applications;
- having alliances with other key suppliers to the industry.

As Moore observes, pragmatists like to hear companies talk about their new products as "industry standards." What they hate to hear is products described as "state-of-the-art." This makes them extremely edgy. Pharmaceutical companies are well known for targeting their new drugs at hospital specialists working in the leading teaching hospitals. However, they do not neglect the pragmatists either. Amgen has assembled a sales team of about 50 people to promote its new hepatitis C drug to all the hematologists and gastroenterologists working in hospitals who may have to treat patients with the ailment.

Target Conservatives

The "conservatives," or "late adopters," really are not that keen on new technology. By and large, they would really rather not adopt any if they could get away with it, but competitive pressures may force them to do so. They are not that confident in their ability to adapt to new technology, so they like to see evidence of support. By the time the technology gets to them, there will probably be an established standard. Conservatives like to buy pre-assembled packages, with everything bundled. "They want high-tech products to be like refrigerators," says Moore. "You open the door, the light comes on automatically, your food stays cold, and you don't have to think about it."

However, it can he a big mistake to neglect this section of the market. For one thing, it is large—probably around a third of the whole market. It is often not developed as systematically as it should be, possibly because high-tech companies do not generally find it easy to empathize with this group. The product development costs are apt to be fully amortized at this stage, so extending the product's life should be highly profitable.

Because of conservatives' reluctance to come to grips with a new technology and its implications, a product has to be made increasingly easy to adopt if a high-tech company is to succeed with this group. The DOS PC operating system stalled when it reached the late adopter segment—the home market, the home office, the small business. This segment does not have the support offered in large companies and was disinclined to teach itself DOS. It took the greater simplicity of Windows 3.0 to bring it into the market. Microsoft has aimed its product Works, an integrated, all-in-one word processor, spreadsheet, and database (none of which are state-of-the-art), at the PC conservative market.

Target Current Customers

Existing customers can be an obvious target group for well-established companies. So it makes sense for IBM Software Group, the world's second largest software firm—which has very strong customer relationships with the Global 5000, the world's largest companies—to think first

of its current customers. Although current customers ought to be the most secure market, this is not necessarily the case. They can he hard to satisfy and quite costly to retain. Such is Intel's experience. It is having to cut the prices of some of its computer chips in an attempt to retain big corporate customers such as Compaq and Packard Bell. The latter are threatening to switch to Cyrix, the rival microprocessor producer, as they do everything possible to reduce the costs of their lowest-priced PCs.

Targeting existing customers is a strategy particularly appropriate to rapidly changing, advanced technologies. It can be particularly relevant for complex technologies when the decision to adopt often relies on a high degree of technical expertise and mutual trust between buyer and supplier.

Target Competitors' Customers

Finally, competitors' customers can present a prime opportunity, especially when the company's own product is competitive and the competitor has a large market share. Xerox would claim that this is the case for the new digital copiers designed by its Office Document Product Group. The copiers, which have faxing, scanning, and printing capabilities when connected to the personal computers of Hewlett-Packard's customers, are targeted toward HP and its dominance in the printer market.

Such a practice is commonplace in the pharmaceutical industry. Amgen has pitched its new hepatitis C treatment drug, Infeger, at those customers for whom the existing treatments, such as Schering-Plough's Intron A or Roche Holdings' Roferon A, have not been successful.

Of course, this strategy is very aggressive. For brand new technologies, it may be counterproductive. Aggressive competitive tactics may be seen as undermining the credibility of the entire technology, rather than just the competitor's product, as may have been intended.

POSITIONING

Some new technologies are so specialized that targeting and positioning strategies are too unambiguous and virtually redundant. Other new technologies are so wide-ranging in their potential applications that the market needs some strong clues as to targeting and positioning before it will respond. Many products fall between these two extremes.

Positioning can be based on tangible (technological) or intangible characteris-

tics (such as image), with technologically intensive industrial markets favoring the former. Where the market is not so technologically informed, or the benefits of the new technology are not so easily differentiated from competitors, positioning characteristics are likely to be more intangible. Positioning possibilities can be numerous, but some of those used most often are described here (see Figure 4 for examples).

Emphasize Exclusivity

A way to differentiate the product offer is by emphasizing how exclusive it is. In other words, can the product be placed in the upper segment of the market, where the margins are usually higher? For example, by focusing on quality, engineering, and adjustability, Recaro is offering a top-of-the-range child's safety seat—the Recaro-Start—that appeals to wealthier parents who place high priority on their children's safety. The company is playing heavily on its reputation for producing high-tech safety seats for Porsche and Aston-Martin.

Emphasize a Low Price

It used to be that low prices were considered an inappropriate lever for high-tech products and services. The market's reluctance to purchase was due to the misgivings it held about the new product's performance, which was largely unproven. The best strategy, marketers believed, was to address this reluctance directly by lowering the perceived risk that the product would not come up to expectations, or by reducing the perceived likelihood that it might be made redundant by a superior technology. In any case, high margins were needed to recoup the high costs of development.

Well, not necessarily anymore. Low price is used more and more in high-tech markets. For instance, phone companies will have to pay just $5 per device to use EPOC from Symbian, versus a reported $25 for Microsoft's Windows CE.

Emphasize Technological Superiority

Focusing on the technological superiority of a new high-tech product is common. When technology is changing rapidly and perhaps radically, it would seem that positioning a product on the basis of the latest technology built into it should reflect the product's true *raison d'etre*.

Figure 4
Positioning: Some Examples

Emphasize exclusivity	Recaro (supplier to Porsche and Aston Martin) with its top-of-the-range child's safety seat
Emphasize a low price	Just $5 per mobile phone for the operating system from Symbian ($25 quoted for the alternative)
Emphasize technological superiority	Xerox focusing on the superiority of digital copiers over the old technology
Emphasize a "safe bet"	Lucent Technologies designing its digital phones to be compatible with international standards

Xerox's new digital copiers are priced about 10 percent higher than old-style copiers because of the greater quality and reliability they offer compared to the old "light lens" technology copiers. This practice is also observed in the computer component manufacturing industry, where such new products as "bonded modems," storing units, and processor chips justify their premium pricing through their advanced technological features.

However, emphasizing such superiority does have its drawbacks. First, by stressing technological features, the marketer is assuming a certain level of knowledge that may not be present in at least part of the target market. Second, the preoccupation with technological specifications may obscure the genuine benefits customers could realize from the technology. Given the buying center nature of many high-tech adoption decisions involving technical specialists and nonspecialists, not all of whom are capable of translating technical specifications into everyday benefits, it may be more successful to come up with a more benefit-specific positioning tactic.

Emphasize a 'Safe Bet'

Stressing customer protection in the product is important because it enhances the product's credibility element and reduces the associated risk of moving to a new technology. Lucent Technologies focused on the fact that the specifications of both of its two newly introduced digital phones fall under established standards. One of the phones operates on the Code Division Multiple Access (CDMA) technology standard of the United States. The other, which is a "dual mode/dual band" handset, operates on the Time Division Multiple Access (TDMA) standard introduced by

AT&T to serve the entire European market, where the existence of different networks can otherwise hinder compatibility.

EXECUTION

As the final stage and therefore the one that completes the product's projection into the marketplace, execution is designed to trigger a positive purchase decision. The strategies used depend on the objectives of the launch itself, which in turn depend on the state of technology and the awareness the market has of it. For a very new technology, of which the market is unaware, execution tends to focus on conveying the generic benefits. At the other extreme, where the technology is well known to the market, the launch objectives focus more on establishing a brand name and competitive advantage. Figure 5 provides examples.

Use Opinion Leaders

It makes good sense to obtain the support of opinion leaders. As Moore states, "No company can afford to pay for every marketing contact made. Every programme must rely on some on-going chain-reaction effects, what is usually called 'word of mouth.'" Word-of-mouth is invaluable, of course, but the support of opinion leaders, who are industrial rather than public celebrities, can also be taken on board more formally, such as in advertising or through appearances at company seminars.

Compaq and NEC Technologies have managed to secure the endorsement of a number of well-known technical journalists for their FPDS screen. Pharmaceutical companies try to communicate the views of prominent doctors on their new drugs to influence the views of general practitioners and other doctors.

Reduce the Risk of Adoption

It is sometimes possible to reduce adoption risks. Can the product be offered on an introductory trial? Can it be leased? Luz Engineering, a producer of industrial solar heaters costing between $2–4 million, came up with a novel variation on this approach. Now Luz is prepared to sell its systems. However, it is also prepared to install and operate the solar heaters itself, in which case the client merely contracts to buy steam at 350°F for 20 years at a discount from the prevailing local power company rate. This is a "no-lose deal" from the client's perspective. The client pays for none of the installation and operating costs, but enjoys most of the expected benefits of the technology, without the associated risks.

Cultivate a Winner Image

Individuals and organizations can easily be confused by too much choice. Their first reaction, when faced with a confusing purchasing decision, is to postpone it. But when this is no longer possible, they vote for the safe choice: the market leader. There is safety in numbers. And this position can be reinforcing in technology markets. Other companies will recognize the leadership position and design supporting products and services around the market leader, which will thus become even more the preferred choice. The number one product becomes easier to use, cheaper to use, and better supported. There is a "winner take most" tendency, as Arthur states—the phenomenon of increasing returns. The bigger you get, the more apt you are to get bigger still. Conversely, the smaller you get, the more apt you are to shrink even more. Success breeds success, failure breeds failure. You have to become

Figure 5
Execution: Some Examples

Use opinion leaders	Compaq and NEC Technologies securing endorsements from technical journalists
Reduce the risk of adoption	Luz Engineering installing and running its industrial solar heaters that supply clients with energy at guaranteed prices
Cultivate a winner image	IBM advertising its position as recipient of the most U.S. patents for the fifth year running
Concentrate on a particular application	Lotus Notes focusing on worldwide accounting and consulting firms

a "gorilla," because if you do not, you'll be a "chimpanzee" or, more likely, a "monkey."

Thus, companies should try to cultivate a winner image for themselves and their products. However, this often involves allocating considerable resources to a big media splash aimed at communicating the (preordained) success of the new product. So this strategy is most popular with large companies. When Microsoft launched Windows 95, it did not pull its punches or spare its expenses. In the U.S., the Empire State Building was bathed in Windows colors. In the U.K., the *Times*, sponsored by Microsoft, doubled its print run and was given away free. In Australia, the Sydney Opera House was commandeered. The worldwide event, accompanied by the Rolling Stones' hit "Start Me Up," was said to have cost $200 million, but was hugely successful: one million copies sold in the U.S. in the first four days, compared to the 60 days it took the upgrade to MS-DOS to reach that level.

Of course, the approach to this position can be more subtle. In the last year, IBM received more U.S. patents than any other company, taking the top spot for the fifth consecutive year in a list that used to be dominated primarily by Japanese firms. This achievement has been stressed by IBM through articles in the technology sections of top-rated journals. It has also been the theme of an advertising campaign that aims to build a leader image for the company.

Sometimes the leadership position cannot be established across the entire market, in which case it should be established in a market segment. It is important to be the biggest fish in the pond, even if it means searching out a very small pond.

A market leader position is particularly important for pragmatists. These are the people who are contemplating committing their organizations to the new product—a much less risky gamble if the new product is the market leader.

A company that can establish a lead in a segment is in a very strong position. All the major customers have committed themselves to the product and so want it to remain the standard. The company can only lose such a position by shooting itself in the foot. Moore believes that segments conspire, unconsciously, "to install some company or product as the market leader and then do everything in their power to keep [it] there." This, of course, puts up huge barriers to entry for other competitors. If the leader plays its cards right, it can end up "owning" the segment.

Concentrate on a Particular Application

Concentrating on a particular application is all about crossing the chasm, the huge gulf that separates the techies and visionaries, few in number, from the much larger mainstream market dominated by pragmatists. The way across the chasm is to target the company's resources to one or two very specific niche markets where it can dominate rapidly and force out competitors. It can then use the dominance of the first niche to attack the surrounding niches.

Moore uses the analogy of the Allies' D-Day invasion strategy in World War II: assembling a huge invasion force and focusing it on one narrowly defined target, the beaches of Normandy, routing the enemy, then moving out to dominate surrounding areas of Normandy. In other words, establish a beachhead, then broaden the basis of operations.

Serving the needs of a particular segment is all about focusing the company's resources on customizing the product to the needs of that segment. The segment wants a customized solution. It wants the "whole product" with all relevant services, not 80 percent of the whole product with the responsibility of supplying the missing 20 percent itself. Sales in several segments would soon stretch the company's development resources to the breaking point as it tried to customize the product to each segment's needs. Lotus Notes managed to escape the chasm when it focused on the global account management sector; particularly on worldwide accounting and consulting firms.

In addition, niche sales are driven by references and word-of-mouth within that niche. Failure to build up a core level of business in a particular segment means that momentum in any one single segment is never established. Pragmatists and conservatives talk to people in their own industry and look for solutions that have been proven to work there.

Tactical Alliances. Companies sometimes have the opportunity to form tactical alliances with smaller firms to help put a "complete product" in place. Market niches will coalesce behind a product much more readily—elevating it effectively to the position of a standard—if that product is supported by a number of products that fill in the gaps the market values but that the main product could not possibly supply. Producers of software packages often welcome the entry of smaller firms with their add-on programs to help provide the fully rounded complete product. It is a matter of gathering the appropriate partners and allies to jointly deliver a more complete product.

This is, however, very different from the cooperation/licensing/alliance approach discussed earlier, which is more formal and strategic. Tactical alliances tend to occur spontaneously at a later stage in a technology's development as smaller companies, realizing that a product has the potential to become a standard, desire to become associated with that standard.

Introducing a new technology offers a marketplace the first opportunity to experience the brand new product. So the manner in which the introduction is handled is critical. Everything has to come together in what is usually a narrow window of opportunity. Get it wrong, and there may be little time to put things right. By this stage, the investment in the new technology may be considerable, yet the chances of rejection or indifference are quite high.

The strategies proposed here are all designed to reduce the risks of failure. Of course, a complete and consistent strategy will assemble one or more components from each of the preparation, targeting, positioning, and execution stages.

Technology-intensive products and companies are at the leading edge of many Western countries' economies. By examining the range of illustrations included here, it is hoped that managers can help the new technology take its intended role in these economies.

References

W. Brian Arthur, "Increasing Returns and the New World of Business," *Harvard Business Review*, July–August 1996, pp. 100–109.

Christopher Easingwood and Simon O. Lunn, "Diffusion Paths in a High-Tech Environment: Clusters and Commonalities," *R&D Management*, 22, 1 (1992): 69–80.

Geoffrey A. Moore, *Crossing the Chasm: Marketing and Selling High-Technology Products to Mainstream Customers* (New York: HarperBusiness, 1991).

Geoffrey A. Moore, *Inside the Tornado: Marketing Strategies from Silicon Valley's Cutting Edge* (New York: HarperBusiness, 1995).

Charles P. Wallace, "The Man Bill Gates Fears Most," *Fortune*, November 23, 1998, pp. 257–260.

Chris Easingwood is the Caudwell Professor of Marketing and Head of Marketing and Strategy at Manchester Business School, Manchester, England, where **Anthony Koustelos** was an MBA student before becoming a market analyst with the Competitive Intelligence Unit, Business Development Group, DHL Worldwide Network NV/SA Brussels, Belgium.

Brand Killers

Store brands aren't for losers anymore. In fact, they're downright sizzling. And that scares the soap out of the folks who bring us Tide and Minute Maid and Alpo and ?…

By Matthew Boyle

MELANIE TURNER HAS FORGOTTEN HER SHOPPING LIST. But the 42-year-old pension consultant, who has just entered Costco's 133,000-square-foot warehouse store in Norwalk, Conn., doesn't seem to mind. Turner knows right where she's going. In the dish detergent section, her hand goes past Procter & Gamble's Cascade to grab two 96-ounce bottles of Kirkland Signature, the in-store brand that Costco has plastered on everything from cashews to cross-trainer sneakers. Trolling for some fresh fish for dinner, she hauls in a 2½-pound package of tilapia—it, too, emblazoned with the bold red, white, and black Kirkland logo. Then it's off to the paper aisle, where she picks up mammoth packs of Kirkland dinner napkins, Kirkland toilet paper, and … wait, where are the Kirkland paper towels? Her eyes scan the store's maze of hulking pallets—no sign of them—before coming to rest on a 12-pack of Bounty. A moment of decision. "I'll wait on this," she says finally.

And there, in microcosm, is why Melanie Turner scares the pants off Procter & Gamble, Unilever, Kraft, and just about every consumer goods company out there. Her shopping cart is headed for the checkout aisle, and there's hardly a national brand in it.

Not so long ago the great American brand wouldn't have stood for that sort of treatment. You were a symbol of the good life: the pause that refreshed, the breakfast of champions, the filtered cigarette with the unfiltered taste. Everyone wanted a piece of you. But you've come a long way, baby—down. No, brand loyalty isn't dead. We've heard that knell sounded before,

most notably following Marlboro Friday in 1993, when Philip Morris cut its prices 40%, sending investors into a panic that lopped nearly $50 billion off the market caps of 25 top brandmakers. But there's always been a swoosh or an apple to seduce us back into buying brands. In fact, Melanie Turner is just as brand loyal as her mother was in the 1960s when she kept the cupboard in their Queens home: "We were a Skippy family," Turner recalls. What's different today is who owns and creates the products Turner is loyal to.

An almost imperceptible tectonic shift has been reshaping the world of brands. Retailers—once the lowly peddlers of brands that were made and marketed by big, important manufacturers—are now behaving like full-fledged marketers. And here's the earthquake part: It is their brands—not those of traditional powerhouses like Kraft or Coke—that are winning over the Melanie Turners in the greatest numbers.

Retailers, once the lowly peddlers of brands, are now behaving like full-fledged marketers.

They're brands like Wal-Mart's Ol' Roy dog food, which has quietly surpassed Nestle's venerable Purina as the world's top-selling dog chow—or the George line of apparel, which has knocked Liz Claiborne's duds out of Wal-Mart. They're brands like Charles Shaw wine (a.k.a. Two-Buck Chuck, after its inconceivably

low price), available at gourmet grocer Trader Joe's, where customers have been known to haul away a dozen cases at a time. They're the Michael Graves line of housewares at Target, where an estimated 50% of all products are private brands, and the 4,300 food and drink items that grocery giant Kroger cranks out of the 41 factories it owns and operates. And there's more to come. 7-Eleven has launched its own beer, Santiago, brewed in El Salvador and designed to steal market share from Mexican import Corona. Barnes & Noble recently expanded its imprint of store-brand books. Rite Aid will add about 250 private-label items this year, some under its new brands Pure Spring and 411. One out of two ceiling fans sold in the U.S. is from Home Depot, and most of those are its Hampton Bay brand. Once happy to serve as passive landlords of shelf space, "retailers are now becoming brand managers," says Dan Stanek, executive vice president at consulting company Retail Forward.

Private-label goods are nothing new, of course, having been around since the days when A&P owned vast coffee plantations in South America. Back in 1930, a new magazine called FORTUNE, commenting on the struggle between retailers and manufacturers, noted, "No issue, except Prohibition, is more violently discussed." But there are big differences this time around—beginning with the products themselves. Picturing those no-name, black-and-white cans labeled simply beans? Picture instead a slender glass bottle of Harvest Moon asparagus spears from Texas grocery chain H-E-B, with an elegant label (a soft crescent moon, interlocking o's) that makes the Del Monte canned product sitting next to it look cheap—except that Harvest Moon is 20 cents cheaper. The quality can be better too: Take Winn-Dixie's chocolate ice cream, which *Consumer Reports* magazine ranked ahead of Breyers. Or Kroger's potato chips, found to be tastier than Ruffles and Pringles—for less money. Wal-Mart employs a creative team devoted to designing logos and writing marketing copy, while everyone from France's Carrefour to Wegmans in Rochester, N.Y., is developing branding programs that emphasize quality, image, and innovation—not just price. "Get rid of the term 'private label,'" says Merrill Lynch analyst Mark Husson. "They possess an independent personality. They are brands."

The New No-Names

One in five items sold in U.S. stores is store branded, and more and more retailers are getting in on the action. They're selling better products and designing spiffier packaging. Free samples on the following pages.

Retailers love this trend. Because overhead is low and marketing costs are nil, private-label products bring 10% higher margins, on average, than branded goods do. But more than that, a trusted store brand can differentiate a chain from its competitors. Shoppers will drive the extra mile to Costco to buy Kirkland cashews, filling their carts with other goods while they're at it.

The numbers look good for the retailers too. According to A.C. Nielsen, unit sales of store-brand goods grew 8.6% during the past two years, vs. 1.5% for national brands. All told, one in five items sold in U.S. stores is now store branded, which sounds like a lot—until you learn that in Europe that percentage has reached 40%. Consumers here keep warming to them. A 2001 Gallup poll found 45% of shoppers more likely to switch to a store brand, while only 31% said so in 1996.

If your job is assistant brand manager at Duracell, those are the numbers that keep you awake at night. "It's a mistake to think that store brands are not 'real' brands," P&G chief A.G. Lafley said in a February speech to employees. "In some categories these brands are tougher competitors than tradi-

tional brands." (Neither Lafley nor executives from most major consumer-products companies would comment for this story.) The immediacy of the threat has been clear in Lafley's actions. While flagships like Tide still have a magnetic pull for shoppers, a second-tier P&G offering like Era detergent is in a whole different world of hurt: P&G slashed its ad spending on Era from $13.9 million to $5.3 million last year, according to TNS Media Intelligence/CMR. Rival Unilever, meanwhile, has pared its brands from 1,600 in the mid-1990s to just 200. A spokesperson explains that "all our innovation and marketing support" will focus on leading brands like Dove, Hellmann's, and Lipton. "The future is three and out," says Ken Harris of Cannondale Associates, which is a consultant to consumer packaged-goods makers. "Either you're among the top three brands or you're out."

Yet even as they cull their stables to the strongest horses, many branded manufacturers are pursuing a fallback strategy. Years ago a Gillette executive equated producing private-label razors to "selling your soul." Now Kraft, Nestle, Kimberly-Clark, H.J. Heinz, Del Monte, Unilever, and others have selectively taken an "if you can't beat 'em, join 'em" strategy. "Ten or 15 years ago branded manufacturers wouldn't [make] private labels, or, if they did, they lied about it," says retail consultant Bill Bishop. "Today more and more have a strategy to do both." Even Campbell Soup—its classic label iconized by Andy Warhol in the '60s—turns out soup for European retailers. "Many of our products are made by the same guys that pack national brands," says Bill Moran, CEO of the 1,170-store "extreme value" chain Save-a-Lot. "We have to be careful how we tell people about that. For instance, [Con-Agra's] Chef Boyardee packs our canned pasta products. They wouldn't want you to know that."

Nor would P&G want you to know that it's making other people's brands. But it is. Quietly, and until now undetected by the outside world—including analysts who have followed the company for years—its paper products division has been churning out store-brand toilet paper and paper towels in Europe. (It has done so in the U.S. in the past, but no longer.) A spokesperson at the maker of Charmin and Bounty stresses that it is a "tiny, tiny" piece of its business—less than 5% of its Family Care division, valued at $4 billion by analysts—and that it produces private labels only to fulfill contracts of acquired companies or

to maximize production at its plants. That makes sense: P&G needs to keep its works running full and steady.

Still, that the world's leading brand company would even consider a reduction to subcontractor status speaks volumes about the seismic shifts taking place. And now the role reversal seems complete: Grocery giant Albertsons has appointed a "vice president of corporate brands" to roll out a premium brand called Essensia. We'll learn of its merits later this year, when TV spots featuring Everybody Loves Raymond star Patricia Heaton hit the air. When store brands go prime time, something has changed.

P & G's A.G. Lafley told employees: "It's a mistake to think that store brands are not real brands."

THE CHANGE CAN BE BOILED DOWN TO THIS: The retail universe has consolidated, and the media universe has shattered. In brands' golden age the three big TV networks gave brand giants like Colgate a direct conduit to the American public. But as the mass media have de-massified into 1,000 bits—500 channels, DirecTV, blogs, and the mass marketer's worst nightmare, TiVo—you don't see as many Colgate ads on TV. In short, brandmakers are losing their connection to the consumer. Willard Bishop Consulting found that in 1995 it took three TV commercials to reach 80% of 18- to 49-year-old women. In 2000, just five years later, it took 97 ads to reach the same group. "Short of being embroiled in a scandal," concludes ad agency Doremus in a recent newsletter, "it's almost impossible to get your name in enough channels to build substantial awareness."

Meanwhile, guess who's been building a direct connection to more and more American consumers? That's right, the "mass channel," as the big superstores are known in the trade. The consolidation of retail into a few mega-megachains means the ten biggest account for some 80% of the average manufacturer's business, vs. about 30% a decade ago. It's that mass channel, not the mass media, that is now attracting the bulk of marketing dollars. Almost 60% of manufacturers' marketing budgets flow to retailers in the form of so-called trade spending (ads in shopper circulars, merchandising displays), compared with 36% two decades ago, according to Cannondale.

In other words, the news for manufacturers is doubly bad: Not only are your customers launching their own brands, but more and more they are managing yours. Looking for a big TV audience to push your new deodorant? Try Wal-Mart's in-store TV screens, said to reach 100 million shoppers every month. Want to sell your tasty new cupcakes? Have Costco whip up a batch for customers to nosh on while they shop. It makes you wonder how far-fetched Forrester Research was when it came to this conclusion in a 2002 report: "Wal-Mart will become the next P&G."

In 1995 it took **three TV spots** to reach 80% of women. Five years later it took 97 spots to reach them.

As incredible as that sounds, don't discount it. P&G's Lafley speaks often about how the customer is, in fact, two separate people: the consumer and the shopper. P&G's job, his logic goes, is to prime the consumer to want a given product. The retailer's job is to close the deal with the shopper. But here again, the numbers aren't on Lafley's side: 72% of purchasing decisions are made in the store, not in front of the tube, according to Point-of-Purchase Advertising International. Time isn't on his side either: The longer a store brand is on the shelves—Ol' Roy has been around since 1983—the more comfortable shoppers become with it. So while merchants act like marketers, marketers like P&G are forced to act like … merchants.

An odd but increasingly common sight is that of the FORTUNE 500 CEO in aisle four muttering about the placement of his products. Lafley has been spotted pondering P&G's Swiffer floor cleaner in a department store in Greece. Visiting a Wal-Mart store in Maryland last fall, Newell Rubbermaid CEO Joseph Galli took copious notes on the display of his company's Sharpie pens. Hasbro CEO Alan Hassenfeld frequently traipses the aisles of Targets and Wal-Marts. "One of our very important jobs is to figure out how to get more people in the stores," Hassenfeld said earlier this year.

If the makers of Crest, PaperMate, and Play-Doh are scrambling for shelf space, it's easy to imagine what life is like for a lesser-known brand like Mrs. Paul's frozen seafood. It gives new meaning to the term shelf life. Frank Weise, CEO of Cott, which makes store-brand soft drinks, including Wal-Mart's huge-selling Sam's Choice, says he's stealing market share mainly from Orange Crush, Shasta, and Hires Root Beer. "You don't see them much anymore," he says. Nor do you see Nuprin, the pain reliever from Bristol Myers-Squibb that tennis great Jimmy Connors used to shill for. It got caught between Advil and store-brand ibuprofen. "Just Nupe it," indeed.

So what happens if your company's whole strategy consists of pushing Nuprins and Orange Crushes? Ask Aurora Foods. In the mid-1990s it got the idea of buying up "orphaned brands"—Mrs. Butterworth's and Log Cabin syrups, Duncan Hines cake mix, Van de Kamp's frozen fish—and giving them the love they weren't getting from their caretakers. Though at first applauded by Wall Street, the company soon discovered it was marching backward into the future: What the orphans really lacked was love from retailers, not marketers. Retail giants wanted to deal with Jolly Green Giants, not a bunch of lovable but underweight orphans. After searching in vain for a home for its orphans—and oh, yeah, seeing its CEO jailed for securities fraud—Aurora recently announced its intention to declare Chapter 11 bankruptcy. (It will continue to do business while in bankruptcy.)

Occasionally a castoff can return to haunt its parent. In the late 1990s, P&G dropped its White Cloud toilet paper label to focus on the stronger Charmin. It made good sense—until an entrepreneur named Tony Gelbart noticed that thanks to the use-it-or-lose-it policy that governs trademarks, P&G's claim to the White Cloud label had lapsed. Gelbart snapped it up for a song before offering Wal-Mart the rights to the White Cloud label. Today Wal-Mart's aisles are filled with White Cloud toilet tissue and even diapers—it's an "undead" brand, as one observer puts it, that gives P&G the unenviable distinction of having to compete against a label it created.

YOU WOULDN'T THINK THAT A TREND AS diffuse as this could be traced to one man. Then you meet Dave Nichol. Picture a grumpier Dave Thomas with a law degree, a master's from Harvard, the paunch of a lifelong food lover, and an ego to match. "Where are those softshell crabs?" he roars to his assistant from his thickly wooded living room. In the stately South Forest Hill section of Toronto, Nichol has recreated a tropical resort, with fountains and palm trees, the glow of a big-screen TV penetrating the fauna. Tonight he's not only storyteller but chef. "This wine is from my own vineyard," he crows, pouring his visitor a glass of cabernet and diving into his tale.

After a stint at McKinsey & Co., Nichol was hired by Canadian grocer Loblaws in 1972 and three years later was named president of its supermarkets. "I started off running Loblaws like every other retailer in North America, which is getting people in the store by giving Coke and Tide away below cost. I remember one time I ran chuck steaks at 99 cents. I killed every cow between here and Moose Jaw," he deadpans. "It was a disaster. I finally said, 'This is a fool's errand.'"

It was time for a new plan. Nichol remembered seeing how London retailer Marks & Spencer had featured its own store brand, St. Michael, which was not only less expensive but also higher in quality than the leading brands. "This stuck in my head," says Nichol, who also got private-label inspiration from England's J. Sainsbury, Germany's Aldi, and France's Carrefour. He began simply in 1978, offering basic knock-off products under the brand name No Name. (He nicked that idea from Carrefour.) "For five or six years I did nothing but go into people's living rooms and say, 'Here's one basket of national brands for $150, and here are the same products from No Name for $100. If you don't like them, we'll give you the national brands free.'"

No Name was a commercial success—but Nichol wasn't happy selling canned veggies. "I was food-obsessed," he says. "That was my passion. So I started creating products." The first—a coffee he called President's Blend, which was modeled after the brew sold in a top Toronto restaurant—was good, but nothing compared to his ambitions for his next project. Nichol would bake the world's tastiest chocolate chip cookie. It took him two years. The prototypes exchanged real butter for hydrogenated coconut oil, and quality chocolate for artificial chips, but the recipe ultimately hinged on this: "I tried to find the maximum amount of chips you could cram into a cookie," says Nichol. "That turned out to be 39%. Chips Ahoy was 19%."

The product that emerged from the lab—Nichol dubbed it the Decadent—wasn't just tasty; it was truly delicious. And it swept all of Canada, becoming the country's top seller within a year or two. Shoppers began to take notice. "If you liked my chocolate-chip cookie," Nichol recalls thinking, "you will really like my cereal." His approach here was identical: "Kellogg's had two scoops of raisins, so I said, 'We've got twice the number of raisins. And oh, yes, it's cheaper.'"

This strange idea—a store brand whose quality was better than national brands—was only one in a series of firsts. His next had to do with packaging. Toronto-based Cott, at the time an also-ran in soda, was making President's Choice cola using a formula based on RC Cola. Don Watt, a package-design expert then working with Cott, took the logo for President's Choice cola and reduced it to a simple, highly stylized "PC." That fresh visual representation "became the next wave," Watt recalls, and sales shot up from 680,000 cases per year to two million.

Nichol's next brainstorm was to export President's Choice products to North America, so he brought in a man named Tom Stephens to sign deals with regional grocers, like D'Agostino in New York and Jewel in Chicago. He told them a strong store brand would free them from the tyranny of manufacturers. Many American grocers scoffed at the idea, calling it "Canadian lunacy," Stephens remembers. "The stores that took President's Choice," he says over a plate of risotto at a quiet Toronto trattoria, "were either desperate or brilliant." By 1994, 15 chains in 36 states were carrying President's Choice, Stephens says. That's how, around 1990, Nichol ended up in the office of Sam Walton.

Walton's proposition was simple: He didn't want to carry President's Choice in his stores. But could he tap the expertise of Nichol and his team to develop a private-label strategy for Wal-Mart?

Nichol's initial recommendation was a radical one: Build a Sam Walton Innovation Center dedicated to new-product development while simultaneously buying up faded but still-resonant brands like the detergent Purex. Wal-Mart could flood each category and dominate it with its own brands. "If Wal-Mart had adopted that strategy, they would rule the world," Nichol says. Wal-Mart rejected the proposal because it insisted—and still does—that it needed national brands to pull customers into its stores. "The food business in the U.S.— when they say their prayers, they should thank God I did not convince them that that was the way to go," says Nichol.

But the actual outcome was big enough. In 1991, Wal-Mart launched its premium Sam's Choice brand, modeled after President's Choice. Two years later Great Value, an even less expensive store brand, hit the shelves. In 2000 the company devoted an entire page of its annual report to its store brands, which now make up 40% of total sales, according to *Private Label* magazine estimates. The stable includes Equate nasal spray and ibuprofen, Great Value beef jerky and bleach, Spring Valley vitamins, Sam's Choice tuna, and, of course, Ol' Roy. "Everything that a brand would do, we have to live up to," says Bob Anderson, Wal-Mart's head of store-brand food products, who helped launch Great Value in 1993 and is now moving the brand into China. While Wal-Mart won't disclose sales of its store brands, one analyst estimated to *Private Label Buyer* magazine that Wal-Mart was responsible for 75% of the growth of store-brand sales last year.

No doubt aware of what he helped create, Nichol dives into his dinner of delectable soft-shell crab and yams, washed down with some of his wine. "When you think about private label in North America," he says between bites, "you think about Dave Nichol."

WHERE WILL IT STOP? WHEN WAL-MART launched an in-house line of batteries called EverActive in 1999, Rayovac CEO David Johnson called the competition "much ado about nothing," predicting the store-brand share would stay below 3%. Three years later sales were at 8%—"which I think is where they're going to be," he said last December: "8% to 10%." Tops.

By focusing on their best brands and going after unlikely targets, manufacturers can fight back.

But as each line in the sand turns out to be just that, manufacturers are finding they have few moves left. They could never compete with store brands on price. Now many of them can't compete on quality either. So besides getting into private-label production, how do you compete against the store brands? One answer: You don't. You go after other targets—like the $600 visit to the dentist. That's what P&G has done with its do-it-yourself $25 Whitestrips (marketed under the Crest umbrella, along with the equally successful SpinBrush), notes Harvard Business School professor Clayton Christensen. That, along with Lafley's main strategy— refocusing around 12 superbrands like Iams, Pantene, and Pampers and selling the heck out of them—has produced cheering results. P&G's stock is up a dividend-adjusted 34% over the past two years.

P&G and others had better keep moving. The cycle of innovation followed by imitation is faster than ever. In fact, Whitestrips are now up against Colgate Simply White and store-brand whitening gel.

The manufacturers' reliance on old standbys raises another question: Why do we buy brands, anyway? Above all else, it's about trust. There's also the intangible aspirational quality. For Susana MacLean, 40, store brands conjure memories of growing up without luxuries. But already there are signs that the store-brand stigma is disappearing. First, shoppers are catching on to the quality thing—seven out of ten polled by Gallup in 2001 said that the quality of store brands was equal to or better than national brands. Trust? Shoppers trust Wal-Mart's Equate nasal spray enough to stick it up their nose. Aspiration? How's this: "I really like the Michael Graves brand," says 32-year-old Jean Trujillo of Hillsborough, N.J., "and have gone out of my way to see if they sell something I'm looking for."

Most store brands will never attain the heights of Ol' Roy and Michael Graves: Branding is a tricky business, as much art as science, and brand loyalties die hard. "House brands have no appeal to me," says Susan Gifford, 46. If she subbed Shop Rite's store brand "sandwich cookies" for Oreos, her kids would throw a fit. But if you listen closely, you can almost hear the tectonic plates shifting. "I definitely still have the perception—which I suspect is wrong—that the quality of store-brand products is not as high," she says. Her self-questioning deepens when she thinks about how Target brands appeal to her. "I might even buy them if they were offered in another store," Gifford says. "Now that I think about it, I'd probably give a lot of store brands a try, just to see how we liked them, and then stick with them if they're just as good." When asked why she isn't trying them now, Gifford has an answer that would put the fear of God into the most self-possessed branded manufacturer: "Good question. Maybe I will."

Pitching It To Kids

On sites like Neopets.com, brands are embedded in the game. Is children's marketing going too far?

By DAREN FONDA
GLENDALE

*C*hirita isn't feeling well. A furry green creature with four legs and a pair of wings, she has come down with a case of the Neomites, a common affliction in the mythical online world of Neopia. The Neopian pharmacy sometimes stocks a cure, but it's pricey, costing about 330 Neopoints. What's Chirita's owner, Wendy Mendoza, 10, of Atlanta, to do? One way to rack up the points would be to play any of the 110 free games on Neopets.com, trying activities like bumper cars or chemistry for beginners. Then again, Wendy could also score by hunting for secret images in the site's virtual McDonald's, trying her hand at the Lucky Charms Super Search game or watching cereal ads in the General Mills theater—earning 150 points a commercial. Wendy visits the site several days a week. "I like playing on it better than watching TV," she says.

Wendy may not realize it, but in Neopia she's the target of the latest twist in children's marketing—a burgeoning and increasingly controversial business. In the past decade, corporate America's annual budget for advertising products and services to kids has more than doubled, to an estimated $15 billion. The pot of gold: $600 billion in family spending that children under 13 are said to influence, along with $40 billion in pocket money that they spend on purchases from candy to clothes, an amount projected to hit nearly $52 billion in 2008, according to the market research firm Mintel. As many a besieged parent can attest, children's marketing seems to be raining down everywhere, from the Internet to video games to coloring books. And with kids increasingly splitting their time among all manner of media, not to mention extracurricular activities, "marketers are targeting children younger and younger in every way they can," says James McNeal, a children's marketing consultant based in College Station, Texas.

Is the ad parade getting out of hand? Consumer advocates say it is, claiming that an explosion of ads for junk food, aimed primarily at children, is fueling the obesity epidemic. (The food industry's lobbying group, the Grocery Manufacturers of America, denies that claim, saying there's no definitive data linking advertising to obesity.) Another issue: that the lines between advertising, entertainment and educational materials are increasingly blurring, as you may have noticed if you have seen schooling materials like the Pepperidge Farm Goldfish Counting Fun book or toys like the Play-Doh George Foreman Grill. "It's unfair. Children don't even know they're being advertised to," says Susan Linn, author of *Consuming Kids: The Hostile Takeover of Childhood.*

Even professionals devoted to marketing seem concerned about some of the brand-building tactics. According to a poll of youth marketers conducted by Harris Interactive earlier this year, 91% of those surveyed said that kids are being pitched to in ways that they don't even notice, and 61% believe that advertising to children starts too young. At what age do they think it's O.K.? A majority of the pros in the poll think it's appropriate to start advertising to kids at age 7, even though they feel that children can't "effectively separate fantasy from reality in media and advertising" before age 9 or make intelligent purchase decisions before 12. A recent study by the American Psychological Association confirmed that children under 8 have a tough time distinguishing ads from entertainment. But don't expect those findings to kill the product-placement party. "Kids' marketing just grows as businesses realize that children have more purchasing potential than any other demographic," says consultant McNeal, who advises FORTUNE 500 firms on marketing policies.

Sites like Neopets are taking the old concept of product placement to sophisticated new heights. With 11 million users, 39% under 13, Neopets is one of the Internet's most popular and "stickiest" destinations. Users visit on average for 3½ hours a month, according to Nielsen/NetRatings. But unlike sites that generate ad revenues by inserting pop-ups or banners along a page that are easily identified (and ignored), Neopets offers marketers what company CEO Doug Dohring calls "immersive

RETAILING
Brand-Name Field Trips

The field trip for the 24 kindergartners from Woodside Avenue School has all the noisy excitement of the old-fashioned kind, with kids tumbling out of a school bus eager to see, hear and touch things outside their classroom. But the field-trip destination is not the usual venue, like a museum or zoo. It's a Petco store. Tour guide Jennifer Rohan, manager of the Ramsey, N.J., pet-supply emporium, lets the kids pet a quivering chinchilla ($129.99, food and shelter sold separately), squawk at a taciturn macaw named Oscar ($2,399.99) and find Nemo the clown fish ($14.99). An hour later, the children are back on the bus clutching handout Petco-logo Frisbees and debating the merits of dogs vs. Hermit crabs.

The retail field trip is part education, part marketing, and all the rage. Groups of children from schools, summer camps and Girl and Boy Scout troops are taking organized tours through establishments ranging from Sports Authority stores to Saturn dealerships to Krispy Kreme outlets. With school budgets squeezed in recent years, these free excursions are in some cases replacing trips to more traditional destinations. While companies are eager to polish their community image, critics say the real goal is to turn kids into brand-loyal consumers.

Leading the boom is Field Trip Factory, a five-year-old Chicago outfit founded by former marketing consultant Susan Singer that designs educational tours for corporate clients. Bookings have nearly doubled in 2004, to 12,000. One big reason: cost. The trip to Petco cost $5.25 a child for the bus ride, says Woodside teacher Stacey Melhorn, while a zoo visit can cost $15. "When it's free, it's easier for everybody," says Melhorn. Says Dan Fuller, director of federal programs for the National School Boards Association: "In a perfect world, schools would have the funds to send kids to where they feel is the most educationally appropriate."

Dominick's supermarket pay Field Trip Factory up to $300,000 a year to fill the void. On a recent tour, second-graders from Universal School, a Muslim school in Bridgeview, Ill., learned how sugar-laden kids' cereals are placed on lower shelves. Li Schiavitti, 75, the store's star field-trip guide, advised them to reach instead for something healthier—like Toasted Oats, Dominick's house brand.

It's subtle, but the message sticks. At stores where kids received free samples of V8 Splash Fruit Medley, it became the top-selling flavor, according to Field Trip Factory. In another case, sales of children's toothpaste shot up 18%. "These field trips are nothing more than a way to clobber a captive audience of impressionable children with ads," says Gary Rushkin of Commercial Alert, a watchdog group. But Abbie Levi, whose daughter Sarah asked for a hamster after attending the Petco field trip, says simply, "Parents have the power to say no." Easier said than done.

—By Lisa Takeuchi Cullen.
With reporting by Leslie Whitaker/Chicago

advertising." The company integrates ad messages into the site's content, creating "advergames" for clients based on a product-or brand-awareness campaign. The company then tracks site activity and provides demographic and usage data to customers, offering a window into kids' purchasing habits.

At the Neopia food shop, for instance, Uh Oh Oreo cookies, Nestle SweeTarts and Laffy Taffy candy (along with unprocessed foods) have occasionally been available to buy with Neopoints to feed virtual pets. Kids can also win points by watching cereal ads or movie trailers in the Disney theater. And they can fatten their Neopoints accounts by participating in marketing surveys. Universal Pictures recently ran a survey on the site to assess and build awareness of a forthcoming kids' movie, *Two Brothers.* Another pitch on the Neopets home page: click through to a website called Dealtime.com and compare such consumer electronics as Sharp and Sony camcorders, getting to know brands in the process.

"It's sneaky," says Clancy Mendoza, mother of Neopets fan Wendy, who forbids her daughter to take the surveys. Even with the more playful features, the marketing messages are seeping through. After Wendy tried a Neopets game with a tie-in to Avril Lavigne's new CD, she told her mom she wanted the music. After an advergame's launch, says Neopets' Dohring, surveys have shown double-digit increases in the number of users who have tried a product embedded in the game.

At company headquarters in Glendale, Calif., posters of Neopets dolls decorate the walls, and dozens of young workers sit in cubicles programming and creating content for Neopia. Speaking in a conference room, Dohring emphasizes that branded content is less than 1% of the site's total. "We're not trying to be subliminal or deceive the user. We label all the immersive ad campaigns as paid advertisements."

But critics say websites like Neopets enable advertisers to skirt TV-industry practices that alert children to commercials with bumper announcements like, "Hey, kids, we'll be right back after these messages." Neopets Inc. press materials declare that advertisers can embed their brands "directly into entertaining site content." The practice isn't illegal, and Dohring says Neopets complies with the Children's Online Privacy Act, which bars companies from collecting personal information from Internet users under 13. Still, by embedding brand characters into games and activities, the ad "just goes unnoticed by the child, much less the parent," says McNeal, a critic of such practices. Democratic Senator Tom Harkin of Iowa plans to introduce a bill this week that would reinstate the Federal Trade Commission's ability to issue rules on unfair advertising to children (the ad industry now abides by voluntary guidelines).

Whatever one's opinion of it, the Neopets franchise is expanding. Neopets Inc. has revenues of more than $15 million annually and is turning a profit after just four years in business, says Dohring. Neopia now exists in nine languages, including Chinese (Dutch is next). The company is growing with a line of merchandise, including stuffed animals, toys and a trading-card game. Fueling that growth is Dohring's advertising pitch, which has attracted some major, if reticent, clients. Disney, General Mills and Universal Pictures, contacted by TIME to discuss their business with Neopets, declined to comment. Asked about

McDonald's association with the site, Kathy Pyle, the fast-food company's director of kids' marketing, said, "McDonald's wants to be integrated into the online experience. We have been doing it for entertainment purposes, not directly selling." McDonald's, however, is offering Neopets toys in Happy Meals, cross-promoted on the site.

Internet advergaming isn't limited to Neopets. Food manufacturers in particular are luring kids to their brands with similar offerings. Postopia.com, a popular Kraft Foods site, offers a full arcade of games, some (like the Pebbles Quarry Adventure) linked to sweetened cereals and drinks like Kool-Aid. Look closely at the bottom of the home page and you can see the fine print: "We, at Post, want to let you know that this page contains commercial advertising where we mention products we sell."

Plenty of other corporate initiatives are under way to grab kids' attention. WalMart has been drawing kids (and their parents' pocketbooks) to its stores with a marketing concept called "retailainment." In one version last fall, kids visiting Wal-Mart received Bob the Builder coloring books and could go on a "safety scavenger hunt" that led them to the toy, hardware and infant-and-toddler departments. What's going on? Preschoolers are now considered a "highly marketable segment for certain products," says a recent report by MarketResearch.com. Though you probably already know that if you have a toddler in the house.

From *Time* Magazine, June 28, 2004, pages 52–54. Copyright © 2004 by Time Inc. Reprinted by permission.

E-Biz Strikes Again!

**The Internet has rewritten the rules for books, music, and travel.
Which industries are next? Here are six.**

By Timothy J. Mullaney

AS THE INTERNET BOOM TURNED INTO BUST, COR-PORATE America could be forgiven for allowing itself a small sigh of relief. When all was giddy, and the stock market giddiest of all, big companies feared the disruptive power of the Net. Look what happened to Barnes & Noble, they fretted, as Amazon.com changed the game of bookselling. Or how Expedia Inc. overran travel agents. No one wanted to be the next to get "Amazoned." So when the NASDAQ buckled in 2000, the corporate giants relaxed—relieved that things weren't going to change as radically or as rapidly as they had feared.

Uh-oh—the threat is back. Net companies have survived their nuclear winter, and throughout the economy, big companies are again under assault. Again, the Web is threatening to force down the prices charged by traditional players, squeeze their margins, and even put some out of business. New technology, new ways of doing business, and new approaches to cutting out the middleman mean the old pricing power is collapsing in a series of industries—and existing leaders will be forced to find new ways to make money. The pressing question is: How many more industries will be transformed by the Net? "How high is the sky?" answers Barry Diller, CEO of InterActiveCorp, which owns Expedia and other Net properties.

In the first wave of disruption, Amazon, Expedia, and others rewrote the rules for books, music, and air travel. Now the Web is poised to remake at least six more major industries: jewelry, bill payments, telecom, hotels, real estate, and software. In the jewelry business, online players are set to wreak havoc on traditional players. Amazon CEO Jeffrey P. Bezos, who jumped into the business on Apr. 22, says he can buy a diamond wholesale for $500 and resell it for $575. Never mind that Tiffany, Zale, and neighborhood stores are used to getting $1,000 for the same stone. Five-year-old Blue Nile Inc. has proved that this strategy can be very profitable. The online jeweler made $27 million on $129 million in sales last year. The upstarts "are going to kill everyone," says analyst Ken

Gassman of New York-based Rapaport, which publishes a diamond industry newsletter.

Brave talk like that is surfacing again because this show turned out to star more than just eBay and the Failures. Companies that made it through the dot-com bust worked hard to get their houses in order. Nearly 60% of the remaining public Internet companies made money in the fourth quarter of last year, based on standard accounting measurements. Those profits are luring investors back to the market. Venture-capital investments topped $5 billion in the first quarter for the first time in nearly two years, while 14 Net companies are registered to go public.

That's not to say this is 1996 redux. The Net is no secret, and most established players know exactly what's coming. Instead of burying their heads in the sand, they're devising strategies to strike back against Net insurgents. In some cases, the incumbents simply plan to co-opt the upstarts' technology. Consider Verizon Communications Inc. Once CEO Ivan G. Seidenberg saw Vonage Holdings Corp. and other newcomers start using Net technology to offer phone services for a third less than existing rates, he played his trump card: He said the New York phone giant would invest $2 billion in Net technology over the next two years. "It's a dynamic process, where you get new players, but old players also can reinvent themselves," says Paul Saffo, research director at Institute for the Future, a Silicon Valley think tank. "Only the dumbest players die in this process."

Still, some incumbents are bent on fighting the digital evolution. Hotel chains are cracking down on franchisees that get too cozy with Web travel agencies. InterContinental Hotels Group is slapping hotel owners with fines and threatening to pull their franchise licenses if they offer special discounts through Net partners. At the same time, real estate giant Cendant Corp. pressed the National Association of Realtors to make it harder for Net upstarts to get home-sale listings. "The time for being scared was

1998. It's not today," says Richard A. Smith, CEO of Cendant's real estate division.

The tactics may prove ineffective, however. Hotel owners barred from giving Web players discounts may see travelers book rooms across the street at rival hoteliers. And Cendant's parry in real estate is on hold while the Justice Dept. conducts an antitrust probe.

As the battle is joined, expect another round of productivity gains to cascade through the economy. Many economists have been predicting productivity will slow from its torrid pace of the past few years. But the Web's impact on more industries suggests that productivity growth may continue over 3% a year, near its 3.6% average clip of the past five years. Moving to digital check writing is just one example. Write a paper check, and it costs your bank about 30 cents to process. Pay the same bill online, and it's a dime. Online bill payment is exploding: Gartner Inc. estimates that 65 million people paid at least one bill online last year, up 97% from the year before. "The Internet economy is in full swing again," says Mark M. Zandi, chief economist at Economy.com Inc.

As e-biz strikes again, key questions arise: Why these industries? And why now? In the first round of Net disruption, the online players were selling commodities: books, music, or stock trades. Customers didn't need to see, squeeze, or sniff the stuff—all they cared about was price. Today's Net upstarts are pulling together more complex information and boiling it down so consumers can become smarter purchasers of a broader array of products and services. In real estate, for instance, zipRealty and others have learned how to use software to show potential home buyers photos and floor plans for scores of potential houses. Because that reduces the agent's work, zipRealty can save consumers 20% to 25% off standard commissions. In the jewelry biz, Blue Nile offers loads of educational information on diamonds so lovestruck men feel comfortable buying gems based on a collection of independent ratings on color, cut, clarity, and carat size.

Broadband has been instrumental in the Net's advance, too. A critical mass of people around the world now have high-speed Net access, including 27 million U.S. households. That means consumers can handle the huge loads of information dished up by the second wave of online players. Lickety-split Net links let them browse through dozens of photos of hotel rooms, check out a variety of gold necklaces, or take virtual tours of scores of homes for sale. Speedy Net connections also have made it easier for programmers around the world to cooperate in developing new open-source software, which is changing the economics of the $200 billion software market.

The Web players' new assault should keep the productivity gains coming

The industries under assault have other more subtle characteristics in common, as well. Several, including jewelry and hotels, have long supply chains with many middlemen, each of whom takes a cut of the profits, driving up retail prices. A South African white diamond can pass through five different hands, including rough-diamond brokers, cutters, and jewelry and diamond wholesalers. Blue Nile connects over the Internet to its key suppliers, who buy their stones directly from South Africa's powerful DeBeers Consolidated Mines Ltd. That eliminates three middlemen or more. "Businesses are learning to drive process change by combining it with technology," says John T. Chambers, CEO of networking giant Cisco Systems Inc.

So, who will win, the upstarts or the established companies? This time, with incumbents attuned to the advantages of the Net, there will be victors on both sides. A Blue Nile here, a Verizon there. More important, though, is that the Internet will continue to have sweeping impact on the economy, giving consumers more choices and making everyone more efficient. "It's going to be a wonderful mess," says Al Lill, a fellow at tech-research firm Gartner. In these six industries, and more.

JEWELRY HEIST Online sales are soaring as e-tailers—now including Amazon—offer big savings and still make a profit

JEWELRY

HUNTERS Blue Nile, eBay, Amazon.com, Diamond.com.

HUNTED Zale, Tiffany, neighborhood jewelry stores.

AT STAKE A $45 billion U.S. industry

OUTLOOK Only $2 billion in jewelry sales are conducted online now, but e-tailers are coming on strong. Blue Nile boosted revenues 9% last year—12 times faster than the industry. While Tiffany is more insulated because it sells image and cachet, Zale and neighborhood stores face trouble.

AMY SMITH IS WHAT HAPPENS WHEN TRUE LOVE meets the Internet. The 31-year-old admits she oohed and aahed over engagement rings at the Tiffany & Co. store near her Potomac Falls (Va.) home. But when she got engaged last October, Smith checked out other stores, including online jeweler Blue Nile Inc. After using Blue Nile's guides to master the Four Cs of diamonds (color, cut, clarity, and carats) and picking out a $10,000 ring there, Smith had one question left. "Blue Nile beat them by almost $6,000," she says. "I thought, 'Why are these so much more expensive?'"

Jewelry e-tailers are the leading players in the Web's second act. Selling diamonds, double-strand pearl necklaces, sterling silver bangle bracelets, and more, online jewelers made up about $2 billion of the industry's $45 billion in U.S. revenues last year. Startups such as Blue Nile, Ice.com, Diamond.com, and now Amazon.com, which opened its jewelry store on Apr. 22, are textbook cases of how the Web fundamentally undercuts traditional ways of doing business. The secret? Knock out the middlemen and expensive stores to lower costs, then slash prices. Amazon.com Inc., for example, is betting it can make money on 15% markups instead of the industry's usual 60% to 100%. Amazon charges $1,000 for a pair of oval emerald and diamond earrings that it gets from a supplier for $850. Traditional jewelers typically charge $1,700. "We believe over time customers figure these things out," says Thomas J. Szkutak, Amazon's chief financial officer.

The diamond market is where changes are happening first, and Blue Nile is the leader there. The five-year-old Seattle company, which has filed to go public, has become the eighth-largest specialty jeweler in the U.S. Last year, sales jumped 79%, to $128.9 million, and net income hit $27 million. Selling diamonds for up to 35% less than rivals, Blue Nile is not just profitable—it has higher margins than No.1 chain Zale Corp.

Commoditization

BLUE NILE PACKS a punch by streamlining a famously byzantine business. It has just 115 full-time staffers and a 10,000-square-foot warehouse. To sell $129 million worth of jewelry, a chain would need 116 stores and more than 900 workers, estimates analyst Ken Gassman of Rapaport Research. Blue Nile also bypasses the industry's tangled supply chain, where a stone can pass through five or more middlemen before reaching a retailer. Instead, Blue Nile deals directly with major suppliers through its own network online.

To get to where they are, the Net upstarts had to defy conventional wisdom that diamonds couldn't be sold online. The companies solved this problem by giving people the same information a jewelry expert would give them. They dish up educational guides in plain English and independent quality ratings for every stone. For example, a customer at Diamond.com can pore over the rating scales for cut, clarity, and color, pick out a one-carat stone with the preferred criteria—and then shop around for a better price. These resources are now standard practice, as is a 30-day money-back guarantee. "The comfort level came from that guarantee," says Pat Grobelny, a California college student who bought his girlfriend a Valentine's Day ring at Ice.com.

This commoditization of diamond selling is making it progressively harder for small jewelers to make money. That's one reason some 465 jewelry stores closed last year.

Even among survivors, profits are lean, and many small try, such as Roger Thompson, a jeweler in Lambertville N.J., say they're specializing in custom crafted pieces that don't include diamonds. "Anyone with half a brain who wants a diamond engagement ring will go to the Internet," he says.

Larger rivals have more options. Although Zale declined comment, analysts say the chain is reducing costs through more efficient purchasing. Helzberg Diamonds emphasizes the customer service it can deliver in its 265 stores. "Our kind of customer really wants our kind of service levels. E-commerce does not do that," says Helzberg CEO Jeffrey W. Comment. Of all the major jewelers, Tiffany may be the most insulated from the Web threat thanks to the cachet of its coveted blue box and a flagship Fifth Avenue store that provides 9% of sales amid an ineffable whiff of Audrey Hepburn.

Still, for a growing number of people, a Web-purchased ring can replace the idyll of taking your girl to Tiffany's. Just ask Pete Dignan of Littleton, Colo. When he was planning to give Kelly Gilmore a Blue Nile ring, Dignan had a limo whisk them to a park where he proposed over an outdoor dinner overlooking the Rockies. "It was a really romantic proposal, and that was more important," he says. He saved about $4,000, and the experience was priceless.

—By Timothy J. Mullaney

CHECKS CHECK OUT With online bill payment and processing, use of paper checks is headed for a steep decline

PAYMENTS

HUNTERS Startups, including Viewpointe, Endpoint Exchange and NetDeposit that manage archives of disital checks and provide check exchange software and services.

HUNTED Check-printing companies such as Deluxe, check transport specialists like Airnet, and community banks.

AT STAKE A $30 billion industry that handles the printing, transporting, and processing of checks.

OUTLOOK The number of checks written in the U.S., currently around 40 billion a year, is expected to decline 25% over the next three years.

A FUNNY THING HAPPENS WHEN YOU WRITE A check at some Wal-Marts: It gets handed right back to you. Hoping to speed payments, reduce costs, and cut fraud, the world's largest retailer now scans paper checks for pertinent information such as the bank and account number—and then gives them back to customers in the checkout line.

Remember the old saw, the check's in the mail? Drop it. Digital processing technologies such as those used by Wal-Mart Stores Inc. and the skyrocketing adoption of online bill payment are reshaping the $30 billion business of printing, transporting, and processing checks. Driving the transformation are banks, credit-card companies, and merchants eager to simplify an antiquated system that involves as many as 28 middlemen. They have plenty of motivation: Handling an online payment costs only 10¢, roughly one-third that of processing a paper check, according to Atlanta consultant Global Concepts. The result: The number of checks written annually should decline by about one quarter by 2007, to 30 billion, estimates researcher Celent Communications LLC. "This is a transformational moment," says Jonathan Wilko senior vice-president at Bank of America Corp.

The age-old practice of printing checks and shuttling them around the country in armored cars is in upheaval. No.1 check printer Deluxe Corp. is closing three of its 13 printing plants and fighting for its margins by pushing higher-priced check designs and fraud-prevention services. One of the Web's unlikeliest victims is AirNet Systems Inc., in Columbus, Ohio, which gets nearly 70% of its $140 million in revenues from flying checks between cities on Learjets. AirNet is shifting its focus to passenger charters and express shipments of donor organs. "We've seen this bogeyman coming," says Wynn D. Peterson, AirNet's vice-president for corporate development.

Fostering Loyalty

AND HE'S COMING FAST. This year, 65 million U.S. consumers are paying some of their bills online, almost twice as many as last year, according to Gartner. And that's expected to jump to 73 million in four years. This growth is a boon for companies such as Wells Fargo, American Express, and Sprint, which work with online bill payment pioneers CheckFree Corp., edocs Inc., and others. Gartner figures that the average company with 1.9 million customers can cut $26 million in costs per year by persuading customers to receive and pay their bills over the Web.

Cost savings are just the start. Customers are more likely to stay with a bank if they pay bills online there. At Wells Fargo & Co., customers who pay bills online are 75% less likely to leave the bank than other customers. "No doubt, the benefits far outweigh the expenses," says Jim Smith, executive vice-president for consumer Internet products at Wells Fargo.

Even when payments are not made online, paper checks are going digital. Behind this modernization is the Check Clearing for the 21st Century Act, known as Check 21. This law, which goes into effect in October, is expected to kick off a mass adoption of check imaging by putting electronic images of checks on equal legal footing with paper originals for the first time. Even banks that aren't equipped to handle digital checks have to accept printouts of them, known as "substitute checks," as payment. During the past three years, startups Viewpointe Archive Services, Endpoint Exchange, and NetDeposit have rolled out software and services that convert checks into digital files so they can be stored and swapped electronically. Banks could reap big savings. The cost of upgrading to digital check handling will reach $1.9 billion next year, but the industry could save $2.1 billion annually from the shift, estimates Celent.

The changes will allow the banking behemoths to compete more fiercely with community banks. The corner florist and local Wal-Mart typically do business with a nearby bank because they want to get credit for their daily deposits as quickly as possible. With digital check processing, proximity no longer matters. Merchants can choose banks that offer quick and secure processing for the lowest price wherever they happen to be located.

Shuttered printing plants. Grounded Learjets. Struggling community banks. They're all signs of how the business of checks is changing in the Digital Age.

—By Andrew Park, with Ben Elgin and
Timothy J Mullaney

TELECOM TURMOIL Internet phone services are undercutting the telecom giants and creating new rivals

TELECOM

HUNTERS Vonage, Net2Phone, and other upstarts.

HUNTED Telecom giants from Verizon and France Télécom to AT&T and NTT.

AT STAKE Leadership of the $300 billion U.S. phone market and the $750 billion international market.

OUTLOOK Phone calls with Net technology, which are about 33% cheaper than regular phone service, are expected to hit $6.7 billion in U.S. revenues in 2007, up from $281 million last year. Even more significant, Net technology will make it easier and cheaper for a host of small outfits to compete with the big phone companies.

ALAN BELL, A PROFESSIONAL NUMBER CRUNCHER, thought he was paying too much for phone service. So last year he dropped Sprint Corp. and turned to Vonage Holdings Corp. for its Internet phone service, which sends voice calls over the same networks that transport Net data. Now his auditing firm, ARB Consulting Inc. in Plant City, Fla., gets unlimited domestic phone service and a dedicated fax line for $55 a month, about 75% less than what he paid before. He also enjoys new features, such as the ability to check records of calls on the Web. "It does the same thing that a regular phone does, and more. Why not save the money?" Bell says.

More and more people are asking that question. Tens of thousands a month are turning to Vonage, Net2Phone, i2 Telecom International, and other upstarts for telephone service based on Net technology. The service, dubbed Voice over Internet Protocol, or VOIP, is expected to surge next year as broadband providers like Comcast, Time Warner, and AT&T roll it out en masse. "We are crossing over into a new era. In three years, telecom companies won't look anything like they do today," says analyst Farooq Hussain of researcher Network Conceptions LLC.

The Internet is quickly refashioning telecom in its image. Revenues in the $120 billion traditional phone business are declining several percentage points a year, and capital investment in basic gear has all but dried up. Yet revenue from telecom services based on Net technology is expected to hit $6.7 billion in 2007, up from $281 million last year, according to researcher IDC.

"We Were Wrong"

THE TRULY REVOLUTIONARY promise of the technology is that it could break the grip that local phone companies have on their customers. Until now, the Bells have been able to decide the conditions under which rivals could connect to their networks. The result is that the Bells control about 80% of the U.S. local phone market. But with Net technology, rivals can bypass the Bells because Net phone service can simply be plugged into any broadband connection. Already under pressure from wireless, the Bells may lose an additional 20% to 30% of their market over the next few years. That will drive down margins and will spark consolidation.

Incumbents hope to co-opt the technology to limit the damage. Verizon Communications Inc. is investing billions in new technologies so that it can offer its own low-cost Net phone and other services beginning this spring. "The VOIP market is bigger than we would have guessed. We were wrong," admits Stuart Elby, Verizon's vice-president for network architecture.

International traffic is getting cheap. A nickel a minute to China, anyone?

Consumers will be the winners. Vonage offers unlimited service for $35 a month. That's about 33% cheaper than the $50 to $55 Verizon charges for a similar service over its traditional network.

Internet telephony is unleashing a wave of new features, too. ReadyTech-Go, a staffing agency for the health-care industry, switched to a Net phone system six months ago. Instead of a separate phone line, workers simply plug a headset into laptops loaded with phone software. As they travel around the country, co-workers can reach one another using the same extension, as if they were down the hall. The application costs about $125 per user, cheaper than many phones.

Net technology also is helping drive down the cost of international phone traffic. Net2Phone's rate to China is only 5¢ a minute, half that of a regular calling plan. Some forms of IP phone service are even free. Skype, a software program that can be downloaded from the Web, lets people make free calls to other people who use the same program. Net technology now accounts for about 13% of cross-border international phone traffic, compared with 1% five years ago, according to TeleGeography Research Corp.

Expect the phone giants to fight back hard now that they've been awakened to the risks of Vonage and other Net upstarts. Still, regardless of who wins the battle, customers can look forward to one sure thing: phone service that's cheaper and loaded with new features.

—*By Steve Rosenbush in New York*

HOTEL CRUNCH Online bookers are getting better rates by offering hotels volume. That has the chains scrambling

HOTELS

HUNTERS Expedia, Travelocity, Orbitz.

HUNTED Chains, including Hilton Hotels, Starwood Hotels & Resorts, and InterContinental Hotels Group.

AT STAKE Pricing and profits in the $80 billion U.S. hotel biz.

THE OUTLOOK Hotel chains are trying to get Expedia to pay more for the rooms it resells. But that will be tough. Online agencies have legions of loyal customers that they can direct to the most cooperative hostelries. By 2006, the online upstarts are expected to account for 17% of the lodging market, up from 8% in 2003.

JIM YOUNG HAD HAD ENOUGH. THE SENIOR VICE-president for global distribution at InterContinental Hotels Group had seen IHG's 3,300 franchisees flirt too much with the Internet. Some locally owned hotels had allowed online travel agents, such as InterActiveCorp.'s Expedia Inc. and Travelocity, to offer lower rates than those charged by InterContinental. That gave the Web services a bigger slice of revenues per room than they pay the InterContinental chain. On Apr. 20, he threw down the gauntlet at TravelCom Expo, an annual confab of

1,200 hotel owners and other travel execs. Franchisees have to choose between doing business on the Web travel agencies' terms or on InterContinental's. "If a hotel chooses not to comply, it won't be a Holiday Inn or a Crowne Plaza any longer," Young told a packed room.

Of all the battles between Big Business and Web insurgents, the one raging between hotel chains and online travel agencies may be the fiercest. At stake: who sets hotel prices and who gets the biggest profits in an $80 billion industry. Traditionally, franchisers such as Marriott International, Hilton Hotels, and InterContinental chains have been the hotel industry's dominant middlemen. Hotel owners pay the chains 8% to 10% of their revenues in exchange for marketing and booking services and for the right to call themselves a Marriott or Hilton. Now, Expedia, Travelocity, and Orbitz are homing in on the chains. Using the power of the Net, the online agencies last year booked 35 million rooms worth $5.8 billion, 8% of the market. Consultant PhoCusWright Inc. estimates they will hit $13.3 billion in rooms in 2006, for 17% market share.

With more people booking rooms online, Web travel agencies are changing the hotel industry's fundamental economics. Because they can fill beds with a fury, Net agents are getting a bigger cut of hotel owners' revenues than the chains get for the same room. Expedia, for instance, gets a $106 nightly wholesale rate from the Dana Inn and Marina in San Diego for a June Sunday night, then charges the customer $132. Customers pay less than the $145 rate they would receive if they booked over the phone, and Expedia pockets a 25% markup, or $26.

Losing Sleep

WHY ARE HOTEL owners willing to give Internet travel agents more money? The Web sites can move market share to the hotels that give the agencies the discounts they want. That's crucial in an industry that's chronically overbuilt. A hotel owner's choice often is to give Web agents discounted rooms or let them sit empty. The Snow King Resort Hotel in Jackson Hole, Wyo., began getting up to 100 reservations a week from Travelocity after the site started promoting the 209-room hotel in January. "We're more than willing to discount to them because they more than make up the difference," says Kristine Myers, Snow King's marketing and development director.

Most threatened in this new world are the hotel chains. The danger is that hotel owners who give a hefty slice of their revenues to Web agents to get customers may begin to trim marketing expenses elsewhere. They could push the chains to lower their 8% to 10% fees—or drop them altogether. "If we're going to pay the Web sites, we're going to find someone else to cut out," says Chip Conley, CEO of Joie de Vivre Hospitality, which manages 25 California hotels.

Chains are fighting to save their position. Every major chain has forced franchisees to agree to a best-rate guarantee policy that prevents them from selling rooms for less on Expedia, Orbitz, or Travelocity than they do through the chain's Web site or over the phone. If Starwood Hotels & Resorts Worldwide Inc. catches a hotelier discounting through a Web agency, it fines the owner $75. That takes away Travelocity's ability to sell, say, a Sheraton room for less than Sheraton does, and gives brand-loyal consumers more reason to use the chain's own site. Starwood and Hilton lavish benefits on customers who stay loyal, including upgrades and frequent-stay points. Starwood says the changes have increased the share of Net bookings done through its Web site, but won't say how much. "It's working. It's more than a dent," says Steven M. Hankin, Starwood's chief marketing officer.

The strategy may not be a long-term solution, however. Hotel owners barred from giving Web players discounts may discover the policy is hurting their business. The Radisson Lexington in New York is sticking with the chain rate of $199, while Expedia visitors can stay at the more upscale Hudson for $190 because the independent hotel gives the Web agent bigger discounts. With the Net at their fingertips, travelers can easily figure which hotels are the most hospitable.

—By Timothy J. Mullaney

REAL ESTATE'S NEW REALITY Speed and heft will let Net players drive down brokerage fees—and gain share

REAL ESTATE

HUNTERS Lending Tree, zipRealty.

HUNTED Real estate brokerage franchises run by giants such as Cendant and RE/MAX International.

AT STAKE Control of $60 billion in U.S. residential real estate commissions.

OUTLOOK In a highly fragmented market, upstarts like Lending Tree are projected to grab a 4% share within three years.

IT'S PRETTY CLEAR THAT THE INTERNET IS changing how people look for new homes. These days, more than 70% of home buyers shop online before inking a deal, up from 41% in 2001. Little wonder. With a few mouse clicks, up pop photos and floor plans for a $1 million estate in St. Petersburg or a $100,000 condo in St. Louis.

What's less obvious is how all these Web-surfing home buyers are changing the real estate industry. With a flood of data at their fingertips, they're becoming savvier and starting to chip away at the 6% commission that real estate brokers collect on each home sold. For example, by using the Web to cut costs, upstart zipRealty Inc. can refund 20% of its commission back to buyers and 25% to sellers.

Net insurgents HomeGain.com Inc. and LendingTree Inc., already a leader in mortgages, may have a bigger impact. They're using the power of the Net to gather home sellers and buyers, and funnel them to realtors. They're bucking tradition, giving potential clients' names to several agents and letting them fight it out. That pressures existing middlemen, from realtors to franchisers, including RE/MAX International Inc. and Cendant Corp., to be more competitive, offer better service, and cut rates.

These cyber-middlemen likely will flourish in the next few years. While they collected less than 1% of the $60 billion paid in U.S. real estate commissions last year, they're expected to hit 4% in 2007, according to analyst Steve Murray of research firm Real Trends Inc. in Littleton, Colo. It may not sound like much, but in such a fragmented industry, small shifts in market share affect consumer expectations. Once your neighbor gets a lower commission, you'll want one too. "The standard 6% commission is no longer standard at HomeGain," says CEO Brad Inman.

What forces are at work? Consider zipRealty. The Emeryville (Calif.)-based brokerage cuts costs by having its agents work via the Net from home, rather than in offices. Agents get online training and sales tools, which helps them sell two to three times more homes than typical realtors. Last year, the startup turned profitable as its home sales doubled, to $1.6 billion.

Web referral services, such as LendingTree and HomeGain.com, are taking a different tack Their strategy is to help brokers find clients more cheaply and quickly. In exchange, brokers pay LendingTree up to 35% of their commission when they close a sale. On a $300,000 house, for example, LendingTree would get up to $6,300. If the services deliver more clients, brokers can get enough extra deals to make up for sharing commissions. Last year, LendingTree's referrals led to about 7,000 home sales.

The big franchisers have more defenses than incumbents in other industries. Cendant and RE/MAX sued Lending/tree to stop advertising that local brokers franchised by them accept LendingTree referrals. With the case pending, LendingTree is under an injunction to stop using the names. Lawsuits aside, Cendant says agents make more money when they get clients from the franchisers and don't split commissions.

But changes are underway. Murray reports that in recent focus groups, agents said they're cutting rates, amid pressure from customers. Like termites, the Web is eating away at the old homestead.

—By Timothy J. Mullaney

SOFTWARE SHIFT Open-source developers are looking beyond Linux to databases, e-mail, search—even desktop PCs

---

SOFTWARE

HUNTERS Red Hat, JBoss, MySQL.

HUNTED Traditional software makers, including Microsoft, BEA Systems, and Oracle.

AT STAKE Profits in the $200 billion worldwide software industry.

OUTLOOK Open-source packages are gaining momentum. MySQL has 5,000 customers for its database software. Established software makers will be forced to lower prices and innovate to stay ahead of open-source alternatives.

LINUX. FOR YEARS IT WAS AN OBSCURE WORD, known mostly to idealistic programmers who contributed chunks of software to help develop a free, open-source alternative to operating systems from Microsoft Corp. and others. With its friendly penguin mascot, it seemed more like a feel-good social movement than a serious threat. But in the past four years, Linux has torn into the once fat-and-happy operating-systems biz, raising its share of the server market to 23%—second only to Microsoft.

Now, the open-source crowd is setting its sights well beyond Linux, to huge new swaths of the software industry. Upstarts such as MySQL AB and JBoss Inc. are coming out with second generation open-source software: everything from databases and search engines to programming tools and desktop PC software. If this stuff follows the trajectory of Linux, it could cut into the sales and profits of incumbents, altering the financial landscape of the $200 billion business.

None of this would be possible without the Web. The Net lets thousands of people worldwide contribute code, fixes, and ideas to the small tribes that put open-source programs together. At data-management developer Sleepycat Software Inc., its 20 programmers are aided by a small army of volunteers. "Hundreds of people have added small pieces," says Chief Technology Officer Margo Seltzer.

"Playing the Linux Card"

THE NEW PLAYERS are gaining traction. Sweden's MySQL has signed up 5,000 customers for its $495 database program. A March Forrester Research Inc. survey of 140 large North American companies showed that 60%

are either using opensource software or plan to. "We're starting to see a big change," says Andy Miller, vice-president for technical architecture at Corporate Express Inc., a Broomfield (Colo.) office-products distributor.

There's no mystery to open source's appeal: The price is unbeatable. Corporate Express has saved up to $6.1 million over three years with open-source programs, says Miller. Many corporations simply download open-source packages from the Net for free. Others get the software from such companies as Red Hat Inc. as part of a package that includes services. Even when businesses pay for the software, it often costs a fraction of what traditional software makers charge. MYSQL's $495 program, while not as capable as Oracle Corp.'s $4,995 database, is being used as an alternative for certain applications. "Open source shifts the balance of power to tech buyers," says Forrester analyst Ted Schadler.

Software incumbents are retooling their strategies. IBM and Novell Inc. are embracing open source and selling customers a package of software and services. Microsoft at times discounts Windows to compete. "The word you hear from customers is that playing the Linux card is worth a 25% to 30% discount," says Scott Lundstrom of AMR Research Inc.

Many corporate buyers still want the security and predictability of a proprietary package that is sold and serviced by a proven supplier. Microsoft tries to persuade customers that Linux costs more over time to maintain and update. "Linux used to be this weird, mystical phenomenon," says CEO Steven A. Ballmer, but now that it's a commercial product, Microsoft knows how to compete with it. Maybe so. But as open source moves beyond Linux, this shape-shifting phenomenon is shaking up the software biz.

—*By Steve Hamm*

Marketing myopia

(With Retrospective Commentary)

Shortsighted managements often fail to recognize that in fact there is no such thing as a growth industry

Theodore Levitt

How can a company ensure its continued growth? In 1960 "Marketing Myopia" answered that question in a new and challenging way by urging organizations to define their industries broadly to take advantage of growth opportunities. Using the archetype of the railroads, Mr. Levitt showed how they declined inevitably as technology advanced because they defined themselves too narrowly. To continue growing, companies must ascertain and act on their customers' needs and desires, not bank on the presumptive longevity of their products. The success of the article testifies to the validity of its message. It has been widely quoted and anthologized, and HBR has sold more than 265,000 reprints of it. The author of 14 subsequent articles in HBR, Mr. Levitt is one of the magazine's most prolific contributors. In a retrospective commentary, he considers the use and misuse that have been made of "Marketing Myopia," describing its many interpretations and hypothesizing about its success.

Every major industry was once a growth industry. But some that are now riding a wave of growth enthusiasm are very much in the shadow of decline. Others which are thought of as seasoned growth industries have actually stopped growing. In every case the reason growth is threatened, slowed, or stopped is *not* be-cause the market is saturated. It is because there has been a failure of management.

Fateful purposes: The failure is at the top. The executives responsible for it, in the last analysis, are those who deal with broad aims and policies. Thus:

• The railroads did not stop growing because the need for passenger and freight transportation declined. That grew. The railroads are in trouble today not because the need was filled by others (cars, trucks, airplanes, even telephones), but because it was *not* filled by the railroads themselves. They let others take customers away from them because they assumed themselves to be in the railroad business rather than in the transportation business. The reason they defined their industry wrong was because they were railroad-oriented instead of transportation-oriented; they were product-oriented instead of customer-oriented.

• Hollywood barely escaped being totally ravished by television. Actually, all the established film companies went through drastic reorganizations. Some simply disappeared. All of them got into trouble not because of TV's inroads but because of their own myopia. As with the railroads, Hollywood defined its business incorrectly. It thought it was in the movie business when it was actually in the entertainment business. "Movies" implied a specific, limited product. This produced a

fatuous contentment which from the beginning led producers to view TV as a threat. Hollywood scorned and rejected TV when it should have welcomed it as an opportunity—an opportunity to expand the entertainment business.

Today TV is a bigger business than the old narrowly defined movie business ever was. Had Hollywood been customer-oriented (providing entertainment), rather then product-oriented (making movies), would it have gone through the fiscal purgatory that it did? I doubt it. What ultimately saved Hollywood and accounted for its recent resurgence was the wave of new young writers, producers, and directors whose previous successes in television had decimated the old movie companies and toppled the big movie moguls.

There are other less obvious examples of industries that have been and are now endangering their futures by improperly defining their purposes. I shall discuss some in detail later and analyze the kind of policies that lead to trouble. Right now it may help to show what a thoroughly customer-oriented management can do to keep a growth industry growing, even after the obvious opportunities have been exhausted; and here there are two examples that have been around for a long time. They are nylon and glass—specifically,

E. I. duPont de Nemours & Company and Corning Glass Works.

Both companies have great technical competence. Their product orientation is unquestioned. But this alone does not explain their success. After all, who was more pridefully product-oriented and product-conscious than the erstwhile New England textile companies that have been so thoroughly massacred? The DuPonts and the Cornings have succeeded not primarily because of their product or research orientation but because they have been thoroughly customer-oriented also. It is constant watchfulness for opportunities to apply their technical knowhow to the creation of customer-satisfying uses which accounts for their prodigious output of successful new products. Without a very sophisticated eye on the customer, most of their new products might have been wrong, their sales methods useless.

Aluminum has also continued to be a growth industry, thanks to the efforts of two wartime-created companies which deliberately set about creating new customer-satisfying uses. Without Kaiser Aluminum & Chemical Corporation and Reynolds Metals Company, the total demand for aluminum today would be vastly less.

Error of analysis: Some may argue that it is foolish to set the railroads off against aluminum or the movies off against glass. Are not aluminum and glass naturally so versatile that the industries are bound to have more growth opportunities than the railroads and movies? This view commits precisely the error I have been talking about. It defines an industry, or a product, or a cluster of know-how so narrowly as to guarantee its premature senescence. When we mention "railroads," we should make sure we mean "transportation." As transporters, the railroads still have a good chance for very considerable growth. They are not limited to the railroad business as such (though in my opinion rail transportation is potentially a much stronger transportation medium than is generally believed).

What the railroads lack is not opportunity, but some of the same managerial imaginativeness and audacity that made them great. Even an amateur like Jacques Barzun can see what is lacking when he says:

"I grieve to see the most advanced physical and social organization of the last century go down in shabby disgrace for lack of the same comprehensive imagination that built it up. [What is lacking is] the will of the companies to survive and to satisfy the public by inventiveness and skill."[1]

Shadow of obsolescence

It is impossible to mention a single major industry that did not at one time qualify for the magic appellation of "growth industry." In each case its assumed strength lay in the apparently unchallenged superiority of its product. There appeared to be no effective substitute for it. It was itself a runaway substitute for the product it so triumphantly replaced. Yet one after another of these celebrated industries has come under a shadow. Let us look briefly at a few more of them, this time taking examples that have so far received a little less attention:

• *Dry cleaning*—This was once a growth industry with lavish prospects. In an age of wool garments, imagine being finally able to get them safely and easily clean. The boom was on.

Yet here we are 30 years after the boom started and the industry is in trouble. Where has the competition come from? From a better way of cleaning? No. It has come from synthetic fibers and chemical additives that have cut the need for dry cleaning. But this is only the beginning. Lurking in the wings and ready to make chemical dry cleaning totally obsolescent is that powerful magician, ultrasonics.

• *Electric utilities*—This is another one of those supposedly "no-substitute" products that has been enthroned on a pedestal of invincible growth. When the incandescent lamp came along, kerosene lights were finished. Later the water wheel and the steam engine were cut to ribbons by the flexibility, reliability, simplicity, and just plain easy availability of electric motors. The prosperity of electric utilities continues to wax extravagant as the home is converted into a museum of electric gadgetry. How can anybody miss by investing in utilities, with no competition, nothing but growth ahead?

But a second look is not quite so comforting. A score of nonutility companies are well advanced toward developing a powerful chemical fuel cell which could sit in some hidden closet of every home silently ticking off electric power. The electric lines that vulgarize so many neighborhoods will be eliminated. So will the endless demolition of streets and service interruptions during storms. Also on the horizon is solar energy, again pioneered by nonutility companies.

Who says that the utilities have no competition? They may be natural monopolies now, but tomorrow they may be natural deaths. To avoid this prospect, they too will have to develop fuel cells, solar energy, and other power sources. To survive, they themselves will have to plot the obsolescence of what now produces their livelihood.

• *Grocery stores*—Many people find it hard to realize that there ever was a thriving establishment known as the "corner grocery store." The supermarket has taken over with a powerful effectiveness. Yet the big food chains of the 1930s narrowly escaped being completely wiped out by the aggressive expansion of independent supermarkets. The first genuine supermarket was opened in 1930, in Jamaica, Long Island. By 1933 supermarkets were thriving in California, Ohio, Pennsylvania, and elsewhere. Yet the established chains pompously ignored them. When they chose to notice them, it was with such derisive descriptions as "cheapy," "horse-and-buggy," "cracker-barrel storekeeping," and "unethical opportunists."

The executive of one big chain announced at the time that he found it "hard to believe that people will drive for miles to shop for foods and sacrifice the personal service chains have perfected and to which Mrs. Consumer is accustomed."[2] As late as 1936, the National Wholesale Grocers convention and the New Jersey Retail Grocers Association said there was nothing to fear. They said that the supers' narrow appeal to the price buyer limited the size of their market. They had to draw from miles around. When imitators came, there would be wholesale liquidations as volume fell. The current high sales of the supers was said to be partly due to their novelty. Basically people wanted convenient neighborhood grocers. If the neighborhood stores "cooperate with their suppliers, pay attention to their costs, and improve their service," they would be able to weather the competition until it blew over.[3]

It never blew over. The chains discovered that survival required going into the supermarket business. This meant the wholesale destruction of their huge investments in corner store sites and in established distribution and merchandising methods. The companies with "the courage of their convictions" resolutely stuck to the corner store philosophy. They kept their pride but lost their shirts.

Self-deceiving cycle: But memories are short. For example, it is hard for people who today confidently hail the twin messiahs of electronics and chemicals to see how things could possibly go wrong with these galloping industries. They probably also cannot see how a reasonably sensible businessman could have been as myopic as the famous Boston millionaire who 50 years ago unintentionally sentenced his heirs to poverty by stipulating that his entire estate be forever invested exclusively in electric streetcar securities. His posthumous declaration, "There will always be a big demand for efficient urban transportation," is no consolation to his heirs who sustain life by pumping gasoline at automobile filling stations.

Yet, in a casual survey I recently took among a group of intelligent business executives, nearly half agreed that it would be hard to hurt their heirs by tying their estates forever to the electronics industry. When I then confronted them with the Boston streetcar example, they chorused unanimously, "That's different!" But is it? Is not the basic situation identical?

In truth, *there is no such thing* as a growth industry, I believe. There are only companies organized and operated to create and capitalize on growth opportunities. Industries that assume themselves to be riding some automatic growth escalator invariably descend into stagnation. The history of every dead and dying "growth" industry shows a self-deceiving cycle of bountiful expansion and undetected decay. There are four conditions which usually guarantee this cycle:

1. The belief that growth is assured by an expanding and more affluent population.
2. The belief that there is no competitive substitute for the industry's major product.
3. Too much faith in mass production and in the advantages of rapidly declining unit costs as output rises.
4. Preoccupation with a product that lends itself to carefully controlled scientific experimentation, improvement, and manufacturing cost reduction.

I should like now to begin examining each of these conditions in some detail. To build my case as boldly as possible, I shall illustrate the points with reference to three industries—petroleum, automobiles, and electronics—particularly petroleum, because it spans more years and more vicissitudes. Not only do these three have

excellent reputations with the general public and also enjoy the confidence of sophisticated investors, but their managements have become known for progressive thinking in areas like financial control, product research, and management training. If obsolescence can cripple even these industries, it can happen anywhere.

Population myth

The belief that profits are assured by an expanding and more affluent population is dear to the heart of every industry. It takes the edge off the apprehensions everybody understandably feels about the future. If consumers are multiplying and also buying more of your product or service, you can face the future with considerably more comfort than if the market is shrinking. An expanding market keeps the manufacturer from having to think very hard or imaginatively. If thinking is an intellectual response to a problem, then the absence of a problem leads to the absence of thinking. If your product has an automatically expanding market, then you will not give much thought to how to expand it.

One of the most interesting examples of this is provided by the petroleum industry. Probably our oldest growth industry, it has an enviable record. While there are some current apprehensions about its growth rate, the industry itself tends to be optimistic.

But I believe it can be demonstrated that it is undergoing a fundamental yet typical change. It is not only ceasing to be a growth industry, but may actually be a declining one, relative to other business. Although there is widespread unawareness of it, I believe that within 25 years the oil industry may find itself in much the same position of retrospective glory that the railroads are now in. Despite its pioneering work in developing and applying the present-value method of investment evaluation, in employee relations, and in working with backward countries, the petroleum business is a distressing example of how complacency and wrongheadedness can stubbornly convert opportunity into near disaster.

One of the characteristics of this and other industries that have believed very strongly in the beneficial consequences of an expanding population, while at the same time being industries with a generic product for which there has appeared to be no competitive substitute, is that the individual companies have sought to outdo their competitors by improving on what they are already doing. This makes sense, of

course, if one assumes that sales are tied to the country's population strings, because the customer can compare products only on a feature-by-feature basis. I believe it is significant, for example, that not since John D. Rockefeller sent free kerosene lamps to China has the oil industry done anything really outstanding to create a demand for its product. Not even in product improvement has it showered itself with eminence. The greatest single improvement—namely, the development of tetraethyl lead—came from outside the industry, specifically from General Motors and DuPont. The big contributions made by the industry itself are confined to the technology of oil exploration, production, and refining.

Asking for trouble: In other words, the industry's efforts have focused on improving the *efficiency* of getting and making its product, not really on improving the generic product or its marketing. Moreover, its chief product has continuously been defined in the narrowest possible terms, namely, gasoline, not energy, fuel, or transportation. This attitude has helped assure that:

• Major improvements in gasoline quality tend not to originate in the oil industry. Also, the development of superior alternative fuels comes from outside the oil industry, as will be shown later.

• Major innovations in automobile fuel marketing are originated by small new oil companies that are not primarily preoccupied with production or refining. These are the companies that have been responsible for the rapidly expanding multipump gasoline stations, with their successful emphasis on large and clean layouts, rapid and efficient driveway service, and quality gasoline at low prices.

Thus, the oil industry is asking for trouble from outsiders. Sooner or later, in this land of hungry inventors and entrepreneurs, a threat is sure to come. The possibilities of this will become more apparent when we turn to the next dangerous belief of many managements. For the sake of continuity, because this second belief is tied closely to the first, I shall continue with the same example.

Idea of indispensability: The petroleum industry is pretty much persuaded that there is no competitive substitute for its major product, gasoline—or if there is, that it will continue to be a derivative of crude oil, such as diesel fuel or kerosene jet fuel.

There is a lot of automatic wishful thinking in this assumption. The trouble is that most refining companies own huge amounts of crude oil reserves. These have value only if there is a market for products into which oil can be converted—hence the tenacious belief in the continuing competitive superiority of automobile fuels made from crude oil.

This idea persists despite all historic evidence against it. The evidence not only shows that oil has never been a superior product for any purpose for very long, but it also shows that the oil industry has never really been a growth industry. It has been a succession of different businesses that have gone through the usual historic cycles of growth, maturity, and decay. Its overall survival is owed to a series of miraculous escapes from total obsolescence, of last-minute and unexpected reprieves from total disaster reminiscent of the Perils of Pauline.

Perils of petroleum: I shall sketch in only the main episodes.

First, crude oil was largely a patent medicine. But even before that fad ran out, demand was greatly expanded by the use of oil in kerosene lamps. The prospect of lighting the world's lamps gave rise to an extravagant promise of growth. The prospects were similar to those the industry now holds for gasoline in other parts of the world. It can hardly wait for the underdeveloped nations to get a car in every garage.

In the days of the kerosene lamp, the oil companies competed with each other and against gaslight by trying to improve the illuminating characteristics of kerosene. Then suddenly the impossible happened. Edison invented a light which was totally nondependent on crude oil. Had it not been for the growing use of kerosene in space heaters, the incandescent lamp would have completely finished oil as a growth industry at that time. Oil would have been good for little else than axle grease.

Then disaster and reprieve struck again. Two great innovations occurred, neither originating in the oil industry. The successful development of coal-burning domestic central-heating systems made the space heater obsolescent. While the industry reeled, along came its most magnificent boost yet—the internal combustion engine, also invented by outsiders. Then when the prodigious expansion for gasoline finally began to level off in the 1920s, along came the miraculous escape of a central oil heater. Once again, the escape was

provided by an outsider's invention and development. And when that market weakened, wartime demand for aviation fuel came to the rescue. After the war the expansion of civilian aviation, the dieselization of railroads, and the explosive demand for cars and trucks kept the industry's growth in high gear.

Meanwhile, centralized oil heating—whose boom potential had only recently been proclaimed—ran into severe competition from natural gas. While the oil companies themselves owned the gas that now competed with their oil, the industry did not originate the natural gas revolution, nor has it to this day greatly profited from its gas ownership. The gas revolution was made by newly formed transmission companies that marketed the product with an aggressive ardor. They started a magnificent new industry, first against the advice and then against the resistance of the oil companies.

By all the logic of the situation, the oil companies themselves should have made the gas revolution. They not only owned the gas; they also were the only people experienced in handling, scrubbing, and using it, the only people experienced in pipeline technology and transmission, and they understood heating problems. But, partly because they knew that natural gas would compete with their own sale of heating oil, the oil companies pooh-poohed the potentials of gas.

The revolution was finally started by oil pipeline executives who, unable to persuade their own companies to go into gas, quit and organized the spectacularly successful gas transmission companies. Even after their success became painfully evident to the oil companies, the latter did not go into gas transmission. The multibillion dollar business which should have been theirs went to others. As in the past, the industry was blinded by its narrow preoccupation with a specific product and the value of its reserves. It paid little or no attention to its customers' basic needs and preferences.

The postwar years have not witnessed any change. Immediately after World War II the oil industry was greatly encouraged about its future by the rapid expansion of demand for its traditional line of products. In 1950 most companies projected annual rates of domestic expansion of around 6% through at least 1975. Though the ratio of crude oil reserves to demand in the Free World was about 20 to 1, with 10 to 1 being usually considered a reasonable work-

ing ratio in the United States, booming demand sent oil men searching for more without sufficient regard to what the future really promised. In 1952 they "hit" in the Middle East; the ratio skyrocketed to 42 to 1. If gross additions to reserves continue at the average rate of the past five years (37 billion barrels annually), then by 1970 the reserve ratio will be up to 45 to 1. This abundance of oil has weakened crude and product prices all over the world.

Uncertain future: Management cannot find much consolation today in the rapidly expanding petrochemical industry, another oil-using idea that did not originate in the leading firms. The total United States production of petrochemicals is equivalent to about 2% (by volume) of the demand for all petroleum products. Although the petrochemical industry is now expected to grow by about 10% per year, this will not offset other drains on the growth of crude oil consumption. Furthermore, while petrochemical products are many and growing, it is well to remember that there are nonpetroleum sources of the basic raw material, such as coal. Besides, a lot of plastics can be produced with relatively little oil. A 5,000-barrel-per-day oil refinery is now considered the absolute minimum size for efficiency. But a 5,000-barrel-per-day chemical plant is a giant operation.

Oil has never been a continuously strong growth industry. It has grown by fits and starts, always miraculously saved by innovations and developments not of its own making. The reason it has not grown in a smooth progression is that each time it thought it had a superior product safe from the possibility of competitive substitutes, the product turned out to be inferior and notoriously subject to obsolescence. Until now, gasoline (for motor fuel, anyhow) has escaped this fate. But, as we shall see later, it too may be on its last legs.

The point of all this is that there is no guarantee against product obsolescence. If a company's own research does not make it obsolete, another's will. Unless an industry is especially lucky, as oil has been until now, it can easily go down in a sea of red figures—just as the railroads have, as the buggy whip manufacturers have, as the corner grocery chains have, as most of the big movie companies have, and indeed as many other industries have.

The best way for a firm to be lucky is to make its own luck. That requires knowing what makes a business successful. One of the greatest enemies of this knowledge is mass production.

Production pressures

Mass-production industries are impelled by a great drive to produce all they can. The prospect of steeply declining unit costs as output rises is more than most companies can usually resist. The profit possibilities look spectacular. All effort focuses on production. The result is that marketing gets neglected.

John Kenneth Galbraith contends that just the opposite occurs.[4] Output is so prodigious that all effort concentrates on trying to get rid of it. He says this accounts for singing commercials, desecration of the countryside with advertising signs, and other wasteful and vulgar practices. Galbraith has a finger on something real, but he misses the strategic point. Mass production does indeed generate great pressure to "move" the product. But what usually gets emphasized is selling, not marketing. Marketing, being a more sophisticated and complex process, gets ignored.

The difference between marketing and selling is more than semantic. Selling focuses on the needs of the seller, marketing on the needs of the buyer. Selling is preoccupied with the seller's need to convert his product into cash, marketing with the idea of satisfying the needs of the customer by means of the product and the whole cluster of things associated with creating, delivering, and finally consuming it.

In some industries the enticements of full mass production have been so powerful that for many years top management in effect has told the sales departments, "You get rid of it; we'll worry about profits." By contrast, a truly marketing-minded firm tries to create value-satisfying goods and services that consumers will want to buy. What it offers for sale includes not only the generic product or service, but also how it is made available to the customer, in what form, when, under what conditions, and at what terms of trade. Most important, what it offers for sale is determined not by the seller but by the buyer. The seller takes his cues from the buyer in such a way that the product becomes a consequence of the marketing effort, not vice versa.

Lag in Detroit: This may sound like an elementary rule of business, but that does not keep it from being violated wholesale. It is certainly more violated than honored. Take the automobile industry.

Here mass production is most famous, most honored, and has the greatest impact on the entire society. The industry has hitched its fortune to the relentless requirements of the annual model change, a policy that makes customer orientation an especially urgent necessity. Consequently the auto companies annually spend millions of dollars on consumer research. But the fact that the new compact cars are selling so well in their first year indicates that Detroit's vast researches have for a long time failed to reveal what the customer really wanted. Detroit was not persuaded that he wanted anything different from what he had been getting until it lost millions of customers to other small car manufacturers.

How could this unbelievable lag behind consumer wants have been perpetuated so long? Why did not research reveal consumer preferences before consumers' buying decisions themselves revealed the facts? Is that not what consumer research is for—to find out before the fact what is going to happen? The answer is that Detroit never really researched the customer's wants. It only researched his preferences between the kinds of things which it had already decided to offer him. For Detroit is mainly product-oriented, not customer-oriented. To the extent that the customer is recognized as having needs that the manufacturer should try to satisfy, Detroit usually acts as if the job can be done entirely by product changes. Occasionally attention gets paid to financing, too, but that is done more in order to sell than to enable the customer to buy.

As for taking care of other customer needs, there is not enough being done to write about. The areas of the greatest unsatisfied needs are ignored, or at best get stepchild attention. These are at the point of sale and on the matter of automotive repair and maintenance. Detroit views these problem areas as being of secondary importance. That is underscored by the fact that the retailing and servicing ends of this industry are neither owned and operated nor controlled by the manufacturers. Once the car is produced, things are pretty much in the dealer's inadequate hands. Illustrative of Detroit's arm's-length attitude is the fact that, while servicing holds enormous sales-stimulating, profit-building opportunities, only 57 of Chevrolet's 7,000 dealers provide night maintenance service.

Motorists repeatedly express their dissatisfaction with servicing and their apprehensions about buying cars under the present selling setup. The anxieties and problems they encounter during the auto buying and maintenance processes are probably more intense and widespread today than 30 years ago. Yet the automobile companies do not *seem* to listen to or take their cues from the anguished consumer. If they do listen, it must be through the filter of their own preoccupation with production. The marketing effort is still viewed as a necessary consequence of the product, not vice versa, as it should be. That is the legacy of mass production, with its parochial view that profit resides essentially in low-cost full production.

What Ford put first: The profit lure of mass production obviously has a place in the plans and strategy of business management, but it must always *follow* hard thinking about the customer. This is one of the most important lessons that we can learn from the contradictory behavior of Henry Ford. In a sense Ford was both the most brilliant and the most senseless marketer in American history. He was senseless because he refused to give the customer anything but a black car. He was brilliant because he fashioned a production system designed to fit market needs. We habitually celebrate him for the wrong reason, his production genius. His real genius was marketing. We think he was able to cut his selling price and therefore sell millions of $500 cars because his invention of the assembly line had reduced the costs. Actually he invented the assembly line because he had concluded that at $500 he could sell millions of cars. Mass production was the *result* not the cause of his low prices.

Ford repeatedly emphasized this point, but a nation of production-oriented business managers refuses to hear the great lesson he taught. Here is his operating philosophy as he expressed it succinctly:

"Our policy is to reduce the price, extend the operations, and improve the article. You will notice that the reduction of price comes first. We have never considered any costs as fixed. Therefore we first reduce the price to the point where we believe more sales will result. Then we go ahead and try to make the prices. We do not bother about the costs. The new price forces the costs down. The more usual way is to take the costs and then determine the price; and although that method may be scientific in the narrow sense, it is not scientific in the broad sense, because what earthly use is it to know the cost if it tells you that you cannot manufacture at a price at which the article can be sold? But more to the point is the fact that, although one may calculate what a cost is, and of course all of our costs are carefully calculated, no one knows what a cost ought to be. One of the ways of discovering … is to name a price so low as to force everybody in the place to the highest point of efficiency.

The low price makes everybody dig for profits. We make more discoveries concerning manufacturing and selling under this forced method than by any method of leisurely investigation."[5]

Product provincialism: The tantalizing profit possibilities of low unit production costs may be the most seriously self-deceiving attitude that can afflict a company, particularly a "growth" company where an apparently assured expansion of demand already tends to undermine a proper concern for the importance of marketing and the customer.

The usual result of this narrow preoccupation with so-called concrete matters is that instead of growing, the industry declines. It usually means that the product fails to adapt to the constantly changing patterns of consumer needs and tastes, to new and modified marketing institutions and practices, or to product developments in competing or complementary industries. The industry has its eyes so firmly on its own specific product that it does not see how it is being made obsolete.

The classical example of this is the buggy whip industry. No amount of product improvement could stave off its death sentence. But had the industry defined itself as being in the transportation business rather than the buggy whip business, it might have survived. It would have done what survival always entails, that is, changing. Even if it had only defined its business as providing a stimulant or catalyst to an energy source, it might have survived by becoming a manufacturer of, say, fanbelts or air cleaners.

What may some day be a still more classical example is, again, the oil industry. Having let others steal marvelous opportunities from it (e.g., natural gas, as already mentioned, missile fuels, and jet engine lubricants), one would expect it to have taken steps never to let that happen again. But this is not the case. We are now getting extraordinary new developments in fuel systems specifically designed to power automobiles. Not only are these developments concentrated in firms outside the petroleum industry, but petroleum is almost systematically ignoring them, securely content in its wedded bliss to oil. It is the story of the kerosene lamp versus the incandescent lamp all over again. Oil is trying to improve hydrocarbon fuels rather than develop *any* fuels best suited to the needs of their users, whether or not made in different ways and with different raw materials from oil.

Here are some things which nonpetroleum companies are working on:

• Over a dozen such firms now have advanced working models of energy systems which, when perfected, will replace the internal combustion engine and eliminate the demand for gasoline. The superior merit of each of these systems is their elimination of frequent, time-consuming, and irritating refueling stops. Most of these systems are fuel cells designed to create electrical energy directly from chemicals without combustion. Most of them use chemicals that are not derived from oil, generally hydrogen and oxygen.

• Several other companies have advanced models of electric storage batteries designed to power automobiles. One of these is an aircraft producer that is working jointly with several electric utility companies. The latter hope to use off-peak generating capacity to supply overnight plug-in battery regeneration. Another company, also using the battery approach, is a medium-size electronics firm with extensive small-battery experience that it developed in connection with its work on hearing aids. It is collaborating with an automobile manufacturer. Recent improvements arising from the need for high-powered miniature power storage plants in rockets have put us within reach of a relatively small battery capable of withstanding great overloads or surges of power. Germanium diode applications and batteries using sintered-plate and nickel-cadmium techniques promise to make a revolution in our energy sources.

• Solar energy conversion systems are also getting increasing attention. One usually cautious Detroit auto executive recently ventured that solar-powered cars might be common by 1980.

As for the oil companies, they are more or less "watching developments," as one research director put it to me. A few are doing a bit of research on fuel cells, but almost always confined to developing cells powered by hydrocarbon chemicals. None of them are enthusiastically researching fuel cells, batteries, or solar power plants. None of them are spending a fraction as much on research in these profoundly important areas as they are on the usual run-of-the-mill things like reducing combustion chamber deposit in gasoline engines. One major integrated petroleum company recently took a tentative look at the fuel cell and concluded that although "the companies actively working on it indicate a belief in ultimate success … the

timing and magnitude of its impact are too remote to warrant recognition in our forecasts."

One might, of course, ask: Why should the oil companies do anything different? Would not chemical fuel cells, batteries, or solar energy kill the present product lines? The answer is that they would indeed, and that is precisely the reason for the oil firms having to develop these power units before their competitors, so they will not be companies without an industry.

Management might be more likely to do what is needed for its own preservation if it thought of itself as being in the energy business. But even that would not be enough if it persists in imprisoning itself in the narrow grip of its tight product orientation. It has to think of itself as taking care of customer needs, not finding, refining, or even selling oil. Once it genuinely thinks of its business as taking care of people's transportation needs, nothing can stop it from creating its own extravagantly profitable growth.

'Creative destruction': Since words are cheap and deeds are dear, it may be appropriate to indicate what this kind of thinking involves and leads to. Let us start at the beginning—the customer. It can be shown that motorists strongly dislike the bother, delay, and experience of buying gasoline. People actually do not buy gasoline. They cannot see it, taste it, feel it, appreciate it, or really test it. What they buy is the right to continue driving their cars. The gas station is like a tax collector to whom people are compelled to pay a periodic toll as the price of using their cars. This makes the gas station a basically unpopular institution. It can never be made popular or pleasant, only less unpopular, less unpleasant.

To reduce its unpopularity completely means eliminating it. Nobody likes a tax collector, not even a pleasantly cheerful one. Nobody likes to interrupt a trip to buy a phantom product, not even from a handsome Adonis or a seductive Venus. Hence, companies that are working on exotic fuel substitutes which will eliminate the need for frequent refueling are heading directly into the outstretched arms of the irritated motorist. They are riding a wave of inevitability, not because they are creating something which is technologically superior or more sophisticated, but because they are satisfying a powerful customer need. They are also eliminating noxious odors and air pollution.

Once the petroleum companies recognize the customer-satisfying logic of what another power system can do they will see that they have no more choice about working on an efficient, long-lasting fuel (or some way of delivering present fuels without bothering the motorist) than the big food chains had a choice about going into the supermarket business, or the vacuum tube companies had a choice about making semiconductors. For their own good the oil firms will have to destroy their own highly profitable assets. No amount of wishful thinking can save them from the necessity of engaging in this form of "creative destruction."

I phrase the need as strongly as this because I think management must make quite an effort to break itself loose from conventional ways. It is all too easy in this day and age for a company or industry to let its sense of purpose become dominated by the economies of full production and to develop a dangerously lopsided product orientation. In short, if management lets itself drift, it invariably drifts in the direction of thinking of itself as producing goods and services, not customer satisfactions. While it probably will not descend to the depths of telling its salesmen, "You get rid of it; we'll worry about profits," it can, without knowing it, be practicing precisely that formula for withering decay. The historic fate of one growth industry after another has been its suicidal product provincialism.

Dangers of R&D

Another big danger to a firm's continued growth arises when top management is wholly transfixed by the profit possibilities of technical research and development. To illustrate I shall turn first to a new industry—electronics—and then return once more to the oil companies. By comparing a fresh example with a familiar one, I hope to emphasize the prevalence and insidiousness of a hazardous way of thinking.

Marketing shortchanged: In the case of electronics, the greatest danger which faces the glamorous new companies in this field is not that they do not pay enough attention to research and development, but that they pay *too much* attention to it. And the fact that the fastest growing electronics firms owe their eminence to their heavy emphasis on technical research is completely beside the point. They have vaulted to affluence on a sudden crest of unusually strong general receptiveness to new technical ideas. Also, their success has been shaped in the virtually guaranteed market of military subsidies and by military orders that in many cases actually preceded the existence of facilities to make the products.

Their expansion has, in other words, been almost totally devoid of marketing effort.

Thus, they are growing up under conditions that come dangerously close to creating the illusion that a superior product will sell itself. Having created a successful company by making a superior product, it is not surprising that management continues to be oriented toward the product rather than the people who consume it. It develops the philosophy that continued growth is a matter of continued product innovation and improvement.

A number of other factors tend to strengthen and sustain this belief:

1. Because electronic products are highly complex and sophisticated, managements become top-heavy with engineers and scientists. This creates a selective bias in favor of research and production at the expense of marketing. The organization tends to view itself as making things rather than satisfying customer needs. Marketing gets treated as a residual activity, "something else" that must be done once the vital job of product creation and production is completed.

2. To this bias in favor of product research, development, and production is added the bias in favor of dealing with controllable variables. Engineers and scientists are at home in the world of concrete things like machines, test tubes, production lines, and even balance sheets. The abstractions to which they feel kindly are those which are testable or manipulatable in the laboratory, or, if not testable, then functional, such as Euclid's axioms. In short, the managements of the new glamour-growth companies tend to favor those business activities which lend themselves to careful study, experimentation, and control—the hard, practical realities of the lab, the shop, the books.

What gets shortchanged are the realities of the *market*. Consumers are unpredictable, varied, fickle, stupid, shortsighted, stubborn, and generally bothersome. This is not what the engineer-managers say, but deep down in their consciousness it is what they believe. And this accounts for their concentrating on what they know and what they can control, namely, product research, engineering, and production. The emphasis on production becomes particularly attractive when the product can be made at declining unit costs. There is no more in-

viting way of making money than by running the plant full blast.

Today the top-heavy science-engineering-production orientation of so many electronics companies works reasonably well because they are pushing into new frontiers in which the armed services have pioneered virtually assured markets. The companies are in the felicitous position of having to fill, not find markets; of not having to discover what the customer needs and wants, but of having the customer voluntarily come forward with specific new product demands. If a team of consultants had been assigned specifically to design a business situation calculated to prevent the emergence and development of a customer-oriented marketing viewpoint, it could not have produced anything better than the conditions just described.

Stepchild treatment: The oil industry is a stunning example of how science, technology, and mass production can divert an entire group of companies from their main task. To the extent the consumer is studied at all (which is not much), the focus is forever on getting information which is designed to help the oil companies improve what they are now doing. They try to discover more convincing advertising themes, more effective sales promotional drives, what the market shares of the various companies are, what people like or dislike about service station dealers and oil companies, and so forth. Nobody seems as interested in probing deeply into the basic human needs that the industry might be trying to satisfy as in probing into the basic properties of the raw material that the companies work with in trying to deliver customer satisfactions.

Basic questions about customers and markets seldom get asked. The latter occupy a stepchild status. They are recognized as existing, as having to be taken care of, but not worth very much real thought or dedicated attention. Nobody gets as excited about the customers in his own backyard as about the oil in the Sahara Desert. Nothing illustrates better the neglect of marketing than its treatment in the industry press.

The centennial issue of the *American Petroleum Institute Quarterly*, published in 1959 to celebrate the discovery of oil in Titusville, Pennsylvania, contained 21 feature articles proclaiming the industry's greatness. Only one of these talked about its achievements in marketing, and that was only a pictorial record of how service station architecture has changed. The issue also contained a special section on "New

Horizons," which was devoted to showing the magnificent role oil would play in America's future. Every reference was ebulliently optimistic, never implying once that oil might have some hard competition. Even the reference to atomic energy was a cheerful catalogue of how oil would help make atomic energy a success. There was not a single apprehension that the oil industry's affluence might be threatened or a suggestion that one "new horizon" might include new and better ways of serving oil's present customers.

But the most revealing example of the stepchild treatment that marketing gets was still another special series of short articles on "The Revolutionary Potential of Electronics." Under that heading this list of articles appeared in the table of contents:

- "In the Search for Oil"
- "In Production Operations"
- "In Refinery Processes"
- "In Pipeline Operations"

Significantly, every one of the industry's major functional areas is listed, *except* marketing. Why? Either it is believed that electronics holds no revolutionary potential for petroleum marketing (which is palpably wrong), or the editors forgot to discuss marketing (which is more likely, and illustrates its stepchild status).

The order in which the four functional areas are listed also betrays the alienation of the oil industry from the consumer. The industry is implicitly defined as beginning with the search for oil and ending with its distribution from the refinery. But the truth is, it seems to me, that the industry begins with the needs of the customer for its products. From that primal position its definition moves steadily back-stream to areas of progressively lesser importance, until it finally comes to rest at the "search for oil."

Beginning & end: The view that an industry is a customer-satisfying process, not a goods-producing process, is vital for all businessmen to understand. An industry begins with the customer and his needs, not with a patent, a raw material, or a selling skill. Given the customer's needs, the industry develops backwards, first concerning itself with the physical *delivery* of customer satisfactions. Then it moves back further to *creating* the things by which these satisfactions are in part achieved. How these materials are created is a matter of indifference to the customer, hence the particular form of manufacturing, processing, or what-have-you cannot be considered as a vital aspect of the industry.

Finally, the industry moves back still further to *finding* the raw materials necessary for making its products.

The irony of some industries oriented toward technical research and development is that the scientists who occupy the high executive positions are totally unscientific when it comes to defining their companies' overall needs and purposes. They violate the first two rules of the scientific method—being aware of and defining their companies' problems, and then developing testable hypotheses about solving them. They are scientific only about the convenient things, such as laboratory and product experiments.

The reason that the customer (and the satisfaction of his deepest needs) is not considered as being "the problem" is not because there is any certain belief that no such problem exists, but because an organizational lifetime has conditioned management to look in the opposite direction. Marketing is a stepchild.

I do not mean that selling is ignored. Far from it. But selling, again, is not marketing. As already pointed out, selling concerns itself with the tricks and techniques of getting people to exchange their cash for your product. It is not concerned with the values that the exchange is all about. And it does not, as marketing invariably does, view the entire business process as consisting of a tightly integrated effort to discover, create, arouse, and satisfy customer needs. The customer is somebody "out there" who, with proper cunning, can be separated from his loose change.

Actually, not even selling gets much attention in some technologically minded firms. Because there is a virtually guaranteed market for the abundant flow of their new products, they do not actually know what a real market is. It is as if they lived in a planned economy, moving their products routinely from factory to retail outlet. Their successful concentration on products tends to convince them of the soundness of what they have been doing, and they fail to see the gathering clouds over the market.

Conclusion

Less than 75 years ago American railroads enjoyed a fierce loyalty among astute Wall Streeters. European monarchs invested in them heavily. Eternal wealth was thought to be the benediction for anybody who could scrape a few thousand dollars together to put into rail stocks. No other form of transportation could compete with the

railroads in speed, flexibility, durability, economy, and growth potentials.

As Jacques Barzun put it, "By the turn of the century it was an institution, an image of man, a tradition, a code of honor, a source of poetry, a nursery of boyhood desires, a sublimest of toys, and the most solemn machine—next to the funeral hearse—that marks the epochs in man's life."[6]

Even after the advent of automobiles, trucks, and airplanes, the railroad tycoons remained imperturbably self-confident. If you had told them 30 years ago that in 30 years they would be flat on their backs, broke, and pleading for government subsidies, they would have thought you totally demented. Such a future was simply not considered possible. It was not even a discussable subject, or an askable question, or a matter which any sane person would consider worth speculating about. The very thought was insane. Yet a lot of insane notions now have matter-of-fact acceptance—for example, the idea of 100-ton tubes of metal moving smoothly through the air 20,000 feet above the earth, loaded with 100 sane and solid citizens casually drinking martinis—and they have dealt cruel blows to the railroads.

What specifically must other companies do to avoid this fate? What does customer orientation involve? These questions have in part been answered by the preceding examples and analysis. It would take another article to show in detail what is required for specific industries. In any case, it should be obvious that building an effective customer-oriented company involves far more than good intentions or promotional tricks; it involves profound matters of human organization and leadership. For the present, let me merely suggest what appear to be some general requirements.

Visceral feel of greatness: Obviously the company has to do what survival demands. It has to adapt to the requirements of the market, and it has to do it sooner rather than later. But mere survival is a so-so aspiration. Anybody can survive in some way or other, even the skid-row bum. The trick is to survive gallantly, to feel the surging impulse of commercial mastery; not just to experience the sweet smell of success, but to have the visceral feel of entrepreneurial greatness.

No organization can achieve greatness without a vigorous leader who is driven onward by his own pulsating *will to succeed*. He has to have a vision of grandeur, a vision that can produce eager followers in vast numbers. In business, the followers are the customers.

In order to produce these customers, the entire corporation must be viewed as a customer-creating and customer-satisfying organism. Management must think of itself not as producing products but as providing customer-creating value satisfactions. It must push this idea (and everything it means and requires) into every nook and cranny of the organization. It has to do this continuously and with the kind of flair that excites and stimulates the people in it. Otherwise, the company will be merely a series of pigeonholed parts, with no consolidating sense of purpose or direction.

In short, the organization must learn to think of itself not as producing goods or services but as *buying customers*, as doing the things that will make people *want* to do business with it. And the chief executive himself has the inescapable responsibility for creating this environment, this viewpoint, this attitude, this aspiration. He himself must set the company's style, its direction, and its goals. This means he has to know precisely where he himself wants to go, and to make sure the whole organization is enthusiastically aware of where that is. This is a first requisite of leadership, for *unless he knows where he is going, any road will take him there.*

If any road is okay, the chief executive might as well pack his attaché case and go fishing. If an organization does not know or care where it is going, it does not need to advertise that fact with a ceremonial figurehead. Everybody will notice it soon enough.

Retrospective commentary

Amazed, finally, by his literary success, Isaac Bashevis Singer reconciled an attendant problem: "I think the moment you have published a book, it's not any more your private property.... If it has value, everybody can find in it what he finds, and I cannot tell the man I did not intend it to be so." Over the past 15 years, "Marketing Myopia" has become a case in point. Remarkably, the article spawned a legion of loyal partisans—not to mention a host of unlikely bedfellows.

Its most common and, I believe, most influential consequence is the way certain companies for the first time gave serious thought to the question of what businesses they are really in.

The strategic consequences of this have in many cases been dramatic. The best-known case, of course, is the shift in think-ing of oneself as being in the "oil business" to being in the "energy business." In some instances the payoff has been spectacular (getting into coal, for example) and in others dreadful (in terms of the time and money spent so far on fuel cell research). Another successful example is a company with a large chain of retail shoe stores that redefined itself as a retailer of moderately priced, frequently purchased, widely assorted consumer specialty products. The result was a dramatic growth in volume, earnings, and return on assets.

Some companies, again for the first time, asked themselves whether they wished to be masters of certain technologies for which they would seek markets, or be masters of markets for which they would seek customer-satisfying products and services.

Choosing the former, one company has declared, in effect, "We are experts in glass technology. We intend to improve and expand that expertise with the object of creating products that will attract customers." This decision has forced the company into a much more systematic and customer-sensitive look at possible markets and users, even though its stated strategic object has been to capitalize on glass technology.

Deciding to concentrate on markets, another company has determined that "we want to help people (primarily women) enhance their beauty and sense of youthfulness." This company has expanded its line of cosmetic products, but has also entered the fields of proprietary drugs and vitamin supplements.

All these examples illustrate the "policy" results of "Marketing Myopia." On the operating level, there has been, I think, an extraordinary heightening of sensitivity to customers and consumers. R&D departments have cultivated a greater "external" orientation toward uses, users, and markets—balancing thereby the previously one-sided "internal" focus on materials and methods; upper management has realized that marketing and sales departments should be somewhat more willingly accommodated than before, finance departments have become more receptive to the legitimacy of budgets for market research and experimentation in marketing, and salesmen have been better trained to listen to and understand customer needs and problems, rather than merely to "push" the product.

A mirror, not a window

My impression is that the article has had more impact in industrial-products compa-nies than in consumer-products companies—perhaps because the former had lagged most in customer orientation. There are at least two reasons for this lag: (1) industrial-products companies tend to be more capital intensive, and (2) in the past, at least, they have had to rely heavily on communicating face-to-face the technical character of what they made and sold. These points are worth explaining.

Capital-intensive businesses are understandably preoccupied with magnitudes, especially where the capital, once invested, cannot be easily moved, manipulated, or modified for the production of a variety of products—e.g., chemical plants, steel mills, airlines, and railroads. Understandably, they seek big volumes and operating efficiencies to pay off the equipment and meet the carrying costs.

At least one problem results: corporate power becomes disproportionately lodged with operating or financial executives. If you read the charter of one of the nation's largest companies, you will see that the chairman of the finance committee, not the chief executive officer, is the "chief." Executives with such backgrounds have an almost trained incapacity to see that getting "volume" may require understanding and serving many discrete and sometimes small market segments, rather than going after a perhaps mythical batch of big or homogeneous customers.

These executives also often fail to appreciate the competitive changes going on around them. They observe the changes, all right, but devalue their significance or underestimate their ability to nibble away at the company's markets.

Once dramatically alerted to the concept of segments, sectors, and customers, though, managers of capital-intensive businesses have become more responsive to the necessity of balancing their inescapable preoccupation with "paying the bills" or breaking even with the fact that the best way to accomplish this may be to pay more attention to segments, sectors, and customers.

The second reason industrial products companies have probably been more influenced by the article is that, in the case of the more technical industrial products or services, the necessity of clearly communicating product and service characteristics to prospects results in a lot of face-to-face "selling" effort. But precisely because the product is so complex, the situation produces salesmen who know the product more than they know the customer, who are more adept at explaining what they have and what it can do than learning what the customer's needs and problems are. The result has been a narrow product orientation rather than a liberating customer orientation, and "service" often suffered. To be sure, sellers said, "We have to provide service," but they tended to define service by looking into the mirror rather than out the window. They *thought* they were looking out the window at the customer, but it was actually a mirror—a reflection of their own product-oriented biases rather than a reflection of their customers' situations.

A manifesto, not a prescription

Not everything has been rosy. A lot of bizarre things have happened as a result of the article:

- Some companies have developed what I call "marketing mania"—they've become obsessively responsive to every fleeting whim of the customer. Mass production operations have been converted to approximations of job shops, with cost and price consequences far exceeding the willingness of customers to buy the product.
- Management has expanded product lines and added new lines of business without first establishing adequate control systems to run more complex operations.
- Marketing staffs have suddenly and rapidly expanded themselves and their research budgets without either getting sufficient prior organizational support or, thereafter, producing sufficient results.
- Companies that are functionally organized have converted to product, brand, or market-based organizations with the expectation of instant and miraculous results. The outcome has been ambiguity, frustration, confusion, corporate infighting, losses, and finally a reversion to functional arrangements that only worsened the situation.

- Companies have attempted to "serve" customers by creating complex and beautifully efficient products or services that buyers are either too risk-averse to adopt or incapable of learning how to employ—in effect, there are now steam shovels for people who haven't yet learned to use spades. This problem has happened repeatedly in the so-called service industries (financial services, insurance, computer-based services) and with American companies selling in less-developed economies.

"Marketing Myopia" was not intended as analysis or even prescription; it was intended as manifesto. It did not pretend to take a balanced position. Nor was it a new idea—Peter F. Drucker, J. B. McKitterick, Wroe Alderson, John Howard, and Neil Borden had each done more original and balanced work on "the marketing concept." My scheme, however, tied marketing more closely to the inner orbit of business policy. Drucker—especially in *The Concept of the Corporation* and *The Practice of Management*—originally provided me with a great deal of insight.

My contribution, therefore, appears merely to have been a simple, brief, and useful way of communicating an existing way of thinking. I tried to do it in a very direct, but responsible fashion, knowing that few readers (customers), especially managers and leaders, could stand much equivocation or hesitation. I also knew that the colorful and lightly documented affirmation works better than the tortuously reasoned explanation.

But why the enormous popularity of what was actually such a simple preexisting idea? Why its appeal throughout the world to resolutely restrained scholars, implacably temperate managers, and high government officials, all accustomed to balanced and thoughtful calculation? Is it that concrete examples, joined to illustrate a simple idea and presented with some attention to literacy, communicate better

than massive analytical reasoning that reads as though it were translated from the German? Is it that provocative assertions are more memorable and persuasive than restrained and balanced explanations, no matter who the audience? Is it that the character of the message is as much the message as its content? Or was mine not simply a different tune, but a new symphony? I don't know.

Of course, I'd do it again and in the same way, given my purposes, even with what more I now know—the good and the bad, the power of facts and the limits of rhetoric. If your mission is the moon, you don't use a car. Don Marquis's cockroach, Archy, provides some final consolation: "an idea is not responsible for who believes in it."

Notes

1. Jacques Barzun, "Trains and the Mind of Man," *Holiday*, February 1960, p. 21.

2. For more details see M. M. Zimmerman, *The Super Market: A Revolution in Distribution* (New York, McGraw-Hill Book Company, Inc., 1955), p. 48.

3. Ibid., pp. 45–47.

4. *The Affluent Society* (Boston, Houghton Mifflin Company, 1958), pp. 152–160.

5. Henry Ford, *My Life and Work* (New York, Doubleday, Page & Company, 1923), pp. 146–147.

6. Jacques Barzun, "Trains and the Mind of Man," *Holiday*, February 1960, p. 20.

At the time of the article's publication, Theodore Levitt was lecturer in business administration at the Harvard Business School. He is the author of several books, including The Third Sector: New Tactics for a Responsive Society *(1973) and* Marketing for Business Growth *(1974).*

Why Customer Satisfaction Starts with HR

There's convincing evidence that HR drives customer satisfaction—and corporate revenues—by careful attention to who is hired, how they are trained, how they are coached, and how they are treated on the job.

By Patrick J. Kiger

In a conference room at Philadelphia-based Rosenbluth International, one of the country's most successful travel agencies, a dozen new employees are participating in a customer-service training exercise. What's astonishing is that the new company associates are practicing how to provide *bad* customer service.

One group is asked to dream up the rudest ways a motor-vehicle bureau staff member could treat a hapless customer who comes in to apply for a driver's license. After a few minutes of preparation, the associates perform a skit for an audience of other new employees. The trainee who plays the customer arrives at the ersatz office and stands in line. Just as he reaches the counter, the trainee portraying the clerk posts a sign proclaiming that he'll be back in 15 minutes. Other trainees make the hands move on a fake clock to simulate the wait stretching to 20 minutes, then 30, then 40. As the customer pleads for service, the clerk—who is sitting behind the counter, reading a magazine and loudly cracking gum—berates him for his impatience. The ultimate indignity comes when the customer proceeds to the license-photo area and learns that the camera is broken.

Rosenbluth's HR team uses the exercise because it's fun, but mainly to focus trainees on a serious lesson: Customer service arguably is the most critical factor in an organization's long-term success and even survival.

There was a time when customer service was seen as the responsibility of sales managers and tech-support team leaders. Today that attitude is as dated as rotary telephones at corporate call centers. Increasingly, companies are recognizing that HR plays a seminal role in building a customer-friendly culture. Throughout the business world, HR departments are focusing their efforts on improving customer satisfaction. They're using HR activities—hiring, training, coaching, and evaluation pro-

grams—to give employees the tools and support they need to develop and nurture positive, lasting relationships with clients.

The evidence is compelling that HR practices can promote customer satisfaction—and, in the process, improve corporate revenues. A landmark 1999 analysis of 800 Sears Roebuck stores, for example, demonstrated that for every 5 percent improvement in employee attitudes, customer satisfaction increased 1.3 percent and corporate revenue rose a half-percentage point.

Most service-quality gurus say that hiring is not only the first, but the most critical step in building a customer-friendly company.

Moreover, subtle changes in hiring or training sometimes can produce major improvements in customer happiness. One of this year's *Workforce* Optimas Award winners, NCCI Holdings Inc., discovered in a survey last year that its customers wanted more help in using the company's insurance-data software products. As a result, NCCI created a training initiative to give its customer-service reps more technical expertise. By the fourth quarter, the surveys were showing that customers were much more favorably impressed with the reps' technical abilities. Apparently as a result, the overall customer-satisfaction rating rose 33 percent during that period, from 6 to 8 on a 10-point scale.

A company with strong customer satisfaction and loyalty can survive and prosper even when faced with a tough economy or an unforeseen disaster. The salient example: Southwest Airlines, which consistently ranks first among airlines in customer satisfaction. Following the September 11 terrorist attacks, which pushed many airline companies to the brink of demise, Southwest actually managed to post a profit in the fourth quarter of 2001, and was confident enough about the future to add new routes.

Conversely, a company that provides lousy service may have trouble hanging on to its customers over time, and thus may be forced to continually replace lost accounts that have fled in frustration. The cost of acquiring new customers is five times higher than the expense of servicing existing ones, says Michael DeSanto, a consultant for Walker Information, an Indianapolis-based business research firm. At that rate, chronically dysfunctional customer service becomes a monster that can devour whatever gains a company is making in other areas. If that company runs into a stalled economy or an aggressive competitor, its bad customer karma can prove fatal.

For proof, you only have to look at Kmart, the once-mighty discount retailer that went bankrupt in January, at least in part because it couldn't compete with the famously courteous folks at Wal-Mart. (A recent study by MOHR Learning, a New Jersey-based consulting firm, found that 20 percent of customers will immediately walk out of a store when confronted by bad service, and 26 percent will warn their friends and neighbors not to shop there.) Last year, the Dow Jones News Service reported that customer dissatisfaction was costing the McDonald's chain a breathtaking $750 million in lost business annually.

Identifying employees with customer-satisfaction potential

Most service-quality gurus say that hiring is the first and most critical step in building a customer-friendly company. "You need to be selective," says Ron Zemke, president of the consulting firm Performance Research Associates, located in Minneapolis. "It's a lot easier to start with people who've got the right personality qualities to work with customers than it is to struggle to teach those skills to whoever walks in the door."

"We don't want people who are mavericks or into self-aggrandizement. We're looking for a person who plays nicely with others."

Zemke says the key indicator of customer-service potential is a high level of what mental-health professionals call "psychological hardiness"—qualities such as optimism, flexibility, and the ability to handle stressful situations or criticism without feeling emotionally threatened. Those are, of course, good qualities for many jobs. But experts note that the personality of a customer-service maven may be markedly different from those of achievers in other business venues. Verbal eloquence and

persuasiveness, for example, aren't as important as the ability to listen.

"The great customer-relationship person has a very even-handed view of things, a strong sense of fairness," says Dianne Durkin, who teaches customer-satisfaction techniques at Loyalty Factor, an HR consulting firm in New Castle, New Hampshire. "This is a person who tends to balance his or her own interests and the company's interests with the customer's interests."

Ruth Cohen, Rosenbluth's director of HR/learning and development, says her company doesn't want "people who are mavericks or into self-aggrandizement. We're looking for a person who plays nicely with others."

Five HR Tips for Improving the Customer Relationship
tools

- **Look for customer-pleasing personalities**. The ability to empathize with others, flexibility, and emotional resilience under pressure are qualities that aren't easy to teach. Design a structured, situational interviewing process to find those special people.

- **Don't be afraid to emphasize the negative**. Good service isn't always noticed, but bad service invariably is. Use role-playing exercises and encourage trainees to discuss their own experiences as mistreated customers to help them understand the impact on the company's fortunes when they don't make a good impression.

- **Give employees tools for understanding their customers**. Your training program should include training in techniques such as "active listening" and advice on how to interpret customers' verbal cues.

- **Don't neglect "hard" skills**. A nice smile and polite telephone manners aren't enough when a customer needs advice on which hardware to pick or help with a product that isn't working. Make sure your customer-service people have a good working knowledge of whatever you're selling.

- **Promote a service-oriented culture from the top**. A company's customer relationships are heavily influenced by the tone of the management/employee relationship. Sell your top leaders on the importance of company rituals that emphasize service as a core value—for example, an employee tea or luncheon where executives do the serving.

—PJK

What's the best way to distinguish those who are the most likely to please customers from a raft of applicants? Some companies have tried standardized psychological tests. But many consultants and HR professionals say that it's more effective to observe an applicant at work. At Rosenbluth, the scrutiny begins the moment that a job-seeker walks in the door for an interview. "We're looking for a person who shows the same courtesy to everyone he or she encounters," says Cecily Carel, company vice president for HR. "Our receptionist, who's been with the company 20 years, is a pretty good judge of character.

One time she called me from her desk to say, 'This person is not polite.' That applicant wasn't hired."

Patrick Wright, director of the Center for Advanced HR Studies at Cornell University, recommends a carefully structured, situational interview process like the one he helped develop for Whirlpool. "You want to present an applicant with a series of potential scenarios that he might face on the job, and ask him what he would do," Wright says. "Just because a person gives a good answer, of course, doesn't ensure that he's going to actually do that when he becomes an employee. But you want to make sure you've got a person who at least has the right instincts, which you can reinforce through training."

Talent+, Inc., an HR consulting firm in Lincoln, Nebraska, has designed a system for evaluating job applicants that compares their answers in an open-ended interview to analyses of the traits of top performers in that particular field. The company's managing director, Lisa French, says the process can predict a candidate's job performance 80 to 85 percent of the time. In the case of customer service, she says, one of the key determinants is a strong sense of values. A good customer-service performer will work hard on a customer's behalf, not with the hope of getting a raise or a promotion, but because it's the right thing to do. "This is the sort of person who will go down fighting for his or her customers," she says.

Talent+ started working with Ritz-Carlton in 1992, when the rate of "customer defects"—people who complained about the service—had reached a disturbing 27 percent. The consultants helped Ritz-Carlton overhaul its interview and hiring practices, with a focus on identifying applicants with the best customer-service potential. With the new system in place, complaints dropped steadily. By 2000, they had dropped to 1 percent. At the same time, annual job turnover at Ritz-Carlton also decreased from 75 percent to 25 percent.

Turning the knack for niceness into skilled service

Service-quality consultants and HR professionals from service-conscious companies say that even an employee with the right personality traits needs guidance on how to channel positive qualities into developing good customer relationships. At a time of economic uncertainty, when many companies may try to cut costs by scrimping on customer-service training, it's all the more crucial for HR to make a strong case for its vital importance.

One of the most basic steps in teaching good customer-service skills is fostering employees' self-awareness, Durkin says. "You're not going to be good at customer relations unless you first understand yourself. You have to know how you come across to other people, how you react under stress, what your communication style is."

To help an employee become more self-aware, a company may want to use an assessment tool. The Myers-Briggs Type Indicator, for example, helps an employee see her own personality style, such as whether she is a "thinker," a methodical person; a "sensor," one who learns through observation; an "intuitor,"

who is enthusiastic and excitable; or a "feeler," who tends to avoid conflict. With training, a customer-service employee also can learn more about identifying customers' personality types.

Another crucial area of customer-service training is communication skills. "Research shows that only 7 percent of the impact of your communication with another person is in the words you use," Durkin says. "Thirty-eight percent is in the tone of voice. The remaining 55 percent of the message comes from physical appearance, mannerisms, eye contact, and so on." Because so much of communication is nonverbal, customer-service employees who have to deal with customers primarily over the phone find themselves at a major disadvantage in getting across their message—or, conversely, in understanding the customer's need.

One way to compensate for the lack of human contact is by teaching customer-service employees the technique of "active listening"—restating and summarizing what the customer tells them. This not only helps understanding but also conveys a message of attentiveness and concern. Employees also can be taught to notice and respond to subtle cues in a customer's speech.

A big part of achieving great customer service turns out to be keeping customer-service employees happy.

Rosenbluth takes a slightly different approach. The travel agency focuses on educating its customer-service associates to use what it calls "elegant language"—words and phrases intended to create a tone of courtesy, respect, and attentiveness to detail. A company associate uses the word "certainly" instead of "yeah" or "sure," and after helping a customer with a problem, reflexively responds, "It has been my pleasure." And they always, always ask for permission—and wait for the response—before putting a customer on hold. "We think this gives customers a message about how much attention we pay to little details," Cecily Carel says. "It's subtle, but important."

But good customer service requires more than just "soft," or non-technical, skills. Customer-service consultant Zemke notes that organizations frequently neglect to give their customer-service employees adequate product training. "If I order something and it doesn't work, I want somebody who knows the product and can help me, not somebody who's been trained to smile at the right times." Companies such as NCCI have successfully used surveys to find out what kind of technical knowledge and assistance customers most need, and incorporate the information into customer-service training.

Supervising to build a customer-friendly environment

In order for carefully selected, well-trained employees to build great relationships with customers, a company must develop its own good internal relationships, HR professionals say.

Discovering and Fixing Customer-Service Ills

business results

When Don Frye joined Process Software as a manager of technical support and management information systems in August 2001, he quickly found himself in the midst of a customer-service crisis. The company's meal ticket is a narrow technological niche: Internet-related software for business and university computer servers running the VMS platform.

"Basically, we compete against a product that Compaq gives away for free," Frye says. "That's why for us, customer service is really crucial. We need to demonstrate on a daily basis that we treat people well, so that they'll be motivated not only to purchase our product but also to purchase tech support services from us."

But when Frye received the results of an annual customer-satisfaction survey, he was disheartened to see a number of clients who rated their experience with Process as below their expectations. "I contacted every one of those people, to see what was the matter with us," he says. "It wasn't the quality of the product. Basically, the problem was account management. Those customers told me that they felt forgotten, out of the loop. They were frustrated about having to call repeatedly to get updates on their cases."

Hiring new people with better customer skills wasn't an option for Frye, because the company's veteran tech-support staff had accumulated crucial knowledge that wasn't easily replaceable. Instead, he brought in an outside consultant, Loyalty Factor, to analyze the staff's customer woes and develop an individualized prescription for fixing them.

In addition to using the Myers-Briggs test to give employees insight about their own personalities and style of relating to customers, the consultant helped Frye make subtle but important adjustments to the team's communication with customers. A third of contact with customers was through e-mail, a mode that, because it strips away facial expressions, tone of voice, and other nonverbal cues, conveys only about 7 percent of the intended message.

To reduce the number of misunderstandings, employees were coached to choose their words more carefully and to utilize emotions. To lessen customer frustration, the staff studies "active listening" techniques, learning to repeat and summarize what customers told them. "One of the big benefits is that it shows people that you're paying attention to their problems," Frye says. Follow-up and continuity were other problems that emerged in the analysis, so the staff learned to take more thorough and systematic case notes on calls. "That way, when the customer called back, whoever answered the phone could immediately pick up their service without missing a beat."

The fix worked, even better than Frye had hoped. Within a month of tech-support completing its training, complaints were down by more than 50 percent. More important, one of the company's most critical indicators, the renewal rate for customers, actually rose 2 percent over the previous year.

—PJK

Walker Information's Michael DeSanto says that he's noticed an intriguing phenomenon: customers' and employees' relationships with companies tend to have striking parallels.

Research at Cornell University's Center for Advanced HR Studies and at other institutions indicates that there's a strong link between customer and employee satisfaction. "The really crucial issues are retention and, more important, loyalty," DeSanto says. "Both of them tend to operate in a three- to five-year cycle. Brand-new employees tend to love you, because they're still learning new skills and have the potential to move up in the company. New customers love you because you'll do anything to keep them happy." Three years down the road, both the employee and customer relationships with the company suddenly are different, he notes. "The employee may feel like he's buried in the organization. Chances are, he's already got whatever training you're going to give him. He's hearing from headhunters. And the customer is in a similar rut. He's being taken for granted, and he's already learned about the business from you, so maybe he doesn't need you as much."

Strong relationships between employees and customers may actually keep both from fleeing the company. "Good customer relationships may actually be a factor in employee retention," DeSanto says.

A large part of achieving great customer service is keeping the employees happy. Service-quality experts say that customer-service employees tend to model externally the treatment they receive from management. An intensely top-driven, autocratic corporate culture with spotty internal communication leads to tense, confused customer relations. A company with a collegial atmosphere and good channels of communication will be a lot better at keeping its customers happy.

There are many things HR can do to help create an environment that nurtures good service and customer relationships. Rosenbluth International has developed a culture that encourages associates to seek one another's help in solving customer problems, and emphasizes its concern for the customer with "elegant language." CEO Hal Rosenbluth often personally serves tea and cookies to new associates at the completion of their training. "It's a little corporate ritual that sets the mood," Carel says. At the same time, it helps Rosenbluth talk with new employees about what they can do to serve customers.

Rosenbluth's HR team has discovered an important truth. Just as subtle qualities such as a facial expression, choice of words, or a nuance of etiquette can help make a good impression on a customer, any comprehensive HR strategy for customer satisfaction depends on attention to detail. In designing hiring, training, evaluation, and other programs, nothing should be left to chance.

Patrick J. Kiger is a freelance writer in Washington, D.C. E-mail editors@workforce.com to comment.

Start With the Customer

At top-performing service companies, the customer always comes first.

By Stephen W. Brown

THIS COLUMN IS THE first in a series of three that will explore the best practices of truly excellent service companies like Disney, Southwest Airlines, Marriott, and Harley-Davidson Motor Co. The second column in the series will focus on "The Employee Experience" and the last will focus on "The Leadership Experience."

These best practices represent the business fundamentals of firms that are masterful at exceeding customer expectations. Deceptively simple yet highly effective for attracting and retaining customers, they can be applied to both service and non-service firms alike. The columns are derived in part from the recent article, "Delivering Excellent Service: Lessons from the Best Firms" by Robert Ford, Cherrill Heaton, and Stephen Brown, which appeared in the Fall 2001 issue of *California Management Review*.

The common ground between all truly excellent service firms is they know it "all starts with the customer" and they look first to the customer to define quality and value. Any company—whether they're primarily a product, service, or distri-

bution company—can benefit from applying these essential best practices of top-performing service companies.

Think and act in terms of the entire customer experience. There's more to a customer's experience than the product itself. Leading companies realize that every interaction with the customer can make or break the relationship. Harley-Davidson customers don't simply buy a motorcycle; they buy into a brand experience and a way of life. Successful firms know how to emulate Harley's ability to create an experience around a product or service. These organizations look beyond the core product or service to also carefully study the "where" and "how" of customer experience.

For example, benchmark service organizations have learned that if the physical environment is not in keeping with the rest of the experience, customer satisfaction diminishes. The "servicescape" extends from ambient temperature and lighting that affect the physiological responses of customers to the character and feel of the experience. Dis-

ney spends considerable time, thought, and money designing the optimal environment for the experiences it provides customers. One example is the diligence of the Main Street painters. Their only responsibility, all year long, is to start at one end of Main Street and paint all the buildings and structures until they get to the other end and then start all over again. This high level of cleanliness and upkeep supports the guests' fantasies of the Disney image.

A good example of managing the "how" of the customer experience is looking at the ways great companies manage wait time. Disney is the master of this. It knows the exact relationship between wait times at the parks and customer satisfaction and makes sure it has sufficient attractions, food service, and merchandise available to handle the number of guests in the park without unacceptable waits. Disney knows guests want to be kept informed, so it posts the estimated wait times. It also sends mobile entertainment teams to entertain people in long lines.

Continuously improve all parts of the customer experience. Although "continuous improvement" is a mantra for many organizations, benchmark service organizations feature two important aspects to this concept. First, they start with the customer and find out what the customer expects to be improved. Second, they consider all parts of the customer experience as potential areas for improvement. These firms not only try to improve the product and service itself, but also the setting in which the product is delivered and the quality of the delivery system.

Even small, low-cost changes based on customer feedback can produce higher levels of customer retention. Disney's customers indicated that the Tower of Terror—a ride designed to simulate the feeling of an elevator dropping—seemed like it was over too quickly. By making some adjustments to the sequencing of the drops, the customers felt the ride time was just long enough without Disney changing the actual length of the ride.

Empower customers to help co-produce their own experience. Outstanding organizations know customer involvement leads to a number of positive organizational benefits. First, whatever customers can do for themselves, the organization does not have to do for them. This outcome can have a cost and convenience benefit to customers as well. Second, the organization knows that the more customers are involved in producing their own ser-

vice experience, the greater the likelihood the experience will meet each customer's expectations. If the experience does not, the customer bears part of the responsibility. It's hard to find fault with a physician if you fail to follow the treatment plan for an illness or injury. Third, the organization can gain loyalty from participating customers who think of themselves as part of the organization's family.

A great example of creating a "family feeling" is Southwest Airlines. Southwest invites its frequent flyers to help interview new flight attendants. This involvement not only brings customer expertise to the selection process, but also sends a strong message to the customers participating—you're so important to us that we want you to help us pick the people you think can best serve your needs.

Build-a-Bear Workshop, a growing national retailer, engages customers of all ages in creating customized stuffed animals, including naming, dressing, and accessorizing each animal. Research I've been involved with in information technology services also demonstrates the effectiveness of customer co-production in B2B settings.

Treat all customers like guests. Disney insists on everyone using the term guest instead of customer for their millions of visitors. Looking at a customer as a genuine guest changes everything the organization

and its employees do. Creating a hospitable experience instead of merely selling a product or service is an important way to turn customers into loyal patrons or repeat guests. It's cheaper to retain loyal customers than it is to recruit new ones, and repeat business is the key to long-term profitability. Although treating customers as guests is a simple sounding lesson, it represents a major challenge that organizations have to master in order to compete successfully in an increasingly customer-driven marketplace.

In short, the benchmark service organization has a key lesson to teach companies of all types: The customer experience is the key element to consider when shaping your business practices. The time and energy spent on accurately understanding the totality of your customer's needs and wants and finding cost-effective ways to address those factors will be rewarded with greater levels of customer retention—the ultimate driver of long-term profitability.

About the Author

Stephen W. Brown holds the Edward M. Carson Chair in Services Marketing and is a professor of marketing at Arizona State University and director of ASU's Center for Services Leadership. He may be reached at stephen.brown@asu.edu. For more information on ASU's Center for Services Leadership visit, www.cob.asu.edu/csl.

From *Marketing Management*, January/February 2003, pp. 12-13. © 2003 by the American Marketing Association. Reprinted by permission.

Talking Shop

Wonder what makes shoppers tick? 5 retail superstars reveal how to please customers and, more important, how to keep them coming back for more.

By Elizabeth Goodgold

Is it a trend or a fad? Will it sell or wind up on the clearance rack? Will it turn my customers on or off? These are questions retailers face every day. Make the wrong decision, and witness a sales dive. Make the right decision, and become a retail hero.

Assembled here are a diverse group of retailers: ESPN Zone, Hot Topic, Starbucks, Anthropologie and Build-A-Bear Workshop. Each one is succeeding because it has discovered an innovative solution to a unique retail problem. Read closely to find out how to target a fickle customer, develop an enduring brand, create a destination, sell a lifestyle and build a relationship with your clientele.

ESPN ZONE
The Power of the Brand

When you step foot into any of ESPN Zone's eight locations, you know you've entered a place like no other. Huge HDTV screens broadcast nonstop sports, an enormous glacier wall tempts you to climb to the top, and interactive sports games urge you to compete.

This is a world where the ESPN brand is king, and you never forget it. From live ESPN TV and radio broadcasts from the restaurant to its aptly named Season Ticket Holder frequent dining card, the establishment is a veritable shrine to the sports-frenzied fan.

ESPN Zone understands the connection it has with its core audience of males between the ages of 25 and 39. Its menu boasts the ESPN Burger, the Zone Cheesesteak and a full pound of chicken wings. Visitors, of course, have ample opportunity to purchase branded merchandise, allowing them to become walking billboards.

In essence, ESPN and ESPN Zone are one, or, as George Whalin, a retail expert with Retail Management Consultants in San Marcos, California, explains, "ESPN Zone has created great synergy between the franchises."

If the ultimate goal of branding is to create an emotional relationship with your customers, then ESPN Zone has succeeded admirably. It presents a case study of how you, too, can create a retail environment where your brand is reinforced through all five of the senses: Ensure that within all lines of sight your brand name and colors are prominently displayed, choose music appropriate for your target demographics, tempt your customers to touch the merchandise, encourage sampling in a food-based establishment and (if applicable) infuse the environment with a compelling scent.

The never-ending sports coverage at ESPN Zone "[keeps] the wallpaper changing every day," says John Pierce, the company's director of marketing and creative content. "Our coverage gives customers something new to talk about every day." The entire experience encourages diners to linger an average of about 90 minutes. And the longer they stay, the more they spend.

HOT TOPIC
Knowing Its Target to a T

It's 9 p.m. Do you know where your teenager is? If she's into punk or goth (short for gothic), she's probably hanging out at Hot Topic, the retailer for this fickle market. "Come in or you suck" challenges a welcome sign that lets you know you've entered a world targeted toward 12-to-22-year-olds. Surrounded by brands such as Morbid Threads and Vamp, excruciatingly loud music, racks upon racks of body jewelry and tons of insulting T-shirts (like "Wow, you're ugly" and "I know how you feel, I just don't care"), the stores exude attitude. More important, Hot Topic rings up big sales.

With 418 stores, annual sales of $443 million and consistent double-digit quarterly growth, clearly this chain has discovered a key retailing secret: Know your target better than anyone else. How does Hot Topic do it? By encouraging employees to report on trends, paying buyers to attend teen venues and events, religiously responding to the 1,400 e-mails it receives each week, and stuffing a Report Card (comment card) into every shopping bag. All managers, including CEO Betsy McLaughlin, read the scores and comments and make adjustments to the merchandise accordingly.

Since the teen scene is so heavily influenced by music, Hot Topic also sells CDs and patrols concert halls to discover the band of the moment. By working with U.S.-based suppliers, it can jump in and out of fads quickly.

One of this retailer's greatest strengths is its low markdown rate—less than 10 percent of sales. It's achieved, of course, by understanding its consumer. Teenagers are often spending someone else's money and are therefore less price-sensitive. Management smartly encourages the sale of gift cards in lieu of merchandise and has introduced licensed gift cards featuring images such as SpongeBob SquarePants and the rock group Korn. The cards act as collectibles, so the unredeemed rate surpasses the industry average of 5 to 10 percent, further contributing to profitability.

STARBUCKS
Creating a Destination Point

Starbucks CEO Howard Schultz often recalls the moment in Milan, Italy, when he knew he could turn his dream of great coffee within a cafe environment into a destination point selling $3 cups of java. He has created a brand so desirable and a customer base so loyal that the average Starbucks consumer visits a location 18 times per month! But how does Starbucks keep what it internally refers to as "enthusiastically satisfied customers"?

One way is through its friendly environment and comfortable seating, which encourages drinkers to visit with friends, catch up on reading or merely relax. The recent introduction of Wi-Fi, allowing users at 2,000 stores to connect to the Internet, not only encourages lingering, but is relevant to its cosmopolitan customers.

Just as important, Starbucks continually brews up new ideas. Earlier this year, the company announced a twist on the gift card: It teamed up with Bank One to create a Starbucks credit card that also functions as a rechargeable store card. Its debut of the Artist's Choice CD series, featuring musical talent from Tony Bennett to Sheryl Crow to the Rolling Stones, adds another revenue stream while honing its hip appeal.

Starbucks has adopted a saturation strategy to offer a convenient way to connect to the brand. It has licensing deals with Kraft for the production and distribution of its products to grocery stores and agreements with Albertson's Inc. for store-within-a-store concepts. The company also has arrangements with Host Marriott International for airport kiosks and is opening stores virtually next to each other to increase brand awareness, create operational efficiencies and provide faster customer service.

In addition, in every one of its 6,000 coffeehouses in 30 countries, Starbucks is committed to giving back to the community. With net earnings of $215 million for fiscal 2002, it follows in the footsteps of Ben & Jerry's, proving that you can do well by doing good.

Says Gary Wright, retail marketing consultant with direct marketing and fulfillment company GA Wright Marketing Inc. in Denver, "Obviously, the brand has extended beyond the coffee; customers are willing to pay a premium for the experience."

ANTHROPOLOGIE
Selling a Lifestyle

Anthropologie doesn't sell merchandise—it sells a lifestyle. Founder Richard Hayne took lessons learned from his successful creation of Urban Outfitters, which sells hip clothing and accessories for twentysomethings, and transformed them into a concept where the focus is not on the fashion of the moment, but on merchandise that soothes women's souls while getting them to open their pocketbooks.

Anthropologie stores are a carefully orchestrated attack on the senses, from the French music to the aromatic candles burning to the rough-hewn signs throughout. Each retailing quadrant acts as its own island, displaying a theme and flavor all its own. Customers enter "The Washroom" and find exotic soaps, lotions, dispensers and even a medicine cabinet for sale. They step into "The Boudoir" and discover sumptuous sheets, duvet covers and pillows luxuriously displayed on a wrought-iron bed (also available for purchase). In fact, selling the props makes the stores seem as if the customer has uncovered a rare artifact—a piece that she alone can own.

The store flies in the face of traditional retailing: It focuses not on one category of goods, but on disparate merchandise that's centered around a theme. Books, clothing, jewelry and patio furniture can be found there. As market expert Jon Schallert of The Schallert Group, a management and marketing consulting firm in Sorrento, Florida, explains, "a 'controlled clutter' design works because it keeps the customer interested." He advises his own clients to display merchandise in an unconventional way so the customer discovers the merchandise as if on a special treasure hunt. Anthropologie has mastered this strategy.

To foster originality in each of its 50 stores, Anthropologie hires two artists for every location to create art unique to that store. This helps bolster the image of Anthropologie as an independent, free-spirited retailer, not a cookie-cutter franchise.

Anthropologie's buyers are on a mission to scour the globe for interesting, relevant and unusual items for its core customer. They see her as a professional woman aged 30 to 45, well-read, well-traveled and well-educated, with a household income approaching $200,000.

And she is a devout fan. Customers spend an average of $80 per visit, leading to average sales per square foot of approximately $600—not bad for a store that is all about creating a mood.

BUILD A BEAR WORKSHOP
Creating a Relationship With Customers

Who would have thought creating teddy bears could generate revenues in excess of $160 million in 2002 alone? Founder Maxine Clark of Build-A-Bear Workshop sure did. Her strategy was to target girls up to age 12 and let them select, stuff, stitch and dress a teddy bear (or one of the other stuffed animals they offer). What's the goal? "To create memories," Clark explains.

Although bears start at just $10, souped-up versions with sound, clothes and shoes can ring the register at $50. By acting as a fashion retailer with seven changes of merchandise per year, the Workshop lures its customers back an average of five times per year, resulting in sales per square foot of twice the industry average.

One of its unique marketing strategies is the Build-A-Party concept: Host a birthday party, and introduce new guests to the franchise. The tactic creates contagious awareness.

As part of its tireless research, Build-A-Bear discovered its customers wanted to dress their bears just like themselves. And the No. 1 retailer the girls selected was Limited Too. The two retailers share similar demographics and are often retail tenant neighbors. In February of this year, Clark inked Limited Too's first brand extension, affording each retailer the opportunity to promote and sell the other's merchandise both in-store and online, providing innovative cross-pollination of customers.

The company also fervently embraces causes relevant to kids and animals. It is part of a partnership with the World

---

YOUR SERVICES ARE REQUIRED

Many a service professional has said selling a service isn't like selling a product, but isn't it? Try some of these tactics to help you bolster sales.

- Use an expiration date. Virtually all retailers offer a coupon or promotion that includes an expiration date— the longer the time period, the higher the redemption rate. If you're trying to motivate your customers to act quickly, put a short timeline on your proposals.
- Bundle your services. Using the Costco approach, price your services according to how many your customers buy. The more they buy, the steeper the discount.
- Employ upselling. Retailers like Claire's, a fashion accessory chain, offer a surprise goody bag with every purchase for just $1 more. Nordstrom offers ties when it sells shirts and socks when it sells shoes. Encourage your customers to purchase more by asking if they need any additional services at the end of every contract.
- Give a free sample. Cinnabon isn't the only company that can offer a free taste. Offer your customers a complimentary audit, in-home survey, evaluation or any other introduction to your services. And don't forget to give speeches in your area of specialty—the ultimate sampling technique.

Wildlife Federation and The Humane Society, donating a portion of its proceeds on selected merchandise. Retail strategist Whalin concurs with its philosophy: "The company that understands cause marketing today will do very well."

Lessons to Be Learned

What did each of these five retailers do exceptionally well? They transformed their brand into an experience. Translating the ESPN brand to ESPN Zone has provided an outlet for like-minded sports fans to share the excitement of a game. Tempting angst-ridden teens with macabre and sarcastic apparel has allowed Hot Topic to shatter retail records nationwide. Grabbing a cup of java at Starbucks has less to do with what's in your cup than with the relaxing environment. Stepping into the world of Anthropologie is like stepping into an international oasis, replete with faraway sounds, smells and merchandise. And creating a birthday bear at Build-A-Bear Workshop becomes a treasured memory.

Instead of trying to be all things to all people, these merchandisers zeroed in on a niche target and never looked back. They mastered the nuances of their demographics, psychographics and geographics to bring the right products to the right customer at the right time.

Elizabeth Goodgold is Entrepreneur's "Marketing Buzz" columnist.

From *Entrepeneur*, September 2003, pp. 64–66. Copyright © 2003 by Entrepreneur Media, Inc. Reprinted by permission.

What **Drives** Customer **Equity**

A company's current customers provide the most reliable source of future revenues and profits.

By Katherine N. Lemon, Roland T. Rust, and Valarie A. Zeithaml

Consider the **issues** facing a typical brand manager, product manager, or marketing-oriented CEO: How do I manage the brand? How will my customers react to changes in the product or service offering? Should I raise price? What is the best way to enhance the relationships with my current customers? Where should I focus my efforts?

Business executives can answer such questions by focusing on customer equity—the total of the discounted lifetime values of all the firm's customers. A strategy based on customer equity allows firms to trade off between customer value, brand equity, and customer relationship management. We have developed a new strategic framework, the Customer Equity Diagnostic, that reveals the key drivers increasing the firm's customer equity. This new framework will enable managers to determine what is most important to the customer and to begin to identify the firm's critical strengths and hidden vulnerabilities. Customer equity is a new approach to marketing and corporate strategy that finally puts the customer and, more important, strategies that grow the value of the customer, at the heart of the organization.

For most firms, customer equity is certain to be the most important determinant of the long-term value of the firm. While customer equity will not be responsible for the entire value of the firm (eg., physical assets, intellectual property, and research and development competencies), its current customers provide the most reliable source of future revenues and profits. This then should be a focal point for marketing strategy.

Although it may seem obvious that customer equity is key to long-term success, understanding how to grow and manage customer equity is more complex. How to grow it is of utmost importance, and doing it well can create a significant competitive advantage. There are three drivers of customer equity—value equity, brand equity, and relationship equity (also known as retention equity). These drivers work independently and together. Within each of these drivers are specific, incisive actions, or levers, the firm can take to enhance its overall customer equity.

Value Equity

Value is the keystone of the customer's relationship with the firm. If the firm's products and services do not meet the customer's needs and expectations, the best brand strategy and the strongest retention and relationship marketing strategies will be insufficient. Value equity is defined as the customer's objective assessment of the utility of a brand, based on perceptions of what is given up for what is received. Three key levers influence value equity: quality, price, and convenience.

EXECUTIVE
briefing

Customer equity is critical to a firm's long-term success. We developed a strategic marketing framework that puts the customer and growth in the value of the customer at the heart of the organization. Using a new approach based on customer equity—the total of the discounted lifetime values of all the firm's customers—we describe the key drivers of firm growth: value equity, brand equity, and relationship equity. Understanding these drivers will help increase customer equity and, ultimately, the value of the firm.

Quality can be thought of as encompassing the objective physical and nonphysical aspects of the product and service offering under the firm's control. Think of the power FedEx holds in the marketplace, thanks, in no small part, to its maintenance of high quality standards. Price represents the aspects of "what is given up by the customer" that the firm can influence. New e-world entrants that enable customers to find the best price (e.g., www.mysimon.com) have revolutionized the power of price as a marketing tool. Convenience relates to actions that help reduce the customer's time costs, search costs, and efforts to do business with the firm. Consider Fidelity Investments' new strategy of providing Palm devices to its best customers to enable anytime, anywhere trading and updates—clearly capitalizing on the importance of convenience to busy consumers.

Brand Equity

Where value equity is driven by perceptions of objective aspects of a firm's offerings, brand equity is built through image and meaning. The brand serves three vital roles. First, it acts as a magnet to attract new customers to the firm. Second, it can serve as a reminder to customers about the firm's products and services. Finally, it can become the customer's emotional tie to the firm. Brand equity has often been defined very broadly to include an extensive set of attributes that influence consumer choice. However, in our effort to separate the specific drivers of customer equity, we define brand equity more narrowly as the customer's subjective and intangible assessment of the brand, above and beyond its objectively perceived value.

The key actionable levers of brand equity are brand awareness, attitude toward the brand, and corporate ethics. The first, brand awareness, encompasses the tools under the firm's control that can influence and enhance brand awareness, particularly marketing communications. The new focus on media advertising by pharmaceutical companies (e.g., Zyban, Viagra, Claritin) is designed to build brand awareness and encourage patients to ask for these drugs by name.

Second, attitude toward the brand encompasses the extent to which the firm is able to create close connections or emotional ties with the consumer. This is most often influenced through the specific nature of the media campaigns and may be more directly influenced by direct marketing. Kraft's strength in consumer food products exemplifies the importance of brand attitude—developing strong consumer attitudes toward key brands such as Kraft Macaroni and Cheese or Philadelphia Cream Cheese. The third lever, corporate ethics, includes specific actions that can influence customer perceptions of the organization (e.g., community sponsorships or donations, firm privacy policy, and employee relations). Home Depot enhanced its brand equity by becoming a strong supporter of community events and by encouraging its employees to get involved.

Relationship Equity

Consider a firm with a great brand and a great product. The company may be able to attract new customers to its product with its strong brand and keep customers by meeting their expectations consistently. But is this enough? Given the significant shifts in the new economy—from goods to services, from transactions to

relationships—the answer is no. Great brand equity and value equity may not be enough to hold the customer. What's needed is a way to glue the customers to the firm, enhancing the stickiness of the relationship. Relationship equity represents this glue. Specifically, relationship equity is defined as the tendency of the customer to stick with the brand, above and beyond the customer's objective and subjective assessments of the brand.

The key levers, under the firm's control, that may enhance relationship equity are loyalty programs, special recognition and treatment, affinity programs, community-building programs, and knowledge-building programs. Loyalty programs include actions that reward customers for specific behaviors with tangible benefits. From airlines to liquor stores, from Citigroup to Diet Coke, the loyalty program has become a staple of many firms' marketing strategy. Special recognition and treatment refers to actions that recognize customers for specific behavior with intangible benefits. For example, US Airways' "Chairman Preferred" status customers receive complimentary membership in the US Airways' Club.

Affinity programs seek to create strong emotional connections with customers, linking the customer's relationship with the firm to other important aspects of the customer's life. Consider the wide array of affinity Visa and MasterCard choices offered by First USA to encourage increased use and higher retention. Community-building programs seek to cement the customer-firm relationship by linking the customer to a larger community of like customers. In the United Kingdom, for example, soft drink manufacturer Tango has created a Web site that has built a virtual community with its key segment, the nation's youth.

Finally, knowledge-building programs increase relationship equity by creating structural bonds between the customer and the firm, making the customer less willing to recreate a relationship with an alternative provider. The most often cited example of this is amazon.com, but learning relationships are not limited to cyberspace. Firms such as British Airways have developed programs to track customer food and drink preferences, thereby creating bonds with the customer while simultaneously reducing costs.

Determining the Key Drivers

Think back to the set of questions posed earlier. How should a marketing executive decide where to focus his or her efforts: Building the brand? Improving the product or service? Deepening the relationships with current customers? Determining what is the most important driver of customer equity will often depend on characteristics of the industry and the market, such as market maturity or consumer decision processes. But determining the critical driver for your firm is the first step in building the truly customer-focused marketing organization.

When Value Equity Matters Most

Value equity matters to most customers most of the time, but it will be most important under specific circumstances. First, value equity will be most critical when discernible differences exist between competing products. In commodity markets, where products and competitors are often fungible, value equity is difficult to build. However, when there are differences between competing products, a firm can grow value equity by influencing customer perceptions of value. Consider IBM's ThinkPad brand of notebook computers. Long recognized for innovation and advanced design, IBM has been able to build an advantage in the area of value equity by building faster, thinner, lighter computers with advanced capabilities.

Second, value equity will be central for purchases with complex decision processes. Here customers carefully weigh their decisions and often examine the trade-offs of costs and benefits associated with various alternatives. Therefore, any company that either increases the customer benefits or reduces costs for its customers will be able to increase its value equity. Consider consumers contemplating the conversion to DSL technology for Internet access. This is often a complex, time-consuming decision. DSL companies that can reduce the time and effort involved in this conversion will have the value equity advantage.

Third, value equity will be important for most business-to-business purchases. In addition to being complex decisions, B2B purchases often involve a long-term commitment or partnership between the two parties (and large sums of money). Therefore, customers in these purchase situations often consider their decisions more carefully than individual consumers do.

Fourth, a firm has the opportunity to grow value equity when it offers innovative products and services. When considering the purchase of a "really new" product or service, customers must carefully examine the components of the product because the key attributes often may be difficult to discern. In many cases, consumers make one-to-one comparisons across products, trying to decide whether the new product offers sufficient benefits to risk the purchase. New MP3-type devices that provide consumers with online access to music are examples of such innovative products and services. Consumers will seek out substantial information (e.g., from the Web, friends, and advertisements) to determine the costs and benefits of new products. Firms that can signal quality and low risk can grow value equity in such new markets.

Finally, value equity will be key for firms attempting to revitalize mature products. In the maturity stage of the product life cycle, most customers observe product parity, sales level off, and, to avoid commoditization, firms often focus on the role of the brand. But value equity also may grow customer equity. By introducing new benefits for a current product or service, or by adding new features to the current offering, firms can recycle their products and services and grow value equity in the process. Consider the new Colgate "bendable" toothbrush. It seeks to revitalize the mature toothbrush market with a new answer to an age-old problem. The success of this new innovation increases Colgate's value equity.

Clearly then, the importance of value equity will depend on the industry, the maturity of the firm, and the customer decisionmaking process. To understand the role of value equity within your organization, ask several key customers and key executives to assess your company using the set of questions provided in the Customer Equity Diagnostic on the following page.

When Brand Equity Matters Most

While brand equity is generally a concern, it is critical in certain situations. First, brand equity will be most important for low-involvement purchases with simple decision processes. For many products, including frequently purchased consumer packaged goods, purchase decisions are often routinized and require little customer attention or involvement. In this case, the role of the brand and the customer's emotional connection to the brand will be crucial. In contrast, when product and service purchase decisions require high levels of customer involvement, brand equity may be less critical than value or relationship equity. Coca-Cola, for example, has been extremely successful making purchases a routine aspect of consumer's shopping trips by developing extremely strong connections between the consumer and the brand.

Second, brand equity is essential when the customer's use of the product is highly visible to others. Consider Abercrombie & Fitch, the home of in-style gear for the "Net Generation." For A&F aficionados, the brand becomes an extension of the individual, a "badge" or statement the individual can make to the world about himself or herself. These high-visibility brands have a special opportunity to build brand equity by strengthening the brand image and brand meanings that consumers associate with the brand.

Third, brand equity will be vital when experiences associated with the product can be passed from one individual or generation to another. To the extent that a firm's products or services lend themselves to communal or joint experiences (e.g., a father teaching his son to shave, shared experiences of a special wine), the firm can build brand equity. The Vail ski resort knows the value of this intergenerational brand value well. The resort encourages family experiences by promoting multigenerational visits.

Fourth, the role of the brand will be critical for credence goods, when it is difficult to evaluate quality prior to consumption. For many products and services, it is possible to "try before you buy" or to easily evaluate the quality of specific attributes prior to purchase. However, for others, consumers must use different cues for quality. This aspect of brand equity is especially key for law firms, investment banking firms, and advertising agencies, which are beginning to recognize the value of strong brand identities as a key tool for attracting new clients.

Customer Equity Diagnostic

How much do your customers care about value equity?

☐ Do customers perceive discernible differences between brands? Do they focus on the objective aspects of the brand?

☐ Do you primarily market in a B2B environment?

☐ Is the purchase decision process complex in your industry?

☐ Is innovation a key to continued success in your industry?

☐ Do you revitalize mature products with new features and benefits?

How are you doing?

☐ Are you the industry leader in overall quality? Do you have initiatives in place to continuously improve quality?

☐ Do your customers perceive that the quality they receive is worth the price they paid?

☐ Do you consistently have the lowest prices in your industry?

☐ Do you lead the industry in distribution of your products and services?

☐ Do you make it most convenient for your customers to do business with you?

How important is brand equity?

☐ Are the emotional and experiential aspects of the purchase important? Is consumption of your product highly visible to others?

☐ Are most of your products frequently purchased consumer goods?

☐ Is the purchase decision process relatively simple?

☐ Is it difficult to evaluate the quality of your products or services prior to consumption or use?

☐ Is advertising the primary form of communication to your customers?

How are you doing?

☐ Are you the industry leader in brand awareness?

☐ Do customers pay attention to and remember your advertising and the information you send them?

☐ Are you known as a good corporate citizen? Active in community events?

☐ Do you lead your industry in the development and maintenance of ethical standards?

☐ Do customers feel a strong emotional connection to the brand?

How does relationship equity weigh in?

☐ Are loyalty programs a necessity in your industry?

☐ Do customers feel like "members" in your community?

☐ Do your customers talk about their commitment to your brand?

☐ Is it possible to learn about your customers over time and customize your interactions with them? Do your customers perceive high switching costs?

☐ Are continuing relationships with customers important?

How are you doing?

☐ Do customers perceive that you have the best loyalty program in your industry?

☐ Do you lead the industry in programs to provide special benefits and services for your best customers?

☐ To what extent do your customers know and understand how to do business with you?

☐ Do customers perceive you as the leader in providing a sense of community?

☐ Do you encourage dialogue with your customers?

Therefore, brand equity will be more important in some industries and companies than others. The role of brand equity will depend on the level of customer involvement, the nature of the customer experience, and the ease with which customers can evaluate the quality of the product or service before buying it. Answering the questions in the Customer Equity Diagnostic will help determine how important brand equity is for your organization.

When Relationship Equity Matters Most

In certain situations, relationship equity will be the most important influence on customer equity. First, relationship equity will be critical when the benefits the customer associates with the firm's loyalty program are significantly greater than the actual "cash value" of the benefits received. This "aspirational value" of a loyalty program presents a solid opportunity for firms to strengthen relationship equity by creating a strong incentive for the customer to return to the firm for future purchases. The success of the world's frequent flyer programs lies, to some extent, in the difference between the "true" value of a frequent flyer mile (about three cents) and the aspirational value—the customer's perception of the value of a frequent flyer mile ("I'm that much closer to my free trip to Hawaii!").

Second, relationship equity will be key when the community associated with the product or service is as important as the product or service itself. Certain products and services have the added benefit of building a strong community of enthusiasts. Customers will often continue to purchase from the firm to maintain "membership" in the community. Just ask an active member of a HOG (Harley-Davidson Owners Group) to switch to a Honda Gold Wing; or ask a committed health club member to switch to an alternate health club. Individuals who have become committed to brand communities tend to be fiercely loyal.

Third, relationship equity will be vital when firms have the opportunity to create learning relationships with customers. Often, the relationship created between the firm and the customer, in which the firm comes to appreciate the customer's preferences and buying habits, can become as important to the customer as the provision of the product or service. Database technology has made such "learning" possible for any company or organization willing to invest the time and resources in collecting, tracking, and utilizing the information customers reveal. For example, Dell has created learning relationships with its key business customers through Dell's Premier Pages—customized Web sites that allow customers to manage their firm's purchases of Dell computers. The benefit: It becomes more difficult for customers to receive the same personal attention from an alternative provider without "training" that new provider.

Finally, relationship equity becomes crucial in situations where customer action is required to discontinue the service. For many services (and some product continuity programs), customers must actively decide to stop consuming or receiving the product or service (e.g., book clubs, insurance, Internet service providers, negative-option services). For such products and services, inertia helps solidify the relationship. Firms providing these types of products and services have a unique opportunity to grow relationship equity by strengthening the bond with the customer.

As with value and brand equity, the importance of relationship equity will vary across industries. The extent to which relationship equity will drive your business will depend on the importance of loyalty programs to your customers, the role of the customer community, the ability of your organization to establish learning relationships with your customers, and your customer's perceived switching costs. Answer the questions in the Customer Equity Diagnostic framework to see how important relationship equity is to your customers.

A New Strategic Approach

We have now seen how it is possible to gain insight into the key drivers of customer equity for an individual industry or for an individual firm within an industry. Once a firm understands the critical drivers of customer equity for its industry and for its key customers, the firm can respond to its customers and the marketplace with strategies that maximize its performance on elements that matter.

Taken down to its most fundamental level, customers choose to do business with a firm because (a) it offers better value, (b) it has a stronger brand, or (c) switching away from it is too costly. Customer equity provides the diagnostic tools to enable the marketing executive to understand which of these three motivators is most critical to the firm's customers and will be most effective in getting the customer to stay with the firm, and to buy more. Based on this understanding, the firm can identify key opportunities for growth and illuminate unforeseen vulnerabilities. In short, customer equity offers a powerful new approach to marketing strategy, replacing product-based strategy with a competitive strategy approach based on growing the long-term value of the firm.

Additional Reading

Aaker, David A. (1995), *Managing Brand Equity*. NY: The Free Press.

Dowling, Grahame R. and Mark Uncles (1997), "Do Customer Loyalty Programs Really Work?" *Sloan Management Review*, 38 (Summer), 71–82.

Keller, Kevin L. (1998), *Strategic Brand Management: Building, Measuring and Managing Brand Equity*. NJ: Prentice-Hall.

Newell, Frederick (2000), *Loyalty.com: Customer Relationship Management in the New Era of Internet Marketing*. NY: McGraw-Hill.

Rust, Roland T., Katherine N. Lemon, and Valarie A. Zeithaml (2000), *Driving Customer Equity: How Customer Lifetime Value Is Reshaping Corporate Strategy*. NY: The Free Press.

Zeithaml, Valarie A. (1988), "Consumer Perceptions of Price, Quality and Value: A Means-End Model and Synthesis of Evidence," *Journal of Marketing*, 52 (July), 2-22.

About the Authors

Katherine N. Lemon is an assistant professor at Wallace E. Carroll School of Business, Boston College. She may be reached at katherine.lemon@bc.edu.

Roland T. Rust holds the David Bruce Smith Chair in Marketing at the Robert H. Smith School of Business at the University of Maryland, where he is director of the Center for E-Service. He may be reached at rrust@rhsmith.umd.edu.

Valarie A. Zeithaml is professor and area chair at the Kenan-Flagler Business School of the University of North Carolina, Chapel Hill. She may be reached at valariez@unc.edu.

From *Marketing Management*, Spring 2001, Vol. 10, No. 1, pp. 20-25. © 2001 by the American Marketing Association. Reprinted by permission.

Creating Growth with Services

In a world of commoditized products, companies are turning to service offerings for growth. The key to success involves redefining markets in terms of customer activities and outcomes, not products and services.

By Mohanbir Sawhney; Sridhar Balasubramanian and Vish V. Krishnan

Faced with saturation of their core product markets, companies in search of growth are increasingly turning to services.[1] A few companies have enjoyed success with this approach—General Electric Co., IBM Corp., Siemens AG and Hewlett-Packard Co., for example. GE's Transportation Systems division had stable revenues and operating profits between 1999 and 2002, despite absorbing a drop of more than 60% in the number of locomotives it sold. Between 1996 and 2002, revenue from services climbed from $500 million to about $1.5 billion, a trend that the division expects will continue.

Not all product manufacturers are so fortunate. Intel Corp., for instance, spent $150 million to launch a unit whose function was to set up data centers to host Web sites for companies. After three years, Intel shut down the unit and announced that it was refocusing on its core microprocessor business.[2] Similarly, Boeing Capital Corp., the financial services subsidiary of Boeing Co., recently reined in its efforts to provide financial services to other industries.[3] A systematic approach to creating services-led growth can help managers of product companies improve the odds of success. Companies must begin by redefining their markets in terms of customer activities and customer outcomes instead of products and services. By mapping the customer-activity chain and relating the map to a service-opportunity matrix, managers can systematically explore opportunities for new services in four directions.[4] Equally important, they must assess the pitfalls and risks that these opportunities represent, and another matrix—on risk mitigation—serves as a tool for that task.

The Customer-Activity Chain

Companies traditionally think about markets in terms of the offerings they sell. But as Peter Drucker has pointed out, "What the customer buys and considers value is never a product. It is always utility—that is, what a product does for him."[5] Customers seek particular outcomes, and they engage in activities to achieve them.

These activities can be mapped along a customer-activity chain, a concept that has been discussed by several authors in different but broadly consistent ways.[6] A customer-activity chain has the following characteristics:

- It must represent an end-to-end temporal sequence of logically related activities. For consumers, these activities can center on a stage of life (education, career, parenting), the pursuit of a specific interest (fishing, golf) or the ownership of a specific asset (home, automobile, camera). For businesses, it can center on a process (logistics management, human resource management) or a set of assets (computer systems, machinery).
- It must lead to defined customer outcomes. For instance, retirees may want "financial independence" and "peace of mind." Purchasers of computer systems may desire "higher employee productivity." Business travelers may seek "to get to a meeting on time and in a positive frame of mind." These outcomes become the basis for defining the quality of the customer experience.
- It must be defined at the segment level, not at the aggregate market level. For instance, it makes no sense to talk about the customer-activity chain for information workers when analyzing productivity. Activities should be mapped according to segments—lawyers, sales executives, health care practitioners and so on.
- It will often cross industry and product-market boundaries. For example, in the home ownership customer-activity cycle, customers might engage with contractors, insurance companies, realtors, banks, telecom companies and many other service providers. In fact, services are often the glue that holds the activity sequence together.

The customer-activity chain is the foundation for exploring services-led growth opportunities. Analogous to product-centric growth strategies like product line extension, product line

To identify temporal expansion opportunities, managers should create a blueprint that maps the customer-activity chain from one end to another and reveals the outcomes that customers seek.

filling and brand extensions, customer-activity chains can be extended, filled, expanded or reconfigured with new services. To structure the investigation of these opportunities, it is useful to categorize them on the basis of the impact they have on the customer-activity chain. The service-opportunity matrix provides the necessary framework.

The Service-Opportunity Matrix

Once companies are thinking in terms of the customer-activity chain, they can classify new services along two dimensions: the focus of growth (where does growth occur?) and the type of growth (how does growth occur?). The "where" question can be answered by thinking about primary and complementary, or adjacent, activity chains. For example, visiting a dealership is a primary activity on the auto ownership chain, whereas seeking insurance quotes is a complementary activity that falls on an adjacent chain. Service growth opportunities can be found on both chains and in two ways (the "how" question): first by adding new activities and second by reconfiguring existing activities.

Merging the focus of growth with the type of growth results in the two-by-two service-opportunity matrix. The four elements of the framework include

- Temporal expansion: growth from services that add new activities to a primary activity chain
- Spatial expansion: growth from services that add new activities to an adjacent chain
- Temporal reconfiguration: growth from services that change the structure and control of activities within a primary chain
- Spatial reconfiguration: growth from services that change the structure and control of activities within an adjacent chain (See "The Service Opportunity Matrix")

Temporal Expansion

An activity chain can be thought of in terms of time—the time it takes a customer to perform all the various tasks he or she needs to reach a specific outcome. And companies can expand the temporal nature of the chain, or fill in gaps within it, by adding new services that help people perform activities at every stage of the process.

Eastman Kodak Co. has created new services designed to help consumers "manage and share memories" using digital photography. Until the advent of digital technology, Kodak's involvement with customers ended when they ordered prints. The company has since found ways to add significantly to its interaction with customers. (See "Temporal Expansion by Kodak.")

Kodak acquired a startup called Ofoto Inc., for example, which offers an online printing service that makes it easy for customers to order prints (because it is expensive and inconvenient, only 2% of analog photographs are ever reprinted). Con-

The Service Opportunity Matrix

Companies seeking services-led growth should redefine their markets in terms of customer activities and outcomes. By adding or reconfiguring customer activities along a primary or adjacent activity chain, companies can find opportunities for growth.

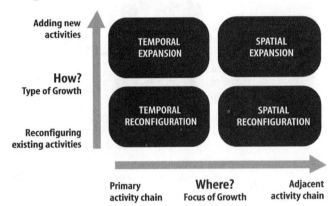

sumers also can create online albums, order greeting cards, archive their photos on a CD, and buy frames and other merchandise. Ofoto has had more than 2 million customers in two years, and its customer base is growing at a rate of 13% per month. Most of that growth is organic—59% of new members come through referrals from other Ofoto members. Almost 12% of all prints ordered on Ofoto are from shared albums.

In addition to the Ofoto acquisition, Kodak has installed 30,000 kiosks in retail locations, where customers can take film or memory cards from digital cameras to make prints. In the future, the company plans to develop a new generation of XML Web services centered on digital photography.[7] While Kodak is struggling as its analog film business declines rapidly, it is the second-largest seller of digital cameras, and its digital camera business turned profitable two years after launch.[8] A big part of the reason for Kodak's success is its deeper presence within the customer's activity chain.

To identify temporal expansion opportunities, managers should create a blueprint that maps the customer-activity chain from one end to another. The blueprint should reveal the outcomes that customers seek, detail the sequence of activities they currently engage in and could potentially engage in, and demarcate the gaps and problems in the existing activity chain. The following questions and examples can guide the exploration for expansion opportunities:

Can Services Be Added That Precede the Sale of the Core Product? Noble House Custom Tailors is based in Hong Kong, where relatively cheap labor allows the company

Temporal Expansion by Kodak

Kodak has added many new digital services along the customer's primary activity chain related to "managing and sharing memories."

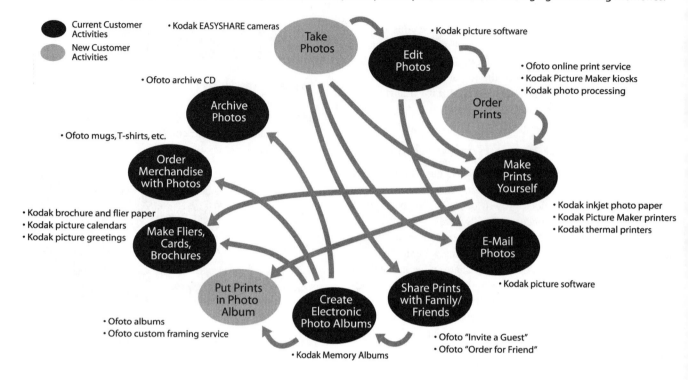

to produce fine clothing at competitive prices. But the clothes really are custom-tailored because the company's master tailor frequently visits dozens of cities across the United States and Europe. During those visits, which are widely advertised locally, he meets scores of customers by appointment, taking their measurements and helping them choose fabrics. People who might normally buy off the rack in order to save money are thus able to enjoy the services of a professional tailor.

Can Services Be Added That Follow the Sale of the Core Product? When a customer selects a casket from Batesville Casket Co. in Batesville, Indiana, the company arranges for a tree to be planted in memory of the deceased. The business thus maintains a connection to people far beyond the primary activity of casket selection. Each year, Batesville Casket receives thousands of letters of appreciation from families for planting the memorial trees.

Can Services Be Added To Accompany the Product? For example, online florists and gift companies could offer to take a digital picture or video clip of the person receiving the flowers or opening the gift and then e-mail the picture or clip to the sender. The gift giver would virtually have the experience of delivering the gift in person.

Can the Product Be Augmented With Network-Based Services? Sewing-machine manufacturer Bernina offers a range of software for its machines that facilitates complex and creative embroidery and stitching projects. The software is thus

a platform for supporting customer relationships over time, as users progress from stitching novices to experts.

Can the Product Be Updated With Services? Computer security specialist McAfee.com offers packaged versions of its VirusScan antivirus software in retail stores. But new computer viruses emerge frequently, so the virus-definition files quickly become outdated. To deal with that problem, McAfee provides an online service that allows VirusScan buyers to update their virus-definition files frequently.

Spatial Expansion

Temporal expansion focuses on the primary activity chain, but companies can also introduce new services into adjacent opportunity spaces. While temporally linked services deepen relationships with customers, spatially linked services broaden them.[9]

To uncover opportunities for spatial expansion, managers need to think about the following questions: Are there activities that are not typically part of the primary chain but are closely associated with it? Can existing products or service platforms anchor the introduction of services in another context? Can the company's reputation related to the primary activity chain be extended to other contexts? The connection between primary and adjacent chains need not be a matter of shared activities. Chains that appear to be unconnected by overlapping activities may be tightly linked along the dimensions of capability or reputation.

General Motors Corp. has leveraged its core automotive business to offer new service platforms for adjacent activity

Spatial Expansion by GM

GM is leveraging its expertise in activity chains that are adjacent to the primary chain of automotive services. (Linked activities appear in blue.)

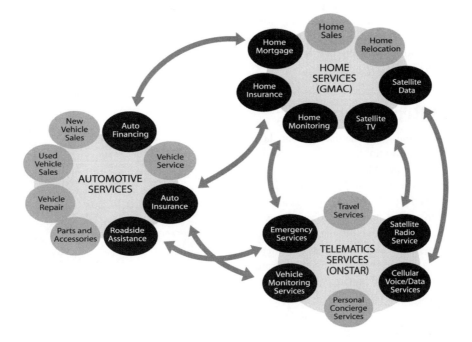

chains. Like most automobile manufacturers, GM offers a comprehensive set of temporally linked services for the primary activity chain of car ownership. Its OnStar platform, however, helps customers with related tasks: emergency services dispatch, stolen vehicle location, roadside assistance, remote diagnostics, route support, convenience and concierge services. Every month, OnStar unlocks about 28,000 doors, dispatches 13,000 roadside assistance vehicles, responds to 700 air-bag deployments and locates 700 lost vehicles.

By the end of 2001, there were almost 2 million OnStar subscribers and the product was offered on more than 40 GM models. While GM offers the first year's OnStar service for free, it claims renewal rates as high as 80%, at annual subscription fees ranging from about $200 to more than $800. In addition, GM has become the country's largest reseller of cellular service thanks to OnStar's Personal Calling service. According to some projections, OnStar may bring in more than $2 billion by 2005.

New services that emerge from spatial linkages can in turn be linked to each other and can themselves become platforms for other services. GMAC Mortgage Corp., another expansion on an adjacent activity chain, is now the fifth-largest mortgage company in the United States. GM is creating an extension of OnStar for the home that will extend its remote monitoring, diagnostics and emergency response services. The company's goal is to be a comprehensive services provider, covering automobile and home ownership, financial services, communications and entertainment. (See "Spatial Expansion by GM.")

The search for spatial expansion opportunities begins with the identification of promising "pivot points" in current activi-

ties and capabilities that can lead to involvement with customers in other areas and continues with the identification of platforms or brands that can support new services. Managers must ask the following questions to identify opportunities in this dimension:

Can Products Become Platforms for Embedded Services? Treadmill manufacturers, for example, have transformed treadmills into platforms for fitness services. Using computers and video equipment, treadmill buyers can log on to iFIT.com for basic workouts (in which the treadmill's speed and incline are remotely controlled), music workouts (which include heart-rate-paced music and verbal encouragements from a trainer) and scenic workouts (which combine virtual landscapes delivered online using streaming video with music, the trainer's voice and treadmill control signals).

Can the Existing Customer Base Be "Rented"? Costco Wholesale Corp. has leveraged the collective bargaining power of its 35 million individual and business members to expand beyond its customers' primary activity chain. The wholesale discounter now contracts with many vendors to provide services and special deals that cover auto and real estate sales, financing, insurance, online software training, communications packages and small-business loans.

Can the Existing Customer Interface Be Leveraged? Recognizing that millions of users are familiar and comfortable with its online interface, eBay Inc. has teamed with Elance Inc. to offer the services of more than 300,000 professionals who work on Web-delivered projects, including software develop-

The search for temporal reconfiguration opportunities requires managers to understand which capabilities are central to their own business but peripheral to those of their customers.

ment and Web and graphic design. Customers post projects online, and service professionals make bids. In addition to receiving the bids, customers can review service providers' profiles, portfolios of sample work and feedback ratings before choosing someone to do the job.

Temporal Reconfiguration

Opportunities for temporal reconfiguration arise again on the primary activity chain. Companies do not add new services in this part of the matrix; they shift the boundary between the activities they perform and those done by customers. Their motivations for undertaking such a shift are threefold. First, companies are better at managing assets or performing business processes that are closely related to their core competencies but not to those of customers. Second, they can aggregate demand across customers to create economies of scale that they can pass on to customers. Third, they can apply knowledge about best practices from the industries in which they provide such services.

United Parcel Service of America Inc., for example, used to focus on a narrow set of activities involved in the package delivery business—picking up, shipping, tracking and dropping off packages. It now takes ownership of the much broader set of activities performed by customers in managing their supply chain, logistics and customer-care operations. Many of the activities performed by UPS for its customers are not new individually, but UPS adds value by integrating them. (See "Temporal Reconfiguration by UPS.")

The UPS Logistics Group has designed transportation networks for customers such as Ford Motor Co. The redesigned network reduced the time Ford needed to deliver vehicles from its plants to dealers by up to 40%. The group also designed and operates a dedicated global distribution center in Singapore for National Semiconductor Corp. The center manages the movement of National Semiconductor's products from its manufacturing plants in Malaysia and Singapore to customers around the world. UPS expects to ship 450,000 orders annually, with an average delivery time of 48 hours. National Semiconductor estimates it will save 15% in shipping and inventory costs with this arrangement. UPS has also partnered with Nike Inc., taking responsibility for managing all the back-end processes for direct selling, including order management, shipping, delivery, returns management, inventory management and customer support.

The search for temporal reconfiguration opportunities often begins inside the company with an evaluation of its capabilities. Specifically, the company's managers must understand which capabilities are central to their own business but peripheral to those of their customers; they must also decide what the firm can do better than its customers in terms of cost, speed, quality or agility.[10] Managers should ask the following questions to identify opportunities for temporal reconfiguration:

Temporal Reconfiguration at UPS

With its logistics-management offerings, UPS handles a much broader set of customer activities than it did when it was only in the package delivery business.

Can Customer Burdens Involving Customization Be Reduced? By taking over activities related to product customization, Dell Inc. embeds itself deeper into the IT operations of its enterprise customers and creates additional revenues from services. For example, Dell provides services related to hardware and software image development, migration and recovery, custom configuration and installation of software, asset tagging, and parts replacement.

Can Customer Burdens Involving Product Storage Be Reduced? Gadue's Dry Cleaning of Burlington, Vermont, stores customers' winter clothes during the summer and vice versa. The clothes are laundered and readied for pickup at a week's notice.

Can Process Expertise Be Leveraged? DuPont is an expert on the application of paint and the minimization of waste and harmful emissions. After DuPont contracted with Ford to run its paint shops, Ford's painting costs were reduced by 35% to 40%, while its emissions of volatile organic compounds declined by 50%. DuPont, which is paid on the basis of the number of painted vehicles, actually sells less paint than before because it has an incentive to paint cars with the least amount of waste. But the company makes more money as a result of the improved efficiency.

Can Customers' Inventory-Control and Stocking Processes Be Replaced? With vendor-managed inventory systems, many manufacturers now track inventory electronically and take charge of ordering, delivery and stocking processes for

The Service Risk Mitigation Matrix

By considering the categories in the matrix, companies can develop a strategy to manage the risks associated with services-led growth.

	Organizational Strategies: "The People"	Design Strategies: "The Offering"	Development Strategies: "The Process"
Capability Risk (Can we do it?)	■ Incubate separately ■ Create, acquire or partner with a company that has a service culture	■ Design services that build on existing product platforms ■ Design product architectures to support services ■ Involve lead users	■ Use partners to fill competency gaps ■ Inventory new competencies
Market Risk (Will they come?)	■ Focus on existing customers ■ Train sales force to build on early adoption success stories while selling ■ Train sales force to clarify "return on investment" ■ Train sales force to manage customer expectations	■ Use partners to fill in reputation gaps ■ Offer trial periods ■ Reduce customer adoption risk (e.g., "pay from savings")	■ Prototype and iterate ■ Blueprint carefully according to customer specifications
Financial Risk (Can we make money?)	■ Use partner assets ■ Use technology and the Internet to decrease labor costs and inconvenience by encouraging customer self-service and/or automated service	■ For smaller customers, create productized versions of services ■ Use annuity payment model to obtain steady revenues	■ Quantify economic value to customers and compare with service delivery cost ■ Perform robust, early and frequent economic value analyses

retailers—a well-known example is Procter & Gamble Co. handling these activities for Wal-Mart Stores Inc.

Can Processes Unrelated to Customers' Core Competencies or Strategic Objectives Be Taken Over? Contract manufacturers such as Solectron Corp. provide manufacturing and assembly services for companies such as Cisco Systems Inc. Over time, Solectron has added services related to product prototyping, customer support, call-center management and repair—freeing customers to focus on innovation, product design and demand creation.

Spatial Reconfiguration

Opportunities for spatial reconfiguration arise when a company that is already present in a customer's primary activity chain can take charge of activities in an adjacent chain.

Nike identified an opportunity to get involved in a secondary customer-activity chain—that of training to play a sport better. Customers often engage coaches or attend sports camps to improve their game. Building on its reputation, Nike entered into a branding arrangement with U.S. Sports Camps; many camps run by the latter are now labeled Nike camps. The camps are held at many locations nationwide and offer mental and physical training for more than a dozen sports. The Nike brand is a vehicle to position and sell the camps; in turn, the camps reinforce the brand and enhance participant loyalty to Nike products.[11]

Spatial reconfiguration calls for a careful analysis of how the relationship between a company and its customers in the primary activity chain can be applied in other contexts. The linkage between the chains may be based on a brand image, a bundling of hitherto distinct activities or the clever design of the value proposition so that it addresses the objectives of an adjacent activity chain. Managers should ask the following questions to identify opportunities for spatial reconfiguration:

Can Services Be Added To Integrate Complementary Customer Activities? Many people think about ordering a pizza to eat while watching a rental movie, but the activity chains associated with eating and viewing are distinct. Movie-rental company Flixrunner.com, however, has teamed up with pizza outlets to offer a "movie plus pizza" delivery service.

Can Services Be Added To Leverage the Brand?
While maintaining its focus on manufacturing and marketing farm and garden equipment, Deere & Co. has entered the adjacent activity chain of financial services. John Deere's brand, forged over 160 years, allows the company to sell credit-card and operating-loan services to farmers and ranchers.

Can Services Be Shifted From Grounded to Mobile Assets? Building expensive, grounded assets in developing nations is risky owing to economic and political uncertainty. To supply power to the Dominican Republic, Smith Cogeneration Management Inc. built a 185-megawatt floating power plant and ran power lines onshore. The plant is a flexible and mobile

Companies need to question continually whether expansion into new service arenas will take them outside the logical scope of their capabilities and organizational culture.

service platform that can be repositioned on short notice. Smith Cogeneration thus supplies power (the primary activity chain) and has taken responsibility for risk management, an adjacent activity chain.

Can Services Change the Way Customers Acquire Products? Most people buy coffee (ground or beans) at a store when they need to restock, and coffee companies usually limit themselves to production and branding. But Gevalia Kaffe of Clifton, New Jersey, sells coffee via direct marketing. Coffees are delivered on a regular schedule and deliveries may be automatically charged to a credit card. Gevalia has built a successful service by questioning and modifying traditional patterns of coffee procurement.

Managing the Risks

The process of migration to services can be difficult and risky. To improve the chances of success, managers must be conscious of the risks involved and be well prepared to manage them. There are three major categories of risk: capability risk (the internal perspective), market risk (the customer perspective) and financial risk (the business model perspective). There are also three categories of risk mitigation strategy: organizational strategies (related to culture, people and organizational design), design strategies (related to design and architecture of the offering) and development strategies (related to the process of developing and testing new services). In combination, these categories form the service risk mitigation matrix, a tool for managers to understand and manage the risks of services-led growth opportunities. (See "The Service Risk Mitigation Matrix.")

Capability Risk: Can We Execute? Companies need to question continually whether expansion into new service arenas will take them outside the logical scope of their capabilities and organizational culture. For instance, Kodak has to determine to what extent a company with a background in technology products should be involved in online photo-printing services or the greeting card business. Significant risks are involved as Kodak's traditional culture and competencies, built on volume production and distribution of cameras and films, adjust to this new perspective.

An organizational strategy for managing such risk is to incubate new service businesses separately until they mature and can be rolled into the parent organization. For example, while OnStar benefits from GM's customer relationships and manufacturing expertise, it operates in a relatively autonomous manner and has created a culture that is distinct from GM's. Almost 80% of OnStar employees are from outside GM. While such separation may be important in the early phases, connections between the core and the services businesses must be

maintained—if they are not, opportunities for mutual leverage may be lost.

Another organizational strategy for mitigating capability risk is to leverage partners' capabilities. The company may need to partner with or acquire other firms that possess the required competencies, as illustrated by Kodak's acquisition of Ofoto. Outsourcing new service development can also mitigate capability risks.[12] The pattern of growth is also important. Companies must carefully decide on the timing, sequence and size of the steps they take as they move away from their core competencies.[13]

Besides organizational adjustments, execution risk can be managed through clever product and process design. Companies can choose product architectures to ease the introduction of new services. For example, the EASYSHARE feature of Kodak's digital cameras provides easy access to its online services. Further, as is the case with product development, the service development process can be augmented with structured tasks and gates that discipline the development process and ensure that key issues are addressed at particular stages.[14] Companies that are new to the services arena must take particular care to document and inventory the tacit knowledge gained during the development process. Those that do so will be better prepared to develop other service offerings in the future.

Market Risk: Will They Come? It's also necessary to address the possibility that customers may not adopt the service or that the service may take so long to reach critical mass of customer adoption that the company cannot continue to fund it. Companies can adopt several strategies to mitigate market risk.

From an organizational viewpoint, selling services can be more challenging than selling a product because the functionality and benefits associated with services are not as clear. A separate organization dedicated to selling services is therefore useful. Selling strategies may include basing the sales pitch on successful, well-documented adoption stories, clarifying the return on investment supported by a detailed statement of expected cost savings, revenue enhancements, and product or process quality improvements; and carefully managing customer expectations.

Market risk is high, particularly when the business is expanding into activity chains where it does not have a proven track record or brand image. In such cases, the company can gain credibility by partnering with, or acquiring, other firms that are trusted names in the adjacent activity chains. For instance, GMAC entered the residential real estate business by acquiring small but well-regarded real estate companies like Koenig & Strey. GMAC employs the brands of these firms in its marketing communications.

To further reduce customer risk and encourage referrals, trial periods and referral bonuses for the new service should be considered. In addition, innovative arrangements in which service providers are paid from the savings realized when a customer

Companies can mitigate the financial risk associated with new services by "productizing" them into standardized offerings that can be cost-effectively replicated and scaled.

adopts the service can dramatically reduce customer risk and encourage adoption. Of course, to support such arrangements, the service providers themselves must be convinced of the value added by the service.[15]

In terms of development, new services should be designed jointly with prospective customers—especially lead users—both to ensure that they have the right features and to prime the pump for adoption. As with products, a company can mitigate market risk during development through carefully planned iterations and test marketing.

Financial Risk: Can We Make Money? Some growth opportunities may offer attractive revenues but not profits. Service margins are sometimes thinner than those for products, especially when the labor-intensive nature of a service makes it difficult to scale. Managers of the core business may question whether services can ever "move the needle" to a sufficient extent and within a reasonable time to justify the use of resources.

Companies can mitigate financial risk by "productizing" their services into standardized offerings that can be cost-effectively replicated and scaled. For instance, Gartner Inc., an information technology consulting firm, has distilled the knowledge of its consultants into industry reports, designed for prospective clients who might not otherwise engage its services. Once knowledge is so embodied, it can be replicated without additional skilled labor. This productized service is much more scalable than the consulting business and is well suited for smaller clients.

Organizations can also leverage Internet-enabled customer connections and resource arbitrage to reduce the cost of services. For example, with its "sure supply" technology for printers, Hewlett-Packard aims to reduce competition from third-party replacement-cartridge sellers and build a customer relationship that extends beyond product purchase. The technology has a sensor that detects when the ink supply is low, and the networked printer automatically orders a new cartridge. By building an automated cartridge-supply service into the printer, Hewlett-Packard not only enhances its revenues but also reduces its costs (for processing a customer's phone order, for example) as well as those of its customers.[16]

Finally, as with any initiative, the economic case for the new service must be rigorously evaluated before embarking on the development process. Managers should keep three points in mind. First, it is incorrect to evaluate the economic case for the service independently of the company's other offerings. Managers must compare the current net present value of the firm with the projected net present value once the service is added. This approach accounts for potential enhancements or cannibalization of revenue across the portfolio of offerings and accommodates the possibility that the new service may intentionally serve as a loss leader.

Second, while existing products may offer high margins and appear more attractive than services, managers must consider whether increased competition and commoditization will reduce that attractiveness in the near future.

Third, the initial costs of service development and launch may be high, but such costs can be reduced substantially as companies learn from experience. For example, management-consulting firms create practice areas and tools that are replicable and reusable by codifying the knowledge gained from service engagements.

Finally, while the issue of time to payoff is important, it must be recognized that new service platforms often have significant option value. Correspondingly, the payoff from new service-related platforms should not be assessed just in terms of discounted cash flows. For example, although OnStar generates limited revenues for General Motors today, it has significant option value if it can become the standard for in-vehicle services and a gatekeeper for delivering interactive services to automobiles.

AN OLD ADAGE IN marketing says "There are no mature markets; there are only mature marketers." In difficult economic times, companies often find themselves stumped as they look for growth in their core businesses. And they are intimidated by the high rate of failure of services-led growth initiatives. But those that systematically employ the frameworks for exploring opportunities and managing risks in services-led growth should find that success is less elusive.

REFERENCES

1. For a general discussion of services, see J.A. Fitzsimmons and M.J. Fitzsimmons, "New Service Development: Creating Memorable Experiences" (Thousand Oaks, California: Sage Publications, 1999); and V. Zeithaml and M.J. Bitner, "Services Marketing," 3rd ed. (New York: McGraw-Hill/Irwin, 2002). For an early discussion of service growth, see J.M. Carmen and E. Langeard, "Growth Strategies of Service Firms," Strategic Management Journal 1 (January-March 1980): 7-22.

2. A. Vance and T.R. Weiss, "Intel and Loudcloud Plan To Quit Web Hosting Business," Computerworld, June 24, 2002, 8.

3. D. Gates, "Boeing Capital To Stop Diversification," Seattle Times, Thursday, Nov. 13, 2003, sec. E, p. 1.

4. The literature that addresses service growth by product companies is limited. For a discussion of the need for manufacturing companies to integrate services and solutions, see R. Wise and P. Baumgartner, "Go Downstream: The New Profit Imperative in Manufacturing," Harvard Business Review 77 (September-October 1999): 133-141. For a discussion of the transition from products to services, see R. Oliva and R. Kallenberg, "Managing the Transition from Products to Services," International Journal of Service Industry Management 14, no. 2 (2003): 160-172.

5. Quoted in P.F. Drucker, "Management: Tasks, Responsibilities, Practices" (New York: Harper & Row, 1973).

6. Sandra Vandermerwe has proposed the customer-activity cycle (consisting of prepurchase, purchase and postpurchase phases) as a basis for managers to redefine how they view their businesses. See S. Vandermerwe, "Jumping Into the Customer's Activity Cycle," Columbia Journal of World Business 28, no. 2 (1993): 46-65. For example, ball-bearing manufacturers may come to see their task as ensuring trouble-free operations, and animal-feed manufacturers may see their objective in terms of enabling productive pig farming. To leverage such thinking, companies should focus on shaping and managing market spaces that are constituted by customer-activity arenas—personal mobility, global-networking capabilities and integrated energy assurance, for example—rather than their product analogs—cars, computers and fuel oil. For a detailed description of market spaces and guidelines to develop them, see S. Vandermerwe, "How Increasing Value to Customers Improves Business Results," Sloan Management Review 42 (fall 2000): 27-37; and S. Vandermerwe, "Customer Capitalism: The New Business Model of Increasing Returns in New Market Spaces" (London: Nicholas Brealey Publishing, 1999).

   A related concept is that of the "metamarket," defined as "an activity-based view of a market consisting of a sequence of related activities customers engage in to achieve a specific set of outcomes." Activities that are tightly and logically related in the cognitive space of customers may be spread across providers, time and space in the physical marketplace. A metamarket is created when the cognitive associations between those activities are reproduced in the physical marketplace, thereby streamlining customer activities and providing them with a seamless experience. In the Internet envionment, such a streamlining may be achieved by a metamediary, such as Edmunds.com for automobiles. For a discussion on cognitive spaces and metamarkets, see M. Sawhney, "Making New Markets," Business 2.0, May 1999, 116–121. The metamarkets concept is mentioned as a fundamental concept in P. Kotler, "Marketing Mangement," 11th ed. (Upper Saddle River, New Jersey: Prentice Hall, 2003), 1–32.

7. For a discussion of how networked digital technologies can be applied to existing products to create new, elastic offerings, see S. Balasubramanian, V. Krishnan and M. Sawhney, "New Offering Realization in the Networked Digital Environment," chap. 12 in "Digital Marketing," eds. V. Mahajan and J. Wind (New York: John Wiley & Sons, 2001), 310-338.

8. The creation of a memorable and complete customer experience can be an important consideration in the choice of activities for temporal expansion. For a discussion of the design of the customer experience, see B.J. Pine II and J.H. Gilmore, "Welcome to the Experience Economy," Harvard Business Review 76 (July-August 1998): 97-105.

9. The concept of an adjacent activity chain is distinct from that of the dependent activity cycle/subcycle in S. Vandermerwe, "The Eleventh Commandment: Transforming To 'Own' Customers" (West Sussex, England: John Wiley & Sons, 1996), in that the connections between activity cycles in the latter are posited mainly in terms of activities.

10. The concept of core versus noncore or contextual activities as the basis for making outsourcing decisions is explained in detail in G. Moore, "Living on the Faultline: Managing for Shareholder Value in Any Economy" (New York: HarperBusiness, 2002).

11. Nike added its brand to sports camps that already existed. From the perspective of the customer of the sports camp, it did not add a new set of activities, but it did add value through branding. Such branding constitutes a spatial reconfiguration rather than a spatial expansion.

12. For a discussion on the outsourcing of innovation, see J.B. Quinn, "Outsourcing Innovation: The New Engine for Growth," Sloan Management Review 41 (summer 2000): 13-28.

13. Companies must grow in measured steps away from their existing core competencies. This allows them to avoid the "Alexander problem," that is, the situation in which they cover so much territory so quickly that they are unable to consolidate and hold on to the captured ground. See C. Zook and J. Allen, "Profit From the Core: Growth Strategy in an Era of Turbulence" (Boston: Harvard Business School Press, 2001).

14. Ideas about and examples of how systematic approaches, methods and tools can be applied to reduce service development risk can be found in H.-J. Bullingera, K.-P. Fähnrichb and T. Meiren, "Service Engineering—Methodical Development of New Service Products," International Journal of Production Economics 85, no. 3 (2003): 275-287; and in R.G. Cooper and S.J. Edgett, "Product Development for the Service Sector: Lessons From the Market Leaders" (Cambridge, Massachusetts: Perseus Books, 1999). However, unlike products, the primary execution risk here relates to the successful rollout and deployment of the new service. These risks typically dominate the technical risks encountered during the prelaunch period.

15. In explaining how to discover new points of differentiation, the case of an energy management company that encountered resistance from residential co-op owners to the upfront capital expenditures for energy control equipment is discussed in I.C. MacMillan and R.G. McGrath, "Discovering New Points of Differentiation," Harvard Business Review 75 (July-August 1997): 134-145. The company succeeded by altering its payment policy so that customers could pay over time out of their energy savings.

16. For recent discussions regarding customer satisfaction and the design of online services, see S. Balasubramanian, P. Konana and N.M. Menon, "Customer Satisfaction in Virtual Environments: A Study of Online Investing," Management Science 49 (July 2003): 871-889; and Z. Iqbal, R. Verma and R. Baran, "Understanding Customer Choices and Preferences for Transaction-Based e-Services," Journal of Service Research 6, no. 1 (2003): 51-65.

Mohanbir Sawhney is the McCormick Tribune Foundation Professor of Technology at Northwestern University's Kellogg School of Management in Evanston, Illinois.

Sridhar Balasubramanian is an assistant professor at the University of North Carolina's Kenan-Flagler Business School in Chapel Hill.

Vish V. Krishnan is an associate professor at the University of Texas' McCombs School of Business in Austin. They can be reached at mohans@kellogg.northwestern.edu. balasubs@bschool.unc.edu and Krishnan@mail.utexas.edu.

Life support

Hospitals must create brand that differentiates

By Lisa Tollner

There are reasons people buy a Montblanc instead of a Bic, drive a Volvo instead of a Kia, stay at a Hilton instead of Motel 6 or drink Coke instead of a generic cola, and it is not just that they are better products. Consumers gravitate to a brand because it embodies real or perceived benefits to the user. The same applies to hospitals as well as any other health product or service.

A hospital's brand is more than a name. Rather, it represents a set of positive associations including corporate personality, image and differentiated benefits to patients, medical professionals, staff and the community in general.

Today, branding is more important than ever due to increasingly assertive patient choices, more complex legal structures of hospital and professional affiliations, improved technologies and expanded specialties at the community and tertiary levels. A successfully articulated brand greatly assists in the choice of your hospital over the competition. It must communicate core beliefs that result in a brand promise that allows various stakeholders to:

- Differentiate you from the competition;
- Recognize the value of your hospital and its services, and how this value appeals to their wants and needs;
- Develop loyalty; and
- Become evangelists.

Differentiation is perhaps the most important aspect of building an effective health services brand. Ask yourself why a patient would choose your hospital and why a doctor would refer one there when they could go someplace else locally or in a distant city. Some possibilities might be:

- Range of diagnostic and treatment services from routine to higher risk

- Specialties or expertise in particular procedures and programs
- Hospital Joint Commission on Accreditation of Healthcare Organizations (JCAHO) accreditation
- Board-certified medical staff
- Associations with any teaching hospitals or conducts research or clinical trials
- Active patient satisfaction surveys
- Social workers or others that facilitate your stay and discharge
- Nonmedical attributes such as compassion, patient-centered focus, access to care regardless of ability to pay, trust, and so forth

Once patients recognize and appreciate the differentiators, they should also begin to recognize the value implied therein, which evolves into brand loyalty. The goal is moving patients from a position of no brand loyalty (will change or choose a hospital for any reason) to a position that is completely loyal to your hospital.

The importance of demographics in determining brand message

Following an in-depth study, the AARP identified five drivers of change within the healthcare environment in a report published in May 2002. "Beyond 50.02: A Report to the Nation on Trends in Health Security," summarized these drivers as reliance on prescription drugs and innovative technology, rise of chronic disease and chronic care, greater longevity, fluctuating cost growth and patients as consumers. The last driver has the most impact on hospital branding issues. The report found that as consumers, patients have become more assertive about their preferences and have become more influential about the types of "products" available in the healthcare marketplace. The most assertive age group is between the ages of 50 and 65. The study found this group tended to be more skeptical, have higher expectations and were more active in their views about the healthcare system. The U.S. Census Bureau's most recent report indicates that the largest population growth was in the 45 to 49 and 49 to 54 age ranges (the heart of the baby boomer generation).

The conclusion to draw from this is that the most demanding patients are also the fastest growing age demographic. Further, if this analysis holds true, the large population bubble coming behind this group (commonly known as Generation X) will mean this demanding age group will continue to be a major issue for years to come. Accordingly, it is increasingly vital to develop an effective brand message that will capture this difficult mindshare and then deliver on it.

Ensuring branding success

As with any marketing program or strategy, there are some proven guidelines that can help ensure the success of your brand:

- **Consider current brand equity**—You have some brand awareness already; the assumption should not automatically be to change things completely.
- **Research**—Understand how your competition is branding themselves and how you can counteract their position.
- **Take your time**—This is an important process that demands in-depth analysis and planning for maximum results.
- **Get buy-in**—Obtain consensus from top management. It will not work otherwise.

- **Engage professional staff and employees**—Ensure that all staff understand the reasoning for what you are doing and are convinced to share the vision (commitment before compliance).
- **Focus on execution**—Every action and interaction is a chance to further your brand.
- **Keep your promise**—Once established, you have to deliver on what you say you are going to do. Not doing so would be devastating to your branding program.

Advantages of high brand equity

Successful branding programs result in increased brand equity. One simple definition of brand equity is the ability to retain current patients while obtaining new ones. Advantages of increasing brand equity include:

- Reduced marketing costs because of consumer brand awareness and loyalty.
- Easier-to-launch extensions because brand name carries higher credibility.
- Increased leverage in bargaining for new facilities, affiliations and medical professional recruitment and retention (people want to do business with you).
- Create higher barriers of entry to competitors.
- Offers defense against present competitive pressures.
- Market value of business is increased. A hospital with high brand recognition is worth more than one without it.

Additionally, it likely is more profitable in current operations as well.

Most importantly, the brand promise you establish needs to be articulated and executed at all levels. Branding programs require research and evaluation in addition to in-depth analysis and careful planning. A unified branding program will reap enormous benefits for your hospital organization, in perpetuity.

Lisa Tollner is founder and CEO of Cintara Corp., an advertising, marketing, branding and marketing communications firm based in San Jose, Calif.

SURVIVING IN THE AGE OF RAGE

Learning to manage angry customers is a crucial part of today's service landscape.

By Stephen J. Grove, Raymond P. Fisk, and Joby John

We seem to live in an age of rage. What once were isolated incidents of volatile customer behavior have become commonplace. News reports from around the world chronicle a growing number of customer rage incidents. These incidents create serious problems for managers of service organizations. Consider the following episodes:

Checkout counter rage: A woman had half her nose bitten off by a fellow shopper when she insisted on remaining in an express lane with more than the 12 permitted items.

Parking rage: Youths screamed, swore at, and verbally abused a man in a dispute over a parking space in front of a Costco store and later severely scratched his automobile.

Air rage: A disruptive passenger who attempted to break into the cockpit on a Southwest Airlines flight to Salt Lake City was beaten, choked, and eventually killed by other passengers. (This happened before Sept. 11, 2001.)

Snowplow rage: Frustrated by the never-ending snowfall and the snowplow generated mountain of white blocking his driveway, a Framingham, Mass., man beat the town's plow driver with his snow shovel.

Pub rage: Incensed for being refused service at a pub at closing time, a man with a tractor repeatedly smashed into the establishment, causing the pub's walls to crumble.

ATM rage: When a bank machine at a convenience store swallowed his card, an enraged patron stuck the ATM machine with a utility knife, cursed a nearby clerk, hurled the knife at a cashier, and smashed an adjacent fax machine to the ground.

These incidents only hint at the breadth and severity of customer rage. Damage caused by rage episodes varies from verbal indignation, to vandalism, to physical injury, and even death. Fellow patrons and workers alike have been unsuspecting targets of rage. Clearly, disruptive customer behaviors pose severe problems for businesses afflicted by rage episodes. These problems might include negative publicity, costs of legal actions, and the untold ramifications of traumatized customers and employees. Service organizations should have policies and procedures to prevent or reduce the occurrence of customer rage.

Many customer rage incidents go unreported, so the precise number of rage episodes is difficult to determine. Indications are, however, that customer rage is on the upswing. Consider the airline industry prior to Sept. 11. A *New York Times* article reported that Swissair witnessed nearly a 100% increase over a three-year period in the occurrence of passenger interference with crew members' in-flight duties. CNN reported that an estimated 4,000 air rage episodes occurred in the United States (where airlines are not required to register such instances) in the year 2000 alone. While the number of air rage incidents has declined since 2001 according to the Federal Aviation Administration, a new phenomenon called "ground rage" is growing. Aggressive behavior toward airline personnel on the ground is now so prevalent that British Airways issues soccer-style yellow cards as a final warning to disruptive travelers that any further disturbance will result in refusal of service.

On another front, a recent survey of call center personnel found that nearly 60% of the respondents reported an increased incidence of phone rage over the past five years. Regardless of the range or severity of customer rage, it's the service sector that is most frequently afflicted with rage incidents. Service organizations, such as hotels, banks, restaurants, airlines, and theme parks, require interaction between customers and employees, often in the presence of multiple consumers sharing a common service setting. In addition, service

EXECUTIVE briefing

With civility on a seemingly downward path, customer rage has become a common problem for many service organizations. This article discusses "the four Ts of customer rage," which include the targets of customer rage behavior, the influence of temperament on customers expressing rage, the triggers that spark customers' rage, and the treatments for preventing or managing customer rage. In this environment, smart service managers are doing all they can to improve the service environment for their customers.

quality provided by such organizations is notoriously variable due to the "real time" character of service delivery and the many uncontrollable elements that combine to create customers' service experience. Further, service organizations are often capacity constrained. It's not surprising then that service encounters are a veritable petri dish for customer rage. According to a 2002 study by the Public Agenda research group, shopping malls, airports, airplanes, and government offices are particularly vulnerable to rude or disrespectful behavior.

Customer behaviors in service settings can range from those that are too friendly to those that constitute rage. Obviously, pleasant interactions between customers and employees are desirable. However, if customers are excessively friendly, they can be a major distraction to employees and may delay service to subsequent customers. Under such circumstances, the service process bogs down and workers search for ways to chill customers' friendly advances. Hence, we label the boundary line between too friendly and the range of acceptable behaviors as the freezing point. Toward the other extreme of acceptable behaviors, unfriendly situations occur when customers are irritating or rude to employees. Unfriendly interactions can escalate to rage if the customer or the employee hits the other's hot button with an inappropriate comment, misguided gesture, or other affront. We label the boundary line between rage and the range of acceptable behaviors as the boiling point.

The Four Ts of Customer Rage

Targets. Since customer rage is a common service phenomenon, it's not surprising that the targets of customer rage are other customers, employees, or elements of the service environment. In reality, no aspect of a service organization is immune from rage. In most cases, the rage exhibited far exceeds the transgression that triggered the anger. An unsolicited comment or an accidental bump by a fellow patron may unleash astonishing fury. Harried employees who snub or overlook demanding customers may experience their uncontrolled wrath. Not even innocent bystanders are sheltered from customer rage. Bottled up angst may find an outlet in the nearest unsuspecting soul. Sometimes it's the adjacent passenger, fellow shopper, or exuberant fan that draws the rage of nearby customers. Sharing the service setting with one who is predisposed to rage is not unfathomable.

When fellow customers or employees are not targets of rage, fury may be directed at inanimate objects or others' possessions. Angry ATM users relentlessly pound the machine that swallowed their debit card. Frustrated golfers hurl the clubs that humiliate them into the nearest water hazard. Enraged diners slam tables and toss food on the floor when offended by a waiter. Clearly, when anger boils over, neither people nor property is safe.

Temperament. Service organizations that cater to large numbers of customers simultaneously must be aware that some people are prone to customer rage. Most people know somebody who can "go off" at the slightest provocation. Perhaps it can be traced to personality or maybe other person al factors are at play. Regardless, not all service customers are equally likely to exhibit rage.

Unfriendly interactions can escalate to rage if the customer or the employee hits the other's hot button with an inappropriate comment, misguided gesture, or other affront.

Modern technology has created a world where the boundaries between work and leisure are blurred. Where can one escape the responsibilities of the workplace? Cell phones, pagers, laptop computers, and Internet access keep us tethered to obligations that follow us everywhere. We seem to live in a world where we're on stage 24 hours a day, seven days a week, and 365 days a year. These stressful circumstances provide ample kindling to ignite rage in some customers.

Is it possible that some people fly into rage more quickly? Perhaps. There is some evidence that anger is inherited, yet it seems more likely that rage behaviors are learned via socialization as appropriate responses to certain situations. Some people may have internalized rage as a typical response for some occasions, possibly through a previous experience or by observing others. Further contributing to the likelihood of rage may be the absence of one's spouse or close friends, whose presence might normally keep one's aggressive behavior in check. At the very least, the enraged customer may lack strong social or personal norms that prevent them from boiling over when faced with challenging circumstances.

Many other temperament factors can make some people susceptible to rage. Aggressive personality types are prone to heated verbal exchanges and attempt retribution for even the smallest perceived transgressions. Customers who exhibit type A behavior patterns (i.e., intense achievement strivings, strong sense of competition) often find themselves in situations where their impatience or obsessive nature sparks confrontation. Those who feel controlled by circumstances may be prone to display aggression as well. Even physiological conditions, such as reduced amounts of serotonin and low levels of cholesterol in one's blood system, have been linked with aggressive tendencies. These are just a handful of individual characteristics associated with rage. In short, some customers enter a service encounter with their rage sensors loaded and ready.

The task of identifying likely candidates for rage is fraught with issues. There is an important but subtle difference between engaging in customer segmentation and discrimination. Customer segmentation involves offering different customers different service based on their distinctive characteristics. (Service businesses that provide a more protective environment for parents with small children engage in customer segmentation.) Discrimination occurs when customers are given poor service because of their race, age, sex, religion, or other distinctive characteristic. Discrimination can take the form of "profiling." For instance, a business may decide that males with beards are prone to rage and subject such customers to obtrusive scrutiny. Since Sept. 11, profiling has become a controversial issue. The U.S. Transportation Security Administration's computer-assisted passenger profiling system (or CAPPS II) classifies prospective passengers with a three-level rating—green, yellow, or red. A green rating yields minimal security screening, a yellow rating leads to extensive searches and interrogation, and a red rating prevents boarding the plane.

Triggers. The interactive nature of services offers many potential triggers for customer rage. Some of the strongest triggers occur when customers believe they have been treated unfairly, neglected, or negated in a service encounter. Perceived unjust treatment, such as a later-arriving patron being seated first at a restaurant, may fuel rage. Customers sometimes become angry when their needs are neglected. One who endures a long wait at an unattended customer service counter may commence yelling when the service representative finally arrives. If customers believe they are being treated with disrespect, hostility may ensue. A patronizing attitude from an employee tells customers that they are unimportant and can send the customer into a fury. Ironically, it seems that some organizations knowingly trigger "righteous indignation" from customers and may deserve the rage responses they prompt.

Situational influences on customer behavior, such as those described by Russell Belk, may play a role in triggering rage in any service encounter. Consider the rage-generating effect of these in the following:

- *Physical surrounding:* Aspects of the service environment may rub customers the wrong way. Room temperatures can be oppressively warm or chillingly cold, noise levels can be painfully loud, filthy service settings can anger customers, and/or cramped facilities can make the service setting seem too crowded.
- *Social surroundings:* Other customers often negatively affect each other by violating normative expectations (e.g., standing too close in line or smoking in nonsmoking areas). Crowded service settings can push customers to their limits and may initiate jostling among customers.
- *Temporal perspective:* Long delays or being rushed for time can ignite rage. Time is one of the most sensitive of situational triggers. For example, most customers detest waiting in line, and time delays can cause tempers to rushed often become aggravated and lash out.

We seem to live in a world where we're on stage 24 hours a day, seven days a week, and 365 days a year. These stressful circumstances provide ample kindling to ignite rage in some customers.

- *Task definition:* Extraordinary obligations Heightened expectations and desires can increase customer sensitivity. For example, a married couple celebrating a special occasion may become quite agitated when things don't go as planned at a fancy restaurant.
- *Antecedent states:* Temporary conditions that customers experience, such as hunger or thirst, may cause people to become easily enraged. But the most troubling of such antecedent states is drunkenness, a circumstance that escalates when businesses such as bars, nightclubs, or sporting events serve large numbers of drinking customers.

Treatment. People's emotions can soar during a rage-precipitating incident to the point where management must get involved during or after the episode. Less astute organizations occasionally find themselves tackling uncomfortable negative publicity and possibly liability issues. Clearly, it's in any organization's best interest to have a well-designed set of procedures and policies to manage customer rage.

The first management step is to prevent customer rage by preempting such situations. To do this, firms should focus on the triggers that activate rage. Organizations that understand the triggers that prompt rage can institute procedures to manage outbursts. For example, an unfulfilled promise of a "freebie" supplemental service, an unbearably long wait for service due to unforeseen circumstances, an aggressive customer in a bad mood, or a poorly trained employee serving an "important customer" may each require different treatment. Consider how Disney Corp. successfully manages waiting time for rides at its theme parks. For years, Disney has communicated average waiting times, kept lines moving, and made the wait entertaining. But the most significant improvement is Disney's Fastpass virtual queue system that allows guests to reserve a place in line without having to queue up.

When rage incidents occur, frontline service staff must scramble to defuse the situation and protect the personal safety of those present. At the very least, customer rage may have harmful effects on frontline employees, on customers who share the service setting, and on the perception of service quality. If an employee is the target of rage, this can affect subsequent encounters with future customers. If other patrons are present, they may witness the rage incident and their own experience may be affected negatively. The 2002 Public Agenda study found that nearly three of every four customers report seeing fellow customers behaving badly toward service personnel, and more than 60% said such incidents bothered them a lot. All in all, the costs of mishandling customer rage are too great to be ignored.

Once a rage episode has occurred, organizations are faced with the difficult task of determining the appropriate remedial action for that specific incident and learning from the event to prevent future occurrences. Service organizations should be attuned to how the nature of services can affect customer rage. Since services occur in real time, the risk of failure is always high. Therefore, it is imperative that organizations take a systematic approach to managing rage incidents. For example, the C.H.A.R.M. School provides lessons in Customer Hostility and Rage Management. Employees learn various identification techniques to spot potential incidents before they happen and plausible tactics to defuse potentially dangerous customers. Forward thinking organizations that prepare employees for rage through such programs are making a commitment to a better service experience.

In Exhibit 1, we suggest how firms might establish customer rage management protocols.

There are several managerial actions that organizations can take before, during, or after a customer rage incident occurs.

Exhibit 1
Living with customer rage

BEFORE

Ensure that people and processes are in place to recognize customers who are prone to rage and potential customer rage situations

DURING

Empower employees with the skills and reward mechanisms to manage customer rage as it occurs

AFTER

Investigate, analyze, and learn from customer rage incidents

"Before" Actions

Before customer rage occurs, managers can take preemptive actions to lock the trigger. First, organizations should identify and institute early warning mechanisms and procedures for handling rage episodes. The specific devices involved may vary across service types. Nevertheless, frontline employees need to be trained, motivated, and rewarded for handling difficult customer rage incidents. These actions demonstrate to employees and customers that management takes rage situations seriously. It also facilitates any legal defense if an unfortunate event should occur. As a manager, you might do the following:

- Train employees to anticipate and manage service failures and customer rage.
- Empower employees to act on the incidents without waiting for supervisory assistance.
- Establish reward systems that motivate all employees to attend to customer rage incidents.
- Design early warning mechanisms to anticipate circumstances and situations leading to customer rage.

As an example, Caterpillar Inc. depends a great deal on service enhancements to its products. The company monitors customer equipment remotely, sending electronic warning signals to its service technicians when necessary. These employees are given information indicating the parts and tools needed to make the repair.

"During" Actions

During a rage incident, other procedures may be engaged. Such procedures might include employee actions that seek to respond to the situation. The status of the customer could dictate the type of procedure to invoke. For example, an important client might be handled by senior management with a just amount of apologies and offers for redemption. During a rage incident, you should do the following:

- Take immediate action
- Maintain decorum and remain calm
- Listen to the customer, show empathy, assume responsibility, apologize, and make amends
- Separate or isolate the enraged customer, especially in a shared customer experience
- Document everything about the incident including witness reports
- Involve superiors, if necessary

Marriott, for example, specifies the situations that call for empowered actions based on the nature of the customer problem and the value of the customer to the company. Employees are given "safe zones" for spending up to $2,500 to compensate a customer grievance or inconvenience.

Exhibit 2
Phases in the treatment of customer rage

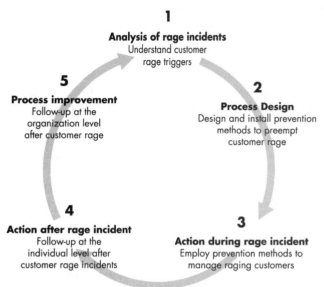

"After" Actions

After a rage incident, management must analyze each episode and follow up with the individuals involved. For long-term actions, incidents must be recorded, categorized by level of severity and frequency of occurrence, stored as information, and then analyzed so that systemic improvements might be designed into the service delivery processes. Managers should take the following steps after an episode of customer rage:

- Investigate causes of the incident
- Follow-up with customers by apologizing, explaining, and reinstating the organization's commitment to preventing similar occurrences in the future
- Depending on the severity and pervasiveness of an incident, involve upper management If service failure was the reason, determine what can be done to prevent it in the future
- If a customer is at fault, determine if an individual or a customer segment should be avoided
- If a service employee is at fault, determine if screening, hiring, training, or supervision is to be changed or improved

Westpac Bank of Melbourne, Australia, has adopted an innovative way to respond to customer rage. It recruits "middle-aged mums" to cool customer rage since mothers tend to have the proper skills from managing their families. They have a general willingness to listen, an increased level of patience, and are naturally empathetic.

Exhibit 2 outlines the series of steps that firms might formally establish to manage customer rage. Step 1 is to

rage. Process design is Step 2, which requires designing and implementing methods for preempting customer rage. Step 3 stresses action during rage incidents by employing prevention methods to manage raging customers. Taking action after a rage incident is Step 4, following up with individuals who became enraged. This is essentially a damage control step. If the customer was enraged about legitimate complaints, then corrective actions must be taken. If, however, the customer was primarily to blame for the rage incident, then it might be necessary to ask the customer to take their patronage elsewhere. Step 5 is process improvement. The organization should follow up on any lessons learned regarding managing customer rage.

The Prognosis

In some ways, it's surprising that the customer rage problem isn't worse. Civility seems to be scarce in modern times. The 2002 Public Agenda study documented a perception of growing rudeness in America with 80% of Americans surveyed viewing rudeness as a very serious problem. Among the reasons that customers become rude or even enraged is that their public and private lives leave them pressed for time. In addition, rising education levels have led to rising customer expectations. Information age technology will continue to present opportunities for customer rage as it provides new methods for interaction between firm and customer, and for interaction among customers. Against this backdrop, it's clear that more needs to be done to manage and prevent customer rage.

Will service encounters in the future contain even more hostility than today? We believe that customer rage is more likely unless service managers reduce common targets of customer rage, manage customer temperaments, prevent triggers, and pursue treatments for customer rage. Smart services managers will do everything possible to make sure that their customer interactions are characterized by civility rather than marred by rage. They know that customers prefer businesses that provide predictably pleasant service environments.

About the Authors

Stephen J. Grove is professor, department of marketing, college of business, Clemson University, Clemson, S.C. He may be reached at groves@clemson.edu. **Raymond P. Fisk** is professor and chair of marketing, department of marketing, college of business administration, University of New Orleans. He may be reached at rfisk@uno.edu. **Joby John** is professor and chair, marketing department, Bentley College, Waltham, Mass. He may be reached at jjohn@bentley.edu.

From *Marketing Management*, March/April 2004, pp. 41–46. Copyright © 2004 by American Marketing Association. Reprinted by permission.

TRUST
IN THE
MARKETPLACE

John E. Richardson and
Linnea Bernard McCord

Traditionally, ethics is defined as a set of moral values or principles or a code of conduct.

> ... Ethics, as an expression of reality, is predicated upon the assumption that there are right and wrong motives, attitudes, traits of character, and actions that are exhibited in interpersonal relationships. Respectful social interaction is considered a norm by almost everyone.
>
> ... the overwhelming majority of people perceive others to be ethical when they observe what is considered to be their genuine kindness, consideration, politeness, empathy, and fairness in their interpersonal relationships. When these are absent, and unkindness, inconsideration, rudeness, hardness, and injustice are present, the people exhibiting such conduct are considered unethical. A genuine consideration of others is essential to an ethical life. (Chewning, pp. 175–176).

An essential concomitant of ethics is of trust. Webster's Dictionary defines trust as "assured reliance on the character, ability, strength or truth of someone or something." Businesses are built on a foundation of trust in our free-enterprise system. When there are violations of this trust between competitors, between employer and employees, or between businesses and consumers, our economic system ceases to run smoothly. From a moral viewpoint, ethical behavior should not exist because of economic pragmatism, governmental edict, or contemporary fashionability—it should exist because it is morally appropriate and right. From an economic point of view, ethical behavior should exist because it just makes good business sense to be ethical and operate in a manner that demonstrates trustworthiness.

Robert Bruce Shaw, in *Trust in the Balance*, makes some thoughtful observations about trust within an organization. Paraphrasing his observations and applying his ideas to the marketplace as a whole:

1. Trust requires consumers have confidence in organizational promises or claims made to them. This means that a consumer should be able to believe that a commitment made will be met.

2. Trust requires integrity and consistency in following a known set of values, beliefs, and practices.

3. Trust requires concern for the well-being of others. This does not mean that organizational needs are not given appropriate emphasis—but it suggests the importance of understanding the impact of decisions and actions on others—i.e. consumers. (Shaw, pp. 39–40)

Companies can lose the trust of their customers by portraying their products in a deceptive or inaccurate manner. In one recent example, a Nike advertisement exhorted golfers to buy the same golf balls used by Tiger Woods. However, since Tiger Woods was using custom-made Nike golf balls not yet available to the general golfing public, the ad was, in fact, deceptive. In one of its ads, Volvo represented that Volvo cars could withstand a physical impact that, in fact, was not possible. Once a company is "caught" giving inaccurate information, even if done innocently, trust in that company is eroded.

Companies can also lose the trust of their customers when they fail to act promptly and notify their customers of problems that the company has discovered, especially where deaths may be involved. This occurred when Chrysler dragged its feet in replacing a safety latch on its Minivan (Geyelin, pp. A1, A10). More recently, Firestone and Ford had been publicly brought to task for failing to expeditiously notify American consumers of tire defects in SUVs even though the problem had occurred years earlier in other countries. In cases like these, trust might not just be eroded, it might be destroyed. It could take years of painstaking effort to rebuild trust under these circumstances, and some companies might not have the economic ability to withstand such a rebuilding process with their consumers.

A *20/20* and *New York Times* investigation on a recent *ABC 20/20* program, entitled "The Car Dealer's Secret" revealed a sad example of the violation of trust in the marketplace. The investigation divulged that many unsuspecting consumers have had hidden charges tacked on by some car dealers when purchasing a new car. According to consumer attorney Gary Klein, "It's a dirty little secret that the auto lending industry has not owned up to." (*ABC News 20/20*)

The scheme worked in the following manner. Car dealers would send a prospective buyer's application to a number of lenders, who would report to the car dealer what interest rate the lender would give to the buyer for his or her car loan. This interest rate is referred to as the "buy rate." Legally a car dealer is not required to tell the buyer what the "buy rate" is or how much the dealer is marking up the loan. If dealers did most of the loans at the buy rate, they only get a small fee. However, if they were able to convince the buyer to pay a higher rate, they made considerably more money. Lenders encouraged car dealers to charge the buyer a higher rate than the "buy rate" by agreeing to split the extra income with the dealer.

David Robertson, head of the Association of Finance and Insurance Professionals—a trade group representing finance managers—defended the practice, reflecting that it was akin to a retail markup on loans. "The dealership provides a valuable service on behalf of the customer in negotiating these loans," he said. "Because of that, the dealership should be compensated for that work." (*ABC News 20/20*)

Careful examination of the entire report, however, makes one seriously question this apologetic. Even if this practice is deemed to be legal, the critical issue is what happens to trust when the buyers discover that they have been charged an additional 1–3% of the loan without their knowledge? In some cases, consumers were led to believe that they were getting the dealer's bank rate, and in other cases, they were told that the dealer had shopped around at several banks to secure the best loan rate they could get for the buyer. While this practice may be questionable from a legal standpoint, it is clearly in ethical breach of trust with the consumer. Once discovered, the companies doing this will have the same credibility and trustworthiness problems as the other examples mentioned above.

The untrustworthiness problems of the car companies was compounded by the fact that the investigation appeared to reveal statistics showing that black customers were twice as likely as whites to have their rate marked up—and at a higher level. That evidence—included in thousands of pages of confidential documents which *20/20* and *The New York Times* obtained from a Tennessee court—revealed that some Nissan and GM dealers in Tennessee routinely marked up rates for blacks, forcing them to pay between $300 and $400 more than whites. (*ABC News 20/20*)

This is a tragic example for everyone who was affected by this markup and was the victim of this secret policy. Not only is trust destroyed, there is a huge economic cost to the general public. It is estimated that in the last four years or so, Texas car dealers have received approximately $9 billion of kickbacks from lenders, affecting 5.2 million consumers. (*ABC News 20/20*)

Let's compare these unfortunate examples of untrustworthy corporate behavior with the landmark example of Johnson & Johnson which ultimately increased its trustworthiness with consumers by the way it handled the Tylenol incident. After seven individuals, who had consumed Tylenol capsules contaminated by a third party died, Johnson & Johnson instituted a total product recall within a week costing an estimated $50 million after taxes. The company did this, not because it was responsible for causing the problem, but because it was the right thing to do. In addition, Johnson & Johnson spearheaded the development of more effective tamper-proof containers for their industry. Because of the company's swift response, consumers once again were able to trust in the Johnson & Johnson name. Although Johnson & Johnson suffered a decrease in market share at the time because of the scare, over the long term it has maintained its profitability in a highly competitive market. Certainly part of this profit success is attributable to consumers believing that Johnson & Johnson is a trustworthy company. (Robin and Reidenbach)

The e-commerce arena presents another example of the importance of marketers building a mutually valuable relationship with customers through a trust-based collaboration process. Recent research with 50 e-businesses reflects that companies which create and nurture trust find customers return to their sites repeatedly. (Dayal.... p. 64)

In the e-commerce world, six components of trust were found to be critical in developing trusting, satisfied customers:

- State-of-art reliable security measures on one's site
- Merchant legitimacy (e.g., ally one's product or service with an established brand)
- Order fulfillment (i.e. placing orders and getting merchandise efficiently and with minimal hassles)
- Tone and ambiance—handling consumers' personal information with sensitivity and iron-clad confidentiality
- Customers feeling that they are in control of the buying process
- Consumer collaboration—e.g., having chat groups to let consumers query each other about their purchases and experiences (Dayal..., pp. 64–67)

Additionally, one author noted recently that in the e-commerce world we've moved beyond brands and trademarks to "trustmarks." This author defined a trustmark as a

> ... (D)istinctive name or symbol that emotionally binds a company with the desires and aspirations of its customers. It's an emotional connection—and it's much bigger and more powerful than the uses that we traditionally associate with a trademark.... (Webber, p. 214)

Certainly if this is the case, trust—being an emotional link—is of supreme importance for a company that wants to succeed in doing business on the Internet.

It's unfortunate that while a plethora of examples of violation of trust easily come to mind, a paucity of examples "pop up" as noteworthy paradigms of organizational courage and trust in their relationship with consumers.

In conclusion, some key areas for companies to scrutinize and practice with regard to decisions that may affect trustworthiness in the marketplace might include:

- Does a company practice the Golden Rule with its customers? As a company insider, knowing what you know about the product, how willing would you be to purchase it for yourself or for a family member?
- How proud would you be if your marketing practices were made public.... shared with your friends....

or family? (Blanchard and Peale, p. 27)

- Are bottom-line concerns the sole component of your organizational decision-making process? What about human rights, the ecological/environmental impact, and other areas of social responsibility?

- Can a firm which engages in unethical business practices with customers be trusted to deal with its employees any differently? Unfortunately, frequently a willingness to violate standards of ethics is not an isolated phenomenon but permeates the culture. The result is erosion of integrity throughout a company. In such cases, trust is elusive at best. (Shaw, p. 75)

- Is your organization not only market driven, but also value-oriented? (Peters and Levering, Moskowitz, and Katz)

- Is there a strong commitment to a positive corporate culture and a clearly defined mission which is frequently and unambiguously voiced by upper-management?

- Does your organization exemplify trust by practicing a genuine relationship partnership with your customers—*before, during, and after* the initial purchase? (Strout, p. 69)

Companies which exemplify treating customers ethically are founded on a covenant of trust. There is a shared belief, confidence, and faith that the company and its people will be fair, reliable, and ethical in all its dealings. ***Total trust is the belief that a company and its people will never take opportunistic advantage of customer vulnerabilities***. (Hart and Johnson, pp. 11–13)

References

ABC News 20/20, "The Car Dealer's Secret," October 27, 2000.

Blanchard, Kenneth, and Norman Vincent Peale, *The Power of Ethical Management*, New York: William Morrow and Company, Inc., 1988.

Chewning, Richard C., *Business Ethics in a Changing Culture* (Reston, Virginia: Reston Publishing, 1984).

Dayal, Sandeep, Landesberg, Helen, and Michael Zeissner, "How to Build Trust Online," *Marketing Management*, Fall 1999, pp. 64–69.

Geyelin, Milo, "Why One Jury Dealt a Big Blow to Chrysler in Minivan-Latch Case," *Wall Street Journal*, November 19, 1997, pp. A1, A10.

Hart, Christopher W. and Michael D. Johnson, "Growing the Trust Relationship," *Marketing Management*, Spring 1999, pp. 9–19.

Hosmer, La Rue Tone, *The Ethics of Management*, second edition (Homewood, Illinois: Irwin, 1991).

Kaydo, Chad, "A Position of Power," *Sales & Marketing Management*, June 2000, pp. 104–106, 108ff.

Levering, Robert; Moskowitz, Milton; and Michael Katz, *The 100 Best Companies to Work for in America* (Reading, Mass.: Addison-Wesley, 1984).

Magnet, Myron, "Meet the New Revolutionaries," *Fortune*, February 24, 1992, pp. 94–101.

Muoio, Anna, "The Experienced Customer," *Net Company*, Fall 1999, pp. 025–027.

Peters, Thomas J. and Robert H. Waterman Jr., *In Search of Excellence* (New York: Harper & Row, 1982).

Richardson, John (ed.), *Annual Editions: Business Ethics 00/01* (Guilford, CT: McGraw-Hill/Dushkin, 2000).

_____, *Annual Editions: Marketing 00/01* (Guilford, CT: McGraw-Hill/Dushkin, 2000).

Robin, Donald P., and Erich Reidenbach, "Social Responsibility, Ethics, and Marketing Strategy: Closing the Gap Between Concept and Application," *Journal of Marketing*, Vol. 51 (January 1987), pp. 44–58.

Shaw, Robert Bruce, *Trust in the Balance*, (San Francisco: Jossey-Bass Publishers, 1997).

Strout, Erin, "Tough Customers," *Sales Marketing Management*, January 2000, pp. 63–69.

Webber, Alan M., "Trust in the Future," *Fast Company*, September 2000, pp. 209–212ff.

Dr. John E. Richardson *is Professor of Marketing in the Graziadio School of Business and Management at Pepperdine University, Malibu, California*

Dr. Linnea Bernard McCord *is Associate Professor of Business Law in the Graziadio School of Business and Management at Pepperdine University, Malibu, California*

Ethics can be gauged by three key rules

By Dillard B. Tinsley

Because the Golden Rule appears in many different cultures, it provides a starting place for analyzing multicultural marketing ethics. Situational variables differ between target markets, but marketers may generally expect multicultural approval of ethical intentions to "do unto others as you would have them do unto you." The admonition is proactive—to do something good for others.

Marketers, target markets, regulatory agencies and other interested parties can agree that the Golden Rule has positive ethical implications. Marketers can apply the Golden Rule to their customers as they seek to beat competitors in satisfying customers' needs, which in essence means: Seek to do good unto customers better than can competitors. For effective use, however, marketers need to understand that different people may understand the Golden Rule in different ways.

One difference is the obvious insight that the other person may be different from you and does not want to be treated as you want to be treated. Marketers have long recognized this insight in their use of market segmentation, where a segment's members have common needs that differ from the needs of other segments. The Golden Rule, therefore, is a reminder to do enough marketing research so that the marketing concept can be implemented in an ethical manner. Marketers who start with the Golden Rule should immediately extend attention to ascertaining the needs of their targeted market segments.

Another difference arises because the exact statement of the Golden Rule varies between cultures. The most significant difference lies in statements in which the admonition focuses on merely not hurting others. The admonition to "not do anything that injures someone else" is sometimes called the Silver Rule. It falls short of the Golden Rule's impetus to actively seek to do something good for others.

The Silver Rule, however, is a useful reminder for marketers to fulfill the relevant laws and regulations. This is an obvious need, but implementation can be challenging, especially when social responsibility requirements vary between multicultural target markets. Even within a single target market, injury may be defined differently by different parties. For example, North-field, Ill.-based Kraft Foods Inc. is reducing portion sizes because of obesity concerns in the United States. Kraft is also reducing marketing in schools because children are a controversial target market—just as other market segments, such as low-income consumers, are controversial target markets with regard to other products. A particularly difficult example in multicultural marketing is injury through cultural pollution, which can be defined as imposing certain aspects of one culture on another culture in a manner that is perceived as detrimental. For example, France tries to prevent the French language from incorporating English words such as "e-mail." In addition, the rise of American-style coffeehouses in Paris is seen by some as a threat to traditional French cafes and coffee.

The Silver Rule reminds marketers of ethical concerns about injuries that go beyond legal baselines, including psychological injuries. The Golden Rule leads marketers toward the goal of satisfying customer needs in ways that better their competitors. This goal, however, involves difficulties that can be approached through the two objectives of marketing promotion—to inform and persuade.

Assuming that marketers offer a product that customers find fulfilling, how much information do customers need about this product? For example, informational food labeling in terms of serving characteristics is controversial for several reasons. A serving is not the same as a portion, but many foods are packaged such that one portion is more than one serving. As recently noted by *The Wall Street Journal*, one 20-ounce soda has 2.5 servings at 100 calories each; one muffin may be several servings; some products that are 100% fat may be legally labeled as fat-free; and one slice of cream pie is defined as one-tenth of that pie, but one slice of lemon meringue is defined as one-eighth of that pie. Just deciding which ingredients to include on labels is controversial, as seen in the new requirements for trans-fat labeling.

Informational labeling may or may not affect consumption, but one ethical justification given for market systems is that they leave final product selections to informed customers. Ethical concerns arise, however, as to how information is presented. What if information is expressed in a persuasive manner? There is no generally accepted theory of ethics with regard to marketing persuasion, and persuasion is endemic in marketing. Marketing persuasion pervades competition. In addition, marketers, as experts in their discipline, often know better what will fulfill customers' needs than do the customers. Do customers *want* to be persuaded by altruistic marketers when something is in their own best interest? Will customers think this ethical? Most people want to feel that their decisions are their own—with no undue influence from others.

Even if marketers fulfill the Golden Rule and offer a product that fulfills the best long-term needs of customers, ethical concerns arise with regard to marketing persuasion. Who determines that the product really is best? For which needs is it best, and how is it best? What about a product that is desired by customers, even though its effects on society are bad, such as SUVs that cause environmental pollution? How thoroughly must marketers understand customer needs in order to justify a claim of adhering to the Golden Rule?

To deal with the situational variables that will influence the answers to concerns about multicultural marketing ethics, marketers can apply the Open Forum Rule. This rule, popularly known as the Television Rule, cautions marketers not to do anything that they cannot explain satisfactorily on television to the concerned stakeholders.

After considering the ethical implications of the Golden Rule and the Silver Rule, marketers should check their programs with the Open Forum Rule. "Would I want to explain my actions on television to the concerned parties?" Such explanations must satisfy ethical requirements as seen by the concerned parties in each market. This means that marketers should know what the cultures in each market deem ethical—not just what the marketers see as ethical in their own culture. These three simple rules provide a basic approach or starting place for achieving adequate multicultural marketing ethics.

Dillard B. Tinsley is a professor of marketing at Stephen F. Austin State University in Nacogdoches, Texas.

UNIT 2
Research, Markets, and Consumer Behavior

Unit Selections

Key Points to Consider

• As marketing research techniques become more and more advanced, and as psychographic analysis leads to more and more sophisticated models of consumer behavior, do you believe marketing will become more capable of predicting consumer behavior? Explain.

• Where the target population lives, its age, and its ethnicity are demographic factors of importance to marketers. What other demographic factors must be taken into account in long-range market planning?

• Psychographic segmentation is the process whereby consumer markets are divided up into segments based upon similarities in lifestyles, attitudes, personality type, social class, and buying behavior. In what specific ways do you envision psychographic research and findings helping marketing planning and strategy in the next decade?

 **Links: www.dushkin.com/online/**
These sites are annotated in the World Wide Web pages.

Canadian Innovation Centre
http://www.innovationcentre.ca/company/Default.htm
CBA.org: Research and Develop
http://www.cba.org/CBA/National/Marketing/research.asp
Industry Analysis and Trends
http://www.bizminer.com/market_research.asp
Marketing Intelligence
http://www.bcentral.com/articles/krotz/123.asp
Maritz Marketing Research
http://www.maritzresearch.com
USADATA
http://www.usadata.com
WWW Virtual Library: Demography & Population Studies
http://demography.anu.edu.au/VirtualLibrary/

If marketing activities were all we knew about an individual, we would know a great deal. By tracing these daily activities over only a short period of time, we could probably guess rather accurately that person's tastes, understand much of his or her system of personal values, and learn quite a bit about how he or she deals with the world.

In a sense, this is a key to successful marketing management: tracing a market's activities and understanding its behavior. However, in spite of the increasing sophistication of market research techniques, this task is not easy. Today a new society is evolving out of the changing lifestyles of Americans, and these divergent lifestyles have put great pressure on the marketer who hopes to identify and profitably reach a target market. At the same time, however, each change in consumer behavior leads to new marketing opportunities.

The writings in this unit were selected to provide information and insight into the effect that lifestyle changes and demographic trends are having on American industry. The article in this subsection describes how a popular research technique helps marketers and consumers get what they really want.

The articles in the *Markets and Demographics* subsection examine the importance of demographic data, geographic settings, economic forces, and age considerations in making marketing decisions. In the first article, there is a description of how some companies are finding ways to market their products to older consumers while making it clear to younger people that their brands are still "cool." The remaining articles scrutinize some unique demographic and psychographic considerations to be reckoned with for women and for various "generational" and multi-cultural groupings.

The articles in the final subsection examine how consumer behavior, social attitudes, cues, and quality considerations will have an impact on the evaluation and purchase of various products and services for different consumers.

A Different Approach for Developing New Products or Services

BY ROBERT BRASS

"When all else fails, ask your customer!" At first utterance, this advice seems to make sense. But it assumes two things:

- A group of potential customers can effectively describe their needs in terms of new products or services.
- These same customers can then rank those needs in terms of importance to offer guidance to development teams.

Both of these "beliefs" have a history of ineffectiveness. Of all new products, 80 to 90 percent fail, and there is no proof that traditional market research techniques would have altered that fact.

Does that mean that market research is useless? The answer is, "No, it doesn't." However, it points to some problems with traditional market research.

INHERENT PROBLEMS WITH TRADITIONAL MARKET RESEARCH

The standard approach to market research is to ask customers in a focus group or one-on-one to describe what they would like to have in a new product or service. Typically, then, after multiple sessions using this approach, the information is sifted, condensed and clarified. To address priorities, a follow-up survey based on a distillation of the discussions is done to quantify the "wants" of the customer. The result is then treated as the basis for defining the features and functions for new products or services.

All problems are not created equal so prioritizing is essential.

The problem with this approach is that it rejects the reality of our lives. If we are to identify the things that make us unhappy, we can usually be precise. On the other hand, if we are asked to formulate the products or the services that would relieve our problems, in most cases, we struggle. However, if you still are tempted to use this old approach, recall the old saying: a camel is a horse designed by a committee.

A DIFFERENT APPROACH

Is there a methodology that would work? The answer is "Yes." Experience demonstrates that the one common denominator for almost all successful products is that they solve high-priority problems in a cost-effective and easy-to-understand manner! Given this clue, there is a process to follow that leverages this wisdom:

1. Find out what problems there are with an existing product or service that you are attempting to improve or replace.
2. Use an objective method to prioritize those problems.
3. Present the results to a very creative individual or to a creative group in a simple and unambiguous manner. Charge them with the goal of developing the actual products or services that would solve the high-priority problems.
4. Create prototypes and implement a preliminary but very different "concept test." Don't ask customers if they like the new product or service. Instead, ask a carefully selected group how well the proposed solution addresses those high priority problems that it was intended to solve.
5. If it passes the test of being an effective solution and it is cost effective, launch it as a new product or service.

PAINSTORMING, NOT BRAINSTORMING

Instead of using brainstorming to get ideas for new products or services, use "painstorming" to identify problems. The key to success in this process is identification of the major problems. All problems are not created equal, so prioritizing is essential. Develop a survey, but don't ask customers to rate the importance of each problem.

First, the human decision process is extremely complex, and the importance or priority of any element varies with circumstances. A totally satisfied customer who has no problems with a new car will have a very different set of priorities from one who needs to go to the dealer every week for repairs. Second, since virtually every purchase decision is emotional, we often consciously or unconsciously support our decisions with rationalizations that may have no real relationship to the actual reason for the decision.

SO IF YOU CAN'T ASK ABOUT IMPORTANCE, THEN WHAT?

Suppose you were designing luggage that would be convenient for traveling. During various focus groups and one-on-one interviews, numerous items continually surface as problems. Among those might be weight, the ability of the luggage to fit under the airline seat, the need to totally unpack to get at all of the clothes, the wrinkling of clothing in the luggage, identification of the luggage on the luggage transport at an airport, and so forth.

True out-of-the-box thinking is a scarce commodity, but is usually the roadmap to successful products or services.

To obtain a good survey sample, you would randomly choose several hundred travelers who matched the market you were interested in. The survey would ask these respondents to express their satisfaction with their current luggage with respect to each of the individual items identified as problems.

Implicit, but subtly buried within the results from all of the surveys, is the actual common complex decision process. What is needed is a method of extracting it. Fortunately, analysis techniques exist that do precisely that, including one based on Neural Networks. As a test of validity, if the results of the overall assessment of a person's current luggage can be predicted knowing only the survey respondents' opinions of their satisfaction with the problem areas, then you will have figured out the decision process. Our experience with Neural Network analysis has demonstrated that over 90 percent of the time it meets that test. Using this model and testing each problem independently allows a clear quantification of the importance of each problem area related to luggage. So, instead of asking for importance, analytical techniques derive the hierarchical irritation level of problems.

DEVELOP CREATIVE SOLUTIONS

Once the problems have been defined and quantified, give the information to the most creative group you know. Let it come up with the solution. You want an unexpected solution. True out-of-the-box thinking is a scarce commodity, but is usually the roadmap to successful products or services. With each potential solution, however, one more task remains: define the savings that accrue. Some may be financial or even personal, but the value needs to be defined.

THE WEAKNESS OF THE CLASSIC CONCEPT TEST

Now you are at the stage where several alternative products or services have been developed. It is time to subject the solutions to a reality test. The Concept Test is a favorite tool of market research. It presents one or more products or services to a group and attempts to obtain their likes, dislikes and general opinions. The skill of the moderator, the choice of the participants and the interpretation of the results of the group are all elements of subjectivity that can inject major biases into the conclusions. The problem with this process stems from the question being asked of the group, which is "What do you think of this concept?" What's missing is the phrase "Compared to what?"

This subtle but important point of view leads to a change in the normal process to create a methodology we call "The Concept Assessment." It leverages our innate and proven ability to identify problems, as opposed to our questionable capability for evaluating solutions. The methodology uses the objective list of prioritized problems that the creative individuals used to develop the products or services. This list then can be considered the answer to the question "Compared to what?"

PRIORITIZE PROBLEMS

We do not ask the group what it likes. Instead, the group is asked to assess how well the various products or services solve the prioritized problems. Participants are chosen for their expertise in the field, not because they are a favorite or knowledgeable customer, and the moderator now has a much less influential role in biasing the conclusions. The group focuses on identifying weaknesses in the products or services with respect to the prioritized problems instead of selecting their favorite solution.

Robert Brass is president of Development II, a market research, survey and new product development company based in Woodbury, CT (www.development2.com).

Product by Design

An increasingly popular research technique helps marketers and consumers get what they really want.

BY DAVID J. LIPKE

This past November, the Lands' End Web site launched "My Personal Shopper," a recommendation engine for customers who want help sorting through the retailer's vast selection of sweaters, skirts, and button-downs. Big whoop, you say—Amazon's been doing this for years. But unlike companies that use past purchases to proffer suggestions to cyber-browsers, Lands' End is the first apparel retailer to use a technique called conjoint analysis. In a brief survey, six pairs of outfits are shown to the shopper, who chooses a preferred outfit among each pair. Through analysis of these six simple choices, and the answers to a few other questions, the site sorts through 80,000 apparel options and presents the most suitable ones to the busy shopper.

While the use of conjoint analysis by Lands' End is unique, the methodology itself is not. It's a research technique that has been around for three decades, but which is increasing in popularity as software developments and the Internet make it easier to use, as well as more powerful and flexible. Understanding how conjoint analysis works, and the innovative ways it's now being used, provides a good opportunity

for any company to increase its chances of giving consumers more of what they want, and less of what they don't. "Use of this method will increase as more marketers realize what it can do, and how well it can work," says John Seal, senior analytical consultant at Burke, Inc., a Cincinnati-based research firm.

So what is conjoint analysis? The rationale underlying the technique is that consumers weigh all the many elements of a product or service—such as price, ingredients, packaging, technical specifications, and on and on—when choosing, say, a sweater, airline ticket, or stereo system. While this may seem obvious to anyone who's faced a wall of DVD players at Circuit City, figuring out how to leverage this concept in the marketing arena can be difficult. Conjoint analysis does this by breaking products down into their many elements, uncovering which ones drive consumer decisions and which combination will be most successful. But rather than directly asking survey respondents to state the importance of a certain component *à la* traditional surveys, participants judge hypothetical product profiles, consisting of a range of defining characteristics called "el-

ements." Their responses are run through an analytical process that indirectly identifies the importance and appeal of each element, based upon their pattern of preferences for the element groups.

If this process sounds more complicated than a traditional survey, it is. And it tends to be more expensive as well. But, as the saying goes, you get what you pay for. While traditional surveys can gauge interest in product features, the results can be misleading. This is because it can be difficult for respondents to directly relate how valuable a particular product feature will be to them. "If you ask respondents how much they are willing to pay for a certain feature, they often can't or won't answer truthfully," says Tom Pilon, a Carrollton, Texas-based consultant who specializes in conjoint research projects. "They'll tend to say they're interested in all the new features." They wouldn't be lying, but they might not actually pay for those features when the product comes to the market. Similarly, focus groups are a good way to draw out consumer opinion on new products, but it's difficult to accurately quantify how a product will perform in the marketplace from this data.

A BRIEF HISTORY OF CONJOINT

1964

The fundamental theories for conjoint analysis are laid out in a paper by R. D. Luce and J. W. Tukey, "Simultaneous Conjoint Measurement: A New Type of Fundamental Measurement," in the *Journal of Mathematical Psychology*.

1971

Conjoint is introduced to market research firm by Professors Paul Green and V. R. Rao, in the guide "Conjoint Measurement for Quantifying Judgemental Data," in the *Journal of Marketing Research*. First commercial use of conjoint analysis is conducted.

1980

Approximately 160 conjoint research projects are completed by market research firms, according to a survey of 17 firms known to conduct this type of research by Professors Philippe Cattin and Richard Wittink. In total, 700 projects are completed from 1971 through 1980.

1983

Choice-based conjoint is introduced to the market research industry by J. J. Louviere and G. G. Woodworth, in an article in the *Journal of Marketing Research*.

1985

Bretton-Clark introduces the first commercial, full-profile conjoint system, called Conjoint Designer.
Sawtooth Software introduces ACA, a software package for adaptive conjoint analysis. It is now the most widely used software for this type of research.

1989

Professors Cattin and Wittink find that 1,062 conjoint research projects have been completed since 1984, and estimate that close to 2,000 conjoint research projects will be conducted that year.

1990

SPSS introduces a full-profile conjoint analysis software package for the computer.

1993

Sawtooth Software introduces the first commercial choice-based conjoint software for the computer.

Source: Sawtooth Software: The Journal of Marketing, Summer 1982: The Journal of Marketing, July 1989; The Journal of Marketing Research, Fall 1995.

"Conjoint mimics the way that consumers actually think," says Joel Greene, director of database marketing at Akron, Ohio-based Sterling Jewelers. Greene first used conjoint research last spring, and is impressed with the results. Fed up with consumers tossing his mailings into the trash, Greene hired White Plains, New York-based market research firm Moscowitz Jacobs Inc. (MJI) to figure out a way to make them more appealing. Using a proprietary research tool called IdeaMap, MJI worked with Greene to systematically break down the brand image and communication efforts of Shaw's (a division of Sterling Jewelers) into bite-size elements. These factors were culled through focus groups and brainstorming sessions that examined previous marketing efforts and possible new approaches. Well over a hundred elements were part of the tested pool, which included different ways to convey messages about Shaw's stores, merchandise, brand differentiation, and emotional appeals. "We wanted to cast a wide net, because we didn't know what would work," says Greene.

MJI recruited a group of more than a hundred survey respondents to its testing facilities in Chicago and White Plains. Seated at computers, they were systematically exposed to the different elements, grouped as words, phrases, and pictures. For each random grouping of elements, the respondent would rate the appeal of the group as a whole. From an analysis of the pattern of ratings, MJI was able to give a utility score to each element. Using these scores, Shaw's could then create marketing messages from this universe of elements appealing to the widest group of customers, or to specific segments. The words, phrases, and pictures (i.e. elements) that scored highest for each segment were then used to create new mailings. And the glittering result? The creative geared toward each segment resulted in significantly higher rates of response, as well as increased dollar sales per response.

Understanding how conjoint analysis works is a good way for any company to increase its chances of giving consumers more of what they want, and less of what they don't.

The effectiveness with which conjoint can be used to understand precisely which aspects and features of a product are driving sales is especially crucial in an industry such as consumer electronics. With an increase in digital convergence, and with hybrid electronic products coming to the market—think refrigerators connected to the Internet, and cameras as MP3 players—the question arises: Will consumers actually pay for these products, and how much? "We really have to avoid the 'if you build it, they will come' pitfall," says Maria Townsend-Metz, a marketing manager at Motorola.

Heeding this warning, Townsend-Metz used conjoint analysis while working on enhancing Motorola's popular TalkAbout two-way radios. "We couldn't put all the different options we were thinking about on the radio, so we needed to know which ones were going to be of most value to the consumer, and help sell the most radios," says Townsend-Metz. Because of the complexity of creating and modeling well-run conjoint studies, she brought in Boise, Idaho-based research firm POPULUS, Inc. In six markets across the U.S., the company conducted conjoint surveys of consumers who participated in activities, such as camping and biking, where a two-way radio would be a natural accessory. POPULUS tested 18 attributes, covering technical specifications, price points, and the appearance of the devices.

Using a conjoint methodology was especially appropriate because all the attributes were interdependent—different features, for example, would affect the look of the radio, as well as the price. "The goal was to find the combination of features that would maximize interest at the lowest production cost," says John Fiedler of POPULUS. The resulting product was right on consumers' wavelength, and the TalkAbout now leads the market for recreational and industrial two-way radios.

CONJOINT ANALYSIS IN A NUTSHELL

Conjoint analysis presents a way for researchers to understand which specific elements (i.e. parts or features) of a product, package design, or marketing message are most valued by consumers when making a decision to purchase. It involves placing a series of product concepts, composed of different elements, in front of survey respondents. The respondents express their preferences for the different concepts, and the importance of each element is determined by analyzing the pattern of the respondents' choices. The elements tested are "attributes" (such as color, brand, and price) and "levels" within those attributes (such as blue or red, Ford or Honda, $100 or $150). After the survey, "utility scores" are calculated for each level showing which ones were most preferred, and which were most important in the hypothetical purchase decision. Many researchers have created their own unique methodology for conducting this type of research, but there are three main types of conjoint analysis:

TYPE	DESCRIPTION	PROS & CONS
TRADITIONAL (a.k.a.: full-profile; preference-based; ratings-based; card-sort)	Respondents are given a series of product profiles to rate. Each profile is composed of one level for each attribute being tested (e.g. How likely are you to buy a blue Ford that costs $150?)	• Easy, straightforward design process • Can be administered on paper or by computer • Encourages respondents to evaluate the product individually, rather than in comparison to others • Because full profiles are used (a level for each attribute is included in every profile), large numbers of attributes can confuse respondents. Respondents can begin to ignore some attributes to simplify the process. This limits the number of attributes that can be successfully tested.
CHOICE-BASED (a.k.a.: discrete choice)	Respondents are given two or more profiles at once and asked to choose the one they prefer, or none (e.g., Which would you purchase: a blue Ford that costs $100 or a red Honda that costs $150, or neither?).	• Allows for measurement of "special effects" (complex interactions between utility scores across attributes and levels in certain types of analysis). • Some researchers believe this method better re-creates the real-life shopping experience, in which consumers choose among products. • Other researchers don't believe consumers always make these side-by-side comparisons and prefer the traditional conjoint rating system. • Comparisons of side-by-side full profiles, with large numbers of attributes, can lead respondents to ignore some attributes, as in traditional conjoint methods.
ADAPTIVE (a.k.a.: Sawtooth Software's ACA)	This technique is divided into three main phases. Respondents first rate or rank the levels within an attribute (e.g., Rank these brands in order of preference: Sony, Toshiba, Compaq). Second, they rate how important a certain attribute is to them (e.g., How important is brand in considering this purchase?). Respondents then rate partial profiles (two to three attributes at a time) that are chosen to test those attributes that mattered most to them.	• Because only "partial profiles" are tested, it can be easier for respondents to make accurate preference choices between the different profiles. • More attributes can be tested in the first phase, and then the questions can hone in on the most important attributes. • Software, such as ACA, makes the design and administration of these surveys easier. • Can only be administered on a computer. • Some researchers dislike the adaptive methodology, as it depends largely on the first questions being answered accurately. If they are not, subsequent questions can focus on the wrong product attributes. • Cannot directly measure certain "special effects."

Source: Information compiled from reports by Maritz Marketing Research; Sawtooth Software, POPULUS, Moscowitz Jacobs, and DSS Research.

The popularity of conjoint research was greatly increased by the development of software in the 1980s that made it easier to design and run these types of studies. The leader in this field is Sequim, Washington-based Sawtooth Software, whose ACA brand of conjoint is the most widely used in the world. Other software suppliers include SPSS Inc. and SAS Systems. Prior to computer-assisted research, conjoint surveys were conducted using cards that had groups of attributes printed on them, and which were sorted by preference. The number of attributes that could be tested in this manner was severely limited, as was the concluding analysis.

The trend toward conducting survey research on the Web will further increase the use of conjoint, according to experts in the field. The Web provides an easy way to present respondents with groups of attributes, something that was much more difficult to do over the phone (people can only remember so many features at once). Fuji Film, for one, has used conjoint Web surveys to uncover the effects of price, brand, and package configurations (i.e. the number of rolls in a package) on sales. "Film is a low-involvement category, the product is standardized, and the effects of price and packaging are significant," says Doug Rose, president of Austin, Texas-based DRC Group, who worked on conjoint projects last year for Fuji.

By showing respondents side-by-side attribute profiles of different brand, price, and packaging configurations, Fuji was able to analyze their patterns of preference, and deduce what was driving their choices. The film manufacturer was further able to estimate exactly what effect a certain price point on a particular package of film would have on market share. This conjoint study was so accurate that its estimates perfectly matched ACNielsen data on price elasticity in the film sector, which appeared after the Fuji study.

One research firm taking conjoint analysis a step further on the Web is Burlingame, California-based Active Research. Its proprietary "Active Buyer's Guide" is a powerful research tool for marketers, disguised as a shopping search engine for consumers. Licensed to over 70 popular sites, such as Lycos and MySimon, it helps Web shoppers find the computers, appliances, and financial services (135 categories in all) that most closely match their needs, both online and offline. By filling out a conjoint survey that hones in on what features, price points, and attributes they are looking for, the Guide delivers a list of products that are most likely to interest the shopper.

But Active Research doesn't do this just to help out consumers. By answering the questions required by the search engine, shoppers are providing the company with a gold mine of continuous information on what kind of products they want, and at what price. In effect, Active Research is compiling 1.5 million surveys a month. What's more, these surveys are from people who are providing the most accurate information possible and are in the market, at that moment, to buy a particular product. By compiling and analyzing this data, Active Research provides up-to-the-minute information for clients such as Ford, GE, and Sony on which aspects of a product are driving consumer decisions, which demographic segments are driving sales, and who's interested in different features.

In addition, clients of Active Research can create hypothetical products and measure what their likely market share would be. Using the conjoint-produced utility scores of different product features, marketers can preview how a new product will sell in the marketplace, without the time and cost of a test launch. Because of the size of its sample, Active Research can slice-and-dice hypothetical products in an array of categories, demographics, and configurations. "It's not an exaggeration to say that what they are doing is an absolutely unique way to do primary research," says client Suzanne Snygg, futures product manager at Palm, Inc. The dual nature of their service is highlighted by the fact that Snygg herself has used Active Research data not only to shape product concepts for Palm but also to find the best mini-stereo system for her home. As the Web makes conjoint analysis more popular, it's important to note that conjoint research is still more complicated to conduct than straightforward survey research. To produce worthwhile results, it is crucial to create a pool of attributes that actually influences consumer choice. This requires careful and creative brainstorming. Researchers have to choose the correct conjoint method (there are several types, with many researchers creating their own unique variants). They have to show groupings of elements to respondents that cover many possible combinations, in a balanced and useful way. The final results are only as good as the design and analysis of the research, which can be complicated. Keith Chrzan, director of marketing sciences at Maritz Marketing Research, goes so far as to say that "a lot of people are using conjoint who shouldn't be," due to the easy-to-use software.

That said, the effectiveness and accuracy of conjoint techniques make them powerful tools for marketers who use them properly. Says Tom Pilon, the Texas-based consultant, "once a company has done it once, they always come back for more."

Marketing Surprise:
Older Consumers Buy Stuff, Too

Sony, Ford Look to Boomers and Beyond, Challenging Obsession with Youth

BY KELLY GREENE

Linda Carter, a 51-year-old hotel manager in Palm Desert, Calif., was planning last year to spend $1,000 or so on a new engine for her 1970 Volkswagen Beetle. Then a TV ad for a Sony digital camcorder caught her eye.

The spot featured a gray-haired astronaut filming Earth from space. The tagline: "When your kids ask where the money went, show them the tape." Soon after, Carter walked into a local electronics store and walked out with a $1,200 Sony camcorder.

Ms. Carter was impressed by the ad's focus on her age group. "As we got older, we stopped getting attention," she says. "But we're still spending a lot of money."

The push by Sony Corp. to hook people such as Ms. Carter is part of a budding revolution in marketing. After decades of obsessing over people in their 20s, some of the world's best-known companies are setting their sights on older consumers, an audience habitually written off as poor, excessively frugal or stuck in a rut of buying the same brand.

Ford Motor Co. plans to sell a sedan for empty-nesters with a trunk that holds eight golf bags. Target Corp. stores are carving out large chunks of space for khaki pants and flowing linen separates aimed at older bodies. Music retailer Virgin Megastores is redesigning its stores to appeal to Led Zeppelin and Miles Davis fans.

Driving the shift are big numbers. The 78 million Americans who were 50 or older as of 2001 controlled 67 percent of the country's wealth, or $28 trillion, according to data collected by the U.S. Census and Federal Reserve. What's more, households headed by someone in the 55-to-64 age group had a median net worth of

$112,048 in 2000—15 times the $7,240 reported for the under-35 age group. And within five years, about a third of the population is going to be at least 50 years old.

One challenge: How do you get the attention of older customers while making it clear to younger people that your brands are still cool? Some companies are discovering that ads featuring older people can speak to younger people, too. Sony found its commercials showing a grandmother taking underwater pictures of sharks scored well with young viewers, who related to the adventure. Other companies continue to use young models but slip in messages that are likely to resonate with older audiences—the approach used by Anheuser-Busch Cos. in its successful marketing of the low-carb Michelob Ultra beer.

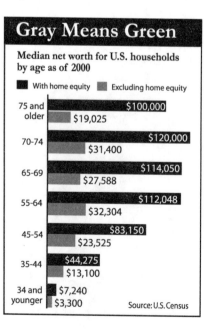

Gray Means Green

Median net worth for U.S. households by age as of 2000

■ With home equity   ■ Excluding home equity

Age	With home equity	Excluding home equity
75 and older	$100,000	$19,025
70-74	$120,000	$31,400
65-69	$114,050	$27,588
55-64	$112,048	$32,304
45-54	$83,150	$23,525
35-44	$44,275	$13,100
34 and younger	$7,240	$3,300

Source: U.S. Census

Sony has poured more than $25 million into advertising to make the company's camcorders, digital cameras and other high-end gadgets more appealing to people between 50 and 64. Sony calls them "zoomers" to reflect their increasingly active lifestyles. The push is successful so far: camcorder sales shot up to a "high double-digit growth" rate last year, says Chris Gaebler, market intelligence and strategy director for the company's U.S. electronics unit. "Ten percent growth is considered good."

Walt Disney Co.'s Walt Disney World rolled out a program called "Magical Gatherings" last year. It allows customers to use a Web site to plan trips and is largely aimed at people over 50 who are organizing outings with golfing buddies, old schoolmates or their grandchildren.

And Microsoft Corp. started publicizing software tools in February—with easier-to-read text, audio alerts and mouse alternatives—to help older workers who are developing vision, hearing and wrist problems.

David Wolfe, a Reston, Va., marketing consultant who studies the 45-plus population, believes the traditional view of older consumers started to crack in early 2002. That's when Disney's ABC television network tried to grab comedian David Letterman and his younger audience for the 11:30 p.m. time slot held by 64-year-old newscaster Ted Koppel's "Nightline." Koppel stuck up for his age group, saying at the time that "60- and 70-year-old people buy things." Ultimately, he kept his show, and "the imbroglio made it OK for the first time to really question Madison Avenue's thinking," Wolfe says.

Recent research has begun to cast doubt on the conventional wisdom that marketing should mainly be directed at young people. One argument runs that it's best to "get them young" because older people have already decided their brand loyalties. But a 2002 study by AARP, the Washington-based advocacy group for people over 50, and Roper ASW found that for most products, the majority of people over 45 aren't loyal to a single brand.

Anheuser-Busch, the largest U.S. beer maker, attempted to reach the 50-plus age group and wound up creating one of its top-selling brands. The push was sparked by the realization around 2000 that "another 29 million people would be in [the 50-to-69] age bracket by 2010, and they're living a more active lifestyle," says Bob Lachky, vice president of brand management for Anheuser-Busch's U.S. beer unit. "We thought, 'There is an opportunity here that nobody else is capitalizing on.'"

In an attempt to woo older drinkers back to beer from wine and other less-filling beverages (which people tend to prefer as they grow older), Anheuser-Busch created a low-carb formula and tagged it "Michelob Ultra." The name plays off a brand better known to older drinkers than younger ones. In 2001, the company started rolling out the product in three retirement hot spots in Florida—Punta Gorda, Naples and Fort Myers—and then in a few larger markets.

The beer maker initially hired seven "mature marketers" age 50 and older to talk up the new brand at golf clubs, retirement communities and veterans' halls. It has since expanded the team to 36 people. As it turned out, the target audience didn't want Anheuser-Busch to "talk to my age" or show people with gray hair in Michelob Ultra ads, says Lachky. "They said, 'Talk to my lifestyle.' They were more interested in learning about lower carbs and lower calories." So advertising shifted to younger models in active pursuits.

The pitch seems to be working. The Ultra brand, rolled out nationally in September 2002, is now on the verge of breaking into the top 10 beer brands sold in the U.S. by volume, says Mr. Lachky. The boom in low-carb foods has helped greatly but Mr. Lachky says, "You can't lose sight of what got us here. There was a nugget of knowledge in this 50-plus demographic that spawned this power brand."

Ford is attempting to solve the riddle facing all auto makers: What will baby boomers, who have snapped up sport-utility vehicles, start driving as their kids move away from home? It's a crucial question, since the average American household buys 13 new cars over the course of a lifetime—including seven after the head of the household turns 50, according to CNW Marketing Research Inc., of Bandon, Ore.

About five years ago, as U.S. car buyers started buying more SUVs than cars for the first time, Ford's marketers started asking them why. "They told us, 'We don't feel like we're in the game when we're driving cars. There's and SUV in front of us and a big truck behind us, and it doesn't feel safe,'" recalls Amy Marentic, marketing manager for the Ford Five Hundred, a car being rolled out this fall to target older drivers. "We took that information and said, 'because we know deep down they love sedans. Once they're done driving their kids to soccer games and hockey games, they won't need SUVs.'"

The Five Hundred will include popular SUV features such as raised seating, all-wheel drive, space to haul a 10-foot ladder and a roomy trunk for all those golf bags. It's also the first Ford to be built on a Volvo chassis, in an attempt to appeal to boomers' affinity for European styling, Ms. Marentic says.

The sedan's marketing won't mention that the Five Hundred is designed for an aging population because Ford believes boomers are fighting the idea that they're getting older. The car would be a good fit for Ms. Marentic's own father, for example, who commutes 60 miles each way to his job in Michigan. "But I would never say, 'Hey, Dad, this will be easy on your back now that you're 63,' because he still runs marathons," Ms. Marentic says.

Older music lovers are an increasingly important audience for retailers at a time when many young people are downloading music free or at low-cost Web sites. Music sales slipped to $12.6 billion in 2002 from a peak of $14.6 billion in 1999. Retailers would like to take a cue from the concert business, where boomers have made $100-plus ticket prices routine and many of the biggest-grossing acts are boomer favorites such as the Eagles.

In November, the Virgin Group's Virgin Megastores revamped its San Francisco store to include sections that appeal mostly to older listeners. In the jazz section, virgin added reproductions of 1930s jazz posters from famous clubs, reference books and Miles Davis T-shirts. In the new "mind, body and spirit" zone, there are relaxation CDs, self-help books, personal journals, yoga balls and DVDs about the Pilates exercise method. Rather than explicitly label the sections by era or age

group, Virgin says they target different "lifestyles."

"There are a lot of people who want to buy music but aren't quite sure where to start," says Dvae Alder, senior vice president of product and marketing for Virgin Entertainment Group, North America. (He's 39 and plays guitar in a rock band.) "If you liked Led Zeppelin in the '70s, there's no reason you wouldn't like the Darkness of Jet." virgin started adding kiosks three years ago, with more than two million clips of songs, along with staff recommendations and reviews, to help older listeners make such links.

Virgin declined to release sales figures, but Mr. Alder says the experimental store is outperforming the company's other 21 U.S. locations. Several of those sites are set to get the same sort of makeover later this year, a spokeswoman says.

Many companies are just starting to reach out to older adults. When Procter & Gamble Co. began research 18 months ago to pinpoint a variety of consumer "segments" it should target, "it quickly became very clear, due to the sheer number of people who fall into (the 50-plus) segment, that this is … an important group to focus on in ways that we haven't before," says P&G spokeswoman Stefani Valkonen.

P&G has started to shake up stereotypes among its own marketers and managers. One tool: a video depicting a day in the life of an older consumer. So far, P&G has pinpointed about 30 existing products—such as Puffs tissues and Downy fabric softener—that it can market more directly to people 50 and older. Work has begun on advertising plans and on a new partnership with AARP that may include joint marketing and research.

Marketers at Sony had to overcome skepticism within the company before targeting older consumers. "It's very easy to convince executives here that we have to target generations X and Y, because it's easy to think that if you get that first purchase, you get set in your brand ways," says Mr. Gaebler, the market-intelligence director. He used demographic research to show the significant differences in buying power between generations.

"A hundred dollars is a lot of money for a 20-year-old, but it's not a lot of money for a lot of people over the age of 50. You're at the senior end of your earning career, and you might contemplate buying a $5,000 home-theater system," he says.

Sony's commercials featuring older videographers resulted not only in a sales spurt but, even more surprisingly, in a boost to younger generations' "youthful perception of Sony." Chris Gaebler, market intelligence and strategy director of the company's U.S. electronics unit, thinks the younger crowd could relate to the risky feats played out in the spots, including that ad in which the grandmother gets into an underwater cage and takes pictures of sharks attacking.

The results convinced "executives inside our company that this is a group worth targeting," Gaebler says. "Now, it's almost as if we don't have a distinct 'zoomer' effort. From executives to engineers, they're thinking about zoomers when they make decisions."

WHAT *WOMEN* WANT

The growing economic power of women consumers
is transforming today's marketplace. Find out how to tap
into the desires of women—and watch your business take off.

By Joanne Cleaver

Freud famously wondered, "What does a woman want?" He never figured it out, but many business owners have—and are making money in the process. What women want right now is attention to detail in product design and service; the right choices, not endless choices; and a nuanced, longer selling process that respects their desire to understand what they're buying before they take it home.

This prevailing wisdom doesn't just apply to the obvious categories like clothes, kids' stuff and cosmetics. Marketers of any product or service can adopt a service philosophy that delivers what women want. Once you translate these expectations to your market niche, you'll win the hearts and pocketbooks of women.

That pocketbook is big and carries plenty of cash. Trend watchers say the escalating economic power of women is emerging as one of the biggest business stories of this decade.

Management guru Tom Peters discovered the importance of women in 1996 when a colleague dragged him to a meeting of high-powered women. Listening to their stories of how businesses brushed aside their requests was a shock. "The more I talked, the more people brought me stories," says Peters. "I thought, How weird is [it] that nobody talks about this?" Peters made the economic power of women a central point in his new book, *Re-imagine! Business Excellence in a Disruptive Age.* (DK Publishing)

Women have been ignored because they're in plain sight. It's standard marketing wisdom that women control 80 percent of all household purchases. That's why marketers of household supplies, kids' gear, food, cosmetics and clothes are good at reaching women. But women buy gender-neutral stuff, too: cars, auto services, technology—the list includes everything but Viagra.

Women's earning power is escalating: They comprise over half of all college students and about 38 percent of small-business owners, according to 2002 figures from the Bureau of Labor Statistics. A February 2002 study by Prudential Financial found that, of the 400 American women surveyed, 37 percent live in households with incomes of $50,000 to $100,000, and 12 percent live in households with more than $100,000 in annual income. Nearly half of adult women are solely responsible for saving money for their households.

Margaret Gardner of marketing consulting firm Yankelovich reports that 60 percent of women 16 and older are working. In nearly two-thirds of households, women are the primary shoppers, but 72 percent of married women who work full time are the primary shoppers. No business owner can afford to ignore women, and few would admit to doing so. But not ignoring them is not the same as attracting them, and attracting them is not the same as winning their loyalty.

Sweat the Details

Get the little stuff right, and the big stuff will take care of itself. Women develop a collage of impressions about a business from a hundred small factors. Everything from its cleanliness to the design of the shopping bag gets a woman's attention. While men tend to make judgments based on first impressions and key interactions, women never stop gathering information. Smart business owners turn this to their advantage by investing in small amenities women can appreciate.

Nancy Poisson, area director for 333 Curves franchises in northern New England, always looks for ways to draw new customers to the fitness centers. While each new franchise advertises locally when it first opens and offers free trials, customers renew memberships based on experiences at the training centers. Poisson has new franchisees plant free membership bags in waiting rooms of businesses ranging from pediatricians' offices to quick-lube shops. That gets potential members to come by the clubs for a week's worth of free sessions.

SEE IT NOW

TO WATCH AN INTERVIEW ON MARKETING TO WOMEN—PROVIDED BY SBTV.COM—GO TO WWW.ENTERPRENEUR.COM/SBTV.

Then it's up to franchisees to keep the excitement going. New Curves owner Tammy Latvis of Hanover, New Hampshire, got 500 leads when she opened her second location in spring 2003. She ensures that workout leaders never flag in their encouragement of women clients who are self-conscious about how they look in workout clothes. Women turn into the centers' best missionaries when they invite friends to join them for free sessions. Latvis is always cooking up rewards for women who recruit new members. "It's like the 'free with purchase' mentality," she says. "It works!"

The Right Choices

Women have so many work and family responsibilities, they don't have time to research and ponder every buying decision. Offering carefully selected choices will win business over an overwhelming A-to-Z plethora. "One way to get women excited is to have fewer but better choices," says Carrie McCament, managing director of the Winston-Salem, North Carolina, consultancy Frank About Women (www.frankaboutwomen.com). This is a strategy adopted by designer Eileen Fisher, who offers simple clothes in a limited palette; and some furniture stores, such as Storehouse Furniture in Atlanta, that have pared their selections to an "everything goes with everything else" array.

SEEING GREEN

Plenty of marketers think they know how to appeal to 18-to-24-year-old women, but there are surprising crosscurrents among college-age women. In August 2003, Frank About Women, a marketing consulting firm in Winston-Salem, North Carolina, released a survey of women's attitudes about shopping. Enthusiasm for shopping peaks when a woman is in her 20s and when she's 55 and older, says Frank About Women marketing director Carrie McCament. "Younger shoppers' discretionary income is all theirs," she says. "They want to be the best-dressed person in their groups." Shopping and socializing are entwined for young women, she adds. Not only do friends' opinions count on everything, but young women also conduct buying excursions with friends.

So what's the surprise? Their moms count as friends. The generation gap doesn't exist anymore, say marketing consultants and executives at companies that target women. Having seen their moms manage careers and households, young women consider them a resource for smart consumer choices.

The key is to avoid assuming that today's young women are just like boomers were at the same age, warns Mary Lou Quinlan, CEO of Just Ask a Woman (www.justaskawoman.com), a New York City consulting firm. Many young women have traveled widely and are accomplished and picky consumers. At the same time, a high proportion of them live at home. Though many carry student loan debt, they also have a lot of disposable income because they have no household expenses.

"They're not like [the characters in] *Sex and the City*," says Quinlan. "They're more conservative. They are optimists, but not activists." One thing they have in common: They expect purchasing and customer relations to be thoroughly supported by technology. This is one group, says Quinlan, that expects businesses to relate to them through e-mail and online ordering.

That's the core of Gretchen Schauffler's strategy to build a new brand of house paint. In the past three years, she has taken Devine Color Inc.'s paint from a nonentity to a boutique brand available on the Web, in West Coast stores and through more than 300 dealers nationwide. Schauffler saw an opportunity to reinvent wall paint and the way it's sold in the mid-90s when she and her friends were decorating their houses and getting frustrated with the paint available. Because traditional paint companies offer thousands of shades on tiny strips, there were too many choices. Schauffler, 42, and her friends would make choices according to the chips and end up with walls that looked nothing like they expected.

She created a palette of just over 100 colors, and collaborating with a regional paint manufacturer, she came up with a new way to merchandise the paint: daubs of paint on palette-shaped boards in coordinated groups. "Women would understand [if] color was organized in a way that they could recognize the subtleties. They do it with makeup and fabric all the time," she says. It's working. Devine Color Inc. is growing at 30 percent per year, bringing in 2003 revenues of $8 million.

Peggy McCloud, 49, owner of Jill's Paint, a home decorating boutique in Los Angeles, sees women customers walk into her store and gravitate to the Devine display. "They love the palettes of complementary colors and that you can go home and experiment," she says. Customers can buy pouches of each paint color for about $3, take them home and paint their walls to get a read on whether it's right for their rooms.

A Selling Spiral

Whether buying for themselves or for the businesses they own or manage, women make final purchasing decisions based on the relationship with the seller, not on statistics and quantitative data, says Peters. Given a choice between two nearly identical products, women are likely to choose based on customer service and the ongoing relationship with the vendor, while men focus on statistics, such as the breakdown rate of the equipment.

"Men want [to buy] the product then leave. Women want to know 'How will it work?'" says Andy Andre, owner of Prescott True Value Hardware in Prescott, Arizona. By having enough staff to guide customers through installing shelves or hanging a picture, Prescott True Value has developed a loyal following of older women running households on their own for the first time due to divorce or widowhood. They have a lot in common with women who have just purchased their first homes and want to get down and dirty with drills and brushes.

Every time Prescott True Value adds a product line in response to the requests of women customers, it has a winner. Andre says the store doesn't need to focus its advertising specifically on women; all it takes is one visit to hook them. "Customer service is all about respect," he says. "It's taking the time to explain things to a customer and not talk down to them."

There is no shortage of cosmetics companies, but Sandi Hwang Adam, 32, felt that major cosmetics companies were limiting the color spectrum of their products. Maven Cosmetics, which she founded with Noreen Abbasi in 2002, markets

WHAT ABOUT DAD?

James Chung is happy to announce the demise of the soccer mom. With more dads adjusting their work hours to pitch in with the kids, the president of marketing consulting firm Reach Advisors has discovered a new niche: dads who identify with the home-with-the-kids lifestyle. Whether they're working part time, telecommuting or working flexible hours, dads are tackling more child-rearing responsibilities. They're going to the grocery store, schlepping kids to and from violin lessons, and showing up for parent-teacher conferences. And because they're taking a more active role in domestic management, these "engaged dads" are starting to have more say in how the household budget is spent. In fact, Irene Dickey, a lecturer with the department of management and marketing at the University of Dayton in Dayton, Ohio, estimates that men now control upwards of 24 percent of household spending. They're at home to spend it, too.

"There's a dramatic shift in generational perception of a dad's role," says Chung, who works partly from his home office and shares family responsibilities with his wife. The recently folded Women's United Soccer Association, for instance, made the mistake of trying to appeal primarily to moms, says Chung, who researched the league's marketing strategy. In fact, dads were the ones who bought tickets to attend with their daughters. "If your services are purchased by families," Chung says, " you need to question the old wisdom that mom controls everything that goes on inside the house."

makeup for women of all skin types, including very dark and very light. The Chicago-based company's sales are expected to grow by about 75 percent between 2003 and 2004, thanks to newly signed contracts with the likes of department store Marshall Field's.

Customers are enthusiastic because the company constantly tests and retests its shades by literally pulling women off the streets to give them makeovers, says Adam. She and Abbasi, 31, ditched their high-paying corporate consulting jobs to work at department store makeup counters for six months before launching their line. That experience has helped them present Maven products with a "we're on your side" attitude instead of the "we're the expert" tone many cosmetics conglomerates adopt.

Entrepreneurs assume marketing to women is all about discounts and giveaways, but creativity and care are what really attract women, says Martha Barletta, president of Winnetka, Illinios, consulting firm The TrendSight Group (www.trendsight.com) and author of *Marketing to Women: How to Understand, Reach, and Increase Your Share of the Largest Market Segment* (Dearborn Trade Publishing). When women find a business that speaks their language, they'll talk about it with their friends. While men make decisions by "stripping away extraneous information, women add information to the process," says Barletta. "We notice the small things. If a man is ignored by a sales clerk, he thinks 'What a jerk.' A woman will think 'I hate this company.' The small things, good and bad, make more of an impact."

ONLINE EXCLUSIVE

For more resources that can help you market you business to women, visit www.entrepreneur.com/features/marketingto women.

JOANNE CLEAVER *has written for a variety of publications, including the* Chicago Tribune *and* Executive Female.

RACE, ETHNICITY AND THE WAY WE SHOP

Understanding the different attitudes and behaviors of Asian, black, Hispanic and white consumers.

BY REBECCA GARDYN AND JOHN FETTO

They may be outnumbered at the shopping mall, but minority consumers and their buying power should not be underestimated. In 2002, blacks, Hispanics and Asians wielded significant discretionary income: $646 billion, $581 billion and $296 billion, respectively, according to the Selig Center for Economic Growth at the University of Georgia, which defines "buying power" as the total personal income available, after taxes, for spending on goods and services—that is, disposable income. And while whites continue to account for the majority of total consumer spending ($6.3 trillion), their market share is dwindling. In 1990, whites represented 87 percent of the total consumer marketplace, but they accounted for 82 percent by 2002, according to the Selig Center. By 2007, analysts expect white consumers' share to shrink to 80 percent of all U.S. consumer spending.

whites continue to account for the majority of consumer spending, **$6.3 trillion**, but their market share is **dwindling.**

As the buying power of blacks, Hispanics and Asians increases, understanding the differences between these groups in terms of how, when, where and why they shop for goods and services becomes even more important to businesses' bottom lines. Here, we highlight some of the more interesting differences between the attitudes and behaviors of Asian, black, Hispanic and white Americans. The data was culled from a Simmons Market Research study of about 22,000 consumers (18,542 whites; 1,444 blacks; 1,349 Hispanics; and 640 Asians) fielded between January and May 2002.

35 percent of **Asians** have made an Internet purchase in the past year. They are also more than **twice as likely** as the average consumer to use the Internet to help plan their **shopping.**

asians

How do you say "shop till you drop" in Japanese or Korean? Not only are Asian consumers the most frequent shoppers of all racial and ethnic groups, they are also the most brand-conscious. Almost half (43 percent) say that they always look for a brand name when they shop. Yet, interestingly, they are also the least brand-loyal. Fully a quarter of Asians say they change brands often, compared with 22 percent of Hispanics, 20 percent of blacks and 17 percent of whites. Asian consumers are also the most concerned about keeping up appearances. More than a quarter (26 percent) say they buy what they think their neighbors will approve of, compared with 12 percent each of Hispanics and blacks and just 10 percent of whites. Asians also do not like to shop alone: 31 percent say they prefer shopping with their friends, compared with 25 percent each of Hispanics and blacks, and 23 percent of whites. And Asians never leave home without a plan. They are 125 percent more likely than the average consumer to rely on the Internet to help them plan their shopping trips.

by the numbers
The facts and figures below show how shopping behaviors and motivations differ by race and ethnicity.

frequent shoppers

White shoppers are the most likely of all racial and ethnic groups to have visited a home improvement store at least five times in the past three months. But they are the least likely to have made frequent trips to electronics and home furnishings stores.

INDEX* OF AMERICANS WHO HAVE GONE TO THE FOLLOWING TYPE OF STORE FIVE OR MORE TIMES IN THE PAST THREE MONTHS, BY RACE AND ETHNICITY.

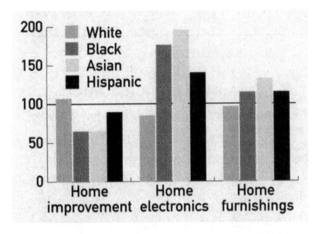

*The national average is 100. For example, Asians are significantly more likely than the average American to have made five or more trips to a home electronics store in the past three months, but they are less likely to have shopped at a home improvement store as frequently.

Source: Simmons Market Research, 2002

dressed to impress

Minority consumers are far more likely than whites to say they enjoy wearing the latest fashions.

	WHITE	BLACK	ASIAN	HISPANIC
I like to dress in the latest fashions	36%	58%	46%	46%
I like to impress people with my lifestyle	17%	20%	28%	20%
I'm very likely to buy new technology products and services	41%	42%	49%	39%
I like to look in hardware or automotive stores	46%	40%	44%	45%

Source: Mediamark Research, Inc., 2002

on the cheap

Americans of all colors like a bargain, but whites are the most likely of all racial and ethnic groups to shop at discount stores. Many Asians also look for a discount, but they are the most likely to buy their clothes, housewares and cosmetics at a traditional department store.

PERCENT OF AMERICANS WHO HAVE SHOPPED AT LEAST ONCE IN THE PAST THREE MONTHS AT DEPARTMENT STORES OR DISCOUNT STORES FOR THE FOLLOWING TYPES OF PRODUCTS, BY RACE AND ETHNICITY:

	WHITE	BLACK	ASIAN	HISPANIC
CLOTHING AND ACCESSORIES				
Department store	47%	43%	51%	48%
Discount store	60%	50%	54%	57%
FOOTWEAR				
Department store	15%	16%	18%	20%
Discount store	24%	15%	19%	21%
HOUSEWARES AND FURNITURE				
Department store	8%	5%	10%	6%
Discount store	20%	14%	18%	17%
COSMETICS				
Department store	6%	5%	8%	7%
Discount store	21%	11%	16%	19%

Source: Simmons Market Research, 2002

joining in on the fun

In 1998, whites were almost twice as likely as blacks or Hispanics to have made an online purchase. Today, the share of Hispanics and whites going online to shop is the same, and almost half of all blacks do so as well.

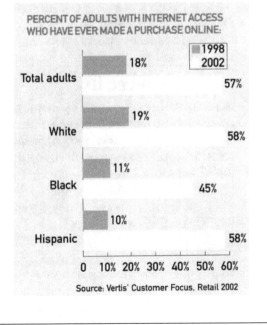

PERCENT OF ADULTS WITH INTERNET ACCESS WHO HAVE EVER MADE A PURCHASE ONLINE:

Source: Vertis' Customer Focus, Retail 2002

diversified dollars

Black, Asian and Hispanic consumers' buying power is growing while the whites' share is shrinking. By 2007, whites are expected to make up 80 percent of the consumer marketplace, down from 87 percent in 1990.

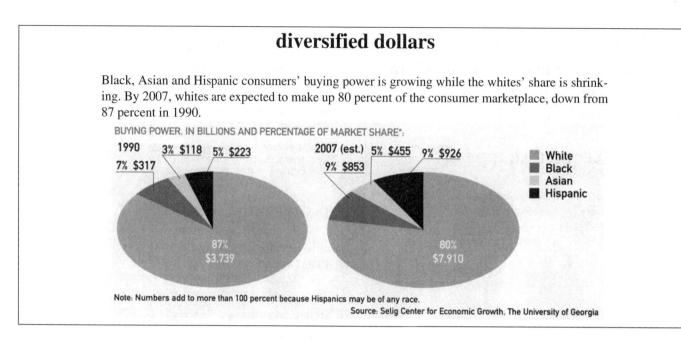

BUYING POWER, IN BILLIONS AND PERCENTAGE OF MARKET SHARE*:

Note: Numbers add to more than 100 percent because Hispanics may be of any race.

Source: Selig Center for Economic Growth, The University of Georgia

whites

Whites may make up the majority of the shopping hordes, but they are the least likely to enjoy the process. Just 35 percent of white consumers say that they enjoy shopping, even when they don't buy anything, compared with almost half (47 percent) of Asian, 43 percent of black and 42 percent of Hispanic shoppers who say the same. Almost two-thirds (62 percent) of white consumers say they go shopping only when they absolutely need something, versus 57 percent of Asians, 54 percent of Hispanics and 47 percent of blacks who say they do the same. And nearly half of white consumers don't stick around to browse: 49 percent say that when they do go shopping, they usually just get what they want and leave. Interestingly, white consumers are the most likely to say they make spur-of-the-moment purchases (41 percent, versus 37 percent of Hispanics, 35 percent of Asians and 34 percent of blacks). Yet they are also more likely (59 percent) to plan far ahead to buy expensive items than are Asians (53 percent), Hispanics (52 percent) or blacks (44 percent).

charge it

More than 1 in 10 Asians (12 percent) say they have used their credit card 20 times or more in the prior month, compared with only 2 percent of blacks who say the same.

HOW MANY TIMES IN THE PAST 30 DAYS HAVE YOU USED A CREDIT CARD?

	WHITE	BLACK	ASIAN	HISPANIC
1–5	47%	28%	49%	39%
6–19	21%	9%	27%	15%
20 or more	8%	2%	12%	5%

*Note: Numbers do not add to 100 percent because some people had not used a credit card at all in the prior 30 days, and others did not answer the question.

Source: Simmons Market Research, 2002

know your customer

The principal shopper in a black household is likely to be single, divorced or widowed.

PERCENT OF HOUSEHOLDS IN WHICH THE PRINCIPAL SHOPPER* IS...

	WHITE	BLACK	ASIAN	HISPANIC
Married	65%	43%	70%	64%
Single	15%	32%	19%	21%
Divorced/ separated	12%	18%	6%	12%
Widowed	7%	7%	5%	3%

*"Principal shopper" refers to the person responsible for making the majority of the everyday purchases (groceries and household necessities) for the family.

Source: Mediamark Research, Inc., 2002

black consumers make 19 trips to convenience stores each year.

hispanics

Hispanics, who may be of any race, tend to make shopping a family affair. More than a third (36 percent) say they prefer shopping with their families and 30 percent report they like shopping with their children, compared with 29 percent and 26 percent, respectively, of the total population. A quarter of Hispanics say their kids have a significant impact on the brands they buy. Hispanics are almost twice as likely as white consumers to go out of their way to find new stores (13 percent versus 7 percent). And they would rather shop at national chains than at local mom-and-pop stores. Just 26 percent of Hispanics

everyday needs

Warehouse clubs, like Costco and Sam's Club, depend heavily on Asian and Hispanic consumers. The typical Asian shopper, for example, makes 14 trips a year to such stores, whereas blacks report that they shop at a warehouse club just eight times a year.

NUMBER OF TRIPS MADE ANNUALLY TO THE FOLLOWING VENUES, BY RACE AND ETHNICITY:

	WHITE	BLACK	ASIAN	HISPANIC
Grocery stores	72	70	65	67
Drugstores	15	17	16	15
Mass merchants	24	20	21	24
Supercenters	19	16	12	15
Warehouse clubs	10	8	14	12
Gas/convenience stores	14	19	6	11
Dollar stores	10	16	7	10

Source: ACNielsen

shopping by proxy

Asians are the least likely to buy merchandise by phone or mail order, but they are the most likely to buy things over the Internet.

PERCENT OF AMERICANS WHO HAVE MADE ANY PURCHASE IN THE PAST YEAR OVER THE PHONE OR BY MAIL, OR VIA THE INTERNET:

	WHITE	BLACK	ASIAN	HISPANIC
Phone or mail order	39%	32%	28%	29%
Internet	28%	14%	35%	20%

Source: Simmons Market Research, 2002

say they would rather shop at a local store than at a national chain, compared with 28 percent of blacks and 30 percent each of Asians and whites.

blacks

Blacks are the most fashion-conscious of all racial and ethnic groups. In fact, 34 percent of black consumers say they like to keep up with changes in trends and fashion, compared with 28 percent of Asians, 27 percent of Hispanics and 25 percent of whites. Blacks are the most likely of all groups to be willing to travel an hour or more to shop at their favorite store and almost twice as likely as the average consumer to go out of their way

to find new stores, especially if a bargain is to be had. The Simmons study found that a third (34 percent) of the black respondents will travel an hour or more to shop at a factory outlet store, compared with 27 percent of all consumers. And once they get there, black consumers, more than anyone else, prefer conquering the sales racks alone, rather than with friends. Indeed, blacks simply enjoy shopping, even for something as mundane as the groceries.

it's in the mail

Across most product categories, black consumers are more likely than the average American to buy items based on direct mail advertisements.

INDEX* OF AMERICANS WHO HAVE PURCHASED THE FOLLOWING TYPES OF PRODUCTS IN THE PAST YEAR IN RESPONSE TO DIRECT MAIL ADVERTISING, BY RACE AND ETHNICITY:

	WHITE	BLACK	ASIAN	HISPANIC
New/used car	87	144	112	126
CDs/tapes/records	91	132	93	119
Children's clothing	89	139	105	128
Computer hardware	94	117	151	104
Computer software	97	125	131	83
Cosmetics/perfume/skin care products	95	119	94	108
Fast food	100	110	91	91
Furniture	91	146	109	109
Groceries	105	103	89	73
Mattress	91	140	101	109
Women's lingerie	94	132	98	104
Women's sportswear	110	89	73	61

*An index of 100 is the national average. For example, black consumers are 44 percent more likely than the average American to have bought a new or used car as a result of direct mail advertising, but they are 11 percent less likely to have bought women's sportswear as a result of direct mail.

Source: Scarborough Research

TOP NICHE

Growth in Asian-Am. spending fuels targeted marketing

Deborah L. Vence

Unceasing population growth and increasing buying power among Asian-Americans in the United States has prompted more companies in recent years to work even harder and put more resources behind researching and marketing to this group.

"The Asian-American segment remains a 'segment of superlatives.' Per 2000 (U.S.) Census data, Asian-Americans are the fastest growing, most affluent, educated and reachable segment, because Asian-Americans are condensed in the top metro areas and states in this country," says Wanla Cheng, president of Asia Link Consulting Group, a full-service multicultural marketing and research consultancy based in New York.

According to the 1990 U.S. Census, the Asian-American population grew by 98%, to 6.9 million from 3.5 million, between 1980 and 1990, largely as a result of Asian immigration during those years; and to 10.7 million from 6.9 million between 1990 and 2000, which represents a 55% increase. Today, some three-fourths of Asian-Americans reside in California, New York, New Jersey, Hawaii, Texas and Illinois. Data as recent as March 2004 from the U.S. Census Bureau predicts that the Asian-American population will grow 213%, to about 33.4 million people, by 2050.

"Growth among the Filipino population has been (particularly) dramatic because of political upheaval. Filipinos are seeking better economic opportunities and have the highest overseas money transfer levels than any Asian segment," she adds.

Meanwhile, buying power has grown among Asian-Americans as well. Census 2000 indicates that Asian-American buying power increased by 116%, to $254.6 billion from $117.6 billion recorded in 1990, according to data from the Selig Center for Economic Growth at the Terry College of Business at the University of Georgia in Athens.

Such rapid growth has influenced more companies to start marketing to Asian-Americans if they haven't been, and prompted firms already reaching out to Asians to target the top six segments (Chinese, Filipinos, Indians, Vietnamese, Koreans and Japanese) independently, using three strategies: language-specific promotions, grassroots marketing and Asian television ads and TV programs.

Asian-American Distribution: Top markets

Experts say the Asian-American population is easier to reach than many marketers realize. The percentages below indicate that more than half the number of Asian-Americans in the country reside in five cities—and in fact, the population is more concentrated now than it was 10 years ago. Meanwhile, other metropolitan markets known for their growing Asian-American populations include Seattle, Boston, Atlanta, Washington, Houston, Dallas, according to information from the New York-based Asia Link consulting Group, a multicultural marketing research consultancy.

	Los Angeles	San Francisco	New York	Honolulu	Chicago
1990 percentage out of 6.6 million in the U.S.	18.4%	12.6%	12.0%	7.2%	3.5%
2000 percentage out of 6.6 million in the U.S.	18.8%	13.9%	15.2%	6.9%	4.2%

Larry Moskowitz, vice president of strategic marketing for New York-based Kang & Lee Advertising Inc., says that in the early 1990s, only long distance telephone carriers, airlines, banks and insurance companies marketed to Asian Americans.

"Now, we have every major automobile company, a wide variety of financial services firms, pharmaceutical companies, health insurance companies, regional hospitals, casinos, the NBA and much more (advertising to Asian-Americans)," he says.

Take Northbrook, Ill.-based Allstate Insurance Co., a property and casualty insurance firm that has been making greater efforts at marketing to Chinese-Americans through a language-specific integrated marketing campaign unveiled in September 2003. The increase in Asian-American population growth together with the company's success at reaching Hispanic consumers prompted Allstate to go beyond its standard Chinese-language brochures and corporate advertising material that it had been distributing to Chinese consumers prior to the start of the campaign.

"Based on the rapid growth of the Asian-American market, (we knew that) if we wanted to continue to grow, and faster than the rate of the industry, we had to go into new markets," says Jennifer Davis, director of multicultural marketing for Allstate. "With the help of Kang & Lee, we did consumer research that gave us insight into the things that would likely resonate with (Chinese) consumers. So, we (more or less) reintroduced Allstate to the Chinese market and reestablished our brand. Allstate is very well-known among general market consumers, but not as well known among Chinese consumers."

One of the main goals of Allstate's brand campaign, which premiered in New York and was later introduced in Seattle and Portland, was to translate the firm's "You're in good hands" slogan into Chinese.

"The truth is that all (Asian) segments … want to be talked to in their native language not because they don't understand English, but because they feel that companies are reaching out to them, bonding with them and showing respect for their community in a way that means that this consumer segment is important to them," says Asia Link's Cheng.

The integrated marketing campaign involves Cantonese- and Mandarin-language TV and radio commercials and print ads. In addition, the company launched a Web site (www.Chinese.Allstate.com) for Chinese consumers to learn more about Allstate in their native language.

To prepare for the campaign, Kang & Lee conducted focus group sessions over the course of a year with Chinese consumers and Chinese-speaking Allstate agents who consumed at least five hours of Chinese language media a week. The goal was to learn more about what Chinese-speaking consumers really looked for in an insurance product. As a result, Kang & Lee put together a tagline that informed Chinese consumers about the value behind Allstate insurance and emphasized Allstate's 70-year history.

Firms step up efforts to address each group

The company's long-term existence was important to Asians—"the stability and wisdom that comes with age and the sense that we would be around into the future," Davis says.

Meanwhile, Moskowitz points out that Kang & Lee wanted to create a tagline that "got to the heart of what 'you're in good hands' meant as opposed to being a slave of the actual words. It's about turning over something of value into our hands, and to (make the Chinese consumers) feel relaxed and free of worry."

"We took a rigorous research approach and went about creating a long list of interpretations (as opposed to doing a literal translation of the logo). Chinese is a language that has poetic (dialects) and daily colloquial forms. So, we went back to the original tagline in English to find out more about its development and why (Allstate) used it," Moskowitz explains.

The main goal was to create a campaign that would establish overall awareness of the Allstate brand among Chinese-Americans. So, Kang & Lee set out, essentially, to educate Chinese consumers with the basics about what kind of a company Allstate was and what its attributes were.

For example, a 30-second TV commercial, titled "Nostalgia," that advertised the Allstate brand shows a background in faded colors of black and white, and opens up with a boy peering into a window of an old toy shop. The boy goes into the store and buys a toy car and then plays with it underneath his kitchen table at home. His dog then runs into the room, snatches it and runs away with it.

During the commercial, a narrator of Asian descent says: "When I was young, there were a lot of things I loved but was unable to protect. Now, I know how important it is to have the right protection that fits my needs."

At the end of the commercial, another voiceover says: "For your auto, home and life insurance needs, Allstate Chinese-speaking agents can provide you with a variety of options. In America, one in every eight American households chooses Allstate." The tagline in Chinese then emerges at the bottom of the screen and reads: "Take control of today in the future, please call your local agent (name), at (number) now."

This ongoing marketing campaign has prompted Allstate to hire more Chinese-speaking insurance agents to work in markets with an abundance of Chinese prospects. (Although Allstate does not have the exact number of Chinese-speaking agents, the company has more than 3,200 agencies whose agents speak languages other than English.)

Like Allstate, Western Union Financial Services Inc., a Greenwood Village, Colo.-based company that provides money transfer and message services, also took a step forward in the last couple of years in how it targets Asian-Americans, says Ming-Ren Shiu, marketing manager with Western Union.

"Since I joined Western Union five years ago, there has been an evolution in the way we target Asian-Americans. There has been increased focus on taking a (grassroots) approach to deliver our consumer message to Asian-Americans. We've always relied on traditional media, like TV, radio and newspapers, which is still dominant, but (now we are) focusing more on the lifestyles of (Asian) consumers," Shiu says.

For instance, Western Union is a major sponsor of many Asian cultural events held throughout the year, such as the Asian-American Expo in Los Angeles for the Chinese New Year, as well as the Vietnamese and Filipino Independence parades, in target markets that include New York, San Francisco, Chicago, Washington, Seattle, Boston, Houston and Honolulu. In addition, Western Union works with media partners and community leaders and organizations in reaching out to Asian communities to address community needs.

One recent example involves Western Union's partnership that began in 2003 with *World Journal*, a Chinese newspaper circulated in the United States and Canada, to publish and distribute the *Chinese Immigrant Handbook* in the New York metropolitan area through key Chinese associations and retail outlets.

Asian-American buying power intensifies

Buying power among Asian-Americans seems to be picking up speed. Projections for the growth rate in buying power of this group by 2007 are faster than the increases seen between 1990 and 2000. According to data from Selig Center for Economic Growth at the Terry College of Business at Athens-based University of Georgia, buying power among Asian-Americans should jump by $200.3 billion by 2007, which would represent a 79% increase since 2000 and a compound annual growth rate of 8.43%. The compound annual growth rate in buying power among U.S. Asians between 1990 and 2000 was 8.03%.

Through the growth rate in buying power among Asian-Americans doesn't surpass U.S. Hispanics, the group is ahead of the African-American population—whose CAGR between 2000 and 2007 is projected to drop to 5.44% a year, compared with 6.4% for a decade earlier—and Caucasians, whose CAGR in buying between 2000 and 2007 is estimated at 4.51%, essentially the same growth as during the '90s.

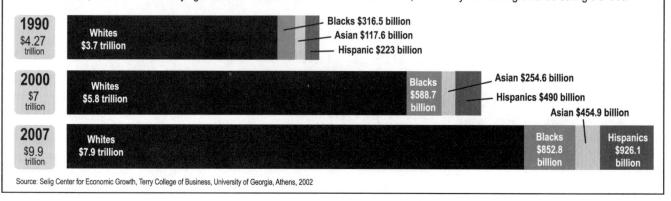

Source: Selig Center for Economic Growth, Terry College of Business, University of Georgia, Athens, 2002

"The booklet contains practical, in-language information, such as how to apply for a driver's license and how to learn more about Asian government organizations and community associations, to help new immigrants to start assimilating their lives in the U.S. This particular booklet was well-received in the Chinese community and now we are replicating the same success and plan to customize the booklets and introduce it in Los Angeles and San Francisco," Shiu says.

"These are many opportunities (for us) to establish relationships with Asian consumers," he adds. "Even going to Chinese grocery stores has become a good touch point. It's important that we are present at (Asian) events or other meeting places and be available to talk with community leaders."

More recently, Western Union sponsored a concert series across six major U.S. cities, including Los Angeles, San Francisco, Las Vegas, Chicago, Washington and Atlantic City. The concert series featured two of the most popular singers in The Philippines: Regine Velasquez and Ogie Alcasid.

"Concerts are a popular form of entertainment and part of the lifestyle for most Filipinos in the United States," Shiu notes.

To get Filipino consumers interested in the concert series, Western Union orchestrated a series of integrated grassroots public relations activities around the concert series.

Flyers that announced the concert were distributed at high-traffic shopping areas in the six markets. In addition, the company arranged for the singers to sign autographs at selected Western Union locations in the six cities, and special-edition music CDs were handed out to Filipino consumers who made transactions at participating Western Union locations.

Ads on TV remain best way to reach audience in their native language

At the concert, a Western Union TV commercial played on the main stage before the start of each concert; flyers were distributed by Western Union representatives who also were on hand to answer any questions Filipino consumers had about the company. In addition, company reps encouraged consumers to enroll in Western Union's loyalty card program, and subsequently had those loyalty cards mailed out to enrolled customers immediately after the concerts.

Shiu says the concert series was successful, overall, and as a result helped Western Union register hundreds of Filipino consumers in its loyalty card program.

"Western Union was able to build strong one-on-one relationships with more than 22,000 Filipino consumers (through pre-concert grassroots PR activities and at the concerts)," Shiu says.

Such grassroots marketing activities are priceless to a company that wants to reach Asian-Americans today. But experts add that TV ads remain dominant in reaching Asian-Americans in both their native language as well as English. Meanwhile, new TV programs for and about Asian-Americans are beginning to emerge.

'over time … you will probably see (more mainstream advertising) with (more Asians depicted in the ads).'

For instance, Allstate runs TV ads in Chinese languages on Chinese-language stations, including KSCI-TV in Los Angeles and Sinovision in New York. Honda Motor Co. also promotes its 2004 Honda Civic on those same Chinese-language stations.

PepsiCo Inc. now is running ads in English on *Stir* TV, an English-language show aimed at the second generation of Asian-Americans, says Greg Chew, creative director at DAE Advertising, a full-service Asian advertising agency in San Francisco. The show, which airs on Seattle's International Channel (Channel 70), a national cable network that reaches nearly 12 million households nationwide, and on KHNL, Hawaii's NBC affiliate, is the first lifestyle program with that target audience. The program, launched on March 3, is a cross between a news magazine and a reality show, and features four hosts whose job is to tackle different issues and trends affecting Asian-Americans. The 30-minute show is shot in San Francisco weekly and sends the four hosts across the country to interview Asian-Americans about the topic of the week.

In addition to *Stir*, another English-language program is in the works to be produced in Los Angeles, called *Object of Desire*. It also will target young, urban Asian-Americans between the ages of 18 and 30. The show is expected to air later this year, Chew says.

Shiu adds: "There is a whole lot of opportunity outside the traditional media. Over time ... you probably will see (more mainstream advertising) with (more Asians depicted in the ads). Marketing or communicating (to Asians) is not enough. It's more about reaching a touch point with Asian consumers and speaking the language they speak."

For more information on the companies mentioned in this story, go to:

www.allstate.com (Allstate Insurance)

www.asialinkny.com (Asia Link Consulting Group)

www.dae.com (DAE Advertising)

www.kanglee.com (Kang & Lee Advertising)

www.westernunion.com (Western Union)

What Makes Customers TICK?

Most businesses have no idea why customers behave as they do.

Lewis P. Carbone

There's never been a better time or a more compelling reason to get to know your customers. Given the challenges facing business today, it's not surprising that the Marketing Science Institute lists "greater insight into the customer experience" as one of its top research needs. Increasingly, we have the means to achieve that end. Innovative new approaches and research tools are now becoming available to help businesses expand their view of customers and dig deeper to understand what truly makes them tick.

In recent years companies have made significant efforts to become more customer-centric. In fact, the notion of "listening to the voice of the customer" has been taken seriously—and quite literally—by countless firms. The practice of going directly to consumers to find out what they think about a product, service, or experience is a basic foundation for business decisions every day.

Implicit in this practice is the assumption that customers will accurately report their thoughts and desires. Yet time and again companies engage in painstaking and expensive research to guide new initiatives, only to find that consumer behavior in the marketplace bears no resemblance to what their research indicated.

Remember New Coke? Its introduction has been heralded as both a brilliant promotional scheme and a major faux pas. But in consumer surveys, even in taste tests, cola drinkers proclaimed their willingness to try and to buy a new refor-

mulation of Coca-Cola's classic beverage. They even responded positively to a more Pepsi-like reformulation. But when the new formula rolled out, it was met with anger and dismay by loyal Coke drinkers and non-drinkers alike. Contrary to the research-based expectations, sales were poor and the product flopped.

The phenomenon isn't unique to the cola business. Marketing has always been based on taking consumers at their word—on grilling them for insights about their tastes, buying habits, and brand attitudes. Yet approximately 60%–80% of all new products fail.

Why? Because traditional research doesn't take into account how the consumer mind works.

How the Brain Works

Up to this point, much of the effort put forth to understand customers has dealt with how they behave and what they have to say. What has not been developed—in large part because the capability hasn't existed—is a deeper understanding of why customers behave the way they do.

Most conventional market research assumes customers understand how they develop preferences and feelings about their experiences. However, we're learning that the conscious choices consumers make are determined almost exclusively through unconscious processes. By relying on consumers to accurately report why they act the way they do, popular re-

search methods like focus groups and surveys very often force customers to develop "intellectual alibis"—to make sense out of things that they simply aren't able to articulate due to their subconscious origins. Instead of the real reason for buying or not buying something, these conscious-centered approaches result in rationalizations based on how people think they ought to be motivated.

This fact affects not only value for consumers, but actions in corporate board rooms. Noted management scholar Peter Drucker states that many CEOs of large U.S. firms who were appointed in the past 10 years "were fired as failures within a year or two in part because they relied on poor paradigms about customer thinking."

The good news is that in the last decade neuroscientists have learned more about how the human brain works—how people process data, both consciously and unconsciously—than in all previous centuries combined. Because of this, we can now begin reaping valuable insights based on how customers formulate their thoughts and preferences about a product, service, or the total experience.

"More may have been learned about the brain and the mind in the 1990s—the so-called decade of the brain—than during the entire previous history of psychology and neuroscience," notes leading neuroscience scholar Antonio Damasio, M.W. Van Allen distinguished professor

EXECUTIVE briefing

How do consumers assess value and arrive at decisions? New insights and approaches into this issue are rewriting the old rules of market research. Science is proving that as much as 95% of human thought, emotion, and action is rooted in the unconscious mind. Organizations that want greater marketing effectiveness must begin to understand the value of these diverse new approaches, as well as the robust capability they offer for designing the delivering far richer customer experiences.

of neurology at the University of Iowa College of Medicine.

In particular, modern neurological research shows that people don't think and draw conclusions in linear, hierarchical ways or in exclusively conscious ways. Instead, they glean cues and bits of information from all the senses, above and below awareness, to form a composite experiential impression that becomes a basis for preference, loyalty, and advocacy.

What Customers Can't Say

One marketing researcher whose work has been devoted to this crucial understanding is Gerald Zaltman, author of *How Customers Think: Essential Insights Into the Mind of the Market* (Harvard Business School Press, 2003). He describes the impressionistic approach to the brain in action as "that wonderful if messy stew of memories, emotions, thoughts, and other cognitive processes we're not aware of or that we can't articulate."

Knowing that humans take in and process information in a multitude of ways, effective marketing researchers like Zaltman are beginning to develop an array of more sophisticated approaches. The new insights into how consumers assess value and arrive at decisions, coupled with the growing weight being given to experience-driven perspectives, are rewriting the old rules of marketing research. And they're creating significant opportunity for companies to design and deliver far richer customer experiences.

The lesson of New Coke and other similar examples is that opinions, even though they are conscious expressions, seldom tell the complete story. Science is proving that the unconscious dynamics of customer thinking provide the richest understanding of attitudes, behavior, and

loyalty tendencies. Studies in neuroscience have revealed that as much as 95% of all thinking occurs in our subconscious, which means it is also the starting point for conscious action.

It's that dynamic linking that explains the failure of conscious-focused research activities to correctly predict consumer responses in the marketplace. Like the tip of a very large iceberg, the rational reasons consumers give for their buying decisions and preferences are highly influenced by the mass of information below the surface of consciousness. By the time people become aware of a decision on a conscious level, it has already happened in their unconscious mind.

Marketers searching for greater marketing efficiencies and effectiveness must understand the value of diverse new approaches that help tap into the underlying 95% and apply them to create more value for customers. Doing so is the key to competitive advantage in the 21st century.

Choose Your Tool

Fortunately, new approaches are emerging that provide windows into unconscious consumer thinking. And "experience management" perspectives and techniques are making it possible to translate that information into more relevant day-to-day interactions. Tools grounded in psychology, anthropology, ethnography, neuroscience, and linguistics, among others, are entering the research arena to help businesses mine for these insights. They range from cross-disciplinary one-on-one interview strategies to using MRI techniques that allow researchers to literally "watch" what parts of the brain are stimulated when people are exposed to particular experiences and stimuli.

These approaches, along with technology-enhanced observation tech-

niques, are leading to far more valuable offerings and experiences for consumers because they are resulting in more relevant and authentic connections with them.

Zaltman is leading the charge in this exploration. In *How Customers Think*, he states that the foundation for understanding customers—and thus surviving in today's rapidly shifting business environment—is to "draw on research from an array of disciplines to extend managers' comfort zones." Those disciplines may range from musicology, neurology, philosophy, and linguistics to the more familiar fields of anthropology, psychology, and sociology. Combined, Zaltman notes, they give marketers powerful new tools to help them "better understand what happens in the complex system of mind, brain, body, and society when consumers evaluate products and the experiences they have with them."

Zaltman cites the example of a client that met for two days with a neurobiologist, a psychiatrist, an Olympic coach, an adult learning specialist, and a public health sociologist to examine new ways to use consumer incentives. The meeting resulted in several innovative and practical ideas that were immediately implemented—some within two weeks. In the next seven months, the effectiveness of the company's consumer-incentive program soared by almost 40%.

And then there is Moen Inc., the showerhead manufacturer that enlisted video specialists, cultural anthropologists, and hydro-therapists to expand its understanding of consumer showering preferences as it developed a new high-end massaging showerhead. Even at more than double the cost of standard showerheads, the "Revolution" has become a top seller in the consumer market. In addition, its commercial use has made it such a point of differentiation in selected Marriott Courtyard Hotels that showerheads are actually sold at the front desk.

What follows are some examples of innovative approaches in the areas of interpersonal, observational, and linguistics research. From them, it will become more obvious how drawing on an array of disciplines offers marketers expanded options for putting together a more complete picture of consumers.

Thinking Metaphorically

One of the most productive of the innovative research strategies pioneered by Zaltman is the study of the metaphors that consumers use to express their thoughts and feelings. The technique is called metaphor elicitation (and has been trademarked by its developer as the Zaltman Metaphor Elicitation Technique, or ZMET for short).

By the time people become aware of a decision on a conscious level, it has already happened in their unconscious mind.

A metaphor is a way to understand one thing in terms of something else. In *Seeing the Mind of the Market* (Harvard Business School Press, 1998), Zaltman and Kathryn Braun show how metaphors are central to human thought and act as organizing frameworks for the expression of abstract or varied concepts.

For example, when someone says a person is a "train wreck" waiting to happen, they're using the idea of a mishap with things coming apart to convey certain, yet unspecified characteristics about an individual who, in starkly physical terms, has nothing in common with a locomotive on a track. But although the message is not supposed to be taken literally, its meaning is clear. Similarly, the metaphor of "being in good hands" has nothing to do with being physically touched or held, but the meaning is clear.

Neuroscience has revealed that humans think more in images than in words. For this reason, metaphor elici-

tation researchers rely on visual images chosen by respondents in one-to-one customer interviews to help surface metaphors. When recognized and probed for the thinking behind them, metaphors are considered reliable vehicles for transporting unconscious thoughts to conscious awareness.

This is enormously useful information because, as Zaltman states, "no matter what the characteristics of a product, experience, or brand, it will always be initially perceived by consumers in some organizing framework or metaphor." What's more, universal metaphors are often revealed after probing just a handful of interview respondents. Once surfaced and recognized, these metaphors become an invaluable form of shorthand for understanding how offerings and experiences fit into people's lives. And those insights often become the basis for new product designs, communications, or experience designs.

Recently, Toronto-based Innerviews Inc. conducted a metaphor elicitation study around employee workspace. Two environments that, at first blush, would seem to have little in common were studied: a state-of-the-art call center and a nurses' station at a children's hospital. Despite their apparent differences, it didn't take long for interview respondents to share the intense nature of how they felt about their surroundings—and in surprisingly similar metaphorical terms. In language and visual images, both groups referred to their workspace as "territory" and their need to feel that it was like "a home." The need to feel "rooted" in workspace, with corresponding visual images of mature, well-anchored trees, was another common description.

But while both groups of respondents aligned on the overarching concept of territory, surprising insights surfaced as each discussed their workspace in very different organizing metaphors.

Call center employees consistently described their state-of-the-art work environment by using combat metaphors.

Language, behavior, and visual images were summed up in words and pictures that conveyed "feeling like East Germany," "feeling invaded," "attacked from all sides," and "nowhere to hide." Through these expressions of vulnerability, an obvious conflict was revealed between the employees' deep desire for their own private space (territory) and the open design and layout of the work area.

The organizing metaphor for the children's hospital was very different. The nurses interviewed had a deep desire for their space to be a place of retreat from their time on the floor with patients. They referred to wanting an area to help them "re-energize," "escape," or "seek serenity." Images that introduced this idea were often garden-like, associated with the color yellow and soft guitar music.

The organizing metaphors for both environments were quite different, largely due to the cultures of the two institutions. But consideration for the "culture" as part of design work is critical to creating clues that will imprint the experience for the intended audience in more dynamic and profound ways. The metaphors in the workspace study suggested very different starting points for design work, but with the need for territory to always play a central role in both.

For the call center, this involved ways to personalize and allow employees to "mark" and privatize their workspaces. For the hospital, it translated to providing a place that had revitalizing and serene characteristics, but was "off stage" and away from the chaos.

When companies are able to surface and understand relevant metaphors, a window into the unconscious is revealed, which can serve as a powerful compass for communications, experience design, and planning.

Learn by Observing

To invoke that great American philosopher, Yogi Berra, "You can observe a lot by watching." Companies are discovering that simply observing customers offers a wealth of information they cannot get with traditional research methods. With enhanced technological capabilities, watching consumers in their natural settings is becoming an important part of the expanded research mix.

When an organization understands the effect of certain words in specific contexts, the impact of its communication can improve exponentially.

Ironically, according to Harvard professor Dorothy Leonard, until marketers developed the tools to gather "hard" numbers from large samples of the population, the kind of "soft" information that observational research captures used to be the norm. Today, most businesses rely on that hard data in lieu of observing consumers in their natural settings—and often miss important insights as a direct consequence.

As a growing number of organizations have discovered, there are many innovative ways to observe customers in action. During development of Quicken, its top-selling accounting software, Intuit brought users into labs and even sent engineers into people's homes to see how they used the product. This took engineers a step beyond what customers verbalized and enabled them to see how clients physically used the product. "This type of observation gives you a depth of understanding beyond which customers can articulate," says Craig Cunningham, CEO of Customer Integrated Solutions, a consultancy that helps companies create client-driven initiatives. "It gets you past what clients think they need and helps you see what they really require."

Paco Underhill, a retail anthropologist, has done considerable research documenting the "science of shopping." Through video observation and customer interviews, he has observed more than 1,000 distinct shopping elements, everything from how shoppers negotiate department store doorways on a busy Saturday to how often they touch the merchandise before buying and the intricate ballet of product placement on the shelf.

Often, it's the most prosaic observations that provide new insights that affect both the customer experience and the bottom line. For example, in *Why We Buy: The Science of Shopping* (Touchstone Press, 2000), Underhill describes a supermarket study for a dog food manufacturer that, through video, revealed that adults bought the dog food, but dog treats were almost always picked out by children or senior citizens. Because of the smaller packaging, however, dog treats were typically stocked near the top of the shelf. Children were observed climbing the shelving to reach the treats and one elderly lady used a roll of aluminum foil to knock down her favorite dog biscuits. Once the treats were moved to lower shelves, sales of dog treats went up.

The Right Words

As Mark Twain put it, "The difference between the right word and the almost right word is the difference between lightning and a lightning bug." When an organization understands the effect of certain words in specific contexts, and is able to cue metaphors where possible, the impact of its communication can improve exponentially.

The fast-deepening science of linguistics offers marketers exciting ways to understand customers and communicate more effectively with them. Charles Cleveland, founder of Communications Development Corporation (CDC) and former director of the Academic Computing Center at Drake University, has developed patented conversation analysis software that can make ultra-fine distinctions in the human communication process. It does this by comparing the language of one context (or group) to another and recommending the necessary language shifts to move to the desired context.

To see the power of even simple nuances, consider this example from "The Little Words in Life," a paper delivered by Cleveland in 2000 as part of the University of Toronto Distinguished Fellow Series. Imagine you are renting a car at an airport. And you're in a hurry. The agent at counter A says, "I'll have a car for you soon." The agent at counter B says, "I'll have the car for you soon." Which car agency would have the edge in making you feel most confident that your need was understood and it would be met? Most likely rental counter B because the words its agent used, "the car," imply it has a specific car picked out, creating an impression that the vehicle is being readied just for you and will be brought down in a minute. At the other counter, "a car" left a more general impression—it's even possible someone might still be out searching for a car in the lot.

The difference in two tiny words in that single situation might seem insignificant. In fact, the customer might not even notice the words. But linguistically, those words register and contribute to a greater or lesser sense of confidence.

And if there's impact to be derived from distinctions as simple as "a" and "the," imagine what may be possible when the linguistics in an entire transaction are analyzed. Cleveland tells of a financial services firm that explored the language effectiveness of its call centers with the goal of improving customer satisfaction scores. By monitoring several hundred random conversations between customer service reps (CSRs) and customers, his contextual linguistics software benchmarked both groups' language and measured the degree of meaningful communication between them. All conversations were found to have communication breakdowns—on average, the gap was 115%.

After the firm trained its CSRs in usage of high performance words that maintain business language but also come closer to the customer's context, the communication gap narrowed to substantially less than 30%. In terms of return on investment, the language effectiveness study resulted in overall customer satisfaction rising 12% for the company and employee turnover dropping by 23%.

The implications for how customers experience businesses in the years to come are profound. Organizations that develop expanded approaches for understanding their customers will gain powerful competitive advantages. It's the difference between trying to make judgments from a single snapshot or having an array of perspectives from different vantage points that offers a far more holistic and truthful picture. The ability to play back a video, assess body language, gain insights from verbal contexts, or surface meaningful metaphors will lead to far more relevant connections with customers, which will lead to greater differentiation, loyalty, and value for all concerned.

Author's Note: The author acknowledges the contribution of Suzie Goan, experience director of Experience Engineering, Inc.

Lewis P. Carbone is founder, president, and chief experience officer of Experience Engineering, a Minneapolis-based experience management consulting firm. He may be reached at lcarbone@expeng.com.

Tough Love

In this economy, maintaining good relationships with customers is vital. So what do you do about clients or prospects you can't stand? Here's how to charm your five most difficult customer types

by Justin Berzon

In the booming 1990s, sales executives and their reps could afford to show pain-in-the-you-know-what customers the door. In this economic climate, losing a prospect, or worse yet, an existing account, can be devastating to the bottom line. Managers and salespeople alike are constantly reminding themselves of the old adage that the customer is always right, as they seek to please their spectrum of clients and court new business. But within that range of valued customers, there's the easy sell and there's the client from hell. When it comes to the latter, strategies exist for dealing with a difficult personality that might turn a tense initial meeting into a beautiful (and profitable) new relationship. We've broken down the tough crowd into five personality types, and we've also consulted experts and sales executives to find out how to deal with clients who roll their eyes, change their minds, and demand over-the-top treatment, all without losing your mind—or the deal.

MR. GREEDY

You've seen this guy many times before: He's the one who makes crazy demands and wants you to shower him with perks and gifts in exchange for business. He brags about what your competitors are giving him in exchange for his business and wants you to do the same. He might as well be wearing a T-shirt that reads, "What's In It for Me?"

Obviously, you have two major options with Mr. Greedy: appease him and make concessions, or refuse, stand by your product, and let him take it or leave it. Steve Rothberg, founder and president of Minneapolis-based Internet job board CollegeRecruiter.com, says he uses a system of categorizing demanding clients, first as large or small customers, and second as rude or polite. For polite clients, he'll go out of his way to meet their special requests. Catering to the de-

mands of big Mr. Greedies can often mean a big payoff. Catering to small-but-polite clients makes sense, too, Rothberg says, because there's always the chance that a small client will someday become a big client if you treat him well.

However, when it comes to clients who are not polite about making special requests for service, he handles large and small clients differently. "For larger clients, I'll grit my teeth and give them what they want," Rothberg says. "You're never going to like all of your customers, but it's still good business and good revenue." But Rothberg stops pursuing small clients who ask for special favors and aren't particularly charming about it. If they are existing customers, he lets them go when their service contracts or agreements run out.

Another way to keep Mr. Greedy in check is to preemptively offer certain bonuses and special deals so he doesn't have any ground to stand on when asking for additional perks. Ron Kern, president and general manager of the Las Vegas branch of Ferguson Enterprises, a Newport News, Virginia–based plumbing supplies wholesale distributor, says his firm takes its best clients on excursions, such as deep-sea fishing trips to Cabo San Lucas, and several golf outings each year. He uses these bonding events to keep clients in the loop year-round and alert them to special discounts and promotions before they ever have the chance to ask, making them feel that they're already getting luxury treatment. "Yeah, these guys want perks, but sometimes if it's a good client or potential client, you just have to factor that in as a cost of doing business," Kern says.

THE WAFFLER

When push comes to shove, this prospect just can't make up his mind. He lacks self-confidence, and as a result, even when the deal is ultimately signed, he'll make a million further revisions and impulsive decisions. He'll run your entire sales team ragged with his constant changes.

When it comes to awaiting that final purchasing decision, make sure that a waffling prospect is in fact the one responsible for making the final call. By the very nature of their indecisiveness, Wafflers are rarely the actual decision makers.

The best way to deal with a Waffler, says Charlotte, North Carolina-based sales trainer Landy Chase, is to assign the most confident salesperson to work with him. "These folks will generally gravitate toward salespeople with a high degree of expertise, because it lowers their risk of making a bad decision," Chase says.

Wafflers often lack technical expertise or confidence, which Chase says salespeople can capitalize on if they go about it the fight way. "These people are afraid to make decisions, lest they make the wrong one. If you can step into a leadership role, they'll likely fall into a follower one," Chase says.

Rothberg, on the other hand, takes a more dismissive approach to indecisive buyers. He says he shifts such clients into a low-maintenance mode, where he follows up through e-malls, not long phone conversations. He says that he can spend up to 100 hours communicating back and forth with a major Waffler, only to get the same amount of business he would from one hour with someone who is willing and able to make a decision. "You've got to realize sometimes that spending a tremendous amount of time on this kind of a client just won't help," Rothberg says. "Sometimes they need time to procrastinate. Oh, they'll come back when it gets to be a crisis, and then they'll finally make their decision."

Joseph Rofe, president of J&A Direct, which operates the automotive Web site MisterCarHead.com, uses reverse psychology when dealing with Wafflers. He tells them they should take more time to carefully think out their decision after he's explained the deal in the most thorough terms. They usually counter by insisting they are ready to buy. It's also essential to eliminate the buyer's reluctance in advance, he says. Using an unconventional method, Rofe hands new clients a package of Smarties candy, telling them to eat a single piece whenever they feel a sense of buyer's remorse coming on or any lack of confidence that they should have made the purchase. "You'd be surprised how well it works," he says. (Such tactics might not play out well in all businesses, but Rofe insists that, they work with his particular client base.)

When it comes to awaiting that final purchasing decision, however, Chase cautions sellers to make sure that a waffling prospect is in fact the one responsible for making the final call. "By the very nature of their indecisiveness, Wafflers are rarely the actual decision makers," Chase says. He recommends using this generic question to find out for sure if the Waffler is indeed the decision maker. "Assuming we were to move forward, who besides yourself would be involved?"

THE DOUBTING THOMAS

This person has had too many encounters with the stereotypical used car salesman. (Either that, or he's seen *Glengarry Glen Ross* one too many times.) He thinks salespeople are sleazy and doesn't want to give them the time of day. He won't let your reps in the door, and if he does, he makes negative comments and rolls his eyes when they tell him they want to help meet his needs.

Should you give up on Thomas? Absolutely not. In fact some managers, such as CollegeRecruiter.com's Rothberg, lure them in by giving them a free service. "I offer a free, no-strings-attached trial," Rothberg says. "That quickly separates the doubters who will try the product at no risk from the people who just simply can't make a decision. By providing this free service, I let them sell themselves on me."

Kristin Anderson, founder and president of Burnsville, Minnesota–based Say What? Consulting, warns that seeing Thomas as a lost sale can quickly become a self-fulfilling prophecy. "You think to yourself that this person is skeptical, dismissive, doesn't care what you have to say, and probably won't buy," she says. "Then you fall into the trap of giving a perfunctory sales pitch and make it all come true."

Anderson also says it's important with this type of person to demonstrate your flexibility. Make it clear that you can always come back later if he prefers, or that you are ready to work around his schedule. "If they see you as a salesperson, it isn't going to work," Anderson says. "With this customer, you've got to step out of character. Stop, laugh, reiterate that you're there to help them, but add comments like, 'Bet you've heard that a million times before' to lighten the atmosphere. You've got to be their buddy and be able to start with a friendly conversation, which should almost certainly be about something outside of work and business."

HOW TO (AMICABLY) DIVORCE YOUR CLIENT

STOP COURTING HIS BUSINESS Just let yourself discreetly fade into the background. Stop pursuing new ventures with him (but be sure to follow through on any current commitments). When his contract with you runs out, don't go out of your way to renew it. And if the two of you were in the process of exploring any new projects, you can claim to be too bogged down to work on them for now.

RECOMMEND A CHANGE IN HANDLERS With great deference, explain to your client that you don't think your firm is a good fit for him anymore. Having pored over his list of service needs, you don't think you'll be able to adequately commit the time and resources he deserves. Tell him that this would be a good time to make a clean break, and recommend a new firm that might be better able to cater to his needs. One caveat: Don't refer to a friend's firm—sending a difficult client to a fellow company or business partner could strain your relationship with that business.

BE FRANK Some people just can't take a hint. In this case, as a last resort, you may have to follow the example of Edina, Minnesota–based marketing consultant Kevin Donlin of Guaranteed Marketing. When Donlin can no longer tolerate a client, he simply tells him, "It looks like we don't have a good fit here, so I'm releasing you as a client, effective immediately. I wish you the best in moving forward."

Sound cold? "No matter how well you serve your clients, about one to three percent will never be happy no matter what you do," Donlin says. "Time isn't money—it's everything. So don't waste yours on people who don't understand or appreciate what your business does for them."

—*J.B.*

THE BEST FRIEND

These guys or gals have a hard time saying "no" because they want to be everybody's best pal. They'll go out with you and tell you that your products or services are their favorite, but meanwhile, they're telling all of your competitors the same thing.

"Tenure and time with that Best Friend is going to offer the biggest amount of ammunition against their wavering on loyalty," Ferguson's Kern says.

Chase says the main motivation of the Best Friend is that "they want to be liked and they don't want to upset anyone or be the one to give bad news." They react negatively to pressure, so try to avoid being overly aggressive or appearing exasperated, he says.

However, Kern says that after the members of your team have developed a rapport with the Best Friend, it's okay to confront him as long as it's in a positive manner. "At some point, you're within your right to make your own demands," Kern says. "If he's telling you that you're the best, you've got to ask him for the opportunity to prove it. You have to cross that bridge of talk and qualify his opinion with action."

Should you take this step, Chase suggests asking for a commitment in the form of a conditional "yes." For instance, ask the question: "If we (the company) can do this action, do we have a basis for moving forward with this deal?"

Chase says it's important to try to positively and unintrusively determine if there's any potential to actually close a deal, because your time and that of the client is very valuable.

And by all means, leave a lasting impression on the Best Friend. "When there are multiple contenders vying for this sort of fickle client's business," Chase says, "always make sure you're the last one to meet with him before he's going to make the final decision."

THE SILENT TYPE

One of the most frustrating client types, these individuals don't ask many questions and don't reveal what they are thinking through body language or other cues. Salespeople have a hard time gauging their level of interest in the product or service. Do they love your product or think it stinks?

Not to fret, though. The problem may not lie in the client's disinterest in your product—or your salesperson. Say What?'s Anderson says silence can stem from a cultural difference or even a simple issue of comprehension. "Saleswomen often think men aren't interested, but it's really because men generally give less nonverbal feedback," she says. "In other words, male clients may be very much interested in your presentation, but they are culturally less inclined to give visual responses and acknowledgement."

It may also be possible that clients don't understand the information you are presenting, Anderson says. Often they feel too insecure to ask questions, because they think it will make them look bad. They're supposed to be knowledgeable about services they already get or are considering purchasing, "The most proactive approach to dealing with this is to check in and say, 'I noticed you are quiet,' or 'I noticed you didn't have any questions. Do you understand everything?'" Anderson says.

But she also concedes that silence may be a negotiation tactic. "Silence is a powerful tool, thus that famous saying that the first one to speak is the loser," Anderson says. "They're hoping if they remain silent, it'll force you into breaking down. Maybe you'll knock off a few bucks for them."

Simma Lieberman, a Berkeley, California–based author and consultant, agrees. She says people use silence as a way of taking power and getting what they want. "If I'm being silent on the phone or in person, it's because I want more than what the person is offering me," she says. In this case, it would be up to the discretion of the salesperson, upon recognizing the prospect is using this tactic, to decide if further negotiation is in his best interest.

Kern tries to get quiet or unresponsive clients to open up by dealing with them in a more comfortable environment. For instance, he has a contractor client who used to send representatives to pick up orders and handle day-to-day relations with Ferguson. The contractor was reticent, rarely becoming too personally involved in dealings, so Kern invited him and his wife over to his house for dinner. They've since developed a more open dialogue, and the contractor has greatly increased his business with Kern. "Mind you, you can't change the stripes on an animal," Kern says. "He's still shy and removed from day-to-day dealings, but our underlying rapport has made him amenable to doing more business."

CUTTING YOUR LOSSES

Of course, there are instances when a nagging client is too much of a drain on your firm's resources (not to mention your patience), and he just isn't worth the hassle. In this case, you may want to consider discontinuing your business relationship with him. However, CollegeRecruiter. com's Rothberg cautions sales executives who drop clients to be

businesslike at all times. "You must always remember it's not the organization you have the problem with, it's the person at that organization who's your contact," Rothberg says. "Be careful not to burn bridges because difficult clients might eventually leave that firm, and then you'll have a whole new opportunity to get that firm's business."

Writer Justin Berzon can be reached at edit@salesandmarketing.com

From *Sales & Marketing Management*, December 2002, pp. 34-40. © 2003 by V N U Business Publications USA. Reprinted by permission.

Defining Moments: Segmenting by Cohorts

Coming of age experiences influence values, attitudes, preferences, and buying behaviors for a lifetime.

By Charles D. Schewe, Geoffrey E. Meredith, and Stephanie M. Noble

Cohorts are highly influenced by the external events that were happening when they were "coming of age" (generally between the years 17–23). For example, those now in their late seventies and early eighties lived through the Great Depression while baby boomers witnessed the assassination of JFK, saw other political assassinations, shared the Vietnam War, and lived through the energy crisis. Such shared experiences distinguish one cohort from another.

Today, many call marketing to birth groups generational marketing. Generations differ from cohorts. Each generation is defined by its years of birth. For example, a generation is usually 20 to 25 years in length, or roughly the time it takes a person to grow up and have children. But a cohort can be as long or short as the external events that defines it. The cohort defined by World War II, for example, is only six years long.

Consider how different cohorts treat spending and saving. Today's Depression cohort, those ages 79 to 88 in 2000, began working during the Great Depression. Their conduct with respect to money is very conservative. Having experienced the worst of economic times, this age group values economic security and frugality. They still save for that "rainy day." Those, however, in the 55 to 78 age category today were influenced by the Depression, but also experienced the boom times of the Post-World War II period. This group has attitudes toward saving that are less conservative; they are more willing to spend than the older group. In sharp contrast to the "Depression-scarred" is the free-wheeling generation that grew up during the "hippie revolution." Russell (1993) calls this birth group the "free agents," since its members defied the establishment, sought individualism, and were skeptical of everything. This cohort can be characterized as "buy now, pay later" and its members will carry this value into the century ahead as they journey through middle age and on into old age.

Cohort effects are life-long effects. They provide the communality for each cohort being targeted as a separate market segment. And since these cohorts can be described by the ages of their constituents, they offer an especially efficient vehicle for direct marketing campaigns.

Six American Cohorts

In 2000, American adults can be divided into six distinct cohorts, or market segments, ranging in age from the Depression cohort (age 79–88) to what many people are calling Generation X (age 24–34). This division is based on intensive content analysis of a wide range of publications and studies scanned over a 10-year period. The roughly 4 million people who are age 89 and older are not included for two reasons. First, this group is much smaller than other cohorts. Also, much of their consumption behavior is controlled by physical need. There also are more than 72 million persons under the age of 24. This newly emerging cohort can be referred to as the "N-Gen," since the impact of the internet revolution appears to be the key defining moment shaping this group's values. Yet it is too early to know their "defining moment-driven" values, preferences, and attitudes because external forces take some time to influence values. A brief description of each of the six cohorts follows.

The Depression Cohort

This group was born between 1912 and 1921, came of age from 1930 to 1939, and is age 79–88 today. Currently this cohort contains 13,054,000 people, or 7% of the adult U.S. population.

This cohort was defined by the Great Depression. Maturing, entering the workforce, trying to build and support families during the '30s had a profound influence on this cohort in so many areas, but most strongly in finances: money and savings. To many of today's business managers, the Depression seems like ancient history, almost apocryphal, like the Great Flood. Yet to this cohort, it was all too real. To put the Depression in perspective, the S&P 400 (the broadest measure of the economy as a whole available at that time) declined 69% between 1929 and 1932 in a relentless and agonizing fall. It wasn't until 1953—24 years and a World War later—before the S&P index got back to where it had been in 1929! People starting out in this environment were scarred in ways they carry with them today. In particular, financial security still rules their thinking as reflected in the following example.

A Depression Cohort Marketing Example. One savings and loan bank on the West Coast took a cohort perspective to boost deposits from this cohort. They used an icon familiar to this age group, George Feneman (Groucho Marx's television sidekick on *You Bet Your Life*), who assured this cohort of the safety of their money. He stressed that the financial institution uses their money for mortgages. "We build houses," he says, which is just what this cohort can relate to, since preserving their homes was central to the financial concerns of this age group.

EXECUTIVE
briefing

Cohorts are groups of individuals who are born during the same time period and travel through life together. They experience similar external events during their late adolescent/ early adulthood years. These "defining moments" influence their values, preferences, attitudes, and buying behaviors in ways that remain with them over their lifetime. We can identify six known American cohorts that include those from age 88 to those coming of age in 2000. While generational cohorts are far from the final solution for marketers, they are certainly a relevant dynamic. Marketers should seriously consider targeting these age groupings, especially in their marketing communications.

The World War II Cohort

Born 1922–1927, this cohort came of age from 1940 to 1945. Its members are age 73–78 today. Currently 9,465,000 people, it represents 5% of our adult population.

World War II defined this cohort. Economically it was not a boom time (the S&P 500 gained 50% from 1940 to 1945, but it was still only half of what it had been in 1929), but unemployment was no longer a problem. This cohort was unified by a common enemy, shared experiences, and especially for the 16 million in the military, a sense of deferment and delayed gratification. In World War I, the average duration of service was less than 12 months; in World War II, the average was 33 months. Marriages, careers, and children were all put on hold until the war was over.

This sense of deferment made the World War II cohort an intensely romantic one. The yearning for loved ones left behind, and for those who left to fight is reflected in the music and literature and movies of the time (e.g., *I've Got My Love to Keep Me Warm, Homesick, That's All, 'Til Then,* and *You'd Be So Nice to Come Home To*). And, while for many the war was an unpleasant experience, for many others it was the apex of their lives. They had a defined role (frequently more important in status than any other they would ever have), a measure of freedom from their particular social norms, and an opportunity to travel, some to exotic foreign shores, others just away from the towns and cornfields of their youth. The horrors and heroism experienced by our soldiers imbedded values that stay with them still. And this influence was clearly depicted in the award-winning and highly acclaimed movies of 1998: *Saving Private Ryan* and *The Thin Red Line.*

A World War II Cohort Marketing Example. Using cohort words, symbols, and memories can bring substantial rewards for marketers. A direct marketing campaign designed for a cable television provider to increase subscriptions is just such an example. Postage stamp-sized pictures of Douglas McArthur were put on the corner of the envelope with the copy "If you remember V-J Day, we've got some new programs you're going to love." This attention-getter immediately communicated that the content is for members of the targeted cohort. When this approach was used, subscription response rates surged from 1.5% to more than 10%.

The Post-War Cohort

Members of this cohort were born from 1928 to 1945, came of age from 1946 to 1963, and are age 55 to 73 in 2000. Currently 42,484,000 people, 22.7% of the adult population are Post-Wars.

This cohort is a very long one—18 years span the youngest to the oldest members. They were the beneficiaries of a long period of economic growth and relative social tranquility. Economically the S&P 500, which had struggled until 1953 just to get back to where it had been before the Depression, then tripled over the next 10 years. There were dislocations during this time—the Korean War in the early '50s, Sputnik in 1957, the first stirrings of the civil rights movement, a brief recession in 1958—but by and large, at least on the surface, things were pretty quiet.

The tenor of the times was conservative, seeking the comfortable, the secure, and the familiar. It was a time that promoted conformity and shrank from individual expression, which is why the overt sexuality of Elvis and the rebellion of James Dean were at once popular and scandalous.

A Post-War Cohort Marketing Example. The Vermont Country Store, highly successful marketers of nostalgic products difficult to find, uses cohort images and memories to target market segments. To capture the attention of Post-War cohort customers, it peppers its catalog with pictures from the '50s and value-reflective copy along the outside of various pages such as:

"When I was young, I knew kids who were allowed in their living rooms only on special occasions—and usually under adult supervision. Now, instead of a chilly room used only to entertain on holidays, we can really relax in our living rooms."
and
"In high school, buying clothes was easy. The more we dressed according to the conventions of the day, the better. If we'd known then what we know now, we could have looked every bit as good—and been a lot more comfortable. But then, that wasn't the point of being a teenager."

Boomers—I

The Baby Boom is usually defined as the 76 million people born between 1946 and 1964, since this is indeed when the annual birthrate bulged to more than 4 million per year. However there are two boomer cohorts. The first of these are the leading-edge boomers and they are 32,531,000 people strong, 17.4% of the adult population. They were born from 1946 to 1954, and came of age from 1963 to 1972. They are age 46 to 54 today.

Due to their numbers, the baby boomers as a whole have dominated marketing in America since they first appeared on the scene. When they were truly babies, they made Dr. Spock's *Infant and Child Rearing* the second best-selling book in the history of the world, after the Bible. As pre-teens, they dominated the media in shows like *Leave It to Beaver* and in merchandising with fads like Davy Crockett caps and Hula Hoops. As teens they propelled Coke, McDonald's, and Motown into corporate giants, and ensured the success of Clearasil.

The "Boomer I" cohort began coming of age in 1963, the start of a period of profound dislocations that still haunt our society today. It ended shortly after the last soldier died in Vietnam. The Kennedy presidency seemed like the natural extension of continued good times, of economic growth and domestic stability. It represented a liberated and early transfer of power from an older leader to a much younger one.

The Kennedy assassination, followed by that of Martin Luther King and Robert Kennedy, signaled an end to the status quo and galvanized a very large boomer cohort just entering its formative years. Suddenly the leadership (LBJ) was no longer 'theirs,' the war (Vietnam) was not their war, and authority and the establishment which had been the bedrock of earlier cohorts disintegrated in the melee of the 1968 Democratic National Convention in Chicago.

However, the Boomer I cohort continued to experience economic good times. Despite the social turmoil, the economy as a whole, as measured by the S&P 500, continued an upward climb. The Boomer I cohort wanted a lifestyle at least as good as they had experienced as children in the '50s, and with nearly 20 years of steady economic growth as history, they had no reason not to spend whatever they earned or could borrow to achieve it.

The Boomer I cohort still heavily values its individualism (remember, they were and are the "Me Generation,") indulgence of self, stimulation (a reflection of the drug culture they grew up with), and questioning nature. Marketing to this cohort demands attention to providing more information to back up product claims and to calm skeptical concerns. And these boomers prize holding on to their youth as the following example shows.

A Boomer I Cohort Marketing Example. The California Prune Board recommended to its plum producers that they plant many more trees, since large numbers of baby boomers were turning 50 and the 50+ age bracket (indeed, the 65+) was the heaviest consumer of prunes. However, boomers did not relate to prunes; they did not come of age with prunes as part of their consumption lives. Why, then, would they eat prunes in later life? In fact, prunes reflect cohort preferences of their parents—those same parents boomers did not want to trust ("Don't Trust Anyone Over 30").

Research into the chemical composition of prunes, however, found that they naturally stimulate the body's production of testosterone and estrogen… just the ingredients aging boomers desire to hold on to their sexual vitality and sense of youth. Clinical studies to provide advertising claim support for the estrogen and testosterone benefits were being undertaken. This approach could lead to, for example, a radio or television commercial featuring Adam and Eve in the Garden of Eden. Eve requests some fruit for sustenance, since they have a big night ahead populating the earth. She is delighted to receive a platter including one lonely prune (no apples, please). Her comment as she gulps the prune: "Well, this should get us through Asia, at least!"

Boomers II

The trailing-edge boomers were born between 1956 and 1965, came of age from 1973 to 1983, and are age 35 to 45 today. Currently 46,794,000 people are Boomer II's, 26% of the adult population.

The external events that separate the Boomer I from the Boomer II cohort were less dramatic than The Depression or World War II, but were just as real. They were composed of the stop of the Vietnam War (it never really ended—just stopped), Watergate (the final nail in the coffin of institutions and the establishment), and the Arab Oil Embargo that ended the stream of economic gains that had continued largely uninterrupted since 1945.

By 1973, something had changed for a person coming of age in America. While faith in institutions had gone, so had the idealist fervor that made the Boomer I cohort so cause-oriented. Instead, those in the Boomer II cohort exhibited a narcissistic preoccupation with themselves which manifested itself in everything from the self-help movement (*I'm OK—You're OK*, and various young and aging gurus imported from India) to self-deprecation (*Saturday Night Live, Mary Hartman, Mary Hartman*).

The change in economic fortunes had a more profound effect than is commonly realized. Throughout their childhood and as they came of age, the Boomer I cohort members experienced good times; their expectations that these good times would continue were thus reinforced, and the cohort mindset formed at that time can be seen today in a persistent resistance to begin saving for retirement. Things had been good, and they were going to stay good—somehow.

For the Boomer II cohort, the money mindset was much different. The Oil Shock of 1973 sent the economy tumbling: the S&P 500 lost 30% of its value between 1973 and 1975! At the same time, inflation began to resemble that of a banana republic. During this period, the real interest rate (Prime minus the CPI) hit a record low of -4%. In those circumstances, debt as a means of maintaining a lifestyle makes great economic sense. And a cohort with a 'debt imprint' will never lose it. Boomers II are spenders just like the Boomer Is, but for a different reason. It's not because they expect good times, but because they assume they can always get a loan, take out a second mortgage on the house, get another credit card, and never have to "pay the piper."

A Boomer II Cohort Marketing Example. A major finance company is currently aggressively promoting home equity loans with radio advertising directly oriented toward this cohort mindset. The commercial in essence states "Everyone else has a BMW, or a new set of golf clubs, and they're not any better than you are. Even if you don't think you can afford them, you can have them, now—with a home equity loan from XYZ company. And, while you're at it, why not take the Hawaiian vacation, too—you deserve it!" The copy brings on severe anxiety attacks for the World War II and Depression cohorts, but it makes perfect sense to the Boomer IIs.

Generation X

Born 1966–1976, Gen Xers came of age from 1984 to 1994. They are age 24 to 34 today. Currently 41,119,000 people, they represent 21.9% of the adult population.

Much has been written about Generation X, most of it derogatory in tone: "Slackers" (from the movie of that name); "Whiners"; "a generation of aging Bart Simpsons," "armed and possibly dangerous." That seems to be unfair. The generation of F. Scott Fitzgerald was widely characterized as "Lost," and that describes Generation X. This cohort has nothing to hang on to—not the institutions of the Post-War cohort, not the Boomer I's idealism and causes and institutions to resist, not the narcissism of the Boomer IIs. These were the children of divorce and daycare, latch-key kids of the 1980s; no wonder they exhibit so little foundation. The fact that they are searching for anchors can be seen in their seemingly contradictory "retro" behavior—the resurgence of proms, coming-out parties, and fraternities that Boomers rejected.

It can be seen in their political conservatism, which is also motivated by a "What's in it for me?" cynicism that repudiates liberal redistribution tendencies. And they feel alienated, reflected in the violence and brutal sex of the popular culture, and resigned to a world that seems to have little hope of offering them the lifestyles of their parents.

A Generation X Cohort Marketing Example. So how does a marketer reach a cohort with no defining moments? One way is with irreverent, rebellious, self-mocking, and sassy portrayals—which helps explain the popularity of South Park, the Simpsons, and the infamous Married With Children. Commercials like Maybelline's ad for Expert Eyes Shadow with Christy Turlington also exemplifies this sassiness. The ad shows the stunning model with beautifully made-up eyes illuminated by moonlight. A voice-over says: "Was it a strange celestial event… that gave her such bewitching eyes?" Then Turlington, sitting on her living room sofa, laughs and says, "Get over it."

Managerial Implications

Cohort segmentation provides a most intriguing additional method for separating consumer markets. Age has long been a segmentation variable, but this innovative approach shows it is defining moments that shape mindsets and provide the true value of age targeting. While not a key behavior driver for all product categories, cohort segmentation is particularly appropriate for food, music, apparel, automotive, financial and insurance, as well as entertainment products. Product creation and management over its life cycle is clearly ripe for cohort implementation.

Cohort analysis can help in designing communication campaigns. Determining music, movie stars, or other icons that cohorts identified with in their past is an effective selling technique. These tactics work because they rely on nostalgia marketing, that is, tapping deep, pleasurable memories of what seemed simpler, better times. They also work by calling out the target in an implicit way. "This message is for you!" Many companies have already engaged in this tactic as evidenced by the growing number of songs, logos, and actual commercial footage from the past.

Additionally, the changing nature of values across cohorts has important implications for marketers. As new cohorts enter the marketplace, organizations need to keep apprised of their changing value structures. In particular, as the age distribution in the United States changes, so will consumers' wants and needs. A cohort analysis can help track and forecast these wants and needs. In the 1980s, for example, the age segment of 50–65 years was comprised mostly of Depression and World War II cohort consumers. Today, it is made up mostly of the Post-War cohort and in 2010 it will be all Boomers. The demographic age segmentation—age 50 to 65—is the same, but the composition of that segment is constantly changing. It's a moving target.

Final Thought

Cohort segmentation works in the United States. But what about outside of the United States? Would cohorts be the same as here? Our research has found cohort values derived from defining moments indeed do exist abroad. Germany, for example, witnessed no Depression as Hitler's war effort energized the economy. In Brazil, the 1970s found a dictatorship imposing severe censorship, which created the need for personal freedoms in individuals coming of age during that time. In Jordan, the Six-Day War in 1967 dramatically displaced Jordanians from their homeland and they now long for stability in maintaining a place to live. As these examples illustrate, cohort segmentation offers a rich opportunity here… and around the world.

Additional Reading

Meredith, Geoffrey and Charles D. Schewe (1994), "The Power of Cohorts," *American Demographics*, December, 22–31.

Rentz, Joseph O. and Fred D. Reynolds (1991), "Forecasting the Effects of an Aging Population on Product Consumption: An Age-Period-Cohort Framework," *Journal of Marketing Research*, 28, (3), 355–60.

——, ——, and Roy G. Stout (1983), "Analyzing Changing Consumption Patterns With Cohort Analysis," *Journal of Marketing Research*, 20, 12–20.

Russell, Cheryl (1993), *The Master Trend: How the Baby Boom Generation Is Remaking America*, Plenum, New York.

Schewe, Charles D. and Stephanie M. Noble (forthcoming), "Market Segmentation by Cohorts: The Value and Validity of Cohorts in America and Abroad," *Journal of Marketing Management* (Scotland).

Schuman, Howard and Jacqueline Scott (1989). "Generations and Collective Memories," *American Sociological Review*, 54, (3), 359–381.

Smith, J. Walker and Ann Clurman (1997), *Rocking the Ages*, Harper Business, New York.

Strauss, William and Neil Howe (1997), *The Fourth Turning*, Broadway Books, New York.

About the Authors

Charles D. Schewe is professor of marketing at the University of Massachusetts and a principal in Lifestage Matrix Marketing. Focusing on the marketing implications of the aging process, Schewe has advised such companies as Coca-Cola, Kellogg's, Kraft General Foods, Time-Life, Lucky Stores, Grand Metropolitan, and K-Mart. He may be reached at schewe@mktg.umass.edu.

Geoffrey E. Meredith is president of Lifestage Matrix Marketing, located in Lafayette, Calif. Formerly a senior vice president at Olgivy & Mather, Ketchum Communications, and Hal Riney and Partners, he also spent two years with Age Wave (see V1,N3 MM). He may be reached at Lifestage@aol.com.

Stephanie M. Noble is a doctoral candidate at the University of Massachusetts. She may be reached at smevans@som.umass.edu.

From *Marketing Management*, Fall 2000, Vol. 9, No. 3, pp. 48-53. © 2000 by the American Marketing Association. Reprinted by permission.

UNIT 3

Developing and Implementing Marketing Strategies

Unit Selections

Key Points to Consider

- Most ethical questions seem to arise in regard to the promotional component of the marketing mix. How fair is the general public's criticism of some forms of personal selling and advertising? Give some examples.

- What role, if any, do you think the quality of a product plays in making a business competitive in consumer markets? What role does price play? Would you rather market a higher-priced, better-quality product or one that was the lowest priced? Why?

- What do you envision will be the major problems or challenges retailers will face in the next decade? Explain.

- Given the rapidly increasing costs of personal selling, what role do you think it will play as a strategy in the marketing mix in the future? What other promotion strategies will play increased or decreased roles in the next decade?

DUSHKIN ONLINE **Links: www.dushkin.com/online/**
These sites are annotated in the World Wide Web pages.

American Marketing Association Homepage
http://www.marketingpower.com

Consumer Buying Behavior
http://www.courses.psu.edu/mktg/mktg220_rso3/sls_cons.htm

Product Branding, Packaging, and Pricing
http://www.fooddude.com/branding.html

"**M**arketing management objectives," the late Wroe Alderson once wrote, "are very simple in essence. The firm wants to expand its volume of sales, or it wants to handle the volume it has more efficiently." Although the essential objectives of marketing might be stated this simply, the development and implementation of strategies to accomplish them is considerably more complex. Many of these complexities are due to changes in the environment within which managers must operate. Strategies that fail to heed the social, political, and economic forces of society have little chance of success over the long run. The lead article in this section provides helpful insight suggesting a framework for developing a comprehensive marketing plan.

The selections in this unit provide a wide-ranging discussion of how marketing professionals and U.S. companies interpret and employ various marketing strategies today. The readings also include specific examples from industry to illustrate their points. The articles are grouped in four sections, each dealing with one of the main strategy areas: product, price, distribution (place), and promotion. Since each selection discusses more than one of these areas, it is important that you read them broadly. For example, many of the articles covered in the distribution section discuss important aspects of personal selling and advertising.

Product Strategy. The essence of the marketing concept is to begin with what consumers want and need. After determining a need, an enterprise must respond by providing the product or service demanded. Successful marketing managers recognize the need for continuous product improvement and/or new product introduction.

The articles in this subsection focus on various facets of product strategy. The first article describes how IDEO is changing the way companies innovate. The second article provides some thoughtful ideas about making and marketing remarkable products. The last article in this subsection describes that from lipstick to cars, a growing array of products can be made to your own taste.

Pricing Strategy. Few elements of the total strategy of the "marketing mix" demand so much managerial and social attention as pricing. There is a good deal of public misunderstanding about the ability of marketing managers to control prices and even greater misunderstanding about how pricing policies are determined. New products present especially difficult problems in terms of both costs and pricing. The costs for developing a new product are usually very high, and if a product is truly new, it cannot be priced competitively, for it has no competitors.

"Kamikaze Pricing" scrutinizes the tremendous pricing pressures that companies face and suggest some ways to make better pricing decisions. "Mind Your Pricing Cues" covers some of the most common pricing cues retailers use and evaluates their effectiveness. In "Which Price Is Right?" the authors discuss how business is at the start of a new era of pricing.

Distribution Strategy. For many enterprises, the largest marketing costs result from closing the gap in space and time between producer and consumer. In no other area of marketing is efficiency so eagerly sought after. Physical distribution seems to be the one area where significant cost savings can be achieved. The costs of physical distribution are tied closely with decisions made about the number, the size, and the diversity of marketing intermediaries between producer and consumer.

Promotion Strategy. The basic objectives of promotion are to inform, persuade, or remind the consumer to buy a firm's product or pay for the firm's service. Advertising is the most obvious promotional activity. However, in total dollars spent and in cost per person reached, advertising takes second place to personal selling. Sales promotion supports either personal selling and advertising, or both. Such media as point-of-purchase displays, catalogs, and direct mail place the sales promotion specialist closer to the advertising agency than to the salesperson.

The articles in this final unit subsection cover such topics as effective advertising campaigns, the significance of a unified global advertisement being adapted to a local market, and the Web's vital role in marketing promotions.

THE VERY MODEL OF A
MODERN MARKETING PLAN

SUCCESSFUL COMPANIES ARE REWRITING THEIR STRATEGIES TO REFLECT CUSTOMER INPUT AND INTERNAL COORDINATION

SHELLY REESE

IT'S 1996. DO YOU KNOW WHERE YOUR MARKETING PLAN IS? *In a world where competitors can observe and rapidly imitate each other's advancements in product development, pricing, packaging, and distribution, communication is more important than ever as a way of differentiating your business from those of your competitors.*

The most successful companies are the ones that understand that, and are revamping their marketing plans to emphasize two points:

1. Marketing is a dialog between customer and supplier.

2. Companies have to prove they're listening to their customers by acting on their input.

WHAT IS A MARKETING PLAN?

At its most basic level, a marketing plan defines a business's niche, summarizes its objectives, and presents its strategies for attaining and monitoring those goals. It's a road map for getting from point A to point B.

But road maps need constant updating to reflect the addition of new routes. Likewise, in a decade in which technology, international relations, and the competitive landscape are constantly changing, the concept of a static marketing plan has to be reassessed.

Two of the hottest buzz words for the 1990s are "interactive" and "integrated." A successful marketing plan has to be both.

"Interactive" means your marketing plan should be a conversation between your business and your customers by acting on their input. It's your chance to tell customers about your business and to listen and act on their responses.

"Integrated" means the message in your marketing is consistently reinforced by every department within your company. Marketing is as much a function of the finance and manufacturing divisions as it is the advertising and public relations departments.

Integrated also means each time a company reaches out to its customers through an advertisement, direct mailing, or promotion, it is sending the same message and encouraging customers to learn more about the product.

WHY IS IT IMPORTANT?

The interaction between a company and its customers is a relationship. Relationships can't be reproduced. They can, however, be replaced. That's where a good marketing plan comes into play.

Think of your business as a suitor, your customers as the object of your affection, and your competitors as rivals. A marketing plan is your strategy for wooing customers. It's based on listening and reacting to what they say.

Because customers' priorities are constantly changing, a marketing plan should change with them. For years, conventional wisdom was 'prepare a five year marketing plan and review it every year.' But change happens a lot faster than it did 20 or even 10 years ago.

For that reason, Bob Dawson of The Business Group, a consulting firm in Freemont, California, recommends that his clients prepare a three year plan and review it every quarter. Frequent reviews enable companies to identify potential problems and opportunities before their competition, he explains.

"Preventative maintenance for your company is as important as putting oil in your car," Dawson says. "You don't wait a whole year to do it. You can't change history but you can anticipate what's going to happen."

ESSENTIAL COMPONENTS

Most marketing plans consist of three sections. The first section should identify the organization's goals. The second section should establish a method for attaining them. The third section focuses on creating a system for implementing the strategy.

Although some plans identify as many as six or eight goals, many experts suggest a company whittle its list to one or two key objectives and focus on them.

"One of the toughest things is sticking to one message," observes Mark Bilfield, account director for integrated marketing of Nissan and Infiniti cars at TBWA Chiat/Day in Los Angeles, which handles national advertising, direct marketing, public relations, and promotions for the automaker. Bilfield argues that a focused, consistent message is easier to communicate to the market place and to different disciplines within the corporation than a broad, encompassing one. Therefore, he advises, "unless there is something drastically wrong with the idea, stick with it."

SECTION I: GOALS

The goals component of your plan is the most fundamental. Consider it a kind of thinking out loud: Why are you writing this plan? What do you want to accomplish? What do you want to achieve in the next quarter? The next year? The next three years?

Like taping your New Year's resolution to the refrigerator, the goals section is a constant reminder of what you want to achieve. The key difference between a New Year's resolution and your marketing goals, however, is you can't achieve the latter alone.

To achieve your marketing goals you've got to convince your customers to behave in a certain way. If you're a soft drink manufacturer you may want them to try your company's latest wild berry flavor. If you're a new bank in town, you need to familiarize people with your name and convince them to give your institution a try. Or perhaps you're a family-owned retailer who needs to remind customers of the importance of reliability and a proven track record in the face of new competition.

The goals in each of these cases differ with the audiences. The soft drink manufacturer is asking an existing customer to try something new; the bank is trying to attract new customers; the retailer wants to retain existing customers.

Each company wants to influence its customers' behavior. The company that is most likely to succeed is the one that understands its customers the best.

There's no substitute for knowledge. You need to understand the demographic and psychographic makeup of the customers you are trying to reach, as well as the best methods for getting their attention.

Do your research. Learn as much as possible about your audience. Trade associations, trade journals and government statistics and surveys are excellent resources, but chances are you have a lot of data within your own business that you haven't tapped. Look at what you know about your customer already and find ways to bolster that information. Companies should constantly be asking clients what they want and how they would use a new product.

"If you're not asking people that use your end product, then everything you're doing is an assumption," argues Dawson.

In addition, firms should ask customers how they perceive the products and services they receive. Too often, companies have an image of themselves that they broadcast but fail to live up to. That frustrates consumers and makes them feel deceived.

Companies that claim to offer superior service often appear to renege on their promises because their definition of 'service' doesn't mesh with their customers', says Bilfield.

"Airlines and banks are prime offenders," says Bilfield. "They tout service, and when the customers go into the airport or the bank, they have to wait in long lines."

The problem often lies in the company's assumptions about what customers really want. While an airline may feel it is living up to its claim of superior service because it distributes warm towels and mints after a meal, a business traveler will probably place a higher value on its competitor's on-time record and policy for returning lost luggage.

SECTION II: THE STRATEGY

Unfortunately, after taking the time and conducting the research to determine who their audience is and what their message should be, companies often fail by zooming ahead with a plan. An attitude of, "OK, we know who we're after and we know what we want to say, so let's go!" seems to take over.

More often than not, that gung-ho way of thinking leads to disaster because companies have skipped a critical step: they haven't established and communicated an internal strategy for attaining their goals. They want to take their message to the public without pausing to get feedback from inside the company.

For a marketing plan to work, everyone within the company must understand the company's message and work cooperatively to establish a method for taking that message to the public.

For example, if you decide the goal of your plan is to promote the superior service your company offers, you'd better make sure all aspects of your business are on board. Your manufacturing process should meet the highest standards. Your financial department should develop credit and leasing programs that make it easier for customers to use

GETTING STARTED

A NINE-STEP PLAN THAT WILL MAKE THE DIFFERENCE BETWEEN WRITING A USEFUL PLAN AND A DOCUMENT THAT GATHERS DUST ON A SHELF

by Carole R. Hedden and the *Marketing Tools* editorial staff

In his 1986 book, *The Goal*, Eliyahu M. Goldratt writes that most of us forget the one true goal of our business. It's not to deliver products on time. It isn't even to manufacture the best widget in the world. The goal is to make money.

In the past, making money depended on selling a product or service. Today, that's changed as customers are, at times, willing to pay for what we stand for: better service, better support, more innovation, more partnership in developing new products.

This section of this article assumes that you believe a plan is needed, and that this plan should weave together your desires with those of your customers. We've reviewed a number of marketing plans and come up with a nine-step model. It is perhaps more than what your organization needs today, but none of the steps are unimportant.

Our model combines some of the basics of a conventional plan with some new threads that we believe will push your plan over the edge, from being satisfactory to being necessary. These include:

• Using and improving the former domain of public relations, image, as a marketing tool.
• Integrating all the business functions that touch your customers into a single, customer-focused strategic marketing plan.
• Borrowing from Total Quality theories to establish performance measures beyond the financial report to help you note customer trends.
• Making sure that the people needed to deliver your marketing objectives are part of your plan.
• "Selling" your plan to the people whose support is essential to its success.

Taking the Plan Off the Shelf

First, let's look at the model itself. Remember that one of the primary criticisms of any plan is that it becomes a binder on a shelf, never to be seen again until budget time next year. Planning should be an iterative process, feeding off itself and used to guide and measure.

Whether you're asked to create a marketing plan or write the marketing section of the strategic plan for your business, your document is going to include what the business is trying to achieve, a careful analysis of your market, the products and services you offer to that market, and how you will market and sell products or services to your customer.

1. Describe the Business

You are probably in one of two situations: either you need to write a description of your business or you can rely on an existing document found in your annual report, the strategic plan, or a capabilities brochure. The description should include, at minimum:

• Your company's purpose;
• Who you deliver products or services to; and
• What you deliver to those customers.

Too often, such descriptions omit a discussion about what you want your business to stand for—your image.

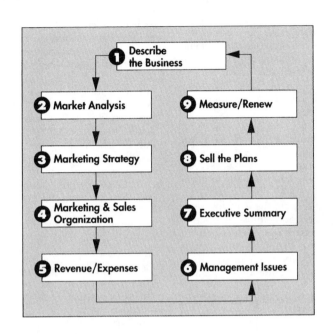

This is increasingly important as customers report they are looking for more than the product or service; they're in search of a partner. The only way to address image is to know who you want to be, who your customers think you are, and how you can bridge the gap between the two.

Part of defining your image is knowing where you are strong and where you are weak. For instance, if your current yield rate is 99.997 percent and customers rate you as the preferred supplier, then you might identify operations as a key to your company's image. Most companies tend to be their own worst critic, so start by listing all your strengths. Then identify weaknesses or the threats you face, either due to your own limitations or from the increased competency of a competitor.

The description also includes what your business delivers to its owners, be they shareholders, private owners, or employees. Usually this is stated in financial terms: revenue, return on investment or equity, economic value added, cash generated, operating margin or earnings per share. The other measures your organization uses to monitor its performance may be of interest to outsiders, but save them for the measurement section of your plan.

The result of all this describing and listing is that you should have a fairly good idea of where you are and where you want to be, which naturally leads to objectives for the coming 6, 12, or 18 months, if not longer.

2. Analyze the Market

This is the section you probably believe you own. *Marketing Tools* challenges you to look at this as a section jointly owned by most everyone working with you. In a smaller company, the lead managers may own various pieces of this section. In a

(continued)

larger organization, you may need to pull in the ideas and data available from other departments, such as logistics, competitor intelligence, research and development, and the function responsible for quality control or quality assurance. All have two things in common: delivering value to customers, and beating the competition.

Together, you can thoroughly cover the following areas:

•**Your target markets**. What markets do you currently compete in? What do you know about them in terms of potential, dollars available, and your share of the market? Something frequently prepared for products is a life cycle chart; you might want to do the same for your market. Is it embryonic, developing, mature or in decline? Are there new markets to exploit?

•**Customer Knowledge**. Your colleagues in Quality, Distribution, Engineering, or other organizations can be helpful in finding what you need. *The customer's objectives.* What threats do your customers face? What goals does the customer have? Work with your customer to define these so you can become a partner instead of a variable component. *How is the customer addressing her or his markets?* Do you know as much about your customer's position as you know about your own? If not, find out. *How big is each customer, really?* You may find you're spending more time on a less important customer than on the customers who can break you. Is your customer growing or in decline? What plans does the customer have to expand or acquire growth? What innovations are in development? *What does your customer value?* Price, product quality,

service, innovation, delivery? The better you know what's driving your customer's purchasing decision, the better you'll be able to respond.

•**Clearly identify the alternatives your customer** has. As one customer told employees at a major supplier, "While you've been figuring out how to get by, we've been figuring out how to get by without you." Is backward integration—a situation in which the customer develops the capability in-house—possible? Is there an abundance of other suppliers? What is your business doing to avoid having your customers looking for alternatives?

•**Know your competition**. Your competitors are the obvious alternative for your customer, and thus represent your biggest threat. You can find what you need to know about your competitors through newspaper reports, public records, at trade shows, and from your customers: the size of expansions, the strengths that competitor has, its latest innovations. Do you know how your competition approaches your customers?

•**Describe the Environment**. What changes have occurred in the last 18 months? In the past year? What could change in the near future and over a longer period of time? This should include any kinds of laws or regulations that might affect you, the entry or deletion of competitors, and shifts in technology. Also, keep in mind that internal change does affect your customers. For instance, is a key leader in your business planning to retire? If so, decision making, operations or management style may change—and your customer may have obvious concerns. You can add some depth to

this section, too, by portraying several different scenarios:

•What happens if we do nothing beyond last year?
•What happens if we capitalize on our strengths?
•What might happen if our image slips?
•What happens if we do less this year than last?

3. The Marketing Strategy

The marketing strategy consists of what you offer customers and the price you charge. Start by providing a complete description of each product or service and what it provides to your customers. Life cycle, again, is an important part of this. Is your technology or product developing, mature or in decline? Depending on how your company is organized, a variety of people are responsible for this information, right down to whoever is figuring out how to package the product and how it will be delivered. Find out who needs to be included and make sure their knowledge is used.

The marketing strategy is driven by everything you've done up to this point. Strategies define the approaches you will use to market the company. For instance, if you are competing on the basis of service and support rather than price, your strategy may consist of emphasizing relationships. You will then develop tactics that support that strategy: market the company vs. the product; increase sales per client; assure customer responsiveness. Now, what action or programs will you use to make sure that happens?

Note: strategy leads. No program, regardless of how good it is, should make the

cut if it doesn't link to your business strategies and your customer.

The messages you must craft to support the strategies often are overlooked. Messages are the consistent themes you want your customer to know, to remember, to feel when he or she hears, reads, or views anything about your company or products. The method by which you deliver your messages comes under the heading of actions or programs.

Finally, you need to determine how you'll measure your own success, beyond meeting the sales forecast. How will you know if your image takes a beating? How will you know whether the customer is satisfied, or has just given up complaining? If you don't know, you'll be caught reacting to events, instead of planning for them.

Remember, your customer's measure of your success may be quite different from what you may think. Your proposed measures must be defined by what your customer values, and they have to be quantifiable. You may be surprised at how willing the customer is to cooperate with you in completing surveys, participating in third-party interviews, or taking part in a full-scale analysis of your company as a supplier. Use caution in assuming that winning awards means you have a measurable indicator. Your measures should be stated in terms of strategies, not plaques or trophies.

4. The Marketing and Sales Organization

The most frequently overlooked element in business is something we usually relegate

(continued)

to the Personnel or Human Resources Office—people. They're what makes everything possible. Include them. Begin with a chart that shows the organization for both Marketing and Sales. You may wish to indicate any interdependent relationships that exist (for instance, with Quality).

Note which of the roles are critical, particularly in terms of customer contact. Just as important, include positions, capabilities, and numbers of people needed in the future. How will you gain these skills without impacting your cost per sale? Again, it's time to be creative and provide options.

5. Revenue and Expense

In this section, you're going to project the revenue your plan will produce. This is usually calculated by evaluating the value of your market(s) and determining the dollar value of your share of that market. You need to factor in any changes you believe will occur, and you'll need to identify the sources of revenue, by product or service. Use text to tell the story; use graphs to show the story.

After you've noted where the money is coming from, explain what money you need to deliver the projected return. This will include staff wages and benefits for your organization, as well as the cost for specific programs you plan to implement.

During this era of budget cuts, do yourself a favor by prioritizing these programs. For instance, if one of your key strategies is to expand to a new market via new technologies, products, or services,

you will need to allocate appropriate dollars. What is the payback on the investment in marketing, and when will revenues fully pay back the investment? Also, provide an explanation of programs that will be deleted should a cut in funding be required. Again, combine text and spreadsheets to tell and to show.

6. Management Issues

This section represents your chance to let management know what keeps you awake at night. What might or could go wrong? What are the problems your company faces in customer relations? Are there technology needs that are going unattended? Again, this can be a collaborative effort that identifies your concerns. In addition, you may want to identify long-term issues, as well as those that are of immediate significance.

To keep this section as objective as possible, list the concerns and the business strategy or strategies they affect. What are the short-term and long-term risks? For instance, it is here that you might want to go into further detail about a customer's actions that look like the beginnings of backward integration.

7. Executive Summary

Since most senior leaders want a quick-look reference, it's best to include a one-page Executive Summary that covers these points:

- Your organization's objectives
- Budget requirements
- Revenue projections
- Critical management issues

When you're publishing the final plan document, you'll want the executive summary to be Page One.

8. Sell the Plan

This is one of the steps that often is overlooked. Selling your plan is as important as writing it. Otherwise, no one owns it, except you. The idea is to turn it into a rallying point that helps your company move forward. And to do that, you need to turn as many people as possible into ambassadors for your marketing efforts.

First, set up a time to present the plan to everyone who helped you with information and data. Make sure that they feel some sense of ownership, but that they also see how their piece ties into the whole. This is one of those instances where you need to say your plan, show your plan, discuss your plan. Only after all three steps are completed will they *hear* the plan.

After you've shared the information across the organization, reserve some time on the executive calendar. Have a couple of leaders review the plan first, giving you feedback on the parts where they have particular expertise. Then, present the plan at a staff meeting.

Is It Working?

You may think your job is finished. It's not. You need to convey the key parts of this plan to coworkers throughout the business. They need to know what the business is trying to achieve. Their livelihood, not just that of the owners, is at stake. From their phone-answering technique to the way they process an

order, every step has meaning to the customer.

9. Measure/Renew

Once you've presented your plan and people understand it, you have to continuously work the plan and share information about it. The best way to help people see trends and respond appropriately is to have meaningful measures. In the language of Total Quality, these are the Key Result Indicators—the things that have importance to your customers and that are signals to your performance.

For instance, measure your ability to deliver on a customer request; the amount of time it takes to respond to a customer inquiry; your productivity per employee; cash flow; cycle time; yield rates. The idea is to identify a way to measure those things that are critical to you and to your customer.

Review those measurements. Share the information with the entire business and begin the process all over again. Seek new ideas and input to improve your performance. Go after more data and facts. And then renew your plan and share it with everyone—all over again.

It's an extensive process, but it's one that spreads the word—and spreads the ownership. It's the step that ensures that your plan will be constantly in use, and constantly at work for your business.

Carole Hedden is a writer and communication/planning consultant living in Elmira, New York.

your product. Finally, your customer relations personnel should be trained to respond to problems quickly and efficiently, and to use the contact as an opportunity to find out more about what customers want.

"I'm always amazed when I go into the shipping department of some company and say, 'What is your mission? What's the message you want to give to your end user?' and they say, 'I don't know. I just know I've got to get these shipments out on time,'" says Dawson.

Because the success of integrated marketing depends on a consistent, cohesive message, employees throughout the company need to understand the firm's marketing goals and their role in helping to fulfill them.

"It's very important to bring employees in on the process," says James Lowry, chairman of the marketing department at Ball State University. "Employees today are better than any we've had before. They want to know what's going on in the organization. They don't want to be left out."

HELP IS ON THE WAY

THREE SOFTWARE PACKAGES THAT WILL HELP YOU GET STARTED

Writing a marketing plan may be daunting, but there is a variety of software tools out there to help you get started. Found in electronics and book stores, the tools are in many ways like a Marketing 101 textbook. The difference lies in how they help.

Software tools have a distinct advantage: They actually force you to write, and that's the toughest part of any marketing plan. Sometimes called "MBA In a Box," these systems guide you through a planning process. Some even provide wording that you can copy into your own document and edit to fit your own business. Presto! A boiler plate plan! Others provide a system of interviewing and questioning that creates a custom plan for your operation. The more complex tools demand an integrated approach to planning, one that brings together the full force of your organization, not just Sales or Advertising.

1. Crush

Crush, a modestly named new product from a modestly named new company, HOT, takes a multimedia approach. (HOT stands for Hands-On Technology; *Crush* apparently stands for *Crushing the Competition*)

Just introduced a few months ago, *Crush* is a multimedia application for Macintosh or Windows PCs. It features the competitive analysis methods of Flegis McKenna, marketing guru to Apple, Intel and Genentech; and it features Mr. McKenna himself as your mentor, offering guidance via on-screen video. As you work through each section of a complete market analysis, McKenna provides germane comments; in addition, you can see video case studies of

marketing success stories like Intuit software.

Crush provides worksheets and guidance for analyzing your products, customers, market trends and competitors, and helps you generate an action plan. The "mentor" approach makes it a useful

I liked the pyramid for a simple reason: It asks you to define messages for your business as part of your tactics. Without a message, it's easy to jump around, reacting to the marketplace instead of anticipating, leaving customers wondering what really is

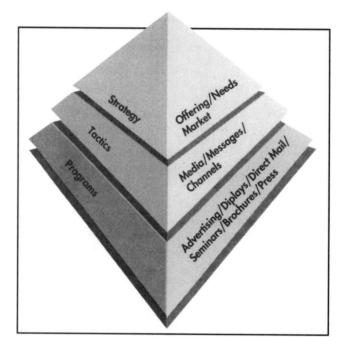

Pyramid Power: Plan Write's pyramid approach asks the user to define the messages for a business as part of the tactics.

tool for self-education; as you work through the examples and develop your company's marketing plan, you build your own expertise.

2. Marketing Plan Pro

Palo Alto's *Marketing Plan Pro* is a basic guide, useful for smaller businesses or ones in which the company leader wears a number of different hats, including marketing. It includes the standard spreadsheet capability, as well as the ability to chart numerical data. *Marketing Plan Pro* uses a pyramid process.

significant about your company or your product.

The step-by-step process is simple, and a sample plan shows how all the information works together. The customer-focus aspect of the plan seemed a little weak, demanding only sales potential and buying capacity of the customers. Targeted marketing is increasingly important, and the user may want to really expand how this section is used beyond what the software requires.

The package displays, at a glance, your strategy, the tactics you develop for each

strategy, and the action plan or programs you choose to support the strategy. That could help when you're trying to prioritize creative ideas, eliminating those that really don't deliver what the strategy demands. Within each of three columns, you can click on a word and get help. Click on the heading program: a list of sample actions is displayed. They may not be what you're looking for, but if this is your first plan, they're lifesavers.

I also really liked *Marketing Plan Pro's* user's manual. It not only explains how the software works with your computer, it helps with business terms and provides a guide to planning, walking you through step-by-step.

3. Plan Write

Plan Write, created by Business Resource Software, Inc., is exponentially more powerful than *Marketing Plan Pro. Plan Write* brings together the breadth of the business, integrating information as far flung as distribution systems and image. And this software places your marketing strategy within the broader context of a business plan, the approach that tends to prove most effective.

As with *Marketing Plan Pro, Plan Write* provides a sample plan. The approach is traditional, incorporating a look at the business environment, the competition, the product or service mix you are offering, the way you will tell customers about that mix, pricing, delivery, and support.

Among the sections that were particularly strong was one on customer alternatives and people planning. Under the heading of customer alternatives, you're required to

(continued)

incorporate competitive information with customer information. If you don't meet the customer's needs, where could he or she go? Most often we look only at the competition, without trying to imagine how the customer is thinking. This exercise is particularly valuable to the company who leads the market.

The people part of planning too often is dumped on the personnel guy instead of being seen as a critical component of your organization's capabilities. *Plan Write* requires that you include how marketing is being handled, and how sales will be accomplished. In addition, it pushes you to define what skills will be needed in the future and where the gaps are between today and the future. People, in this plan, are viewed as a strategic component.

Plan Write offers a fully integrated spreadsheet that can import from or export to most of the popular spreadsheet programs you may already be using. Another neat feature allows you to enter numerical data and select from among 14 different graphing styles to display your information. You just click on the style you want to view, and the data is reconfigured.

Probably the biggest danger in dealing with software packages such as *Marketing Plan Pro* and *Plan Write* is to think the software is the answer. It's merely a guide.

—*Carole Hedden*

Employees are ambassadors for your company. Every time they interact with a customer or vendor, they're marketing your company. The more knowledgeable and helpful they are, the better they reflect on your firm.

At Nordstrom, a Seattle-based retailer, sales associates are empowered to use their best judgment in all situations to make a customer happy.

"We think our sales associates are the best marketing department," said spokeswoman Amy Jones. "We think word of mouth is the best advertising you can have." As a result, although Nordstrom has stores in only 15 states, it has forged a national reputation.

If companies regard marketing as the exclusive province of the marketing department, they're destined to fail.

"Accounting and sales and other departments have to work together hand in hand," says Dawson. "If they don't, you're going to have a problem in the end."

For example, in devising an integrated marketing campaign for the Nissan 200SX, Chiat/Day marketers worked in strategic business units that included a variety of disciplines such as engineers, representatives from the parts and service department, and creative people. By taking a broad view of the business and building inter-related activities to support its goals, Chiat/Day was able to create a seamless campaign for the 200SX that weaves advertising, in-store displays, and direct marketing together seamlessly.

"When everybody understands what the mission is, it's easier," asserts Bilfield. "It's easier to go upstream in the same direction than to go in different directions."

After bringing the different disciplines within your company on board, you're ready to design the external marketing program needed to support your goals. Again, the principle of integrated marketing comes into play: The message should be focused and consistent, and each step of the process should bring the consumer one step closer to buying your product.

In the case of Chiat/Day's campaign for the Nissan 200SX, the company used the same theme, graphics, type faces, and message to broadcast a consistent statement.

Introduced about the same time as the latest Batman movie, the campaign incorporates music and graphics from the television series. Magazine ads include an 800 number

potential customers can call if they want to receive an information kit. Kits are personalized and include the name of a local Nissan dealer, a certificate for a test drive, and a voucher entitling test drivers to a free gift.

By linking each step of the process, Chiat/Day can chart the number of calls, test drives, and sales a particular ad elicits. Like a good one-two punch, the direct marketing picks up where the national advertising leaves off, leveraging the broad exposure and targeting it at the most likely buyers.

While the elaborate 200SX campaign may seem foolproof, a failure to integrate the process at any step along the way could result in a lost sale.

For example, if a potential client were to test drive the car and encounter a dealer who knew nothing about the free gift accompanying the test drive, the customer would feel justifiably annoyed. Conversely, a well-informed sales associate who can explain the gift will be mailed to the test driver in a few weeks will engender a positive response.

SECTION III EXECUTION

The final component of an integrated marketing plan is the implementation phase. This is where the budget comes in.

How much you'll need to spend depends on your goals. If a company wants to expand its market share or promote its products in a new region, it will probably have to spend more than it would to maintain its position in an existing market.

Again, you'll need to create a system for keeping your employees informed. You might consider adding an element to your company newsletter that features people from different departments talking about the marketing problems they encounter and how they overcome them. Or you might schedule a regular meeting for department heads to discuss marketing ideas so they can report back to their employees with news from around the company.

Finally, you'll need to devise a system for monitoring your marketing program. A database, similar to the one created from calls to the 200SX's 800 number, can be an invaluable tool for determining if your message is being well received.

It's important to establish time frames for achieving your goals early in the process. If you want to increase your market share, for instance, you should determine the rate at which you intend to add new customers. Failing to achieve that rate could signal a flaw in your plan or its execution, or an unrealistic goal.

"Remember, integrated marketing is a long-range way of thinking," warns Dawson. "Results are not going to be immediate."

Like any investment, marketing requires patience, perseverance, and commitment if it is to bear fruit. While not all companies are forward thinking enough to understand the manifold gains of integrated marketing, the ones that don't embrace it will ultimately pay a tremendous price.

MORE INFO

Software for writing marketing plans:

Crush, Hands-On Technology; for more information, call (800) 772-2580 ext. 14 or (415) 579-7755; e-mail info@HOT.sf.ca.us; or visit the Web site at http://www. HOT.sf.ca.us.

Marketing Plan Pro, Palo Alto Software: for more information, call (800) 229-7526 or (503) 683-6162.
Plan Write for Marketing, Business Resource Software, Inc.: for more information, call (800) 423-1228 or (512) 251-7541.

Books about marketing plans:

Twelve Simple Steps to a Winning Marketing Plan, Geraldine A. Larkin (1992, Probus Publishing Co.)*

Preparing the Marketing Plan, by David Parmerlee (1993, NTC Business Books)*

Your Marketing Plan: A Workbook for Effective Business Promotion (Second Edition), by Chris Pryor (1995, Oregon Small Business Development Center Network)*

Your Business Plan: A Workbook for Owners of Small Businesses, by Dennis J. Sargent, Maynard N. Chambers, and Chris Pryor (1995, Oregon Small Business Development Center Network)*

Recommended reading:

Managing for Results, Peter Drucker

The One to One Future: Building Relationships One Customer at a Time, by Don Peppers and Martha Rogers, Ph.D. (1993, Currency/Doubleday)*

"Real World Results," by Don Schultz (*Marketing Tools* magazine, April/May 1994)*

* Available through American Demographics; call (800) 828-1133

Shelly Reese is a freelance writer based in Cincinnati.

Reprinted with permission from *Marketing Tools*, January/February 1996, pp. 56-65. © 1996 by American Demographics, a Primedia Company.

THE POWER OF DESIGN

IDEO redefined good design by creating experiences, not just products. Now it's changing the way companies innovate

By Bruce Nussbaum

KAISER PERMANENTE, THE LARGEST HEALTH MAINTENANCE organization in the U.S., was developing a long-range growth plan in 2003 that would attract more patients and cut costs. Kaiser has hundreds of medical offices and hospitals and thought it might have to replace many of them with expensive next-generation buildings. It hired IDEO, the Palo Alto (Calif.) design firm, for help. Kaiser execs didn't know it then, but they were about to go on a fascinating journey of self-discovery. That's because of IDEO's novel approach. For starters, Kaiser nurses, doctors, and facilities managers teamed up with IDEO's social scientists, designers, architects, and engineers and observed patients as they made their way through their medical facilities. At times, they played the role of patient themselves.

Together they came up with some surprising insights. IDEO's architects revealed that patients and family often became annoyed well before seeing a doctor because checking in was a nightmare and waiting rooms were uncomfortable. They also showed that Kaiser's doctors and medical assistants sat too far apart. IDEO's cognitive psychologists pointed out that people, especially the young, the old, and immigrants, visit doctors with a parent or friend, but that second person is often not allowed to stay with the patient, leaving the afflicted alienated and anxious. IDEO's sociologists explained that patients hated Kaiser's examination rooms because they often had to wait alone for up to 20 minutes half-naked, with nothing to do, surrounded by threatening needles. IDEO and Kaiser concluded that the patient experience can be awful even when people leave treated and cured.

What to do? After just seven weeks with IDEO, Kaiser realized its long-range growth plan didn't require building lots of expensive new facilities. What it needed was to overhaul the patient experience. Kaiser learned from IDEO that seeking medical care is much like shopping—it is a social experience shared with others. So it needed to offer more comfortable waiting rooms and a lobby with clear instructions on where to go; larger exam rooms, with space for three or more people and curtains for privacy, to make patients comfortable; and special corridors for medical staffers to meet and increase their efficiency. "IDEO showed us that we are designing human experiences, not buildings," says Adam D. Nemer, medical operations services manager at Kaiser. "Its recommendations do not require big capital expenditures." With corporations increasingly desperate to get in touch with their customers, IDEO's services are in growing demand. As the economy shifts from the economics of scale to the economics of choice and as mass markets fragment and brand loyalty disappears, it's more important than ever for corporations to improve the "consumer experience." Yet after decades of market research and focus groups, corporations realize that they still don't really know their consumers—or how best to connect with them.

Cool and Fast

ENTER IDEO. THE 350-PERSON DESIGN firm has offices not just in Palo Alto but also in San Francisco, Chicago, Boston, London, and Munich. Office-furniture maker Steelcase Inc. owns a majority stake in the firm, which operates as an independent unit. By design industry standards, IDEO is huge, though its $62 million in revenues in 2003 are puny by most corporate measures. But IDEO's impact on the corporate world is far greater than the sum of its sales. It has a client list that spans the globe, including Hewlett-Packard, AT&T Wireless Services, Nestlé, Vodaphone, Samsung, NASA, and the BBC. More than half of the firm's revenue comes from European and Asian clients or work done overseas by U.S. corporations.

IDEO began in 1991 as a merger between David Kelley Design, which created Apple Computer Inc.'s first mouse in 1982, and ID Two, which designed the first laptop computer in the same year. The Grid laptop is in the Museum of Modern Art in New York. Kelley went to Stanford University School of Engineering in the

This Is the **IDEO** Way

Five steps in the process of designing a better consumer experience

1. OBSERVATION

IDEO's cognitive psychologists, anthropologist, and sociologists team up with corporate clients to understand the consumer experience. Some of IDEO's techniques:

SHADOWING Observing people using products, shopping, going to hospitals, taking the train, using their cells phones.

BEHAVIORAL MAPPING Photographing people within a space, such as a hospital waiting room, over two or three days.

CONSUMER JOURNEY Keeping track of all the interactions a consumer has with a product, service, or space.

CAMERA JOURNALS Asking consumers to keep visual diaries of their activities and impressions relating to a product.

EXTREME USER INTERVIEWS Talking to people who really know—or know nothing—about a product or service, and evaluating their experience using it.

STORYTELLING Prompting people to tell personal stories about their consumer experiences.

UNFOCUS GROUPS Interviewing a diverse group of people: To explore ideas about sandals, IDEO gathered an artist, a bodybuilder, a podiatrist, and a shoe fetishist.

2. BRAINSTORMING

An intense, idea-generating session analyzing data gathered by observing people. Each lasts no more than an hour. Rules of brainstorming are strict and are stenciled on the walls:

DEFER JUDGMENT Don't dismiss any ideas.

BUILD ON THE IDEAS OF OTHERS No "buts," only "ands."

ENCOURAGE WILD IDEAS Embrace the most out-of-the-box notions because they can be key to solutions.

GO FOR QUATITY Aim for as many new ideas as possible. In a good session, up to 100 ideas are generated in 60 minutes.

BE VISUAL Use yellow, red, and blue markers to write on big 30-inch by 25-inch Post-its that are put on a wall.

STAY FOCUSED ON THE TOPIC Always keep the discussion on target.

ONE CONVERSATION AT A TIME No interrupting, no dismissing, no disrespect, no rudeness.

3. RAPID PROTOTYPING

Mocking up working models helps everyone visualize possible solutions and speeds up decision-making and innovation. Some guidelines:

MOCK EVERYTHING It is possible to create models not only of products but also of services such as health care and spaces such as museum lobbies.

USE VIDEOGRAPHY Make short movies to depict the consumer experience.

GO FAST Build mock-ups quickly and cheaply. Never waste time on complicated concepts.

NO FRILLS Make prototypes that demonstrate a design idea without sweating over the details.

CREATE SCENARIOS Show how a variety of people use a service in different ways and how various designs can meet their individual needs.

BODYSTORM Delineate different types of consumers and act out their roles.

4. REFINING

At this stage, IDEO narrows down the choices to a few possibilities. Here's how it is done:

BRAINSTORM in rapid fashion to weed out ideas and focus on the remaining best options.

FOCUS PROTOTYPING on a few key ideas to arrive at an optimal solution to a problem.

ENGAGE THE CLIENT actively in the process of narrowing the choices.

BE DISCIPLINED and ruthless in making selections.

FOCUS on the outcome of the process—reaching the best possible solution.

GET AGREEMENT from all stakeholders. The more top-level executives who sign off on the solution, the better the chances of success.

5. IMPLEMENTATION

Bring IDEO's strong engineering, design, and social-science capabilities to bear when actually creating a product or service.

TAP ALL RESOURCES Involve IDEO's diverse workforce from 40 countries to carry out the plan.

THE WORKFORCE Employees have advanced degrees in different kinds of engineering: mechanical, electrical, biomedical, software, aerospace, and manufacturing. Many are experts in materials science, computer-aided design, robotics, computer science, movie special effects, molding, industrial interaction, graphic and Web information, fashion and automotive design, business, communications, linguistics, sociology, ergonomics, cognitive psychology, biomechanics, art therapy, ethnology, management consulting, statistics, medicine, and zoology.

mid-'70s and met Steven P. Jobs. Jobs later introduced Kelley to the woman he married, Kc Branscomb, former senior vice-president at Lotus Development Corp. and CEO of IntelliCorp Inc. ID Two was run by Bill Moggridge, a well-known British interaction designer. Both founders still manage IDEO, along with CEO Tim Brown.

From its inception, IDEO has been a force in the world of design. It has designed hundreds of products and won more design awards over the past decade than any other firm. In the roaring '90s, IDEO was best known for designing user-friendly computers, PDAs, and other high-tech products such as the Palm V, Polaroid's I-Zone cameras, the Steelcase Leap Chair, and Zinio interactive magazine software. It also designed the first no-squeeze, stand-up toothpaste tube for Proctor & Gamble Co.'s Crest and the Oral-B toothbrushes for kids. Now, IDEO is transferring its ability to create consumer products into designing consumer experiences in services, from shopping and banking to health care and wireless communication.

Yet by showing global corporations how to change their organizations to focus on the consumer, IDEO is becoming much more than a design company. Indeed, it is now a rival to the traditional purveyors of corporate advice: the management consulting companies such as McKinsey, Boston Consulting, and Bain. Management consultants tend to look at the corporate world through a business-school prism. By contrast, IDEO advises clients by teaching them about the consumer world through the eyes of anthropologists, graphic designers, engineers, and psychologists. "I haven't seen anything like them before," says Tom Wyatt, president of Warnaco's Intimate Apparel Group, who is turning to IDEO to help battle rival Victoria's Secret Ltd. "They're creative and strategic, eclectic and passionate. They're cool but without attitude."

And IDEO works fast. That's because the company requires its clients to participate in virtually all the consumer research, analysis, and decisions that go into developing solutions. When the process is complete, there's no need for a buy-in: Clients already know what to do—and how to do it quickly. Unlike traditional consultants, IDEO shares its innovative process with its customers through projects, workshops, and IDEO U, its customized teaching program. In IDEO-speak, this is "open-source innovation." "Consulting firms usually come in, go away, and return with heavy binders that sit on the desk," says Kaiser's Nemer. "With IDEO, we partner up and work side-by-side. We are internalizing their methodology to build our own culture of innovation."

Eye Openers

IDEO DOESN'T HAVE the field to itself. Witnessing IDEO's success, management consulting firms are expanding their offerings to corporate clients to include a greater focus on consumers. And other design firms are piling into IDEO's space. Design Continuum in West Newton, Mass., Ziba Design in Portland, Ore., and Insight Product Development in Chicago are all experienced in understanding the consumer experience. Design Continuum, for example, observed consumer cleaning

habits in research that helped P&G launch its $1 billion Swiffer mop business. "IDEO has captured the imagination of the business world," says Craig M. Vogel, director of graduate studies at Carnegie Mellon University's School of Design, "but there are other firms doing similar work, translating user research into products and services."

Even so, IDEO is far ahead of the competition. There is even something of a cult following in the sometimes staid world of business. IDEO's clients don't just like the firm, they love it. "I think the world of them," says P&G CEO Alan G. Lafley, who has teamed up with IDEO to create a more innovative culture at the consumer-goods giant. "They are a world-class strategic partner." Adds Sam Hall, vice-president for mMode at AT&T Wireless Services Inc., who turned to IDEO to redesign its mMode service: "Those guys really get it. They opened our eyes." Since the mMode relaunch in November, 2003, subscriber membership has doubled. "I would work with them again in a heartbeat," he says. "They are a fun bunch."

Fun? Since when is changing corporate culture fun? But that's how most corporate execs describe their experiences with IDEO. Contrast that to the fear and loathing that management consultants sometimes generate when they walk into a corporation's offices. How does IDEO do it? Perhaps it is the unusual techniques it uses to energize corporate clients—"bodystorming," "behavioral mapping," "quick and dirty prototyping," "deep dives," "unfocus groups," "shadowing," and "be your customer."

Or perhaps it is working with interesting polymaths—people with two or three advanced degrees who climb mountains, go birding in the Amazon, and bike through the Alps—instead of the typical B-school grad management consultant. The head of the IDEO group that teaches companies how to innovate, Ilya Prokopoff, is a graduate of the U.S. Naval Academy with a BA in history and a master's degree in architecture. He designs furniture and tinkers with old cars, such as his 1979 Alfa Romeo Giulia Super.

Corporate execs probably have the most fun simply participating in the IDEO Way, the design firm's disciplined yet wild-and-woolly five-step process that emphasizes empathy with the consumer, anything-is-possible brainstorming, visualizing solutions by creating actual prototypes, using technology to find creative solutions, and doing it all with incredible speed.

Here's how it works: A company goes to IDEO with a problem. It wants a better product, service, or space—no matter. IDEO puts together an eclectic team composed of members from the client company and its own experts who go out to observe and document the consumer experience. Often, IDEO will have top executives play the roles of their own customers. Execs from food and clothing companies shop for their own stuff in different retail stores and on the Web. Health-care managers get care in different hospitals. Wireless providers use their own—and competing—services.

The next stage is brainstorming. IDEO mixes designers, engineers, and social scientists with its clients in a room where they intensely scrutinize a given problem and suggest possible solutions. It is managed chaos: a dozen or so very smart people examining data, throwing out ideas, writing potential solutions on big Post-its that are ripped off and attached to the wall.

IDEO designers then mock up working models of the best concepts that emerge. Rapid prototyping has always been a hallmark of the company. Seeing ideas in working, tangible form is a far more powerful mode of explanation than simply reading about them off a page. IDEO uses inexpensive prototyping tools—Apple-based iMovies to portray consumer experiences and cheap cardboard to mock up examination rooms or fitting rooms. "IDEO's passion is about making stuff work, not being artists," says design guru Tucker Viemeister, CEO of Dutch-based designer Springtime USA. "Their corporate customers really buy into it."

That pragmatic attitude is why no-nonsense CEOs are often more comfortable with IDEO than with product designers primarily interested in style. Kelley, born in Barberton, Ohio, says IDEO shares "Midwestern kind of values" with many of his clients. Kelley, who studied engineering at Stanford, now teaches there, holding the Donald W. Whittier Professor of Mechanical Engineering endowed chair. He travels between IDEO's Palo Alto offices and the nearby Stanford campus in a 1954 Chevy pickup truck. "It's all about authenticity, about solutions, not style."

THE FIRM RUN BY BROWN AND KELLEY HAS LONG BEEN **A FORCE** IN THE WORLD OF PRODUCT DESIGN. NOW IDEO IS MOVING INTO SERVICES

Some corporations send their top people to IDEO just to open their minds. P&G CEO Lafley took all the people who report directly to him—his entire Global Leadership Council of 40 business-unit heads—to San Francisco for a one-day immersion. IDEO promptly sent them all out shopping. The goal was to have the execs understand consumer experiences so they could come up with innovations. Lafley's own team went to buy music, first at a small, funky music store, then at a large retail music store, and finally online. IDEO team members shopped alongside them to analyze each experience as it unfolded. Other P&G executives went shopping with poor people so they might better understand what it means for Third World consumers to buy the company's products.

IDEO's strategic relationship with P&G runs deep. In weekly workshops and monthly stays in Palo Alto, P&G managers are taught the techniques that go into observation, brainstorming, prototyping, and fast implementation. CEO Brown sits on P&G's own design board, along with General Motors Corp.'s Robert A. Lutz and other design-minded executives. IDEO has even built an innovation center for P&G called "the Gym," where P&G staffers are inculcated in the IDEO innovation process. "They opened our eyes to new ways of working," says Claudia Kotchka, vice-president for design innovation and strategy at P&G. "They solved problems in ways we would never have thought."

P&G CEO LAFLEY TOOK ALL THE EXECS WHO REPORT TO HIM TO SAN FRANCISCO FOR A **ONE-DAY IMMERSION**. IDEO SENT THEM OUT SHOPPING.

Like a law firm, IDEO specializes in different practices. The "TEX"—or technology-enabled experiences—aims to take new high-tech products that first appeal only to early adopters and remake them for a mass consumer audience. IDEO's success with the Palm V led AT&T Wireless to call for help on its mMode consumer wireless platform. The company launched mMode in 2002 to allow AT&T Wireless mobile-phone customers to access e-mail and instant messaging, play games, find local restaurants, and connect to sites for news, stocks, weather, and other information. Techies liked mMode, but average consumers were not signing up. "We asked [IDEO] to redesign the interface so someone like my mother who isn't Web savvy can use the phone to navigate how to get the weather or where to shop," says mMode's Hall.

Too Many Clicks

IDEO's GAME PLAN: It immediately sent AT&T Wireless managers on an actual scavenger hunt in San Francisco to see the world from their customers' perspective. They were told to find a CD by a certain Latin singer that was available at only one small music store, find a Walgreen's that sold its own brand of ibuprofen, and get a Pottery Barn catalog. They discovered that it was simply too difficult to find these kinds of things with their mMode service and wound up using the newspaper or the phone directory instead. IDEO and AT&T Wireless teams also went to AT&T Wireless stores and videotaped people using mMode. They saw that consumers couldn't find the sites they wanted. It took too many steps and clicks. "Even teenagers didn't get it," says Duane Bray, leader of the TEX practice at IDEO.

After dozens of brainstorming sessions and many prototypes, IDEO and AT&T Wireless came up with a new mMode wireless service platform. The opening page starts with "My mMode" which is organized like a Web browser's favorites list and can be managed on a Web site. A consumer can make up an individualized selection of sites, such as ESPN or Sony Pictures Entertainment, and ring tones. Nothing is more than two clicks away.

An mMode Guide on the page allows people to list five places—a restaurant, coffee shop, bank, bar, and retail store—that GPS location finders can identify in various cities around the U.S. Another feature spotlights the five nearest movie theaters that still have seats available within the next hour. Yet another, My Locker, lets users store a large number of photos and ring tones with AT&T Wireless. The whole design process took only 17 weeks. "We are thrilled with the results," says Hall. "We talked to frog design, Razorfish, and other design firms, and they thought this was a Web project that needed flashy graphics. IDEO knew it was about making the cell phone experience better."

IDEO's largest practice is health care, accounting for 20% of its revenues. In addition to Kaiser Permanente, doctors, nurses, and managers at the Mayo Clinic in Rochester, Minn., SSM DePaul Health Center in Bridgeton, Miss., and Memorial Hospital & Health System in South Bend, Ind., among others, have teamed up with IDEO. They discovered that health providers tend to focus on technology and medicines. Patients, on the other hand, are concerned with service and information.

Fred Dust, head of IDEO's Smart Spaces practice, spent hours in DePaul's emergency rooms. He saw that patients were anxious not just because of their injuries but also because they

Why Corporations Turn to IDEO

Lots of well-known companies—including some we can't talk about—use the firm's services

Company	Problem	Solution
INTEL	Show computer makers the capabilities of its 2005 mobile platform chipset.	Build "concept" notebook–the 17-inch Florence–a wireless consumer appliance that replaces the TV, PC, DVD, and phone.
NESTLE	Kids are eating chocolate less because they are spending more time on their cell phones.	Conceive of new and exciting chocolate-eating experienced for the young set.
GLOBAL AUTO COMPANY (SECRET)	Feared being out of touch with Gen Y, the under-25 generation.	Do research on the values of the young. "Authenticity" turns out to be their most important concern.
LUFTHANSA	Needed to build first wireless remote for inflight entertainment and cabin management.	Design a sleek handheld remote that orders movies, music, and food, dims lights, and cools air.
SAMSUNG	Decided in 1991 to elevate role of design in the corporation to overcome its reputation of making shoddy electronics.	Brought Samsung designers and managers to IDEO U innovation workshops, created an innovation center, and jointly designed a series of products in the 1990s.
PHARMACEUTICAL CO. (SECRET)	Wanted to benchmark its speed of product development.	Produce research called How Fast Is Fast. The best speed: 8 to 14 months from idea to market.

simply didn't know when they were going to be treated. Dust suggested a cheap monitor in emergency rooms that lets patients know when they will be called.

"Shop-a-longs"

SURPRISINGLY, MANY OF THE lessons learned in the health practice work in retail. Just as getting medical care is a shared experience, so is shopping. Warnaco's Wyatt went to IDEO when faced with severe competition from Victoria's Secret. Warnaco was at a disadvantage because its lingerie is sold in department stores rather than in its own private shops. "Consumers were not having a good experience shopping for our products, and we needed to make the department stores more inviting," says Wyatt. "We turned to IDEO because it had done unique things with hospitals and Gap Inc. and Prada that enhanced the shopping experience."

Warnaco and IDEO teams did "shop-a-longs" with eight women. They also visited department stores in three cities to understand something as personal as the lingerie shopping experience. The upshot: Women didn't especially enjoy shopping for Warnaco's products. When they entered a department store, they couldn't find the lingerie section. Once they did, they couldn't find their sizes. The fitting rooms were too small to accommodate a female friend—and there was no place nearby for anyone to sit. The experience was eerily like that of the dissatisfied patient in Kaiser's hospitals: bad.

In 18 weeks, IDEO and Warnaco came up with a solution. They created a new kind of retail space within department stores

with big fitting rooms, a sitting area for couples and friends to talk privately, concierges to guide shoppers, and displays offering fashion options. Now, Warnaco is working with department stores to implement the design.

During the '90s boom, some 35% of IDEO's revenues came from designing products and Web services for Internet and other startups. At its peak in 2002, IDEO generated some $72 million in revenues. The tech bust destroyed that business model. Brown, then the head of IDEO Europe and its London office, was made CEO in 2000 by Kelley. In 2004, Brown reorganized IDEO into a professional consultancy around practices, or fields of expertise. "With practices, you can talk to clients with a voice they can connect to," says Brown. "It allows us to focus on their broader needs and serve them more effectively."

IDEO may yet stumble. Its penchant for zany terminology verging on new-age jargon could potentially turn off no-nonsense CEOs. And companies used to button-down management types may not be attracted to IDEO's fast-paced, open-ended methods. "The first P&G team that worked with IDEO called back in horror," says P&G's Kotchka. "They said, 'These people have no process.' We later saw that they do have a process. It just doesn't look like ours."

Despite—or because of—its iconoclastic ways, IDEO's ideology is gaining traction. Stanford, for one, has bought in. It has committed to raising $35 million so that Kelley can create a "D-school," a new design school that may one day match Stanford's famed B-school. Stanford professors in business, engineering, social sciences, and art will teach there. Sounds a lot like IDEO. If the D-school students are lucky, they might even have as much fun as IDEO's corporate clients.

IN PRAISE OF THE PURPLE COW

REMARKABLY HONEST IDEAS (AND REMARKABLY USEFUL CASE STUDIES) ABOUT MAKING AND MARKETING REMARKABLE PRODUCTS. A MANIFESTO FOR MARKETERS

BY SETH GODIN

For years, marketers have talked about the "five *P*s" (actually, there are more than five, but everyone picks their favorite handful): product, pricing, promotion, positioning, publicity, packaging, pass along, permission. Sound familiar? This has become the basic marketing checklist, a quick way to make sure that you've done your job. Nothing is guaranteed, of course, but it used to be that if you dotted your *i*s and paid attention to your five *P*s, then you were more likely than not to succeed.

No longer. It's time to add an exceptionally important new *P* to the list: Purple Cow. Weird? Let me explain.

While driving through France a few years ago, my family and I were enchanted by the hundreds of storybook cows grazing in lovely pastures right next to the road. For dozens of kilometers, we all gazed out the window, marveling at the beauty. Then, within a few minutes, we started ignoring the cows. The new cows were just like the old cows, and what was once amazing was now common. Worse than common: It was boring.

Cows, after you've seen them for a while, are boring. They may be well-bred cows, Six Sigma cows, cows lit by a beautiful light, but they are still boring. A Purple Cow, though: Now, that would really stand out. The essence of the Purple Cow—the reason it would shine among a crowd of perfectly competent, even undeniably excellent cows—is that it would be *remarkable*. Something remarkable is worth talking about, worth paying attention to. Boring stuff quickly becomes invisible.

The world is full of boring stuff—brown cows—which is why so few people pay attention. Remarkable marketing is the art of building things worth noticing right into your product or service. Not just slapping on the marketing function as a last-minute add-on, but also understanding from the outset that if your offering itself isn't remarkable, then it's invisible—no matter how much you spend on well-crafted advertising.

This is an essay about what it takes to create and sell something remarkable. It is a manifesto for marketers who want to make a difference at their company by helping create products and services that are worth marketing in the first place. It is a plea for originality, for passion, guts, and daring. Not just because going through life with passion and guts beats the alternative (which it does), but also because it's the only way to be successful. Today, the one sure way to fail is to be boring. Your one chance for success is to be remarkable.

And that means you have to be a leader. You can't be remarkable by following someone else who's remarkable. One way to figure out a great theory is to look at what's working in the real world and determine what the successes have in common. With marketing, it's puzzling though. What could the Four Seasons and Motel 6 possibly have in common? Other than the fact that both companies have experienced extraordi-

NOW *THAT'S* REMARKABLE: OTIS ELEVATOR CO.

When is a bank of elevators more than a bank of elevators? When it's smart enough to tell you which elevator will provide the quickest ride to the floor you need to reach. A product *that* smart changes how people move, how buildings get designed—and how companies, in this case Otis Elevator Co., market their innovation.

NOW *THAT'S* REMARKABLE: TOMBSTONE PIZZA

It's good to be first with an innovation that the world is hungry for. Ron Simek learned that lesson when he launched the first successful line of frozen pizza. The product was a hit. Kraft bought it and advertised like mad. The rest is history. Of course, 40 years later, introducing another brand of frozen pizza seems less appetizing. Me-too products lead to also-ran companies.

nary success and growth, they couldn't be more different. Or Neiman Marcus and Wal-Mart, both growing during the same decade? Or Nokia (bringing out new hardware every 30 days or so) and Nintendo (marketing the same Game Boy for 14 years in a row)?

It's like trying to drive looking in the rearview mirror. Sure, those things worked. But do they help us predict what will work tomorrow? The thing that all of those companies have in common is that they have *nothing* in common. They are outliers. They're on the fringes. Superfast or superslow. Very exclusive or very cheap. Extremely big or extremely small.

The reason it's so hard to follow the leader is this: The leader is the leader precisely because he did something remarkable. And that remarkable thing is now taken—so it's no longer remarkable when you decide to do it.

STAND OUT FROM THE HERD I: GOING UP!

Elevators aren't a typical consumer product. They can easily cost more than a million dollars, they generally get installed when a building is first constructed, and they're not much use unless the building is more than three or four stories tall.

How, then, does an elevator company compete? Until recently, selling involved a lot of golf, dinners, and long-term relationships with key purchasing agents at major real-estate developers. No doubt that continues, but Otis Elevator Co. has

radically changed the game by developing a remarkable Purple Cow.

Every elevator ride is basically a local one. The elevator stops 5, 10, 15 times on the way to your floor. This is a hassle for you, but it's a huge, expensive problem for the building. While your elevator is busy stopping at every floor, the folks in the lobby are getting more and more frustrated. The building needs more elevators, but there's no money to buy them and no room to put them. Walk into the Times Square offices of Cap Gemini Ernst & Young, and you're faced with a fascinating solution to this problem.

Otis's insight? When you approach the elevators, you key in your floor on a centralized control panel. In return, the panel tells you which elevator is going to take you to your floor. With this simple presort, Otis has managed to turn every elevator into an express. Your elevator takes you immediately to the 12th floor and races back to the lobby. This means that buildings can be taller, they need fewer elevators for a given density of people, the wait is shorter, and the building can use precious space for people rather than for elevators. A huge win, implemented at a remarkably low cost.

Is there a significant real-estate developer in the world who is unaware of this breakthrough? Not likely. And it doesn't really matter how many ads or how many lunches the competition sponsors: Otis now gets the benefit of the doubt.

10 WAYS TO RAISE A PURPLE COW

Making and marketing something remarkable means asking new questions—
and trying new practices. Here are 10 suggestions.

1. Differentiate your customers. Find the group that's most profitable. Find the group that's most likely to influence other customers. Figure out how to develop for, advertise to, or reward either group. Ignore the rest. Cater to the customers you would choose if you could choose your customers.
2. If you could pick one underserved niche to target (and to dominate), what would it be? Why not launch a product to compete with your own that does nothing but appeal to that market?
3. Create two teams: the inventors and the milkers. Put them in separate buildings. Hold a formal ceremony when you move a product from one group to the other. Celebrate them both, and rotate people around.
4. Do you have the email addresses of the 20% of your customer base that loves what you do? If not, start getting them. If you do, what could you make for them that would be superspecial?
5. Remarkable isn't always about changing the biggest machine in your factory. It can be the way you answer the phone, launch a new brand, or price a revision to your software. Getting in the habit of doing the "unsafe" thing every time you have the opportunity is the best way to see what's working and what's not.
6. Explore the limits. What if you're the cheapest, the fastest, the slowest, the hottest, the coldest, the easiest, the most efficient, the loudest, the most hated, the copycat, the outsider, the hardest, the oldest, the newest, or just the most! If there's a limit, you should (must) test it.
7. Think small. One vestige of the TV-industrial complex is a need to think mass. If it doesn't appeal to everyone, the thinking goes, it's not worth it. No longer. Think of the smallest conceivable market and describe a product that overwhelms it with its remarkability. Go from there.
8. Find things that are "just not done" in your industry, and then go ahead and do them. For example, JetBlue Airways almost instituted a dress code—for its passengers! The company is still playing with the idea of giving a free airline ticket to the best-dressed person on the plane. A plastic surgeon could offer gift certificates. A book publisher could put a book on sale for a certain period of time. Stew Leonard's took the strawberries out of the little green plastic cages and let the customers pick their own. Sales doubled.
9. Ask, "Why not?" Almost everything you *don't* do has no good reason for it. Almost everything you don't do is the result of fear or inertia or a historical lack of someone asking, "Why not?"
10. What would happen if you simply told the truth inside your company and to your customers?

THE SAD TRUTH ABOUT MARKETING JUST ABOUT ANYTHING

Forty years ago, Ron Simek, owner of the Tombstone Tap (named for a nearby cemetery) in Medford, Wisconsin, decided to offer a frozen version of his pizza to his customers. It caught on, and before long, Tombstone Pizza was dominating your grocer's freezer. Kraft eventually bought the brand, advertised it like crazy, and made serious dough. This was a great American success story: Invent a good product that everyone wants, advertise it to the masses, earn billions.

That strategy didn't just work for pizza. It worked for most everything in your house, including aspirin. Imagine how much fun it must have been to be the first person to market aspirin. Here's a product that just about every person on earth needed and wanted. A product that was inexpensive, easy to try, and promised huge immediate benefits. Obviously, it was a big hit.

Today, a quick visit to the drugstore turns up lots of aspirin and aspirinlike products: Advil, Aleve, Alka-Seltzer Morning Relief, Anacin, Ascriptin, Aspergum, Bayer, Bayer Children's, Bayer Regimen, Bayer Women's, BC Powder, Bufferin, Cope, Ecotrin, Excedrin Extra Strength, Goody's, Motrin, Nuprin, St. Joseph, Tylenol, and, of course, Vanquish. Within each of those brands, there are variations, sizes, and generics that add up to more than 100 different products to choose from.

Think it's still easy to be an analgesics marketer today? If you developed a new kind of pain reliever, even one that was a little bit better than the ones that I just listed, what would you do? The obvious answer, if you've got money and you believe in your product, is to spend everything you've got to buy tons of national TV and print advertising.

There are a few problems that you'll face, though. First, you need people who want to buy a pain reliever. While it's a huge market, it's not for everyone. Once you find people who buy pain relievers, then you need people who want to buy a *new kind* of pain reliever. After all, plenty of people want the "original" kind, the kind they grew up with. Finally, you need to find the people who are willing to listen to what you have to say about your new pain reliever. The vast majority of folks are just too busy and will ignore you, regardless of how many ads you buy. So you just went from an audience of everyone to an audience a fraction of that size. Not only are these folks hard to find, they're picky as well. Being first in the frozen-pizza category was a good idea.

Being first in pain relievers was an even better idea. Alas, they're both taken. Which brings me to the sad truth about marketing just about anything, whether it's a product or a service, whether it's marketed to consumers or corporations: Most people *can't* buy your product. Either they don't have the money, they don't have the time, or they don't want it.

NOW *THAT'S* REMARKABLE: U.S. POSTAL SERVICE

The runaway success of "zip+4" might give new meaning to the term "going postal." This simple innovation makes it quicker for the Postal Service to deliver mail, easier for marketers to target neighborhoods, and cheaper for marketers to send bulk mail. But the innovation would never have taken hold without savvy marketing by an organization not famous for its savviness.

And those are serious problems. An audience that doesn't have the money to buy what you're selling at the price you need to sell it for is not a market. An audience that doesn't have the time to listen to and understand your pitch treats you as if you and your product were invisible. And an audience that takes the time to hear your pitch and decides that they don't want it… well, you're not going to get very far.

The old rule was this: Create safe products and combine them with great marketing. Average products for average people. *That's broken*. The new rule is: Create remarkable products that the right people seek out.

As I write this, the top song in France, Germany, Italy, Spain, and a dozen other countries in Europe is about ketchup. It's called "Ketchup," and it's by two sisters you've never heard of. The number-two movie in America is a low-budget animated film in which talking vegetables act out Bible stories. Neither is the sort of product you'd expect to come from a lumbering media behemoth.

Sam Adams beer was remarkable, and it captured a huge slice of business from Budweiser. Hard Manufacturing introduced a product that costs 10 times the average (the $9,945 Doernbecher crib) and opened up an entirely new segment of the hospital-crib market. The electric piano let Yamaha steal an increasingly larger share of the traditional piano market away from the entrenched leaders. Vanguard's remarkably low-cost mutual funds continue to whale away at Fidelity's market dominance. Bic lost tons of market share to Japanese competitors that had developed pens that were remarkably fun to write with, just as Bic had stolen the market away from fountain pens a generation or two earlier.

STAND OUT FROM THE HERD II: MAIL CALL

Very few organizations have as timid an audience as the United States Postal Service. Dominated by a conservative bureaucracy and conservative big customers, the USPS has an awfully

hard time innovating. The big direct marketers are successful because they've figured out how to thrive under the current system, and they're in no mood to see that system change. Most individuals are in no hurry to change their mailing habits either.

The majority of new-policy initiatives at the USPS are either ignored or met with nothing but disdain. But "zip + 4" was a huge success. Within a few years, the USPS was able to diffuse a new idea, making the change in billions of address records in thousands of computer databases.

How? First, it was a game-changing innovation. Zip +4 makes it far easier for marketers to target neighborhoods and much faster and easier to deliver the mail. The product was a true Purple Cow, completely changing the way customers and the USPS would deal with bulk mail. It offered both dramatically increased speed in delivery and significantly lower costs for bulk mailers. That made it worth the time it took for big mailers to pay attention. The cost of ignoring the innovation would be felt immediately on the bottom line.

Second, the USPS wisely singled out a few early adopters. These were organizations that were technically savvy and that were extremely sensitive to both pricing and speed issues. These early adopters were also in a position to sneeze the benefits to other, less astute, mailers.

The lesson here is simple: The more intransigent your market, the more crowded the marketplace, the busier your customers, the more you need a Purple Cow. Half-measures will fail. Overhauling the product with dramatic improvements in things that the right customers care about, on the other hand, can have an enormous payoff.

WHY THERE ARE SO FEW PURPLE COWS

If being a Purple Cow is such an effective way to break through the clutter, why doesn't everyone do it? One reason is that people think the opposite of remarkable is "bad" or "poorly done." They're wrong. Not many companies sell things today that are flat-out lousy. Most sell things that are good enough. That's why the opposite of remarkable is "very good." Very good is an everyday occurrence, hardly worth mentioning—certainly not the basis of breakthrough success. Are you making very good stuff? How fast can you stop?

Some people would like you to believe that there are too few great ideas, that their product or their industry or their company simply can't support a great idea. That, of course, is absolute nonsense. Another reason the Purple Cow is so rare is because people are so *afraid*.

If you're remarkable, then it's likely that some people won't like you. That's part of the definition of remarkable. Nobody gets unanimous praise—ever. The best the timid can hope for is to be unnoticed. Criticism comes to those who stand out.

Playing it safe. Following the rules. They seem like the best ways to avoid failure. Alas, that pattern is awfully dangerous. The current marketing "rules" will ultimately lead to failure. In a crowded marketplace, fitting in is failing. In a busy marketplace, not standing out is the same as being invisible.

In *Marketing Outrageously* (Bard Press, 2001), author Jon Spoelstra points out the catch-22 logic of the Purple Cow. If times are tough, your peers and your boss may very well point out that you can't afford to be remarkable. There's not enough room to innovate: We have to conserve, to play it safe. We don't have the money to make a mistake. In good times, however, those very same people will tell you to relax, take it easy. There's not enough need to innovate: We can afford to be conservative, to play it safe.

So it seems that we face two choices: Either be invisible, uncriticized, anonymous, and safe or take a chance at true greatness, uniqueness, and the Purple Cow. The point is simple, but it bears repeating: Boring always leads to failure. Boring is always the riskiest strategy. Smart businesspeople realize this and work to minimize (but not eliminate) the risk from the process. They know that sometimes it's not going to work, but they accept the fact that that's okay.

STAND OUT FROM THE HERD III: THE COLOR OF MONEY

How did Dutch Boy Paint stir up the paint business? It's so simple, it's scary. They changed the can.

Paint cans are heavy, hard to carry, hard to close, hard to open, hard to pour, and no fun. Yet they've been around for a long time, and most people assumed that there had to be a reason why they were so bad. Dutch Boy realized that *there was no reason*. They also realized that the can was an integral part of the product: People don't buy paint, they buy painted walls, and the can makes that process much easier.

Dutch Boy used that insight and introduced an easier-to-carry, easier-to-pour, easier-to-close paint jug. "Customers tell us that the new Twist & Pour paint container is a packaging innovation that was long overdue," says Dennis Eckols, group vice president of the home division for Fred Meyer stores. "People wonder why it took so long for someone to come up with the idea, and they love Dutch Boy for doing it."

It's an amazing innovation. Worth noticing. Not only did the new packaging increase sales, but it also got them more distribution (at a higher retail price!).

That is marketing done right. Marketing where the marketer changes the product, not the ads.

WHY IT PAYS (BIG) TO BE A PURPLE COW

As the ability to be remarkable continues to demonstrate its value in the marketplace, the rewards that follow the Purple Cow increase. Whether you develop a new insurance policy, make a hit record, or write a groundbreaking book, the money and satisfaction that follow are extraordinary. In exchange for taking the risk, creators of a Purple Cow get a huge upside when they get it right.

Even better, you don't have to be remarkable all the time to enjoy the upside. Starbucks was remarkable a few years ago. Now they're boring. But that burst of innovation and insight has allowed them to expand to thousands of stores around the world. Compare that growth in assets to Maxwell House. Ten years ago, all of the brand value in coffee resided with them, not with Starbucks. But Maxwell House played it safe (they

thought), and now they remain stuck with not much more than they had a decade ago.

Once you've created something remarkable, the challenge is to do two things simultaneously: One, milk the Purple Cow for everything it's worth. Figure out how to extend it and profit from it for as long as possible. Two, build an environment where you are likely to invent an entirely new Purple Cow in time to replace the first one when its benefits inevitably trail off.

These are contradictory goals. The creator of a Purple Cow enjoys the profits, accolades, and feeling of omniscience that come with a success. None of those outcomes accompany a failed attempt at a new Cow. Thus, the tempting thing to do is to coast. Take no chances. Take profits. Fail to reinvest.

AOL, Marriott, Marvel Comics, Palm, Yahoo—the list goes on and on. Each company had a breakthrough, built an empire around it, and then failed to take another risk. It used to be easy to coast for a long time after a few remarkable successes. Disney coasted for decades. Milton Berle did too. It's too easy to decide to sit out the next round, rationalizing that you're spending the time and energy to build on what you've got instead of investing in the future. So here's one simple, tangible suggestion. Create two teams: the inventors and the milkers. Put them in separate buildings. Hold a formal ceremony when you move a product from one group to the other. Celebrate them both, and rotate people around.

STAND OUT FROM THE HERD IV: CHEWING MY OWN CUD

So, how does an author get his new book to stand out from all of the other marketing books? By trying to create a remarkable way to market a book about remarkable marketing. How? By not selling it in stores. Instead, a copy of the book version of *Purple Cow* is available for free to anyone reading this article. You pay for postage and handling ($5), and FAST COMPANY will send you one copy of the book-length version of this article for free (visit www.fastcompany.com/keyword/purplecow67 for details). How does this pay? Visit the site and I'll show you my entire marketing plan.

WHAT IT MEANS TO BE A MARKETER TODAY

If the Purple Cow is now one of the *Ps* of marketing, it has a series of big implications for the enterprise. In fact, it changes the definition of marketing. It used to be that engineering invented, manufacturing built, marketing marketed, sales sold, and the president managed the whole shebang. Marketing, better called "advertising," was about communicating the values of a product after it had been developed and manufactured.

That's clearly not a valid strategy in a world where product attributes (everything from service to design) are now at the heart of what it means to be a marketer. Marketing is the act of inventing the product. The effort of designing it. The craft of producing it. The art of pricing it. The technique of selling it. How can a Purple Cow company not be run by a marketer?

Companies that create Purple Cows, such as JetBlue Airways, Hasbro, Poland Spring, and Starbucks, *have* to be run by marketers. Turns out that the CEO of JetBlue made a critical decision on day one: He put the head of marketing in charge of product design and training as well. It shows. JetBlue sells a time-sensitive commodity just like American Airlines does, but somehow it manages to make a profit doing it. All of these companies are marketers at their very core.

The geniuses who managed to invent 1-800-COLLECT are true marketers. They didn't figure out how to market an existing service. Instead, the marketing is built into the product—from the easy-to-remember phone number to the very idea that MCI could steal the collect-call business from the pay-phone companies.

But isn't the same idea true for a local restaurant, a grinding-wheel company, and Citibank? In a world where anything we need is good enough and where just about all of the profit comes from the Purple Cow, we must all be marketers.

You've got a chance to reinvent who you are and what you do. Your company can reenergize itself around the idea of in-volving designers in marketing and marketers in design. You can stop fighting slow growth with mind-numbing grunt work and start investing in insight and innovation instead. If a company is failing, it's the fault of the most senior management, and the problem is probably this: They are just running a company, not marketing a product. And today, that's a remarkably ineffective way to compete.

Contributing editor **Seth Godin** (sgodin@fastcompany.com) has written some of FAST COMPANY's most influential articles, from "Permission Marketing" (April: May 1998) to "Unleash Your Idea Virus" (August 2000). This essay is adapted from his book, *Purple Cow: Transform Your Business by Becoming Remarkable* (Portfolio, May 8, 2003). The book is available at www.Apurplecow.com and other select locations.

Have It Your Way

From lipsticks to cars, a growing array of products can be custom-made to your own taste—and waist

By LISA TAKEUCHI CULLEN

CANDY SHORT IS A BORN SHOPPER. SHE studies every purchase with the zeal of her hound dogs sniffing out a trail. So she couldn't help herself when, while laid up with a back injury in her Southern California home last month, she chanced upon a curious offer on the Internet. A company called Reflect.com promised it could customize cosmetics for her based on information she entered on its website. Short, 33, formulated a lipstick, a moisturizer, then pretty much an entire product line. Some $500 later, she kissed mass-market makeup goodbye for good.

As a mother of two on workers' compensation, Short isn't given to excess. She would have spent about as much for mass-market makeup at a department store. "Now more than ever," she says, "it made me feel good getting something made just for me."

The custom craze is on. Once a privilege exclusive to the Park Avenue class, customization has come to hoi polloi courtesy of the Internet. A few clicks beget jeans, sneakers, shampoo, cars, candy, furniture, even vampire fangs made just for you and delivered to your door, for not a whole lot more than the mass-market equivalent. Just in time too. In the age of TiVo and iPod, consumers increasingly expect to custom-tailor their lives, and retailers are eager to comply. New manufacturing technologies and the Internet make custom service possible, and the prices, while in most cases modestly higher, are still affordable. As Dell Computer has been proving for years, tooling products individually cuts inventory expense, pleases customers and even lures new traffic.

The trend is driven by the tech-savvy young looking for something unique—and by their parents looking for something that fits. In apparel—the industry charging fastest into customization—the nation's 76 million baby boomers, with their expanding girth and shrinking patience, are fueling the trend. Bill Bass, head of e-commerce for Lands' End, knew there was pent-up demand for better-fitting casual clothing. Two years ago, in a promotional campaign, his company put a high-tech body scanner on a truck and traveled around the country to offer personalized fittings. "People loved it, but they had to stand in line and take their clothes off, and it was a hassle," says Bass.

Therein lay the problem—and the opportunity. For apparel retailers, customizing used to mean high cost and low efficiency; for consumers, the indignity of strangers' circling tape measures around ample waistlines in public storefronts. Levi's has long offered customized jeans, but the Original Spin line is not available on the Internet, and the company says it has never grown to more than a small fraction of sales. At Burberry's flagship store in New York City, custom-made trench coats start at $700 and require an hour of fitting; just 20 sell a week.

Could a virtual tailor change those dynamics? Using new software from Archetype Solutions, Lands' End launched a custom-fit service on its website last fall. Customers measure themselves, detail their style preferences and answer questions about their figure. The data yield a precise pattern that gets beamed to factories in Mexico or the Caribbean, and a pair of customized jeans arrives on the customer's doorstep three weeks later. Bass says he expected the custom-fit line would grow to 10% of sales. But a year later, nearly half of all Lands' End pants sold online are custom.

MAKING MAKEUP FOR ME

HOW IT WORKS

- On Reflect.com's website, I customize makeup, lipstick and other products for my skin and hair. I start by answering a series of questions about skin tone, hair texture, coloring and favorite fragrances

- After I supply the personal data, lab technicians in San Francisco match them with unique, active ingredients and mix those with base formulas. Finally, they inject my chosen scent

- "You're the ultimate brand," Reflect.com CEO Richard Gerstein tells us. So I make like Estee Lauder, Bobbi Brown and J. Lo, naming all my creations after myself

One of the company's happy customers is Alex von Bidder, 52. He has a wardrobe packed with $2,500 suits in which he hobnobs with guests at the Four Seasons, his famed New York City restaurant. "I'm used to the finest things in life," Von Bidder says. "Best wine, best food. Still, I never thought I'd get custom-made jeans." His $54 pair from Lands' End is "the best-fitting thing I've ever owned," swears Von Bidder, who has since ordered custom-fit chinos and shirts

SHOES

Nike iD, the shoemaker's customization website, lets you pick favorite colors and add words to personalize the treads. But it won't let you alter the basic shoe design

Custom mass-consumer products typically cost 10% to 20% more than off-the-rack items. Jupiter Research found in a recent study that more than half of consumers were willing to pay $10 extra to custom-order a pair of $50 slacks—but not much more. "The economy's bad," says Madison Riley of retail consultants Kurt Salmon Associates. "But if it's not going to stop people spending, they'll make for darn sure what they do spend is on the best quality and fit."

Take Jane Miller, 57, a retiree in Knoxville, Tenn. "I don't like to drive, and I'm not a big shopper," she says. "Most of the time you don't know what you're getting.

You make an investment, and it's a crapshoot." She tailors her purchases through Reflect.com and Lands' End and, with her MP3 player and DVD-rental club, customizes her tunes and movies online too.

Car buyers have always added features, a major profit driver for automakers and customizing shops that garners an estimated $26 billion-plus in sales each year. Gary Cowger, president of GM North America, says the trend toward personalization is evident in sales of the Hummer H2, a favorite of affluent baby boomers. Sales of accessories like running boards, brush guards and roof racks are "much better than we expected," he says.

Recession-squeezed automakers salivate at the thought of persuading even more buyers to customize by offering easy, accessible options online. In a study published this month, Forrester Research analyst Baba Sheddy found that 66% of prospective buyers customized vehicles while researching price online. In a bid to turn speculative customizers into real ones, Toyota's Scion, Honda's Element and Saturn's Ion will let customers order personalized cars on their websites with touches like aluminum pedals and gearshifts, and springs that adjust the car's height. Because young buyers "want something that says, 'I'm unique,'" says Toyota's Jim Farley, the youth-targeted Scion will offer 40 accessories.

But customization extends to gearhead items like air intakes, enhanced exhaust systems and rear spoilers. As Jill Lajdziak, a Saturn executive, notes, "Many young

buyers would rather buy an affordable vehicle and then have a couple of thousand dollars to invest in a higher level of performance."

CARS

Many automakers now let car buyers test-drive custom features online. On the Honda website, potential buyers can check out a "bug bra" for the front grille and other accessories

One thing's for sure with young buyers: custom sells. This fall American Eagle Outfitters, a clothing company, instructed its college-age buyers how to tear up T shirts and embroider jeans—and sold 12% more jeans in the process. Nike iD lets customers help design their own sneakers.

But there's a limit to how far retailers will go to let customers fiddle with their products. Jonah Peretti, 28, who works for a new-media arts group in New York, tried to order a pair of Nike iD shoes embroidered with the word sweatshop. That's a swipe at Nike's reputation as a company reliant on cheap foreign labor. Nike's response: Just forget it.

*—**With reporting by Joseph R. Szczesny/Detroit***

Kamikaze Pricing

When penetration strategies run amok, marketers can find themselves in a dive-bomb of no return.

by Reed K. Holden and Thomas T. Nagle

Price is the weapon of choice for many companies in the competition for sales and market share. The reasons are understandable. No other weapon in a marketer's arsenal can be deployed as quickly, or with such certain effect, as a price discount. The advantage is often short-lived, though, and managers rarely balance the long-term consequences of deploying the price weapon against the likely short-term gains.

Playing the price card often is a reaction to a competitor and assumes that it will provide significant gain for the firm. Usually, that's not the case. Firms start price wars when they have little to lose and much to gain; those who react to the initiators often have little to gain and much to lose. The anticipated gains often disappear as multiple competitors join the battle and negate the lift from the initial reductions.

Managers in highly competitive markets often view price cuts as the only possible strategy. Sometimes they're right. The problem is that they are playing with a very dangerous weapon in a war to improve near-term profitability that ends in long-term devastation. As the Chinese warrior, Sun Tzu, put it, "Those who are not thoroughly aware of the disadvantages in the use of arms cannot be thoroughly aware of the advantages."

If marketers are going to use low prices as a competitive weapon, they must be equally aware of the risks as well as the benefits (see "The Prisoner's Dilemma"). They also must learn to adjust their strategies to deploy alternatives when pricing alone is no longer effective. Failure to do so has put companies and entire industries into tail spins from which they never fully recover.

Pricing Options

Marketers traditionally have employed three pricing strategies: skim, penetration, and neutral. Skim pricing is the process of pricing a product high relative to competitors and the product's value. Neutral pricing is an attempt to eliminate price as a decision factor for customers by pricing neither high nor low relative to competitors. Penetration pricing is the decision to price low relative to the product's value and to the prices of similar competitors. It is a decision to use price as the main competitive weapon in hopes of driving the company to a position of market dominance.

EXECUTIVE BRIEFING

Penetration pricing is perhaps the most abused pricing strategy. It can be effective for fixed periods of time and in the right competitive situation, but many firms overuse this approach and end up creating a market situation where everyone is forced to lower prices continually, driving some competitors from the market and guaranteeing that no one realizes a good return on investment. Managers can prevent the fruitless slide into kamikaze pricing by implementing a value-driven pricing strategy for the most profitable customer segments.

All three strategies consider how the product is priced relative to its value for customers and that of similar competitors. When Lexus entered the luxury segment of the automobile industry, the car's price was high relative to

EXHIBIT 1

Experience curve effects

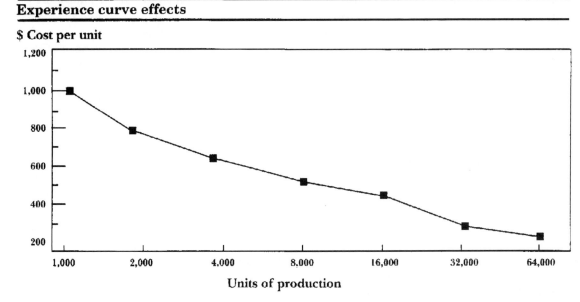

$ Cost per unit

Units of production

standard vehicles but low relative to Mercedes and BMW. The penetration strategy was defined not by the price but by the price relative to the value of the vehicle and to similar competitive products.

The main ingredient to successful penetration pricing is a large segment of customers for whom price is the primary purchase motivation.

Any of these strategies can be associated with a variety of cost structures and can result in either profits or losses. To understand when each strategy is likely to be successful, managers should evaluate their current and potential cost structure, their customers' relative price sensitivities, and their current and potential competitors. All three areas must be carefully considered before employing any pricing strategy.

Penetration Strategies Can Work

If a firm has a fixed cost structure and each sale provides a large contribution to those fixed costs, penetration pricing can boost sales and provide large increases to profits—but only if the market size grows or if competitors choose not to respond. Low prices can draw additional buyers to enter the market. The increased sales can justify production expansion or the adoption of new technologies, both of which can reduce costs. And, if firms have excess capacity, even low-priced business can provide incremental dollars toward fixed costs.

Penetration pricing can also be effective if a large experience curve will cause costs per unit to drop significantly. The experience curve proposes that, as a firm's production experience increases, per-unit costs will go down. On average, for each doubling of production, a firm can expect per-unit costs to decline by roughly 20%. Cost declines can be significant in the early stages of production (see Exhibit 1).

The manufacturer who fails to take advantage of these effects will find itself at a competitive cost disadvantage relative to others who are further along the curve. This is often the case with new technologies and innovative products, where relatively small increments in units sold yield substantial decreases in unit costs. This is also the case for many new entrants to a market who are just beginning to see experience curve cost reductions.

However, the main ingredient to successful penetration pricing is a large segment of customers for whom price is the primary purchase motivation. This can be the case in business markets where original equipment commodities are sold to the production process of a customer's business, but it rarely occurs in consumer markets where image is an important part of the use of a product.

When Omega watches—once a brand more prestigious than Rolex—was trying to improve market share in the 1970s, it adopted a penetration pricing strategy that succeeded in destroying the watch's brand image by flooding the market with lower priced products. Omega never gained sufficient share on the lower price/lower image competitors to justify destroying its brand image and high-priced position with upscale buyers. Similar outcomes were experienced by the Cadillac Cimarron and Lacoste clothing.

A better strategy would have been to introduce a totally new brand as a flanking product, as Heublein did with the Popov, Relska, and Smirnoff vodka brands and Intel did with microprocessors in 1988. After the introduction of the 386 microprocessor, Intel adopted a skim price strategy for the high value and proprietary 386 chips. It also wanted to market a circuit in the 286 market that could compete with AMD and Cirrus on a nonprice, value-added basis. The 386SX was introduced as a scaled down version of the 386, but at a price only slightly higher than the 286. The net result was to migrate price sensitive customers more quickly to the proprietary 386 market with the 386SX, while still capturing increased profit from the high value users with the 386.

In its marketing of the 486, Pentium, and Pentium Pro circuits, Intel continues this flanking strategy with dozens of varieties of each microprocessor to meet the needs of various market segments.

For penetration pricing to work, there must be competitors who are willing to let the penetration pricer get away with the strategy. If a penetration price is quickly matched by a competitor, the incremental sales that would accrue from the price-sensitive segment must now be split between two competitors. As more competitors follow, smaller incremental sales advantages and lower profits accrue to both the initiator and the followers.

Fortunately, there are two common situations which often cause competitors to let penetration pricers co-exist in markets. When the penetration-pricing firm has enough of a cost or resource advantage, competitors might conclude they would lose a price war. Retailers are beginning to recognize that some consumers who are unconcerned about price when deciding which products and brands to buy become price sensitive when deciding where to buy. They are willing to travel farther to buy the same branded products at lower prices. Category killers like Toys 'R' Us use penetration pricing strategies because they are able to manage their overhead and distribution costs much more tightly than traditional department stores. Established stores don't have the cost structure to compete on this basis, so they opt to serve the high-value segment of the market.

When the penetration-pricing firm has enough of a cost or resource advantage, competitors might conclude they would lose a price war.

The second situation conducive to penetration pricing occurs when large competitors have high-price positions and don't feel a significant number of their existing customers would be lost to the penetration pricer. This was the case when People's Express entered the airline industry with low priced fares to Europe in the 1970s. The fares were justified with reduced services such as no reservations or meal service. People's also limited the ability of the high value business traveler to take advantage of those fares by not permitting advanced reservations or ticket sales. This was a key element of their strategy: Focus only on price sensitive travelers and avoid selling tickets to the customers of their competitors.

Major airlines didn't respond to the lower prices because they didn't see People's Express taking away their high value customers. It was only when People's began pursuing the business traveler that the major airlines responded and quickly put People's out of business.

The same strategy is being repeated today by Southwest Airlines in the domestic market far more skillfully. Southwest has a cost and route structure that limits the ability of major airlines to respond. In fact, when United Airlines, a much larger competitor, did try to respond with low-cost service in selected West Coast markets, it had to abandon the effort because it couldn't match Southwest's cost structure.

Penetration or Kamikaze?

An extreme form of penetration pricing is "kamikaze" pricing, a reference to the Japanese dive bomber pilots of World War II who were willing to sacrifice their lives by crashing their explosives-laden airplanes onto enemy ships. This may have been a reasonable wartime tactic (though not a particularly attractive one) by commanders who sacrificed single warriors while inflicting many casualties on opponents. But in the business world, the relentless pursuit of more sales through lower prices usually results in lower profitability. It is often an unnecessary and fruitless exercise that damages the entire dive-bombing company—not just one individual—along with the competitor. Judicious use of the tactic is advised; in as many cases as it works, there are many more where it does not.

Kamikaze pricing occurs when the justification for penetration pricing is flawed, as when marketers incorrectly assume lower prices will increase sales. This may be true in growth markets where lower prices can expand the total market, but in mature markets a low price merely causes the same customers to switch suppliers. In the global economy, market after market is being discovered, developed, and penetrated. High growth, price sensitive markets are quickly maturing, and even though customers may want to buy a low-priced product, they don't increase their volume of purchases. Price cuts used to get them to switch fail to bring large increases in demand and end up shrinking the dollar size of the market.

A prominent example is the semiconductor business, where earlier price competition led to both higher demand and reduced costs. But in recent years, total demand tends to be less responsive to lower prices, and most suppliers are well down the experience curve. The net result is an industry where participation requires huge investments, added value is immense, but because of a penetration price

The Prisoner's Dilemma

A popular exercise in seminars and executive briefings we hold is to ask executives to participate in a prisoner's dilemma pricing game. Each team must decide whether to price its products high or low compared to those of another team in 10 rounds of competition. The objective is to earn the most money; results are determined by the decision that two competitors make in comparison with each other.

The game fairly accurately simulates a typical profit/loss scenario for price competition in mature markets. The objective is to impart several lessons in pricing competition, the first being that pricing is more like playing poker than solitaire. Success depends not just on a combination of luck and how the hand is played but also on how well competitors play their hands. In real markets, outcomes depend not only on how customers respond but, perhaps more important, on how competitors respond to changes in price.

If a competitor matches a price decrease, neither the initiator nor the follower will achieve a significant increase in sales and both are likely to have a significant decrease in profits. In developing pricing strategy, managers need to anticipate the moves of their competitors and attempt to influence those moves by selectively communicating information to influence competitive behavior.

The second lesson is that managers must adopt a very long time horizon when considering changes in price.

Once started, price wars are difficult to stop. A simple decision to drop price often becomes the first shot in a war that no competitor wins. Before initiating a price decrease, managers must consider how it will affect the competitive stability of markets.

Philip Morris discovered this when it initiated a price war in the cigarette business by cutting the prices of its top brands. Competitors followed, and the net result was a $2.3 billion drop in operating profits for Philip Morris, even as the Marlboro brand increased its market share seven points to 29%. The manufacturer of Camels experienced a $1.3 billion drop in profits.

The third lesson from the prisoner's dilemma is that careful use of a value-based marketing approach can reverse a trend toward price-based marketing. This is accomplished through signaling, a nonprice competitive tactic that involves selectively disclosing information to competitors to influence their behavior. The steel and airline industries provide prominent examples of the signaling strategy's use. They often rely on announcements that conveniently appear on the front pages of the Wall Street Journal to signal competitors of pending price moves and provide them with opportunities to follow. The strategy takes time to implement, but it provides a far better long-term competitive position for marketers who employ it.

Most managers who play the prisoner's dilemma adopt a low-price strategy. This mirrors the real world, where 63% of managers who adopt an identifiable strategy use low price, according to an ongoing research project in which we are engaged. In the game, low-price teams fail to earn any profit in a majority of cases. The strategy works in round one, but competitors quickly learn to respond and both parties end up losing any chance for profit.

Executives rationalize that, if their firm can't make money, competitors shouldn't, either. Managers quickly forget that the objective of this game—and the game of business—is profit. Price cuts in the real world can be devastating. A current example is the personal computer business, where Packard Bell sets the low price standard that many competitors follow.

Packard Bell's management is less concerned with profit than with achieving a volume of sales and market share in a growing industry. But unless the company has operational characteristics that distinguish it from competitors and permit Packard Bell to deliver a quality product at those low prices, its ability to leverage market share will be limited. Analysts estimate that Packard Bell has only made $45 million in net profit over the past 10 years and is staying afloat through loans granted by suppliers and massive cash infusions from its Japanese and European co-owners.

—Reed Holden and Thomas Nagle

mentality, suppliers can't pull out of the kamikaze death spiral.

There was a time when large, well-entrenched competitors took a long time to respond to new low-price competitors. That is no longer true; domestic automobiles are now the low priced brands, and even AT&T has learned to respond to the aggressive price competition of Sprint and MCI. The electronics, soft goods, rubber, and steel companies that ignored low-price competitors in the 1970s and '80s have become ruthless cost and price cutters. The days of free rides from nonresponsive market leaders are gone.

Another risk comes in using penetration pricing to increase sales in order to drive down unit costs. Unfortunately, there are generally two reasons managers run into trouble when they justify price discounts by anticipated reductions in costs. First, they view the relationship between costs and volume as linear, when it actually is exponential—the cost reduction per unit becomes smaller with larger increases in volume. Initial savings are substantial, but as sales grow, the incremental savings per unit of production all but disappear (see Exhibit 2). Costs continue to decline on a per-unit basis, but the incremental cost reduction seen from each additional unit of sale becomes insignificant. Managers need to recognize that experience curve cost savings as a percentage of incremental sales volume declines with increases in volume. It works great in early growth phases but not in the later stages.

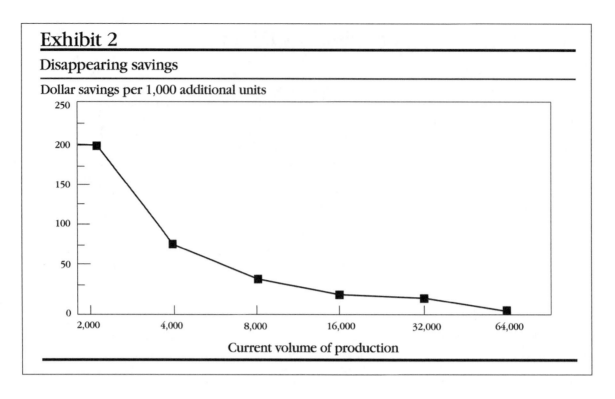

Exhibit 2

Disappearing savings

Dollar savings per 1,000 additional units

(Current volume of production)

Many managers believe that sales volume is king. They evaluate the success of both their sales managers and marketing managers by their ability to grow sales volume. The problem is that their competitors employ the exact same strategy. Customers learn that they can switch loyalties with little risk and start buying lower priced alternatives. Marketers find themselves stuck with a deadly mix of negligible cost benefits, inelastic demand, aggressive competition, and no sustainable competitive advantage. Any attempt to reduce price in this environment will often trigger growing losses. To make matters worse, customers who buy based on price are often more expensive to serve and yield lower total profits than do loyal customers. Thus starts the death spiral of the kamikaze pricers who find their costs going up and their profits disappearing.

Penetration pricing is overused, in large part, because managers think in terms of sports instead of military analogies. In sports, the act of playing is enough to justify the effort. The objective might be to win a particular game, but the implications of losing are minimal. The more intense the process, the better the game, and the best way to play is to play as hard as you can.

This is exactly the wrong motivation for pricing where the ultimate objective is profit. The more intense the competition, the worse it is for all who play. Aggressive price competition means that few survive the process and even fewer make reasonable returns on their investments. In pricing, the long-term implications of each battle must be considered in order to make thoughtful decisions about which battles to fight. Unfortunately, many managers find that, in winning too many pricing battles, they often lose the war for profitability.

Value Pricing

To avoid increasingly aggressive price competition, managers must first recognize the problem and then develop alternate strategies that build distinctive, nonprice competencies. Instead of competing only on price, managers can develop solutions to enhance the competitive and profit positions of their firms.

In most industries, there are far more opportunities for differentiation than managers usually consider. If customers are receiving good service and support, they are often willing to pay more to the supplier, even for commodities. A client in India produced commodity gold jewelry that was sold into the Asian market at extremely low penetration prices. Because of the client's good relationships with wholesale and retail intermediaries, we recommended a leveraging of those relationships to increase prices to a more reasonable level. Despite much anxiety, the client followed suit and major customers accepted the increases.

Opportunities to Add Value

Marketers often fail to recognize the opportunity for higher prices when they get caught up in kamikaze pricing. To avoid this, they need to understand how their customers value different product and company attributes. The objective is to identify segments of customers who have problems for which unique and cost-effective solutions can be developed. Sometimes it's as simple as a minor adjustment in packaging.

Know what customers want. Loctite Corp., a global supplier of industrial adhesives, introduced a specialty

Exhibit 3

Customer purchasing agenda

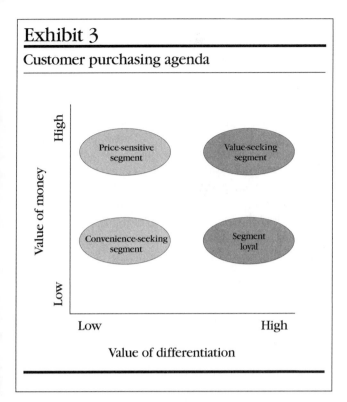

liquid adhesive in a 1-oz. bottle for use in emergency applications. Unfortunately, sales were less than spectacular. After a number of customer interviews, Loctite discovered that the liquid was difficult to apply and the bottle was difficult to carry. What customers really wanted was an easy-to-apply gel in a tube. The product was reformulated to meet these criteria and saw huge success. In the process, Loctite almost doubled the price.

Firms that attract value customers get the loyal buyer as part of the bargain and sell to the price buyer only when it is profitable and reasonable.

Managers should identify features that they can add more cost effectively than their competitors can. IBM has been under intense price pressure in the personal computer segment. Besides introducing lower-priced flanking products (with limited success), IBM also has introduced computers with more internal memory. This feature had significant appeal because of the higher memory demands of the Windows 95 operating system. The value of this feature was greater than a price cut because IBM is arguably the most cost-effective producer of random access memory in the world. It also forced low-price competitors to incur higher relative costs to match IBM, thereby undercutting their ability to price their PCs below IBM's.

In the process of adding value to their products, firms should remember that value is achieved not only from the products themselves, but from the services associated with their use. The manufacturer of a heavy-duty truck oil broke out of commodity pricing when it began analyzing the oil from its customers' trucks to determine if there were excessively high temperatures or metal in the oil that would indicate a breakdown of the internal components of engines. The service was promoted in a mailer included with each large drum of oil. The cost of this service was minimal, and a large segment of small- and owner-operator customers placed a huge value on it. This tactic helped the firm to differentiate its product with a valued service connected to the product.

Offer complete benefits. Another way to avoid downward pricing is to offer complete product benefits, which is especially useful in the early phases of a new product's life. This tactic is not as effective when products mature and customers no longer need as much service support. However, when customers are still developing their expertise, they require complete systems to achieve the maximum benefit to their organization. This is often an expensive affair that needs to be justified by the future business and profit potential that a customer represents.

When marketers correctly assess this type of situation, they often develop a sustainable competitive advantage that makes them impervious to competitive erosion. This was the strategy that Intel employed when it introduced the 8086 microprocessor to the PC industry in the early 1980s. Although the 8086 was slightly inferior technically to Motorola's 6800, Intel adopted sophisticated customer support programs that permitted new PC manufacturers to introduce new products quickly. This and other services were backed by a strong sales and marketing program that focused on specific customer adoptions. The net result was the beginning of Intel's dominance in PC microprocessors.

Understand customer agendas. Marketers make a serious mistake when they assume that all their customers are willing to sacrifice quality to obtain low prices. A few are, but most really want to get high-quality products at the lowest possible price. The seller of a high-quality product can compete against a low-price, low-quality product by recognizing that, despite the words of the purchasing agent, pricing need not be too aggressive.

Sellers who understand why customers buy their products often find that there is a fairly uniform set of reasons underlying purchasing behavior. Price is often important, but it seldom is the sole motivation. In most business situations, there are four types of agendas with regard to the pricing of products and a buyer's desired relationship with the supplying firm (see Exhibit 3). One of the best ways for marketers to avoid the trap of excessive price competition is to develop market- and customer-level strategies that reflect those behaviors.

For example, loyal customers highly value specific things that a supplier does for them, such as technical support, quality products, and customer-oriented service agents. These customers are less concerned about the price than about the care they receive. They often have a single supplier and have no intention of qualifying another. Understanding who the loyal customers are and keeping their loyalty is critical.

> # The purpose of sales is not to use a lower price to close a sale, but to convince the customer that the price of a product is fair.

Conversely, price buyers care little about a long-term relationship with a supplier and want the lowest possible price for products. These commodity buyers have multiple vendors and encourage them to dive into kamikaze price wars. For consumer marketers, price shoppers who switch allegiances at the drop of a coupon provide few incremental dollars to the retailers who cater to them. For business-to-business sellers, these tend to be the buyers who scream loudest and dictate pricing and selling strategies. Unfortunately, the profits they generate rarely justify the attention they demand.

The price buyer's agenda is to get products at the lowest possible prices, so he or she uses tactics that force marketers to employ kamikaze pricing tactics even when it might not be the wisest thing to do. For the marketer, the trick is only to do business with the price buyer when it is profitable to do so and when it doesn't prompt a more profitable customer to purchase elsewhere.

Convenience buyers don't care whose product they purchase, and have little regard for price. They simply want it readily available. This often is the most profitable market segment, provided marketers can deliver their products at the locations preferred by these buyers. Unfortunately, this group exhibits little brand loyalty and provides sellers with no sustainable competitive advantage beyond their distribution systems.

Offer the best deal. Value buyers evaluate vendors on the basis of their ability to reduce costs through lower prices or more efficient operations, or to make the buyer's business more effective with superior features or services. From a customer perspective, this is the place to be; while both price and loyal buying have unique costs, value buying comes with the assumption that these customers are getting the best deal possible, given all factors of consumption. From a marketing perspective, firms that attract value customers get the loyal buyer as part of the bargain and sell to the price buyer only when it is profitable and reasonable.

Organizations that employ kamikaze pricing have a poor understanding of how their products create value for customers. This lack of understanding results in excessive reliance on price to obtain orders. Successful marketers use price as a tool to reflect the value of the product and implement systems in the organization to assure that value is delivered to customers and captured in the pricing.

The Five Cs

"Sell on quality, not on price" was once a popular marketing aphorism. Unfortunately, while product quality can reduce the seller's rework and inventory costs, it does little for customers. Selling the quality of a product is often not enough because buyers have difficulty quantifying its value and may be unwilling to pay for it. By focusing on quality, we miss the opportunity for customers to understand the true value that quality brings to the buyers of our products. Instead, resolving to "sell on value, not on price" focuses on understanding how pricing really should work. To avoid the rigors of price-based competition, marketers should adopt the five "Cs" of the value-based approach:

- Comprehend what drives customer value.
- Create value in product, service, and support.
- Communicate value in advertising.
- Convince customers of value in selling.
- Capture value in pricing strategy.

How a product provides customer value and which value-creation efforts best differentiate a product from the competition must be understood by marketers. When there is additional value that can be created, marketers need to do a better job creating it in their products, service, and support activities. Once a firm provides differentiating value to its customers, the primary responsibility of the marketer is to set up a communications system, including the salesperson, that educates the customer on the components of that value.

The purpose of sales is not to use a lower price to close a sale, but to convince the customer that the price of a product, which is based on its value in the market, is fair. Of course, most sales compensation systems do just the opposite, rewarding salespeople for closing a sale, regardless of the price. Salespeople who lack an understanding of a product's value often bend to a buyer's wishes and match a lower-value competitor's price. Product prices should reflect a fair portion of their value, and they should be fixed so salespeople will have to sell on the basis of value.

Companies that approach pricing as a process rather than an event can effectively break the spiral of kamikaze pricing.

Penetration pricing gains ground in markets against competitors, but extended use of this offensive tactic inevitably leads to kamikaze pricing and calamity in markets as competitors respond, cost savings disappear, and customers learn to ignore value. Good marketers employ such weapons selectively and only for limited periods of time to build profitable market position. They learn how to draw from a broad arsenal of offensive and defensive weapons, understanding how each will affect their overall long-term market conditions, and never losing sight of the overall objective of stable market conditions in which they can earn the most sustainable profit.

Additional Reading

Darlin, Damon (1996), "The Computer Industry's Mystery Man," *Forbes*, (April 8), 42.

Nagle, Thomas and Reed Holden (1995), *The Strategy and Tactics of Pricing*. New York: Prentice Hall.

Reichheld, Frederick F. (1996), *The Loyalty Effect*. Boston: Harvard Business School Press.

Shapiro, Eileen C. (1995), *Fad Surfing in the Boardroom*. Reading, Mass.: Addison-Wesley Publishing.

Taylor, William (1993), "Message and Muscle: An Interview with Swatch Titan Nicolas Hayek," *Harvard Business Review*, (March–April), 99–110.

Tzu, Sun (1988), *The Art of War*, translated by Thomas Cleary. Boston: Shambhala Publications.

About the Authors

Reed K. Holden is President of the Strategic Pricing Group Inc., Marlborough, Mass., where he has conducted numerous industry seminars in the United States and Asia on pricing and competitive strategy, business market research, and loyal buyer behavior. He also works with corporate clients as an educator and strategic analyst. Reed has more than 11 years of experience as a sales and marketing manager in the electrical and electronics industries. During that time, he specialized in the development and implementation of sales training and industrial marketing programs. He also was an Assistant Professor at Boston University's Graduate School of Management for nine years. He coauthored the second edition of *The Strategy and Tactics of Pricing* and "Profitable Pricing: Guidelines for Management" which was published in the third edition of the *AMA Management Handbook*.

Thomas T. Nagle is Chairman of the Strategic Pricing Group Inc., which helps firms in such diverse industries as telecommunications, pharmaceuticals, computer software, semiconductors, wholesale nursery, consumer retailing, and financial services develop pricing strategies. His seminars are offered in public programs and at major corporations in North and South America and in Europe. The second edition of Tom's book, *The Strategy and Tactics of Pricing: A Guide to Profitable Decision Making*, is used extensively as a text on the subject. He is the author of "Managing Price Competition," published in *MARKETING MANAGEMENT* (Spring 1993), and "Financial Analysis For Profit-Driven Pricing," published in *The Sloan Management Review* (1994). His articles also have appeared in the *AMA Handbook of Business Strategy*. Tom has taught at the University of Chicago and at Boston University and is currently on the executive program faculties of the University of Chicago.

Mind Your Pricing Cues

Eric Anderson and Duncan Simester

Quick,
what's a good price to pay for ...

A six-ounce container of
yogurt?

A four-pack of
35-mm film?

A combination
TV-DVD player?

If you aren't sure, you're not alone: For most of the items they buy, consumers don't have an accurate sense of what the price should be. Consider the findings of a study led by Florida International University professor Peter R. Dickson and University of Florida professor Alan G. Sawyer in which researchers with clipboards stood in supermarket aisles pretending to be stock takers. Just as a shopper would place an item in a cart, a researcher would ask him or her the price. Less than half the customers gave an accurate answer. Most underestimated the price of the product, and more than 20% did not even venture a guess; they simply had no idea of the true price.

This will hardly come as a surprise to fans of *The Price Is Right*. This game show, a mainstay of CBS's daytime programming since 1972, features contestants in a variety of situations in which they must guess the price of packaged goods, appliances, cars, and other retail products. The inaccuracy of the guesses is legendary, with contestants often choosing prices that are off by more than 50%. It turns out this is reality TV at its most real. Consumers' knowledge of the market is so far from perfect that it hardly deserves to be called knowledge at all.

One would expect this information gap to be a major stumbling block for customers. A woman trying to decide whether to buy a blouse, for example, has several options: Buy the blouse, find a less expensive blouse elsewhere on the racks, visit a competing store to compare prices, or delay the purchase in the hopes that the blouse will be discounted. An informed buying decision requires more than just taking note of a price tag. Customers also need to know the prices of other items, the prices in other stores, and what prices might be in the future.

Yet people happily buy blouses every day. Is this because they don't care what kind of deal they're getting? Have they given up all hope of comparison shopping? No. Remarkably, it's because they rely on the retailer to tell them if they're getting a good price. In subtle and not-so-subtle ways, retailers send signals to customers, telling them whether a given price is relatively high or low.

In this article, we'll review the most common pricing cues retailers use, and we'll reveal some surprising facts about how—and how well—those cues work. All the cues we will discuss—things like sale signs and prices ending in 9—are common marketing techniques. If used appropriately, they can be effective tools for building trust with customers and convincing them to buy your products and services. Used inappropriately, however, these pricing cues may breach customers' trust, reduce brand equity, and give rise to lawsuits.

Sale Signs

The most straightforward of the pricing cues retailers use is the sale sign. It usually appears somewhere near the discounted item, trumpeting a bargain for customers. Our own tests with several mail-order catalogs reveal that using the word "sale" beside a price (without actually varying the price) can increase demand by more than 50%. Similar evidence has been reported in experiments conducted with university students and in retail stores.

Placing a sale sign on an item costs the retailer virtually nothing, and stores generally make no commitment to a particular level of discount when using the signs. Admittedly, retailers do not always use such signs truthfully. There have been incidents in which a store has claimed that a price has been discounted when, in fact, it hasn't—making for wonderful newspaper articles. Consultant and former Harvard Business School professor Gwen Ortmeyer, in a review of promotional pricing policies, cites a 1990 *San Francisco Chronicle* article in which a reporter priced the same sofa at several Bay Area furniture stores. The sofa was on sale for $2,170 at one store; the regular price was $2,320. And it cost $2,600—"35% off" the original price of $4,000—at another store. Last year, a research team from the *Boston Globe* undertook a four-month investigation of prices charged by Kohl's department stores, focusing on the chain's Medford, Massachusetts, location. The team concluded that the store often exaggerated its discounts by inflating its regular prices. For instance, a Little Tikes toy truck was never sold at the regular price throughout the period of the study, according to the *Globe* article.

So why do customers trust sale signs? Because they are accurate most of the time. Our interviews with store managers, and our own observations of actual prices at department and specialty stores, confirm that when an item is discounted, it almost invariably has a sale sign posted nearby. The cases where sale signs are placed on non-discounted items are infrequent enough that the use of such signs is still valid.

And besides, customers are not that easily fooled. They learn to recognize that even a dealer of Persian rugs will eventually run out of "special holidays" and occasions to celebrate with a sale. They are quick to adjust their attitudes toward sale signs if they perceive evidence of overuse, which reduces the credibility of discount claims and makes this pricing cue far less effective.

The link between a retailer's credibility and its overuse of sale signs was the subject of a study we conducted involving purchases of frozen fruit juice at a Chicago supermarket chain. The analysis of the sales data revealed that the more sale signs used in the category, the less effective those signs were at increasing demand. Specifically, putting sale signs on more than 30% of the items diminished the effectiveness of the pricing cue. (See the exhibit "The Diminishing Return of Sale Signs.")

A similar test we conducted with a women's clothing catalog revealed that demand for an item with a sale sign went down by 62% when sale signs were also added to other items. Another study we conducted with, a publisher revealed a similar falloff in catalog orders when more than 25% of the items in the catalog were on sale. Retailers face a trade-off: Placing sale signs on multiple items can increase demand for those items—but it can also reduce overall demand. Total category sales are highest when some, but not all, items in the category have sale signs. Past a certain point, use of additional sale signs will cause total category sales to fall.

Misuse of sale signs can also result in prosecution. Indeed, several department stores have been targeted by state attorneys general. The cases often involve jewelry departments, where consumers are particularly in the dark about relative quality, but have also come to include a wide range of other retail categories, including furniture and men's and women's clothing. The lawsuits generally argue that the stores have breached state legislation on unfair or deceptive pricing. Many states have enacted legislation addressing this issue, much of it mirroring the Federal Trade Commission's regulations regarding deceptive pricing. Retailers have had to pay fines ranging from $10,000 to $200,000 and have had to agree to desist from such practices.

Prices That End in 9

Another common pricing cue is using a 9 at the end of a price to denote a bargain. In fact, this pricing tactic is so common, you'd think customers would ignore it. Think again. Response to this pricing cue is remarkable. You'd generally expect demand for an item to go down as the price goes up. Yet in our study involving the women's clothing catalog, we were able to increase demand by a third by *raising* the price of a dress from $34 to $39. By comparison, changing the price from $34 to $44 yielded no difference in demand. (See the exhibit "The Surprising Effect of a 9.")

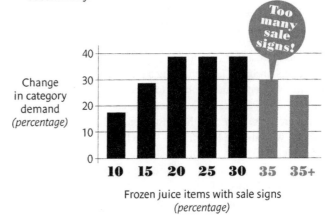

The Diminishing Return of Sale Signs

Our research indicates there is a point at which adding more sale signs yields fewer sales. In a Chicago supermarket's frozen fruit juice category, charted below, putting sale signs on more than 30% of the items reduced demand substantially.

Too many sale signs!

Change in category demand *(percentage)*

Frozen juice items with sale signs *(percentage)*

This favorable effect extends beyond women's clothing catalogs; similar findings have also been reported for groceries. Moreover, the effect is not limited to whole-dollar figures: In their 1996 research, Rutgers University professor Robert Schindler and then-Wharton graduate student Thomas Kibarian randomly mailed customers of a women's clothing catalog different versions of the catalog. One included prices that ended in 00 cents, and the other included prices that ended in 99 cents. The professors found that customers who received the latter version were more likely to place an order. As a result, the clothing company increased its revenue by 8%.

One explanation for this surprising outcome is that the 9 at the end of the price acts the same way as the sale sign does, helping customers evaluate whether they're getting a good deal. Buyers are often more sensitive to price endings than they are to actual price changes, which raises the question: Are prices that end in 9 truly accurate as pricing cues? The answer varies. Some retailers do reserve prices that end in 9 for their discounted items. For instance, J. Crew and Ralph Lauren generally use 00-cent endings on regularly priced merchandise and 99-cent endings on discounted items. Comparisons of prices at major department stores reveal that this is common, particularly for apparel. But at some stores, prices that end in 9 are a miscue—they are used on all products regardless of whether the items are discounted.

Research also suggests that prices ending in 9 are less effective when an item already has a sale sign. This shouldn't be a surprise. The sale sign informs customers that the item is discounted, so little information is added by the price ending.

Signpost Items

For most items, customers do not have accurate price points they can recall at a moment's notice. But each of us probably knows some benchmark prices, typically on items we buy frequently. Many customers, for instance, know the price of a 12-ounce can of Coke or the cost of admission to a movie, so they can distinguish expensive and inexpensive price levels for such "signpost" items without the help of pricing cues.

Research suggests that customers use the prices of signpost items to form an overall impression of a store's prices. That impression then guides their purchase of other items for which they have less price knowledge. While very few customers know the price of baking soda (around 70 cents for 16 ounces), they do realize that if a store charges more than $1 for a can of Coke it is probably also charging a premium on its baking soda. Similarly, a customer looking to purchase a new tennis racket might first check the store's price on a can of tennis balls. If the balls are less than $2, the customer will assume the tennis rackets will also be low priced. If the balls are closer to $4, the customer will walk out of the store without any tennis gear— and the message that the bargains are elsewhere.

The implications for retailers are important, and many already act accordingly. Supermarkets often take a loss on Coke or Pepsi, and many sporting-goods stores offer tennis balls at a price below cost. (Of course, they make up for this with their

The Surprising Effect of a 9

Customers react favorably when they see prices that end in 9. For instance, when a national women's clothing catalog raised the price of one of its dresses from $34 to $39, sales jumped up. But, when the price was raised from $34 to $44, there was no change in demand.

sales of baking soda and tennis rackets.) If you're considering sending pricing cues through signpost items, the first question is which items to select. Three words are worth keeping in mind: *accurate, popular*, and *complementary*. That is, unlike with sale signs and prices that end in 9, the signpost item strategy is intended to be used on products for which price knowledge is accurate. Selecting popular items to serve as pricing signposts increases the likelihood that consumers' price knowledge will be accurate—and may also allow a retailer to obtain volume discounts from suppliers and preserve some margin on the sales. Both of these benefits explain why a department store is more likely to prominently advertise a basic, white T-shirt than a seasonal, floral print. And complementary items can serve as good pricing signposts. For instance, Best Buy sold *Spiderman* DVDs at several dollars below wholesale price, on the very first weekend they were available. The retail giant lost money on every DVD sold—but its goal was to increase store traffic and generate purchases of complementary items, such as DVD players.

Signposts can be very effective, but remember that consumers are less likely to make positive inferences about a store's pricing policies and image if they can attribute the low price they're being offered to special circumstances. For example, if everyone knows there is a glut of computer memory chips, then low prices on chip-intensive products might be attributed to the market and not to the retailer's overall pricing philosophy. Phrases such as "special purchase" should be avoided. The retailer's goal should be to convey an overarching image of low prices, which then translates into sales of other items. Two retailers we studied, Golfjoy.com and Baby's Room, include the phrase "our low regular price" in their marketing copy to create the perception that all of their prices are low. And Wal-Mart, of course, is the master of this practice.

A related issue is the magnitude of the claimed discounts. For example, a discount retailer may sell a can of tennis balls for a regular price of $1.99 and a sale price of $1.59, saving the consumer 40 cents. By contrast, a competing, higher-end retailer that matches the discount store's sale price of $1.59 may offer a regular price of $2.59, saving the consumer $1. By using the phrase "low regular price," the low-price retailer explains to consumers why its discounts may be smaller (40 cents versus $1 off) and creates the perception that all of its products are underpriced. For the higher-end competitor, the relative savings it offers to consumers ($1 versus 40 cents off) may increase sales of tennis balls but may also leave consumers thinking that the store's nonsale prices are high.

Use of signpost items to cue customers' purchases and to raise a store's pricing image creates few legal concerns. The reason for this is clear: Customers' favorable responses to this cue arise without the retailer making an explicit claim or promise to support their assumptions. While a retailer may commit itself to selling tennis balls at $2, it does not promise to offer a low price on tennis rackets. Charging low prices on the tennis balls may give the appearance of predatory pricing. But simply selling below cost is generally not sufficient to prove intent to drive competitors out of business.

Pricing Guarantees

So far, we've focused on pricing cues that consumers rely on—and that are reliable. Far less clear is the reliability of another cue, known as price matching. It's a tactic used widely in retail markets, where stores that sell, for example, electronics, hardware, and groceries promise to meet or beat any competitor's price.

Tweeter, a New England retailer of consumer electronics, takes the promise one step further: It self-enforces its price-matching policy. If a competitor advertises a lower price, Tweeter refunds the difference to any customers who paid a higher price at Tweeter in the previous 30 days. Tweeter implements the policy itself, so customers don't have to compare the competitors' prices. If a competitor advertises a lower price for a piece of audio equipment, for example, Tweeter determines which customers are entitled to a refund and sends them a check in the mail.

Do customers find these price-matching policies reassuring? There is considerable evidence that they do. For example, in a study conducted by University of Maryland marketing professors Sanjay Jain and Joydeep Srivastava, customers were presented with descriptions of a variety of stores. The researchers found that when price-matching guarantees were part of the description, customers were more confident that the store's prices were lower than its competitors'.

Cue, Please

Pricing cues like sale signs and prices that end in 9 become less effective the more they are employed, so it's important to use them only where they pack the most punch. That is, use pricing cues on the items for which customers' price knowledge is poor. Consider employing cues on items when one or more of the following conditions apply:

Customers purchase infrequently. The difference in consumers' knowledge of the price of a can of Coke versus a box of baking soda can be explained by the relative infrequency with which most customers purchase baking soda.

Customers are new. Loyal customers generally have better price knowledge than new customers, so it makes sense to make heavier use of sale signs and prices that end in 9 for items targeted at newer customers. This is particularly true if your products are exclusive. If, on the other hand, competitors sell identical products, new customers may have already acquired price knowledge from them.

Product designs vary over time. Because tennis racket manufacturers tend to update their models frequently, customers who are looking to replace their old rackets will always find different models in the stores or on-line, which makes it difficult for them to compare prices from one year to the next. By contrast, the design of tennis balls rarely changes, and the price remains relatively static over time.

Prices vary seasonally. The prices of flowers, fruits, and vegetables vary when supply fluctuates. Because customers cannot directly observe these fluctuations, they cannot judge whether the price of apples is high because there is a shortage or because the store is charging a premium.

Quality or sizes vary across stores. How much should a chocolate cake cost? It all depends on the size and the quality of the cake. Because there is no such thing as a standard-size cake, and because quality is hard to determine with-out tasting the cake, customers may find it difficult to make price comparisons.

These criteria can help you target the right items for pricing cues. But you can also use them to distinguish among different types of customers. Those who are least informed about price levels will be the most responsive to your pricing cues, and—particularly in an on-line or direct mail setting—you can vary your use of the cues accordingly.

How do you know which customers are least informed? Again, those who are new to a category or a retailer and who purchase only occasionally tend to be most in the dark.

Of course, the most reliable way to identify which customers' price knowledge is poor (and which items they're unsure about) is simply to poll them. Play your own version of *The Price Is Right*—show a sample of customers your products, and ask them to predict the prices. Different types of customers will have different answers.

But is that trust justified? Do companies with price-matching policies really charge lower prices? The evidence is mixed, and, in some cases, the reverse may be true. After a large-scale study of prices at five North Carolina supermarkets, University of Houston professor James Hess and University of California at Davis professor Eitan Gerstner concluded that the effects of price-matching policies are twofold. First, they reduce the level of price dispersion in the market, so that all retailers tend to have similar prices on items that are common across stores. Second, they appear to lead to *higher* prices overall. Indeed, some pricing experts argue that price-matching policies are not really targeted at customers; rather, they represent an explicit warning to competitors: "If you cut your prices, we will, too." Even more threatening is a policy that promises to beat the price difference: "If you cut your prices, we will undercut you." This logic has led some industry observers to interpret price-matching policies as devices to reduce competition.

Closely related to price-matching policies are the most-favored-nation policies used in business-to-business relationships, under which suppliers promise customers that they will not sell to any other customers at a lower price. These policies are attractive to business customers because they can relax knowing that they are getting the best price. These policies have also been associated with higher prices. A most-favored-nation policy effectively says to your competitors: "I am committing not to cut my prices, because if I did, I would have to rebate the discount to all of my former customers."

Price-matching guarantees are effective when consumers have poor knowledge of the prices of many products in a retailer's mix. But these guarantees are certainly not for every store. For instance, they don't make sense if your prices tend to be higher than your competitors'. The British supermarket chain Tesco learned this when a small competitor, Essential Sports, discounted Nike socks to lop a pair, undercutting Tesco by £7.90. Tesco had promised to refund twice the difference and had to refund so much

money to customers that one man walked away with 12 new pairs of socks plus more than £90 in his wallet.

To avoid such exposure, some retailers impose restrictions that make the price-matching guarantee difficult to enforce. Don't try it: Customers, again, are not so easily fooled. If the terms of the deal are too onerous, they will recognize that the guarantee lacks substance. Their reaction will be the same if it proves impossible to compare prices across competing stores. (Clearly, the strategy makes no sense for retailers selling private-label or otherwise exclusive brands.) How much of the merchandise needs to be directly comparable for consumers to get a favorable impression of the company? Surprisingly little. When Tweeter introduced its highly effective automatic price-matching policy, only 6% of its transactions were actually eligible for refunds.

Interestingly, some manufacturers are making it harder for consumers to enforce price-matching policies by introducing small differences in the items they supply to different retailers. Such use of branded variants is common in the home-electronics market, where many manufacturers use different model numbers for products shipped to different retailers. The same is true in the mattress market—it is often difficult to find an identical mattress at competing retailers. If customers come to recognize and anticipate these strategies, price-matching policies will become less effective.

Antitrust concerns have been raised with regard to price-matching policies and most-favored-nation clauses. In one pending case, coffin retailer Direct Casket is suing funeral homes in New York for allegedly conspiring to implement price-matching policies. The defendants in this case have adopted a standard defense, arguing that price-matching policies are evidence of vigorous competition rather than an attempt to thwart it. An older, but perhaps even more notorious, example involved price-matching policies introduced by General Electric and Westinghouse in 1963 in the market for electric

Quality Has Its Own Cues

Retailers must balance their efforts to cultivate a favorable price image with their efforts to protect the company's quality image. Customers often interpret discounts as a signal of weak demand, which may raise doubts about quality.

This trade-off was illustrated in a recent study we conducted with a company that sells premium-quality gifts and jewelry. The merchant was considering offering a plan by which customers could pay for a product in installments without incurring finance charges. Evidence elsewhere suggested that offering such a plan could increase demand. To test the effectiveness of this strategy, the merchant conducted a test mailing in which a random sample of 1,000 customers received a catalog that contained the installment-billing offer, while another 1,000 customers received a version of the catalog without any such offer. The company received 13% *fewer* orders from the installment-billing version, and follow

up surveys revealed that the offer had damaged the overall quality image of the catalog. As one customer cogently put it: "People must be cutting back, or maybe they aren't as rich as [the company] thought, because suddenly everything is installment plan. It makes [the company] look tacky to have installment plans."

Sale signs may also raise concerns about quality. It is for this reason that we see few sale signs in industries where perceptions of high quality are essential. For instance, an eye surgeon in the intensely competitive market for LASIK procedures commented: "Good medicine never goes on sale."

The owner of a specialty women's clothing store in Atlanta offered a similar rationale for why she does not use sale signs to promote new items. Her customers interpret sale items as leftovers from previous seasons, or mistakes, for which demand is disappointing because the item is unfashionable.

generators. The practice lasted for many years, but ultimately the U.S. Justice Department, in the early 1980s, concluded that the policies restrained price competition and were a breach of the Sherman Antitrust Act. GE and Westinghouse submitted to a consent decree under which they agreed to abandon the business practice.

Tracking Effectiveness

To maximize the effectiveness of pricing cues, retailers should implement them systematically. Ongoing measurement should be an essential part of any retailer's use of pricing cues. In fact, measurements should begin even before a pricing cue strategy is implemented to help determine which items should receive the cues and how many should be used. Following implementation, testing should focus on monitoring the cues' effectiveness. We've found that three important concerns tend to be overlooked.

First, marketers often fail to consider the long-run impact of the cues. According to some studies, pricing policies that are designed to maximize short-run profits often lead to suboptimal profits in the long run. For example, a study we conducted with a publisher's catalog from 1999 to 2001 investigated how customers respond to price promotions. Do customers return in the future and purchase more often, or do they stock up on the promoted items and come back less frequently in subsequent months? The answer was different for first-time versus established customers. Shoppers who saw deep discounts on their first purchase returned more often and purchased more items when they came back. By contrast, established customers would stock up, returning less often and purchasing fewer items. If the publisher were to overlook these long-run effects, it would set prices too low for established patrons and too high for first-time buyers.

Second, retail marketers tend to focus more on customers' perceptions of price than on their perceptions of quality. (See the sidebar "Quality Has Its Own Cues.") But companies can just as easily monitor quality perceptions by varying their use of pricing cues and by asking customers for feedback.

Finally, even when marketers have such data under their noses, they too often fail to act. They need to both disseminate what is learned and change business policies. For example, to prevent overuse of promotions, May Department Stores explicitly limits the percentage of items on sale in any one department. It's not an obvious move; one might expect that the department managers would be best positioned to determine how many sale signs to use. But a given department manager is focused on his or her own department and may not consider the impact on other departments. Using additional sale signs may increase demand within one department but harm demand elsewhere. To correct this, a corporate-wide policy limits the discretion of the department managers. Profitability depends both on maintaining an effective testing program and institutionalizing the findings.

* * *

Consumers implicitly trust retailers' pricing cues and, in doing so, place themselves in a vulnerable position. Some retailers might be tempted to breach this trust and behave deceptively. That would be a grave mistake. In addition to legal concerns, retailers should recognize that consumers need price information, just as they need products. And they look to retailers to provide both.

Retailers must manage pricing cues in the same way that they manage quality. That is, no store or catalog interested in collecting large profits in the long run would purposely offer a defective product; similarly, no retailer interested in cultivating a long-term relationship with customers would deceive them with inaccurate pricing cues. By reliably signaling which prices are low, companies can retain customers' trust—and overcome their suspicions that they could find a better deal elsewhere.

Eric Anderson is a visiting assistant professor of marketing at Northwestern University's Kellogg School of Management in Evanston, Illinois. Duncan Simester is an associate professor of management science at MIT's Sloan School of Management in Cambridge, Massachusetts.

THE MONEY ISSUE

WHICH PRICE IS RIGHT?

PREPARE FOR THE COMING REVOLUTION IN HOW BUSINESS SETS PRICES

It is an urgent question: How can we increase profits if we can't raise prices? The answer demands revolutionary thinking—new insights about strategy and human behavior, turbocharged with software, mathematics, and rapid-fire experimentation. Is your company ready to master the new era of pricing? Are you prepared to pay the price of failure?

By Charles Fishman

AIRLINE TICKETS cost 40% less than they did 25 years ago. A two-liter bottle of Diet Coke often has the same price tag as it did in 1985. Light-bulbs, laptops, heck, even the "cost" of a mortgage—all are at historic lows. It's been a good 20 years to be a consumer.

But for companies, the pressure is on. Most companies are desperate to raise prices. And virtually every company has the same lament: We can't. Customers won't stand for it. Competitors will undercut us. And technology will disrupt us—again. Jack Welch saw it back in 1996, when he famously complained, "There is no pricing power at all." The environment is even tougher today.

Anyone who sells anything knows that price is the pivot of business, the ultimate leverage. If you can raise prices—even a bit—you can increase profits dramatically. If you can't raise prices, you feel like your business is struggling, regardless of what is happening with cost, quality, or service.

Meanwhile, anyone who buys anything knows that almost nothing has a single price anymore. Want to know the price of something? Well, you get back a series of questions: Who are you? How long have you been a customer? How much are you buying? How good are you at unblinking negotiation? Did you bring your frequent-shopper card?

So I set out on a mission: to enter the hidden world of prices and pricers. I wanted to talk candidly with the smartest experts, the savviest executives, and the most nimble tacticians about the most urgent subject in business today: pricing. I sensed trouble when the first person I called to interview said after a few minutes, "Wait. I hear typing. I always get nervous when I hear typing." Next came a woman from American Airlines. She kept repeating the official position: "Absolutely not. We just don't discuss prices." Finally, she pleaded, "If I talk about prices, I could go to jail." The spokeswoman for a telecom company said, "We're not going to talk about prices, and the fact that we're not going to talk about it is off the record. You can't use the fact that we won't talk about prices in a story."

But it was not until I traveled to Chicago, to a Professional Pricing Society conference, that I got a full picture of how sensitive the subject is. On my first day, I was asked to leave the trade-show exhibits—the place where vendors beg for attention. A guard was posted at the door, in case I tried to slip in. On the second day, Eric Mitchell, president of the PPS, spotted me standing in the lobby outside the meeting rooms and scowled. I would approach someone and introduce myself, and Mitchell would tag along and stand with his arms crossed as I asked questions. Eventually, his dignity overcame his paranoia, and he assigned an aide to follow me. It didn't matter. Shortly, I was approached by a man who was large enough to play nose tackle for the Chicago Bears. Leval worked security for Marriott. He was extremely polite, and he told me that I would be leaving the hotel. *Immediately.*

So there I was, standing in a biting breeze on Michigan Avenue, wondering what it is about prices that makes otherwise reasonable businesspeople so paranoid. One factor is strategic secrecy: Prices are so important to business that most executives don't want to disclose what they know. But the bigger factor, I came to appreciate, is fear of embarrassment: Most executives are surprisingly in the dark when it comes to setting prices. They guess; they say a prayer; they cross their fingers. They are afraid to disclose what they *don't* know.

Kent Monroe, a professor at the University of Illinois at Urbana-Champaign, is one of the deans of pricing. He's been teaching the subject for nearly 37 years, and he knows that sloppy thinking about pricing is widespread across the U.S. economy. Both consumers and businesspeople assume that price has everything to do with cost. *Wrong.* "You have to know the cost so that you can understand the profitability implications of price," says Monroe, "but not for the purpose of setting price." Businesspeople assume that if they are in a competitive situation, and prices drop, they have to match. *Wrong.* "The natural tendency to match is foolish," he says. Executives who are devoted to using "data" in all kinds of other arenas think it's perfectly acceptable to set prices based on "history" or "experience" or "instinct." *Wrong again.*

Monroe tells a pricing story that shows how even the simplest situation can confound accepted wisdom about prices. "A company is making two versions of the same product," says Monroe. "One has a little more gold and foil on it, but they're essentially the same. One is $14.95; the other is $18.95." Not surprisingly, the $14.95 item is selling better. It's also the lower-profit product.

"Then a competitor comes in with a third product. Again, it's essentially the same thing, but a fancier version. And it's much higher priced: $34.95."

For our original company, asks Monroe, "what becomes the best-seller? Why, the $18.95 version, of course."

It's a small story, but it's true. In fact, you can *feel* how right Monroe is. "The point," he says, "is that economic theory says that can't happen. But it does."

The neat curves and crisp laws of supply and demand, elasticity, and rational behavior that everyone learns in microeconomics class don't work in the real world.

Business is at the start of a new era of pricing. This era is being shaped by a new set of insights into business strategy and human behavior, and these insights are turbocharged with software, mathematics, and rapid experimentation. The result is what might be called "scientific pricing." There is even a blossoming industry of a dozen companies that offer scientific-pricing services.

Changes in pricing will alter every part of the economy. The way that business gets done will change, and companies will flourish or be crushed based in part on their ability to grasp and master the new science of pricing. Among those already using

the new techniques are Best Buy, DHL, Ford Motor Co., the Home Depot, JC Penney, Safeway, Saks, Staples, UPS, and Winn-Dixie. General Electric, perhaps taking Jack Welch's warnings to heart, is not only working with at least two different pricing companies—it has also invested in one.

PRICE CHECK (I): BEFORE THE BAR CODE

The oldest records of prices ever found are clay tablets with pictographic symbols found in a town known as Uruk, in what was ancient Sumer and what is now southern Iraq. These price records are from 3300 BC—they've survived 5,300 years. The documents—records of payment for barley and wheat, for sheep, and for beer—are really receipts. "Uruk was a large city, at a minimum 40,000 people," says UCLA professor Robert Englund, one of the few experts on the Uruk documents. "So some of the quantities are very high—hundreds of thousands of pounds of barley, for instance."

But here's the really remarkable thing. The earliest Uruk tablets aren't just the oldest pricing records ever found. They are the oldest examples of human *writing* yet discovered. In other words, when humans first took stylus to wet clay, the first thing that they were compelled to record was… prices.

INSIDE A PERMANENT PRICE WAR: "YOU'RE ONLY AS SMART AS YOUR DUMBEST COMPETITOR"

If there are pioneers in the world of scientific pricing, they are the airlines. In the 25 years since deregulation, the airlines have honed an obsession with prices—their own and each other's—that is legendary. We all live with the seemingly bizarre inconsistencies that result, such as two people on the same plane, sitting across the aisle from each other, one of whom paid $290 to fly from New York to Miami, one of whom paid $1,290. We also benefit from the pricing obsession: With just a little bit of planning, you can fly for the same price today that you did in 1980.

The airlines know full well that we are puzzled by the frantic pricing and repricing that they do—puzzled, that is, when we aren't infuriated. Jim Compton, senior vice president of pricing and revenue management at Continental Airlines, not only wasn't scared of going to jail if he talked about prices, he was happy to pull back the curtain, to show fliers what he and his 150-person staff are up against. "I do not set the prices," says Compton, a patient, thoughtful man. "The market sets prices." That's point one. Point two: "I have a really perishable product. It's gone when the door of the plane closes. An empty seat is lost revenue."

But here's the first of many oddities of airline pricing. Most other perishable products—milk, bananas, trendy sweaters—get cheaper the closer they are to being "expired." Airline seats get more valuable the closer they get to being "expired." The most valuable airline seat is the one that somebody *must have* an hour before takeoff and is willing to pay almost any price for. Unlike a banana, an airline seat gets more profitable with time—right up to the moment it goes from being worth $1,000 one-way to being worth $0.

Here's how Compton and his colleagues think about this: You always want that seat available to sell at full price—just in case someone wants it. You want to sell every seat on the plane, except that you also want to have a handful left at the very end, for your most profitable (not to mention most grateful) customers.

The airlines could easily sell out every seat, every flight, every day. They'd price 'em pretty low, book 'em up, and wait for takeoff. But that would mean there'd never be any seats available two or three weeks before a flight took off. How exasperated are we to call and find no seats three days out? What if there were no seats three *weeks* out?

When you understand that dilemma, all of a sudden, airline prices don't seem so exploitive. Although all of the seats on that New York– Miami flight are going to the same place, they aren't the same product. You pay less when you commit to a ticket four weeks in advance; Continental assumes a risk for holding a seat until the end—and wants to be paid a lot to balance the times when saving that last seat for you means that the seat flies empty. A ticket sold a month out and a ticket sold a day out are very different things.

The complexity required to pursue this balance is mind-boggling. Continental launches about 2,000 flights every day. Each flight has between 10 and 20 prices. Continental starts booking flights 330 days in advance, and every flying day is different from every other flying day. Monday is a different kind of day than Tuesday; the Wednesday before Thanksgiving is different from the Wednesday before that. At any given moment, Jim Compton and Continental may have nearly 7 million prices in the market.

And that's just the beginning. All of those prices need to be managed, all the time. All of the major airlines (except Southwest) participate in a joint fare-publishing enterprise called ATPCO. ATPCO collects fares and rules (such as advance-purchase requirements, refundability, and so on) from each airline. ATPCO then publishes those fares back out to the airlines and to the reservation services. In the 1980s, fare changes were filed once a day. If someone changed fares, you found out on Monday and filed your competitive response on Tuesday. ATPCO was closed on weekends. Now ATPCO accepts fare changes three times every weekday—at 9 AM, 11:30 AM, and 7 PM Central Time—and once each on Saturday and Sunday. From 5 fare changes a week to 17.

As much as it can look like a kind of silly game—why not just take a pass on a couple of those changes?—it's not. "If a sale comes in at 7 PM from a competitor," says Continental's senior director of pricing, Bob Lancaster, "and you miss the 9 AM filing the next morning—you don't get your changes in until 11:30—you're in trouble." So when Continental has 7 million prices in the market, those prices can change not just every day, but several *times* a day. Typically, says Lancaster, the airlines collectively change 75,000 prices a day. On the morning after someone files a 7 PM sale, there might be 400,000 price changes across the markets.

This frantic tail chasing—which is done with the help of sophisticated computers and software that predicts ticket demand the way "models" predict the weather—is not lost on the smart people who do it. The wry, informal motto of the Continental pricing department is: "You're only as smart as your dumbest competitor." If some airline is taking prices on the Atlanta-Houston route into the ditch, then by gosh, Continental is going right down into the ditch with 'em. Usually.

It's easy to be cynical about the airlines; they could do many things better. But they also live in a business environment that would wilt the rest of us—and might soon. In the airline industry, every competitor knows the price of every product that every other airline offers and knows instantly of any changes. How would you fare if your competitors knew your prices, and your price changes, automatically?

In the airline business, every customer instantly knows every fare available, and a ticket from any airline is equally easy to buy. How would your business fare if your customers instantly knew the prices of your competitors—and could buy their products just as easily as yours?

"Are we addicted to the complexity of our pricing?" asks Continental's chief economist, Paul Thomas. "Yes, we are. But we aren't naive about it. We talk about it all the time."

And this complexity that goes with what the airlines do—this is what's going to sweep through the rest of the economy. Because in just the past few years, the kind of software that the airlines use has become available to any company.

PRICE CHECK (II): SHOPPING FOR AMERICA

Cindy Whittington is standing in a sea of women's coats in a department store in suburban Washington, DC. It is the thick of the Christmas-shopping season, and there are 29 racks of winter coats—perhaps 700 in all. Whittington has a pencil in her teeth, a three-ring binder on her left arm, and a look of calm determination in her eye. She's shopping, and the fate of the nation is balanced on her arm along with her binder.

Whittington is gathering prices used to calculate the U.S. Consumer Price Index. The mood of the stock market, the wages of millions of union workers, and the Social Security checks of nearly 50 million retirees all depend on the CPI. Given the complexity of the consumer economy, the way that the CPI is assembled remains oddly handcrafted. Some 80,000 prices are gathered each month, mostly in person, by 400 people like Cindy Whittington. For the moment, the prices are recorded on paper and keypunched into computers, although pricers will get touch-screen laptops later this year.

It is, in fact, the very complexity of the economy that sends people out into the stores every month. The goal of the CPI is to measure an unchanging (or at least slowly evolving) basket of goods—so that when Whittington plunges into the women's coats this season, she's got a detailed description of the four coats she's seeking. "My friends are very envious, because I get to go 'shopping' for a living," she says. "But it's not shopping, it's pricing." Still, Whittington says she spends so much time in stores, her friends call her "the queen of the deals."

As for the CPI itself, what's the price of that statistic? In an annual economy of $10.2 trillion, measuring the CPI costs $50 million—18 cents a year for each U.S. consumer.

THE SMART WAY TO LOWER PRICES: DISCOUNT LESS, BUT DISCOUNT SOONER

According to a recent study, 63% of noncouture clothing sold in the United States in 2002 was on sale. One way or another, if you're in apparel, managing markdowns matters. Over the years, clothing retailers have gone from being local shops to national chains, and buyers often haven't visited the stores that they are buying for. And even though the buyers have computers on their desks, the buying and pricing process has remained remarkably unchanged in half a century.

"Most retail companies still do a lot of things manually," says Steven Schwartz, senior vice president of planning and allocation at the Casual Male Retail Group, a chain of 475 clothing stores. "Our buyers and planners got reports on sales and inventory weekly," says Schwartz. "And they evaluated those reports, looking for what was selling, what to discount, and deciding the markdown. But they were going through paper 12 inches thick. We took a markdown. If it worked, great. If it didn't work, we took another markdown."

A couple of years ago, Schwartz began to look for a better way, and he found a half-dozen companies offering software to automate the markdown process. It works somewhat like airline-pricing software: The computers absorb several years' worth of data, look at what's in stores and how it's selling, and spit out recommendations for prices on specific clothing items. Casual Male picked ProfitLogic, a company based in Cambridge, Massachusetts that is also working with the Home Depot, JC Penney, and Old Navy. During the first year, Casual Male did a test across six departments in all of its stores. Schwartz's buyers would tell the ProfitLogic software what inventory they wanted to move, what the price was, and, most importantly, when Casual Male wanted to be sold-out (or when the chain wanted to have a certain amount left to be sold at its outlet chain).

ProfitLogic's system not only gave guidance on what to discount, and by how much, it also allowed Casual Male's buyers to ask their own questions, like, "What happens if we mark down 10% instead of 20%?"

The software inspired one basic change in the Casual Male markdown world: Discount less, but discount a lot sooner. "Merchants tend to get emotionally committed to what they buy," says David Boyce, ProfitLogic's vice president of marketing. "Buyers pick styles, colors. In general, they get it right, but once in a while, they don't. They always say, 'Just one more week! It will sell!'"

At Casual Male, the results were immediate. "Sell throughs"—selling all of something—"were much faster, much sooner," says Schwartz. The clothing was still on sale—but not as deeply discounted as it would have been a month later in the season. Schwartz is protective about the exact improvement in profitability. But in June 2002, the software was rolled out for all items at all stores—after Casual Male upgraded its national point-of-sale system.

Saks, with $6.5 billion in sales, is using similar software designed by a ProfitLogic competitor, Spotlight Solutions. After a test done during Christmas 2001, Saks rolled out the software widely this past Christmas. Like at Casual Male, the system is recommending smaller markdowns, but sooner. "What has surprised me," says Bill Franks, CIO of Saks, "is the accuracy of the software's algorithm predicting sales if we move the price. It is uncanny how accurate the software is."

Franks thinks that as the software becomes commonplace, it could have an unintended effect: that of lowering list prices. "What we've had to do up to now is overprice things at the beginning, to compensate for underpricing at the end of the season," he explains. "Ultimately, everything may be a little cheaper, because we won't have to absorb the cost of those deep markdowns at the end."

PRICE CHECK (III): HOW MUCH FOR A COKE?

One of the great moments in the history of price foolishness involved Coca-Cola. On October 28, 1999, the *New York Times* reported that Coke was testing a vending machine that could sense the outside temperature and "automatically raise prices for its drinks in hot weather."

The story came from Coke's then-chairman, Douglas Ivester. He was describing the technology to a Brazilian magazine, bragging that it could increase price during a sports championship in summer heat "when it is fair that it should be more expensive." Coke confirmed the testing; Pepsi said that it would never "exploit" customers in hot weather.

The story ran around the world and was met with outrage. On the day that the story broke, Coke backpedaled furiously, a spokesman saying of temperature-controlled pricing, "We don't see [that] happening anytime soon, if ever."

Of course, Ivester was right according to economic theory and market experience. His customers *already* paid a wild variety of prices for Coke, depending on the setting. What Ivester got wrong was the human part, the perception of price. Consider what the reaction might have been to this headline: "Coke testing machine that automatically discounts prices in cool weather." The tale of the temperature-controlled Coke machine is now taught in business schools across the country.

THE NEW SCIENCE OF PRICING: TEST AND TEST AGAIN

Larry Warnock has only been a new-wave scientific pricer for a few months, but he talks with the zeal of a convert—a zeal that comes from having discovered after 20 years in business something that's been sitting there all along. "How do companies set their prices?" asks Warnock. "Three ways. There's cost-plus. There's 'because my competitor did it.' And then there's what we call OTA pricing. Politely, that's 'out of the air.' Companies say, 'We price what the market will bear.' But they do nothing to *measure* what the market will bear."

Warnock is an executive vice president at Zilliant, an Austin, Texas-based company at the forefront of measuring what the market will bear. Zilliant's offices hardly seem to sit at the epicenter of a strategic revolution. The workspace is pedestrian. The software, however, is not. Zilliant pulls together a growing body of math that can analyze huge amounts of data and then use even more math to predict human behavior in the face of price changes. This isn't the kind of problem solving that even most math-team alumni have any experience with. Zilliant's chief scientist, Ahmet Kuyumcu, sent along a couple of algorithms of the sort that Zilliant uses. Here's one: $P_{win}(R) = \Sigma_N f_N \chi P(R)^N$.

The leap isn't just the computing power, though, or the math. The real leap of Zilliant, and its competitors, is a shrug of modesty. Zilliant says, We're not actually going to get the price *right*. What we're going to do is *look for* the right price.

Zilliant's software runs experiments. You pick a goal—maximizing total profits, for instance—and then you start selling stuff, the *same* stuff, in fact, just at slightly different prices. You don't just take a flier and raise your prices 5% and see if anyone flees to a competitor; you don't just drop your prices 15% and hope that the price brings in 20% more business. You test, you sell, you gather data—you see what works. Then you change your prices—maybe 4% up, maybe 6% down—when you know what's going to happen.

Small changes can make all the difference: Jim Compton and his colleagues at Continental Airlines boarded 44 million passengers in 2001, at an average ticket price of $193. Charging two bucks more per ticket would have swung the firm to profit. That's a price change of 1.04%.

Scientific pricing is really pricing using the scientific method. Let's not guess what's going to happen; let's change prices in a controlled way, watch what happens, then change prices for real after that. And by the way, we'll begin the next set of experiments the next day.

These experiments can reshape how and what companies charge for their services. One of Zilliant's first customers was DHL, the $6 billion-a-year shipping firm. DHL hadn't changed its list prices in five years, and its walk-up (or call-up) business was shrinking in the face of competition from FedEx and UPS.

The typical way that DHL might adjust prices would be to do a market-research study—to *ask* consumers whether they'd ship a five-pound package from Houston to Lyons, France for, say, $81. How about $71? The problem is instantly clear. A "study" like that is marginally better than a guess. As Aman Adinew, director of pricing and yield management for DHL North America, was considering his options, he stumbled onto Zilliant.

"I saw a huge difference between this software and the [survey]," says Adinew. "It is actually testing my customers. They call; we quote a price; they are actually shipping." In DHL's case, the Zilliant software measures something just as important: customers who called, got a quote, and *didn't* ship— a failed price.

The stakes were huge. In the international markets where they competed, FedEx and UPS were underpricing DHL by 20% to 30%. But DHL has a strong international reputation. Did it need to match those discounts to hold its customers? Would less of a discount do the job?

The scale of the problem, in ordinary terms, was vast. DHL was looking at prices in 43 different markets (United States to Mexico, for instance, or United States to Japan), in a range of weights. Just the basic price grid had hundreds of boxes—and DHL needed to test prices in every market for every product.

And the deadline was brutal. DHL and Zilliant talked in September 2001. Prices had to be set by December 17, to make the price-change date of February 1. After Adinew hired Zilliant, the company got its software installed at DHL's Tempe, Arizona call center in 14 days.

The Zilliant software would sit behind DHL's own systems, randomly offering customers the "experimental" prices, then recording the results. "We're taking real orders," says Adinew. "If something happens, and they shut it down, well," he laughs, "I wouldn't be talking to you right now."

Adinew and his staff had guesses about where raising and lowering rates would change volume and profitability. But Zilliant tested a range of prices for every product and every market, just to see. In the end, the system gathered tens of thousands of data points. DHL wound up changing hundreds of prices. And there were plenty of surprises. "Most of our prices went down," says Adinew. "But did we have to match the competition? Not at all." In fact, by lowering prices just a bit, DHL's "ad hoc" business not only stabilized, it grew. People were willing to pay more for DHL.

One key measure of the success of DHL's walk-up rates is the "quote-to-book" ratio. Of people who call to get a quote, how many actually ship? Before the Zilliant test, the number was about 17%. The new prices have increased the ratio to nearly 25% who call and ship. Revenue is up and profitability is up—in the shipping business, in a recession. "That's the beauty of it," says Adinew. The Zilliant experiment paid for itself, he says, "ten thousand times over. I can't tell you the number, but it's huge."

Prices make the world's economy go round. OPEC looks like it's about power; it's really about price. CNBC looks like it's about business; it's really a TV network devoted to prices. Even money, for all its ostensible power, is just a solvent for price. And yet, for all their significance, prices have most often been taken for granted. Scientific pricing ends that.

Adinew, with his airline background, knows the power of what he did. "This was no guessing game," he says. "We will never do this the old way again. This is science." DHL is now starting to use the Zilliant software across all kinds of other segments of its business. And Adinew has seen the future: "In 10 years, no major company will be able to survive without this kind of software. You just won't be able to compete."

Charles Fishman (cnfish@mindspring.com), a FAST COMPANY senior editor, considers himself "extremely price sensitive." His colleagues just think he's cheap.

The Old Pillars of New Retailing

Looking for the silver bullet that will solve your retailing woes? It doesn't exist.
The best retailers lay a foundation for success by creating
customer value in a handful of fundamental ways.

by Leonard L. Berry

EVERYONE WHO GLANCES AT A newspaper knows that the retailing world is brutally competitive. The demise of Montgomery Ward in the realm of bricks and mortar as well as the struggles of eToys on-line—to choose only two recent examples—make it clear that no retailer can afford to be complacent because of previous successes or rosy predictions about the future of commerce.

Despite the harsh realities of retailing, the illusion persists that magical tools, like Harry Potter's wand, can help companies overcome the problems of fickle consumers, price-slashing competitors, and mood swings in the economy. The wishful thinking holds that retailers will thrive if only they communicate better with customers through e-mail, employ hidden cameras to learn how customers make purchase decisions, and analyze scanner data to tailor special offers and manage inventory.

But the truth of the matter is, there are no quick fixes. Yes, technology can help any business operate more effectively, but many new advances are still poorly understood—and in any case, retailing can't be reduced to tools and techniques. Over the past eight years, I've analyzed dozens of retail companies to understand the underlying differences between outstanding and mediocre performers. My research includes interviews with senior and middle managers and frontline employees, observations of store operations, and extensive reviews of published and internal company materials. I've found that the best retailers create value for their customers in five interlocking ways. Doing a good job in just three or four of the ways won't cut it; competitors will rush to exploit weakness in any of the five areas. If one of the pillars of a successful retailing operation is missing, the whole edifice is weakened.

The key is focusing on the total customer experience. Whether you're running physical stores, a catalog business, an e-commerce site, or a combination of the three, you have to offer customers superior solutions to their needs, treat them with real respect, and connect with them on an emotional level. You also have to set prices fairly and make it easy for people to find what they need, pay for it, and move on. These pillars sound simple on paper, but they are difficult to implement in the real world. Taking each one in turn, we'll see how some retailers have built successful operations by attending to these commonsense ways of dealing with customers, and how others have failed to pay them the attention they require.

Pillar 1: Solve Your Customers' Problems

It has become commonplace for companies to talk about selling solutions rather than products or services. But what does this really mean for retailers? Put simply, it means that customers usually shop for a reason: they have a problem—a need—and the retailer hopes to provide the solution. It's not enough, for example, just to sell high-quality apparel—many retailers do that. Focusing on solutions means employing salespeople who know how to help customers find clothing that fits and flatters, having tailors on staff and at the ready, offering home delivery, and happily placing special orders. Every retailer hopes to meet its customers' pressing needs; some do it much better than others.

The Container Store provides its customers with superior solutions. The 22-store chain, based in Dallas, averages double-digit annual sales growth by selling something that absolutely everyone needs: storage and organization products. From boxes and trunks to hangers, trays, and shelving systems, each store carries up to 12,000 different products.

The Container Store's core strategy is the same today as it was in 1978, when the company was founded: to improve customers' lives by giving them more time and space. The company accomplishes this mission well. It starts with the selection of merchandise, which must meet criteria for visibility, accessibility, and versatility. The company's philosophy is that its products should allow people to see what they've stored and get at it easily. The merchandise must also be versatile enough to accommodate customers' particular requirements.

Store organization is another key ingredient of superior solutions at the Container Store. The merchandise is organized in sections such as kitchen, closet, laundry, office, and so on. Many products are displayed in several sections because they can solve a variety of problems. A sweater box, for example, can also store office supplies. Plastic trash cans can also be used for dog food and recyclables. Individual products are often combined and sold as a system—thus, parents in the store who want to equip their children for summer camp may find a trunk filled with a laundry bag, a toothbrush case, a first-aid pouch, leakproof bottles, a "critter catcher," and other items.

Great service is another component of the Container Store's ability to solve its customers' storage prob-

lems. The company is very careful about hiring; it patiently waits until it finds just the right person for a position. Container Store employees are well trained to demonstrate how products work and to propose solutions to complex home organizational problems. They are also treated very well, both in terms of pay and in less tangible ways. In fact, the Container Store was ranked the best place to work in the country in 1999 and 2000 by *Fortune* magazine.

A relentless focus on solutions may sound simple, but it's not. The Container Store has many imitators, but none have matched it. Many businesses have only the fuzziest concept of selling solutions. Department store chains, for example, have stumbled in recent years. They lost their one-stop shopping advantage by eliminating many merchandise categories outside of apparel and housewares. And even as they focused on apparel, they lost ground both to specialty retailers that have larger category selections and to discounters that have lower prices. Finally, they lost their customer service advantage by employing salespeople who often are little more than poorly trained order takers. As a result, these stores do a relatively poor job of solving customers' problems. That's probably why only 72% of consumers shopped in department stores in 2000 compared with 85% in 1996.

Clearly, the lesson here is that you must understand what people need and how you're going to fill that need better than your competitors. The Container Store has figured this out; many department stores and other struggling retailers must go back to the beginning and answer these basic questions.

Pillar 2: Treat Customers with R-e-s-p-e-c-t

The best retailers show their customers what Aretha Franklin sang about: respect. Again, this is absolutely basic, and most retail executives would say that of course they

treat customers with respect. But it just isn't so.

Everyone has stories to tell about disrespectful retailing. You're in an electronics store, looking for assistance to buy a DVD player or a laptop computer. You spot a couple of employees by their uniforms and badges, but they're deep in conversation. They glance in your direction but continue to ignore you. After awhile, you walk out, never to return.

Or you're in a discount store, looking for planters that have been advertised at a low price. You go to the store's garden center but cannot find the planters. This time, you succeed in flagging down an employee. You ask about the planters, but she just mumbles "I dunno" and walks away. Frustrated, you go to the customer service desk and ask the clerk where you might find the advertised planters. He suggests that you try the garden center. Once again, you head for the exit.

It's easy to go on. Stories about women trying to buy cars, as everyone knows, are enough to make your hair curl. The fact is, disrespectful retailing is pervasive. In the 2000 Yankelovich Monitor study of 2,500 consumers, 68% of those surveyed agreed with the statement that "Most of the time, the service people that I deal with for the products and services that I buy don't care much about me or my needs."

Disrespectful retailing isn't just about bored, rude, and unmotivated service workers. Cluttered, poorly organized stores, lack of signage, and confusing prices all show lack of respect for customers.

The best retailers translate the basic concept of respect into a set of practices built around people, policies, and place:

- They select, prepare, and manage their people to exhibit competence, courtesy, and energy when dealing with customers.
- They institute policies that emphasize fair treatment of customers—regardless of their age, gender, race, appearance, or size

of purchase or account. Likewise, their prices, returns policy, and advertising are transparent.

- They create a physical space, both inside and outside the store, that is carefully designed to value customers' time.

In 1971, a 30-year-old entrepreneur named Len Riggio bought a floundering Manhattan bookshop called Barnes & Noble. Today, Barnes & Noble is the nation's largest bookseller, with fiscal 1999 sales of $3.3 billion. Respect for the customer has been at the heart of the company's rise.

Riggio's biggest idea was that books appeal to most everyone, not just to intellectuals, writers, and students in cosmopolitan cities. Riggio listened to prospective customers who wanted bigger selections of books, more convenient locations, and less intimidating environments. He put superstores in all types of communities, from big cities like Atlanta and Chicago, to smaller cities like Midland, Texas, and Reno, Nevada. His respect for the customer led him to create stores with spacious and comfortable interiors, easy chairs for relaxing with a book, and Starbucks coffee bars. To this day, he considers his best decision the installation of easy-to-find public restrooms in the stores. As he said in a recent speech, "You work so hard and invest so much to get people to visit your store, why would you want them to have to leave?"

Besides the large selection of books, the stores also have an active calendar of author signings, poetry readings, children's events, and book discussion groups. Many Barnes & Noble superstores have become a social arena in which busy consumers—who normally rush in and out of other stores—linger.

Riggio sees the Internet as much more than a way to deliver books to customers; it's another opportunity to listen to them and thus show respect for them. He views the store network and Barnesandnoble.com as portals to each other. Customers can ask salespeople at Internet ser-

vice counters to search Barnesandnoble.com for out-of-stock books, for customer reviews of titles that interest them, and for information about authors, such as other books they've published. Customers in a superstore can order the books they want on-line and have them shipped either to that store or to any other address. If a return is necessary, customers can bring their on-line purchase back to the store.

The value of respect often gets little more than lip service from retailers. Some companies wait until it's too late to put words into action.

Pillar 3: Connect with Your Customers' Emotions

Most retailers understand in principle that they need to connect emotionally with consumers; a good many don't know how to (or don't try to) put the principle into practice. Instead, they neglect the opportunity to make emotional connections and put too much emphasis on prices. The promise of low prices may appeal to customers' sense of reason, but it does not speak to their passions.

Many U.S. furniture retailers are guilty of ignoring consumers' emotions. Although the average size of new homes in the country has grown by 25% since 1980, furniture accounts for a lower percentage of total U.S. consumer spending today (1%) than it did in 1980 (1.2%). Making consumers wait up to two months to receive their furniture contributes to these poor results. How can consumers get emotionally involved in products they know they won't see for weeks?

Poor marketing also hurts the industry. Most furniture stores focus strictly on price appeals, emphasizing cost savings rather than the emotional lift that can come from a new look in the home. "We don't talk about how easy it can be to make your home more attractive," says Jerry Epperson, an investment banker who specializes in the furni-

ture industry. "All we talk about is 'sale, sale, sale' and credit terms."

Great retailers reach beyond the model of the rational consumer and strive to establish feelings of closeness, affection, and trust. The opportunity to establish such feelings is open to any retailer, regardless of the type of business or the merchandise being sold. Everyone is emotionally connected to some retailers—from local businesses such as the wine merchant who always remembers what you like; to national companies like Harley-Davidson, which connects people through its Harley Owners Group; to catalog retailer Coldwater Creek, which ships a substitute item to customers who need to make returns before the original item is sent back.

One retailer that has connected especially well with its target market in recent years is Journeys, a Nashville, Tennessee-based chain of shoe stores located primarily in shopping malls. The chain focuses on selling footwear to young men and women between the ages of 15 and 25. Started in 1987, Journeys didn't take off until 1995 when new management took over. The chain has achieved double-digit comparable-store sales increases in five of the six years since then and is now expanding by as many as 100 new stores per year.

Journeys has penetrated the skepticism and fickleness that are characteristic of many teens. By keeping a finger on the pulse of its target market, the company consistently has the right brands available for this especially brand-conscious group of consumers. Equally important, it creates the right store atmosphere—the stores pulsate with music, video, color, and brand merchandising.

A Journeys store is both welcoming and authentic to young people; it is simultaneously energetic and laid-back. Journeys' employees are typically young—the average age of a store manager is about 25—and they dress as they please. Customers frequently visit a store in groups just to hang out; salespeople exert no pressure to buy. And everyone, whether they've made a purchase or not, usually leaves with a giveaway—for instance, a key chain, a compact-disc case, a promotional T-shirt, or one of the 10 million or so stickers the stores give out over the course of a year. The stickers, which usually feature one of the brands Journeys sells, often end up on backpacks, skateboards, school lockers, or bathroom mirrors. Journeys also publishes a bimonthly magazine, *Dig*, that is available in the stores, and it runs a Web site that seeks to replicate the atmosphere of its stores. The number of site visits explodes whenever the company's commercials appear on MTV.

Journeys works in large part because it has created an atmosphere that connects emotionally with the young people it serves. Other retailers should bear in mind that it takes more than a room full of products with price tags on them to draw people in.

Pillar 4: Set the Fairest (Not the Lowest) Prices

Prices are about more than the actual dollars involved. If customers suspect that the retailer isn't playing fair, prices can also carry a psychological cost. Potential buyers will not feel comfortable making purchases if they fear that prices might be 30% lower next week, or if certain charges have only been estimated, or if they are unsure whether an advertised sale price represents a genuine markdown.

Consider some of the pricing tactics commonly used by certain home improvement retailers. One well-known company advertises products as "special buys" even though it has not lowered the regular prices. Another purposely misrepresents a competitor's prices on price-comparison signs within its stores. Still another company promotes lower-grade merchandise implying that it is top quality. One retailer puts a disclaimer in its ads that reads: "Prices in this ad may be different from the actual price at time of purchase. We adjust our prices daily to the lumber commodity market." The disclaimer paves the way for the retailer to raise its prices regardless of the advertised price.

Excellent retailers seek to minimize or eliminate the psychological costs associated with manipulative pricing. Most of these retailers follow the principles of "everyday fair pricing" instead of "everyday low pricing." A fact of retail life is that no retailer, not even Wal-Mart, can truthfully promise customers that it will always have the lowest prices. An uncomfortable truth for many retailers is that their "lowest price anywhere" positioning is a crutch for the lack of value-adding innovation. Price is the only reason they give customers to care.

Retailers can implement a fair-pricing strategy by clearing two hurdles. First, they must make the cultural and strategic transition from thinking value equals price to realizing that value is the total customer experience. Second, they must understand the principles of fair pricing and muster the courage needed to put them into practice. Retailers who price fairly sell most goods at regular but competitive prices and hold legitimate sales promotions. They make it easy to compare their prices with those of competitors, and they avoid hidden charges. They don't raise prices to take advantage of temporary blips in demand, and they stand behind the products they sell.

Zane's Cycles in Branford, Connecticut, is one of the most successful independent bicycle retailers in the United States. Zane's has grown its one-store business at least 20% every year since it was founded in 1981, selling 4,250 bicycles in 2000 along with a full array of accessories. The company's success illustrates the appeal of fair pricing.

Zane's sells better bike brands with prices starting at $250. It stands behind what it sells with a 30-day test-drive offer (customers can return a bike within 30 days and exchange it for another) and a 90-day price protection guarantee (if a buyer finds the same bike in Connecticut at a lower price within 90 days, Zane's will refund the difference plus 10%). Zane's also offers free lifetime service on all new bicycles it sells; it was likely the first bicycle retailer in the United States to take this step. The promise of lifetime service includes annual tune-ups, brake and gear adjustments, wheel straightening and more.

Zane's holds only one promotional sale a year, a three-day spring weekend event featuring discounts on all products. Vendors and former employees come to work at the huge event—some even fly in to participate. Customers who purchase a bicycle at Zane's within 90 days before the sale are encouraged to return during the event for a refund based on the discounted price of their bike. The company refunded about $3,000 during the 2000 sale, but most of that money remained in the store because customers bought more gear. Zane's sold 560 bicycles during the 2000 sale—that's more than the typical one-store U.S. bicycle retailer sells in an entire year. And yet the limited duration of the sale means that Zane's sells about 85% of its bicycles at the regular price.

When Connecticut passed a bike-helmet law in 1992, Zane's sold helmets to kids at cost rather than take advantage of legislated demand. Owner Chris Zane convinced area school administrators to distribute flyers to students under 12 announcing that policy. "We sold a ton of helmets and made a lot of new friends for the store," Zane says. "Our customers trust us. They come in and say, 'I am here to get a bike. What do I need?' They have confidence in our ability to find them just the right bike at a fair price and to stand behind what we sell."

Constant sales, markdowns on over-inflated prices, and other forms of pressure pricing may boost sales in the short term. Winning customers' trust through fair pricing will pay off in the long term.

Are Your Retailing Pillars Solid—or Crumbling?

	Inferior Retailers...	Superior Retailers...
Solutions	gather products, stack them on shelves, put price tags on them, and wonder where their customers are.	consider what people really need and how they can meet that particular need better than competitors can.
Respect	are staffed by people who don't know what customers want and aren't about to interrupt their conversations to find out.	actually train and manage the salespeople they hire so that they are courteous, energetic, and helpful to customers.
Emotions	act as if their customers are Spock-like Vulcans who make purchases solely according to cold logic.	recognize that everything about a retail experience sends a message to customers that goes to the heart, not just the brain.
Pricing	focus exclusively on their supposed low prices, often because they have nothing else of value to offer customers.	focus on having fair prices instead of playing mind games with "special offers," fine print, and bogus sales.
Convenience	are open for business when it's convenient for them, close checkout lanes when it's convenient for them, deliver products when it's convenient for them, and so on.	understand that people's most precious commodity in the modern world is time and do everything they can to save as much of it as possible for their customers.

Pillar 5: Save Your Customers' Time

Many consumers are poor in at least one respect: they lack time. Retailers often contribute to the problem by wasting consumers' time and energy in myriad ways, from confusing store layouts to inefficient checkout operations to inconvenient hours of business. When shopping is inconvenient, the value of a retailer's offerings plummets.

Slow checkout is particularly annoying to busy people. Managers usually know how much money they are saving by closing a checkout lane; but they may not realize how many customers they've lost in the process. For a food shopper waiting behind six other customers in the "10 Items or Fewer" lane to buy a carton of milk, the time invested in the purchase may outweigh the value of the milk. The shopper may follow through this time but find another store next time. Studies by America's Research Group, a consumer research company based in Charleston, South Carolina, indicate that 83% of women and 91% of men have ceased shopping at a particular store because of long checkout lines.

To compete most effectively, retailers must offer convenience in four ways. They must offer convenient retail locations and operating hours and be easily available by telephone and the Internet (access convenience). They must make it easy for consumers to identify and select desired products (search convenience). They need to make it possible for people to get the products they want by maintaining a high rate of in-stock items and by delivering store, Internet, or catalog orders swiftly (possession convenience). And they need to let consumers complete or amend transactions quickly and easily (transaction convenience).

ShopKo, a discount chain based in Green Bay, Wisconsin, illustrates how shopping speed and ease can create value. ShopKo's more than 160 large discount stores operate in 19 midwestern, mountain, and northwestern states; 80% of the customer base is working women. With fiscal 1999 sales of $3.9 billion (including its small-market subsidiary, Pamida), ShopKo is much smaller than Wal-Mart, Kmart, or Target, yet it competes successfully against all three. Since 1995, following the arrival of new management a year earlier, ShopKo has more than doubled sales and achieved record earnings growth.

ShopKo takes possession convenience seriously and is in-stock 98% of the time on advertised and basic merchandise. Search convenience is another strength. ShopKo stores are remarkably clean and neat. Major traffic aisles are free of passage-blocking displays. Customers near the front of the store have clear sight lines to the back. Navigational signs handing from the ceiling and on the ends of the aisles help point shoppers in the right direction. Clothing on a hanger has a size tag on the hanger neck; folded apparel has an adhesive strip indicating the size on the front of the garment. Children's garments have "simple sizing"—extra small, small, medium, and large—with posted signs educating shoppers on how to select the proper size.

ShopKo has a "one-plus-one" checkout policy of opening another checkout lane whenever two customers are waiting in any lane. Ready-to-assemble furniture is sold on a pull-tag system. The customer presents a coded tag at checkout and within three minutes the boxed merchandise is ready to be delivered to the customer's car. These ways of operating give ShopKo an edge in transaction convenience.

ShopKo is succeeding in the fiercely competitive discount sector by focusing on the total shopping experience rather than on having the lowest prices. Shopping speed and ease combined with a pleasant store atmosphere, a well-trained staff, and a carefully selected range of merchandise creates a strong mix of customer value.

While ShopKo creates real convenience for its customers, the term is often used carelessly in retailing. Consider that Internet shopping is commonly referred to as convenient. The Internet does indeed offer superior convenience for some stages of the shopping experience; it is inferior for other stages. On-line shoppers who save a trip to a physical

store must wait for delivery. Christmas shoppers who receive gifts ordered on-line *after* the holiday learn a lesson about possession inconvenience. This is one reason that the most promising path for most retailers is a strategy that combines physical and virtual stores. Increasingly, the best-managed retailers will enable customers to take advantage of the most effective features of physical and virtual shopping, even for the same transaction.

Retail competition has never been more intense or more diverse than it is today. Yet the companies featured in this article, and hundreds of other excellent retailers, are thriving. They understand that neither technology nor promises of "the lowest prices anywhere" can substitute for a passionate focus on the total customer experience. These retailers enable customers to solve important prob-

lems, capitalize on the power of respectfulness, connect with customers' emotions, emphasize fair pricing, and save customers time and energy. In an age that demands instant solutions, it's not possible to combine those ingredients with Redi-Mix, crank out a concrete-block building, and hope the structure will stand. But retailers who thoughtfully and painstakingly erect these pillars will have a solid operation that is capable of earning customers' business, trust, and loyalty.

Leonard L. Berry is Distinguished Professor of Marketing and holds the M.B. Zale Chair in Retailing and Marketing Leadership at Texas A&M University in College Station, Texas. He founded Texas A&M's Center for Retailing Studies and directed it from 1982 to 2000. He is the author of Discovering the Soul of Service *(Free Press, 1999).*

Got Advertising That Works?

How the "Got Milk?" campaign shook consumers out of their milk malaise.

By Jeff Manning and Kevin Lane Keller

THE 10-YEAR-OLD "Got Milk?" campaign—considered one of the most popular ad campaigns of the 1990s—was borne of necessity. In February 1993, the California Milk Processor Board (CMPB) was reviewing reports on per capita U.S. consumption of milk over the last 15 years. To anyone involved in the production and sales of milk, the numbers painted a disturbing picture. Not only had there been a steady decline in milk consumption over the previous two decades, but the decline was now accelerating. The CMPB's ad budget paled in comparison to the big beverage marketers like Coca-Cola and Pepsi. With almost $2 billion in media spending annually in beverages as a category, CMPB had to make the most of its $23 million budget to have milk's message heard among the noise.

To revitalize sales of a product in seemingly perpetual decline, CMPB and its ad agency Goodby, Silverstein & Partners developed the "Got Milk?" campaign. The campaign was based on a milk deprivation strategy that reminded consumers how inconvenient it was to be without milk when eating certain foods such as cereal, brownies, or chocolate chip cookies. The "Got Milk?" campaign was launched in November 1993. Although focus groups indicated that consumers liked the ads, the actual launch exceeded all expectations. The campaign zoomed to a 60% aided-recall level in only three months, enjoyed 70% awareness within 6 months, and surpassed the long-running "It Does a Body Good" campaign in top-of-mind awareness in less than a year. The "Got Milk?" campaign quickly became a consumer favorite, prompting a *Los An-*

geles Times reporter to comment, "Since the ad campaign began, it has reached a near-cult following."

Not only did the campaign get consumers talking, it also exceeded initial expectations of merely stemming the sales decline by increasing actual milk consumption. The number of consumers who reported consuming milk at least "several times a week" jumped from 72% at the start of the campaign to 78% a year later. California household consumption of milk increased every month in the first year after the launch except for the first two months that the campaign began. This performance was in sharp contrast to the rest of the country where consumption actually declined over the same period. In the year prior to the campaign's launch, California milk processors experienced a decline in sales volume of 1.67% or $18 million. A year after the launch, sales volume increased 1.07% or $13 million, for a total turnaround of $31 million. On a month-to-month comparison, sales volume had increased every month to rise 6.8% by the end of the first year.

"Got Milk?" is now deeply entrenched in the American vernacular. The campaign has virtually universal awareness, won just about every marketing and creative competition around, spawned more than 100 rip-offs, led to an unprecedented licensing program, been used in thousands of newspaper articles, justified a book, appeared on hundreds of celebrity moustache ads, and has been mentioned in popular TV shows. Not to mention the fact that it also helped stem the long-term decline in milk sales.

A number of key lessons emerged that help to shed light on arguably

one of the most successful ad campaigns of the last decade and, more importantly, provide guidance to advertising and communication efforts for virtually any brand. On the tenth anniversary of the launch of the program, here are 10 of the most important lessons.

1. Target the right consumers. When sales slide, some firms mistakenly and frantically attempt to attract new users to turn things around. The first step in stopping a sales decline, however, is making sure no other customers leave the brand franchise, especially those most loyal customers who generate much of the brand volume and profit. These customers typically will be most receptive to brand communications and, in fact, may actually be the best short-term source of sales growth. Once brand sales are stabilized, additional sources of growth via new market segments can be targeted.

Accordingly, in order to generate quick results, CMPB decided to target "regular" users of milk who used the product several times a week or more. Regular users constituted 70% of the California market and already had favorable attitudes toward drinking milk and presumably could be influenced in the short term. In contrast, non-users or light users typically refrained from milk for actual or perceived health reasons, which probably could not be changed very quickly.

Consumers could relate to the plight of the poor protagonist and, more important, got the message—running out of milk was no fun.

2. Thoroughly study your target market to find fresh insights. Consumer immersion is critical, and creative research invariably is needed to uncover fresh insights that will yield a stronger brand positioning. Qualitative and quantitative research are increasingly being supplemented by more experiential research where consumers are studied in more naturalistic settings.

To more fully understand their consumers, "Got Milk?" research efforts went beyond traditional focus groups and surveys. Goodby, Silverstein & Partners employed a series of creative, more experiential research studies. For example, to learn how consumers responded to running out of milk, they placed small video cameras in the refrigerators in the agency and took out all the milk to see how employees would react when they found out. One of the most productive research studies involved having a group of consumers go without milk for a week and return to the agency to share their experiences. Consumers' tales of woe and despair made it clear that milk was an integral part of consumers lives, and their anecdotes and recollections even provided inspiration for later advertising creative.

3. Unearth a deeply competitive strategy and stay with it. The challenge in brand building these days is to find competitively unique, but also consumer-relevant, market positions. Because so many potential points of differences between brands have been competed away, it's often difficult to find any viable opportunities in the marketplace. Uncovering those opportunities requires leaving no stone unturned.

The key consumer insight that emerged from CMPB research was almost frighteningly simple and obvious: Sell milk with food. And yet, as CMPB reviewed milk advertising from around the country (and the world), it found that food was almost totally absent. Perhaps in an attempt to compete against soft drinks, the dairy industry had lost contact with its roots. Consumers hadn't, though. They said time and time again that certain foods drive their milk decision.

Nobody doubted that previous milk campaigns successfully achieved positive shifts in consumer attitudes toward milk. What was missing, however, was a corresponding change in consumer behavior. Consumers knew milk was good and thought they should drink more of it, but they never thought enough about milk to be motivated to change their consumption habits. The typical milk campaign, emphasizing calcium and other vitamins, caused consumers to tune out. A new campaign had to break the mold for milk advertising, grab attention, and shake consumers out of their "milk malaise."

Although so many people drank milk every day, milk suffered from a complete lack of consumer mind share. People just didn't think about milk often enough at home, and they almost never thought about milk outside of the home. In order for any campaign to be successful, this lack of mind share had to change. One way to implement the change was to get consumers to stop taking milk for granted, to take them by surprise by creating a new and different image for milk.

Based on the consumer insight, the CMPB and Goodby, Silverstein & Partners decided to reach out to the regular users with a "deprivation strategy." The most effective way to capitalize on milk's relationship with food was to create an advertising campaign that paired the two together. Each ad in the campaign highlighted one of milk's perfect complements: cereal, chocolate chip cookies, peanut butter and jelly sandwiches, and so on. The clever creative twist, however, was to deprive the main character of milk. The end result was delicious food *without milk*—the deprivation strategy. Certain foods without milk represented "cruel and unusual punishment" to most people, and the advertising campaign would set out to drive this message home. In each of the ads, a meal or snack would be essentially ruined because of the absence of milk.

Milk deprivation essentially redefined beverage marketing so that milk won and Coke and Snapple lost. It also spoke directly to an incredibly wide range of consumers: Running out of milk is a pain in the butt regardless of one's age or income or lifestyle!

4. Entertain ... but sell. The right positioning and message is necessary but not sufficient to create a successful ad campaign—there must also be the right creative. In other words, great advertising comes from knowing what to say, as well as how to say it.

The CMPB knew that other beverages had successfully built up strong brand images over the last decade and believed milk could do the same by taking a more lighthearted approach that talked directly to consumers. The dairy industry had taken itself too seriously. Eating is the most popular form of entertainment in California, the United States, and the world. Get people smiling at your advertising and they would look, listen, and consume more milk.

The television ads gradually built the tension that was so critical to the deprivation strategy. Each television ad began with a close-up of one of the food complements such as the peanut butter and jelly sandwich. Once the desire for the food was established, the protagonist took a big bite. While joyfully chewing the food, the protagonist casually reached for a glass of milk. Unfortunately, there was no more milk left in the container. A desperate search for even a single drop ensued, but all efforts were in vain. At the height of anguish, the voice-over pronounced, "Got Milk?"

The ads were funny, but relevant. Consumers could relate to the plight of the poor protagonist and, more important, got the message—running out of milk was no fun. The solution was obvious—be sure to always stock enough milk.

5. Treat the consumer with respect. Advertising doesn't have to aim for the lowest common denominator. In fact, the highest common denominator can be a breath of fresh air to consumers. By not considering what consumers would really like to see, advertisers fail to adopt the right consumer "voice" and thus use a completely wrong approach.

"Got Milk?" is an inherently humble idea. Rather than lecturing (a la Mom), it asks a simple, thought-provoking question: "Do you have enough milk?" It displays a genuine interest in the consumer's opinion that was unheard of in 1993. Think of how much difference one letter would have made—"Get Milk!" instead of "Got Milk?"

6. Adopt a memorable and inspiring brand slogan and signature. Too often, consumers fail to grasp the meaning of ad campaigns or, even worse, draw the wrong conclusions. In such cases, help the consumer out. Devise a few words or a short phrase as a brand slogan or ad tag line that captures the essence of the ad campaign and what it intends to say about the brand. Then use the brand slogan to the fullest extent possible.

For example, the brand slogan can be a vital part of the brand signature—the way the brand is identified at the conclusion of a TV or radio ad or displayed within a print ad. The brand signature must creatively engage the consumer and cause him or her to pay more attention to the brand itself and, as a consequence, increase the strength of brand associations created by the ad. An effective brand signature can dynamically and stylistically provide a seamless connection to the ad as a whole, improving recall and motivating purchase.

"Got Milk?" was a powerful call to action and distilled the brand positioning and message of the ad down to two simple words. Effectively, it functioned as a hook or handle to the intent and main message of the campaign. It was shorthand to consumers that boiled down the key take-away that CMPB wanted to have happen. Moreover, the synonymous brand name and slogan was often used in a manner fitting the ad (e.g., in flames for the "yuppie in hell" ad or in primary school print for the "school lunchroom bully" ad), further enhancing its ability to function as a hook to the brand message.

7. Integrate, integrate, integrate. The days when it was the case that "if you build a great ad, they will come" are long gone. Ad campaigns must incorporate multiple media, taking advantage of the unique characteristics of each and blending them together so that the whole is greater than the sum of the parts.

In order to maximize the impact on consumer behavior, the media strategy for "Got Milk?" focused on consumers in the place where they typically used milk (in the home) and where they typically bought milk (in the supermarket). According to

CMPB, there were three ideal times to communicate the milk message: on the way to the store, in the store, and at home where milk could be immediately consumed. The media strategy complemented the overall communications strategy to reach this goal. The advertising creative strategy motivated consumers to crave the featured food and/or check their refrigerators for the availability of milk. The media strategy focused primarily on television as the medium, thereby catching consumers in their homes where 90% of total milk is consumed. Furthermore, the media buy for the ads typically concentrated on those times of day when consumers drank the most milk (i.e., mornings during breakfast, late evening snacks, and so on). It was thought that timing ads in this manner—given the "call to action" nature of the campaign—could potentially lead to more impulse usage of milk. Each usage occasion was further broken down into the type of user in order to purchase television advertising time. Children were targeted in the early morning hours as well as late afternoons, while adults were targeted at prime time and late night snack times.

It was the magic of TV, outdoor billboards, publicity, cross promotions, and licensing that took "Got Milk?" from an ad to an icon.

To capitalize on the remaining communications expenditures within the store, the "Got Milk?" billboards were located near supermarkets as a reminder to consumers before they entered the store. Billboards and signs at bus shelters reinforced the television campaign and featured the same foods as the television ads with one bite taken out. Of course, each billboard prominently displayed the key question: "Got Milk?" The intention was to get consumers thinking about milk before they entered the store so they would buy milk once they were inside. Other promotions included milk coupons on many recognizable brands of complementary foods located throughout the supermarket, point of purchase displays, shelf talkers at the complementary food locations, and "Got Milk?" check-out dividers.

It could be strongly argued that "Got Milk?" would have failed if it had only been a TV campaign. It was the magic of TV, outdoor billboards, publicity, cross promotions, and licensing that took "Got Milk?" from an ad to an icon.

8. Don't try to make it alone. Increasingly, brands are being built with the assistance and help of other brands. Co-branding, ingredient branding, brand alliances, and joint promotions are all ways to partner with other brands in an attempt to find "win-win" solutions that lead to greater brand equity and better profitability than would have otherwise been possible.

Breaking with the past milk campaigns, CMPB decided to leverage milk's relationship with food by partnering with those foods instead of relying on pulling consumers over to the dairy case. The complementary television, radio, print, and billboard campaigns all leveraged this relationship and capitalized on the advertising budgets of several major brands of cereals and cookies. "Got Milk?" could not have gone far without its host of "co-dependent" brands: Nesquik, Oreos, Cheerios, Girl Scout cookies, even Cookie Monster and Snap! Crackle! & Pop! These alliances helped elevate "Got Milk?" to an unchallenged position in the minds of consumers, the media, and the retail trade.

9. Keep campaigns … but keep them fresh. One common mistake in advertising is that successful campaigns are dropped too soon because marketers and their agencies tire of the campaign sooner than consumers actually do. Unfortunately, more often that not, there is no "Plan B" and an updated, rejuvenated version of the old ad campaign would have had a much greater likelihood of success than an unknown or untested new ad campaign. When your board of directors starts to get bored with your campaign, run it another five years.

Sure we get tired of our own campaigns. We think about them and watch them and talk about them all the time. It would have been easy to drop "Got Milk?" after four or five years, when the first "God, can't we do something new?" remark surfaced. Thankfully, that didn't happen and the tag line is conservatively valued

The "Got Milk?" advertising campaign has also met with critical acclaim.

In 1995, the ads won an Effie Award, as well as top honors from several other major advertising award committees. In September of that same year, "Got Milk?" joined the familiar "milk moustache" program as a national campaign, and the Goodby, Silverstein & Partners ads began receiving national exposure in television, print, and outdoor media.

Though the only commonly shared element of the two commercial series was the prominence of milk, consumers assumed that the two series originated from the same source. In fact, the dairy farmers group, Dairy Management Inc. (DMI), controlled the national "Got Milk?" campaign while the National Milk Processors Education Program (MilkPEP) funded the milk moustache campaign. DMI had approached the CMPB to purchase the licensing rights to "Got Milk?" to replace its own campaign. In California, the CMPB continued to govern the "Got Milk?" campaign, employing Goodby, Silverstein & Partners to develop the ads. Leo Burnett USA handled the national "Got Milk?" creative after Goodby, Silverstein & Partners licensed its work, while Bozell Worldwide did the milk moustache ad work. Perhaps in an effort to consolidate the equity achieved by the separate campaigns, MilkPEP obtained licensing rights to the slogan in 1998 and replaced the milk moustache ads tag line "Milk. What a Surprise" with Dairy Management's "Got Milk?" That same year, the two milk groups forged a partnership that combined their considerable advertising budgets, pooling DMI's $70 million TV and outdoor budget and MilkPEP's $110 million milk moustache budget.

"The Got Milk?" campaign continues to be strong and pay dividends. For 2002 and the first half of 2003, milk sales in California, where the ad campaign is centered, increased roughly 1.5%, whereas sales in the rest of the country remained flat.

at more than $1 billion and an irreplaceable asset to the milk industry.

10. Treat agencies as partners and keep the focus on great work. Adversarial relationships rarely work, and the most successful and longest running ad campaigns often come from establishing a high degree of trust between a core group of decision-makers for the client and agency. Less can be more, and getting the right people involved (no more or no less) is critical. Therefore, streamline, prune, and then cut some more people out of the marketing department. There is a basic, nearly immutable rule: Advertising gets more fractured, self-serving, and plain old dumb with each person that passes judgment on it.

"Got Milk?" creative has been approved (or disapproved) by the same person since day one. At the same time, advertising is often the single largest discretionary expense on the spreadsheet. Yet the CEO is often completely removed from strategic development and the work that goes on the air. The CMPB CEO viewed every single focus group (more than 150).

It's also important to build pliant, trusting, enduring relationships with agency principals. In 1993, the CMPB's stated goal was to become Goodby, Silverstein & Partners best client. Despite his agency having more than quadrupled in size, Jeff Goodby, the agency founder and creative talent, still works on "Got Milk?" Importantly, he doesn't just glance at finished TV spots. Rather, he actually pencils and doodles layouts.

A *New Yorker* cartoon from the early '70s still rings true. It depicts two white-haired, executive types fishing from a rowboat. One says; "We haven't caught a fish all day." The other replies; "Right, let's fire the agency." Client management must take full responsibility for the results of the advertising it approves. Changing CMOs and firing agencies doesn't get rid of mediocre advertising. It only amplifies it.

The principles applied in developing and running the landmark "Got Milk?" ad campaign are relevant to virtually any brand. Ensuring that brand advertising adheres to these principles can be an important means of enhancing the productivity and longevity of any ad campaign.

Authors' Note: The authors would like to thank Keith Richey for his research assistance. It is gratefully appreciated.

Jeff Manning is executive director of the California Milk Processor Board. He may be reached at manning@gotmilk.com. **Kevin Lane Keller** is E.B. Osborn professor of marketing, Amos Tuck School of Business, Dartmouth College. He may be reached at kevin.keller@dartmouth.edu.

Global ads aim for one brand, image

Unified message can be adapted for local market

By Theresa Howard

CANNES, France—It's a small world—and getting smaller for advertisers.

The Web, e-mail and wireless technology give people 24/7 global connections. Carriers such as UPS and FedEx deliver overnight around the world. International travel is cheaper and more available. Alliances led by the expanding European Union and its single euro currency are breaking down trade and political borders.

"The whole communication infrastructure has changed," says Ken Bernhardt, professor of marketing at Georgia State University's Robinson College of Business. "It's easier for businesses to communicate with each other so you truly can have today what people talked about in the past, which was think global, act local."

Nowhere is the trend more evident than with award contenders from around the world here at the 51st annual Cannes Lions International Advertising Festival.

They show that marketing is being altered to fit today's worldly consumers, who expect to see a brand stand for the same thing no matter where they are. That means a global marketer today needs one brand image and message that works worldwide.

"You need to standardize to a greater degree, because consumers will notice differences in different markets more than they would have 10 to 15 years ago," Bernhardt says. "The brand needs to be the same."

Making that easier to do is the fact that ad companies have become worldwide networks of agencies. An idea born in London can be executed with localized sophistication in Tokyo, New York and Amsterdam.

Among one-world marketers:

• **Citibank.** The U.S. financial services brand runs credit card, retail banking and consumer loan businesses worldwide. No matter the locale, "The business is the business, and we want to make sure we're not schizophrenic," says Anne MacDonald, head of global marketing. "We want our brand values consistent around the world." Citibank does so by using one model to develop credit cards, signs and even office interiors.

• **McDonald's.** The fast-food giant last year created its first global ad campaign after finding young adults worldwide were rejecting McDonald's for the same reason—the brand was not contemporary to them—and decided to address the issue with one answer.

"Strategically we said, 'Why would we do it 10 different ways? Let's do it in one voice,'" says Larry Light, global chief marketing officer at McDonald's. That voice now sings, "I'm lovin' it." Supporting the global theme are 25 new ads.

• **Pepsi.** The youthful brand is recognized for its ad humor in the USA and has applied that to ads globally—with local cultural twists. An ad in India, for instance, tells of a boy who, when he drinks a Pepsi, can train elephants to do tricks. His career is shattered, however, when another boy pops open a Pepsi during a performance, and the elephants follow him.

"How consumers experience the personality of the brand should be tempered by the culture," says Dave Burwick, chief marketing officer, North America.

• **Procter & Gamble.** In its drive to be a "high-performance marketing organization," P&G has pushed for broadcast TV and more focus on media that can be better tailored for local needs around the world, says Jim Stengel, global marketing officer. It is perfecting the concept of global brands with regional flair, he says. It sells about 50 of its brands in North and Latin America, Europe, Middle East and Africa.

Stengel says P&G is "reinventing our approach to marketing." It is making media choices based on when and where it can best reach its customers, then creating ads to suit that media.

• **Reebok.** The sports apparel and footwear brand has built a new global marketing campaign around the Olympics that includes print ads of such athletes as basketball player Yao Ming in ancient Greek garb and poses.

Reebok also is creating sculptures of the athletes modeled on poses from the famous Parthenon Frieze. "We try very hard to make a program like this very relevant to cultures around the world," says Denise Kaigler, vice president, global communications.

• **Hewlett-Packard.** Whether in England, Russia, Australia or the USA, H-P's message is that its technology helps businesses handle change. The ads are in a variety of media, but particularly outdoor.

A recent poster outside London's National Gallery promoted H-P technology to restore just the right shade of yellow to a Van Gogh painting. Another ad will go up next week in Moscow's Red Square. Choosing such landmark locations "allows us to become part of the city," says Gary Elliott, vice president, brand marketing.

• **UPS.** The overnight carrier uses just three ads that run in 20 countries for its global message that its service builds businesses.

UPS does so because it has found "that the similarities among decision makers in our category, whether in China, India or Mexico, their needs, wants and fears are amazingly consistent," says Larry Bloomenkranz, vice president, global advertising and brand management.

It varies the faces in the ads—one might have an Asian cast, another white—"so people can recognize themselves in the advertising," Bloomenkranz says.

Web Plays Vital Role in Marketing Push

Online component extends reach

By DEBORAH L. VENCE

Brochures, e-mail, promotions and advertising are far from obsolete, but such marketing tactics increasingly play second fiddle to the Web. For businesses of all sizes, from a new product launch to a brand revival, the Web is the key pivot point in marketing initiatives.

Some recent examples of leading Net-based initiatives include a promotion intended to build awareness and brand identity as a direct marketing and customer retention program, and as a central element in a multipart cause marketing campaign.

The online component "was pivotal in getting outreach to fans. Incentives that we placed in the stores at various times of the promotion (drove) traffic to the Web site. We really mixed up the online element with the retail and network elements for an incredible partnership," says Alyson Dutch, CEO of Brown & Dutch Public Relations Inc. in Malibu, Calif. Her company worked recently with Mrs. Fields' Cookies on a multifaceted cause marketing campaign.

Executives at Salt Lake City snack food retailer Mrs. Fields' Original Cookies Inc., established in 1977, were concerned that after the 9/11 attacks, slowing sales would continue to fall. Seeking to boost sales and increase brand awareness, Mrs. Fields sought the services of Brown & Dutch in early 2002, to help reposition the company in the marketplace.

"What we did first was look for partners and other kinds of retailers and nonprofit partners whose demographics were similar to Mrs. Fields," Dutch explains.

While meeting with various companies that were demographically matched with Mrs. Fields, a friend of Dutch's—a fan of the popular NBC daytime drama *Days of Our Lives*—mentioned that a character on the show was a baker, known for passing down recipes to other characters. Dutch arranged to meet with the show's executives and learned they had some goals of their own: to brand the show beyond the television screen, reach viewers through a retail venue and increase viewer loyalty through an alliance with a brand that reaches women.

"When we met with *Days*, (the executives) told us how excited they were about a partnership because they had been looking for ways to extend their brand," she says. Also, "as we got into more conversations … we found that there was a stow line about a character with leukemia."

That opened the door for a retail and online cross-promotion with a cause marketing element benefiting White Plains, N.Y.-based Leukemia & Lymphoma Society (LLS).

Mrs. Fields and the program created an amateur chef contest, tided "Winning is Sweet—And So Are the Days of Our Lives," and timed the promotion to coincide with the leukemia story line on *Days of Our Lives*. The public was invited to send in their favorite cookie recipes, with the winning formula to be featured at Mrs. Fields' outlets in fall 2002. LLS would receive at least 5% of the net profits of the winning cookie's sales. In addition, the winner would have a walk-on role on the daytime drama.

The cross-promotion campaign also drew in Soap City.com, a division of Culver City, Calif.-based Sony Pictures Digital Networks that provides exclusive daily coverage for all daytime dramas and hosts their official Web sites. SoapCity's objective was to increase traffic to its Web site through the *Days* URL (*www.daysofourlives.com*) and to create a brick-and-mortar connection to its audience through Mrs. Fields' outlets. SoapCity also wanted to garner more attention for the ancillary merchandise it sells related to daytime soaps.

The promotion ran from March 15, 2002, through Feb. 28, 2003, with the four participating organizations: Mrs. Fields, *Days of Our Lives*, SoapCity.com and LLS.

Mrs. Fields stores featured three sets of point-of-purchase materials. The first set featured the *Days of Our Lives'* characters on a freestanding counter card with tear-off contest entry forms, along with a large poster about the contest naming LLS as the beneficiary and encouraging customers to enter the recipe contest, The second round of POP materials focused on the recipe that had won by this time, and included the *Days of Our Lives* characters and information about LLS. The final round of POP materials focused on the new cookie, but was marketed this time for Valentine's Day 2003, and included information about a *Days of Our Lives* seasonal story line.

The promotion's online component made it possible to field contest recipes and vote for favorites through Mrs. Fields' main Web site, the *Days of Our Lives* site or Soap City.com. Fans also could download the recipes off any of the sites and make the cookies at home.

SoapCity.com offered a free *Days of Our Lives* cast photograph and $5 off purchases from The SoapCity Store at www.soapcity.com throughout October 2002. SoapCity coupons also were distributed at participating Mrs. Fields stores nationwide that month.

"We worked heavily with SoapCity.com, which was pivotal in getting online outreach to fans and driving traffic to the Web site with incentives that we placed in the stores at various times of the promotion," Dutch says.

In June 2002, five recipes—out of 1,300 submissions—were chosen and made available to the show's cast and fans. The favorites were each named after the characters in the show, and then posted on the *Days of Our Lives* Web site. The final winning recipe, an Almond White Chip cookie, was selected in September by Mrs. Fields executives and made its debut in Mrs. Fields stores from October through December 2002; anyone who bought three Almond White Chip cookies during the month of October received one free. Texas resident Marrgie Fisher won the contest and received a trip to Los Angeles, a $1,000 check and a walk-on role on *Days of Our Lives*, playing nurse "C. Walker" on an episode that aired Oct. 7, 2002.

The promotion was considered a success on several levels: *Days of Our Lives'* role in the campaign was featured in a variety of magazines and tabloids, including *Soap Opera Digest, Hollywood Reporter, National Enquirer, Soap Talk* (a TV show) and *Soap Opera Weekly.*

The contest did not boost sales for Mrs. Fields, but executives credit the mega-promotion for stabilizing overall sales. In addition, *Days of Our Lives* got a bump in ratings and SoapCity.com increased traffic to its Web site during the period of the promotion, Dutch says.

Meanwhile, $15,000 made from cookie sales was donated to LLS.

"This contest was about getting the Mrs. Fields' brand associated with an entertainment organization," she says. "The biggest result that came out of this promotion was the publicity."

Getting the word out also was the goal for Atlanta-based Parthenon Realty LLC, a 1-year-old real estate management firm. And the company also decided to use an online contest to do that. This contest, launched Feb. I and scheduled to run to the end of calendar year 2004, has

a decided business-to-business bent: Its main objective is to get real estate brokers' clients to lease commercial space from the firm, the market for which is concentrated in the southeastern portion of the United States, including cities in Florida, the Carolinas and Texas.

"(Office) space is really competitive even though the economy is recovering. We really wanted to develop a program that would differentiate us ... (and) give us a competitive edge. We are a new company, and we wanted to develop the Parthenon brand," explains Trey Freeman, senior vice president of Parthenon.

In the "Parthenon Broker Bucks Bonanza" contest, real estate brokers can win a three-year lease on a Lexus SC Convertible, a watercraft and other prizes. The program awards 500 contest points to brokers for showing space to new, qualified tenant prospects, and one point per rentable square foot for new, qualifying leases fulfilled in 2004. The broker with the most points at the end of the year wins the Lexus convertible. The second-place winner receives a 185-horsepower Sea-Doo GTX 4-TEC Limited Supercharged watercraft. Trips and electronics valued from $1,000 to $12,500 comprise the remaining 30 prizes.

The contest is valid at any Parthenon-managed property in its nine contest markets: Atlanta; San Antonio and Austin, Texas; Greenville, S.C.; Memphis and Nashville, Tenn.; the Greensboro-Winston-Salem-High Point area and the Raleigh-Durham-Research Triangle area of North Carolina; and Broward and Palm Beach counties in South Florida. More than 60 brokers are participating in the contest.

The company thought the Web would be an effective vehicle because of its broad geographic reach and the speed with which the Web can disseminate information in many directions simultaneously.

To announce the promotion, Parthenon sent an HTML e-mail message to about 2,500 commercial real estate brokers in the company's nine markets. The initial goal was to drive brokers to Parthenon's Web site to learn more about the company, its locations and available office space in each market.

"We wanted to show our activity to (brokers), and show something desirable. So, in the HTML message, we included a picture of the Lexus convertible in motion. It almost jumps off the (screen) at you," Freeman says.

The company posts a scorecard on the Web site, which is now live. The scorecard shows the competing brokers' names and point total for each market. Updated results are posted on the first Monday of each month.

"Real estate is a competitive industry, so brokers will want to see how they rank with others in their market and across all Parthenon properties," explains Patrick Hill, partner with Jackson Spalding Inc., an independent communications management firm based in Atlanta that launched the promotion for Parthenon.

Parthenon will spend some $70,000 for prizes, as well as additional costs for Web administration, among other expenses. And while the contest is just getting started, Freeman says he's "pleased with the activity so far."

"(Right now), we are seeing tenant prospects from brokers that we've never seen before. In each market, we've been getting three to five new people coming to look at Parthenon properties that might not have been (without the contest). We fully expect significant benefits," Freeman says.

Over the long term, Parthenon's goals are to increase visibility, prompt more showings of its properties and sign more leases.

As Parthenon builds its business via the Web, New Victory Theater, a children's theater company based in New York, uses the technology as more of a direct marketing and customer retention vehicle.

The theater started using the Web for its annual season ticket renewal campaign in summer 2002, when New Victory hired Patron Technology LLC, a New York-based online marketing and software consulting firm that serves the arts and not-for-profit industries.

"We created a Web-based interface program, managed through our system such that people received an e-mail message telling them they could renew (tickets) online. That was followed up by direct mail and phone calls (to theater members)," explains Eugene Cart, founder and president of Patron.

To get members to go to the site, New Victory included a direct link to the Web site (www.newvictory.org) where recipients found directions for renewing ticket subscriptions. The site did double duty as an advertisement for the company's schedule of shows, with information about each show and performing company, video clips of each show and a description of family activities that might be appealing before or after seeing a show, explains Janice Chaikelson, director of marketing for New Victory.

A delay in funding that year meant a delay in mailing out the theater company's print brochures. So, for about two weeks, the Web campaign was the only ticket marketing New Victory was doing for its 2002-03 season. Even so, New Victory received 660 ticket orders online even before the brochures were mailed.

The percentage of member families who renewed tickets for the 2002-03 season was a record high for the theater group. More than three-quarters of the total membership base of 3,026 families renewed their tickets for that season, and about 74.3% of the renewers completed the transaction online. Although comparing ticket sales reve-

nue from year to year is difficult, because the number of performances varies, the 2001-02 season had garnered $1.9 million in sales for a total of 231 performances, and that year, only 33% of member families placed ticket orders online. For the 2002-03 season, $1.67 million was garnered in overall ticket sales.

New Victory was ahead of schedule for the 2003-04 season, with funding already approved when the theater troupe began marketing the new shows with standard direct mail brochures and e-mail blasts in early June. The marketing investment was about $18,000.

"The click-through rate (we had) was pretty high," Chaikelson says. "This season, 65% of (4,051 total) members ordered (tickets) online."

As of March 3, ticket sales revenue for the current season reached $1.58 million for 184 performances.

In 2002-03, New Victory only offered ticket renewals for that season via the Web and through direct mail, not by phone. For this year, although the proportion of members placing orders online dropped, Chaikelson believes 65% is a reasonable drop in online renewals considering that this year orders also could be placed by phone.

"In 2000-01, we only had 20% of our orders placed online, representing 19% of renewing members," she notes.

Meanwhile, additional results for the 2003-04 season from a recent focus group session at the theater showed that six of 10 families indicated they had the New Victory Web site bookmarked and frequently visited the site. Most of the respondents also said the site was a great way to prepare their children for the show, while others said the Web address was easy to remember.

"Our Web site is one of the strongest tools we have as far as letting people know about what we have to offer. You can include information on a Web site that you can't necessarily put into a single brochure. So, we really try to boost our Web address on everything we send out, so people can be more informed about what the shows are all about before they even come to see them," she says. "It's a chance for parents to get their kids excited about a show before going to the theater."

For more information on the companies mentioned in this story, go to:
www.bdpr.com (Brown & Dutch Public Relations Inc.)
www.jacksonspalding.com (Jackson Spalding Inc.)
www.newvictory.org (New Victory Theater)
www.parthenonrealty.com (Parthenon Realty LLC)

UNIT 4
Global Marketing

Unit Selections

Key Points to Consider

- What economic, cultural, and political obstacles must an organization consider that seeks to become global in its markets?

- Do you believe that an adherence to the "marketing concept" is the right way to approach international markets? Why, or why not?

- What trends are taking place today that would suggest whether particular global markets will grow or decline? Which countries do you believe will see the most growth in the next decade? Why?

- In what ways can the Internet be used to extend a market outside the United States?

 **Links: www.dushkin.com/online/**
These sites are annotated in the World Wide Web pages.

CIBERWeb
http://ciber.centers.purdue.edu

International Business Resources on the WWW
http://globaledge.msu.edu/ibrd/ibrd.asp

International Trade Administration
http://www.ita.doc.gov

World Chambers Network
http://www.worldchambers.net

World Trade Center Association On Line
http://iserve.wtca.org

It is certain that marketing with a global perspective will continue to be a strategic element of U.S. business well into the next decade. The United States is both the world's largest exporter and largest importer. In 1987, U.S. exports totaled just over 250 billion dollars—about 10 percent of total world exports. During the same period, U.S. imports were nearly 450 billion dollars—just under 10 percent of total world imports. By 1995 exports had risen to 513 billion dollars and imports to 664 billion dollars—roughly the same percentage of total world trade.

Whether or not they wish to be, all marketers are now part of the international marketing system. For some, the end of the era of domestic markets may have come too soon, but that era is over. Today it is necessary to recognize the strengths and weaknesses of our own marketing practices as compared to those abroad. The multinational corporations have long recognized this need, but now all marketers must acknowledge it.

International marketing differs from domestic marketing in that the parties to its transactions live in different political units. It is the "international" element of international marketing that distinguishes it from domestic marketing—not differences in managerial techniques. The growth of global business among multinational corporations has raised new questions about the role of their headquarters. It has even caused some to speculate whether marketing operations should be performed abroad rather than in the United States.

The key to applying the marketing concept is understanding the consumer. Increasing levels of consumer sophistication is evident in all of the world's most profitable markets. Managers are required to adopt new points of view in order to accommodate increasingly complex consumer wants and needs. The markets in the new millennium will show further integration on a worldwide scale. In these emerging markets, conventional textbook approaches can cause numerous problems. The new marketing perspective called for by the circumstances of the years ahead will require a long-range view that looks from the basics of exchange and their applications in new settings.

The selections presented here were chosen to provide an overview of world economic factors, competitive positioning, and increasing globalization of markets—issues to which each and every marketer must become sensitive. "Segmenting Global Markets: Look Before You Leap" reflects the importance of understanding local and global issues before implementing a global market segmentation strategy. The second article stresses that international marketing research is a very serious and critical undertaking. The third article reveals that India presents an unprecedented economic opportunity for American business. The fourth article contrasts some significant marketing differences between India and China. "Cracking China's Market" describes the dawning reality of China turning into a profitable global market for foreigners in a relatively short time.

Segmenting Global Markets:
Look Before You Leap

Before implementing a global market segmentation strategy,
it's critical to understand both local and global issues.

By V. Kumar and Anish Nagpal

*"I am a citizen, not of Athens or Greece,
but of the world."*

Today we live in a global marketplace that makes Socrates' famous words more valid than ever before. As you read this article, you may be sitting on a chair from Paris, wearing a shirt made in Britain, and using a computer, without which you are handicapped, that probably was made in Taiwan. Have you ever wondered why and how this happens?

Global marketing refers to marketing activities of companies that emphasize four activities: (1) cost efficiencies resulting from reduced duplication of efforts; (2) opportunities to transfer products, brands, and ideas across subsidiaries in different countries; (3) emergence of global customers, such as global teenagers or the global elite; and (4) better links between national marketing infrastructures, which paves the way for a global marketing infrastructure that results in better management and reduced costs.

As the business world becomes more globalized, global market segmentation (GMS) has emerged as an important issue in developing, positioning, and selling products across national boundaries. Consider the global segment based on demographics, global teenagers. The sharing of universal needs and desires for branded, entertaining, trendy, and image-oriented products makes it possible to reach the global teen segment with a unified marketing program. For example, Reebok used a global advertisement campaign to launch its Instapump line of sneakers in the United States, Germany, Japan, and 137 other countries worldwide.

WHAT IS GMS?

Global market segmentation can be defined as the process of identifying specific segments—country groups or individual consumer groups across countries—of potential customers with homogeneous attributes who are likely to exhibit similar buying behavior.

The study of GMS is interesting and important for three reasons. First of all, considering the world as a market, different products are in different stages of the product life cycle at any given time. Researchers can segment the market based on this information, but the membership of the countries in each segment is fleeting. This makes it difficult to reevaluate and update the membership of each segment.

Second, with the advent of the Internet, product information is disseminated very rapidly and in unequal proportions across different countries. The dynamic nature of this environment warrants a continuous examination of the stability of the segment membership. Third, the goal of GMS is to break down the world market for a product or a service into different groups of countries/consumers that differ in their response to the firm's marketing mix program. That way, the firm can tailor its marketing mix to each individual segment.

Targeted segments in GMS should possess some of the following properties:

Measurability. The segments should be easy to define and measure. Objective country traits such as socioeconomic variables (e.g., per capita income) can easily be gauged, but the size of the segments based on culture or lifestyles is much harder to measure. Thus, a larger scale survey may be required for segmenting global markets depending upon the basis of GMS.

EXECUTIVE SUMMARY

The primary purpose of this article is to shed more light on the more complex challenges of global market segmentation (GMS). To provide a complete understanding, we discuss some of the well-known issues in segmenting foreign markets and move on to state the various properties of global target markets. We conclude that companies can implement GMS most effectively by first gaining a full understanding of both local and global concerns.

Size. Segments should be large enough to be worth going after. Britain and Hong Kong can be grouped together in the same segment, because of previous British supremacy in Hong Kong, but their population sizes differ.

Accessibility. The segments should be easy to reach via the media. Because of its sheer size, China seems to be an attractive market. However, because of its largely rural population, it has less access to technology.

Actionability. Effective marketing programs (the four Ps) should be easy to develop. If segments do not respond differently to the firm's marketing mix, there is no need to segment the markets. Certain legal issues need to be considered before implementing an advertisement campaign. For example, many countries, such as India, do not allow direct slandering of the competitor's products.

Competitive Intensity. The segments should not be preempted by the firm's competition. In fact, in global marketing, small companies often prefer entry of less competitive markets and use this as one of the segmentation criteria when assessing international markets.

Growth Potential. A high return on investment should be attainable. Typically, marketers face a trade-off between competitive intensity and growth potential. Currently, Latin American markets have good growth potential, but the instability of local currencies causes major problems.

Companies typically employ the following six-step process for implementing GMS:

- Identify purpose (by introducing a new or existing product and choosing appropriate marketing mix programs in groups of countries)
- Select segmentation criteria (traditional vs. emerging)
- Collect relevant information
- Segment the countries/consumers according to criteria
- Reevaluate the fit of the segment after implementation of the intended program
- Update/reassign segment membership

An interesting aspect of the GMS process is the need to constantly reevaluate segment membership. The process of assigning membership to countries into a segment could be done using traditional procedures, or by evaluating the countries by using emerging techniques.

TRADITIONAL SEGMENTATION BASES

The choice of the segmentation basis is the most crucial factor in an international segmentation study. That a segmentation approach is essential in international markets is no longer questioned. Rather, the basis for segmentation becomes the focus. For example, for its Lexus brand, Toyota would segment the market based upon household income. On the other hand, if Marlboro were planning to introduce a new brand of cigarettes, it would segment the market based on population.

Individual- and country-based segmentation includes the following categories:

Demographics. This includes measurable characteristics of population such as age, gender, income, education, and occupation. A number of global demographic trends, such as changing roles of women, and higher incomes and living standards, are driving the emergence of global segments. Sony, Reebok, Nike, Swatch, and Benetton are some firms that cater to the needs of global teenagers.

Culture. This covers a broad range of factors such as religion, education, and language, which are easy to measure, and aesthetic preferences of the society that are much harder to comprehend. Hofstede's classification scheme proposes five cultural dimensions for classifying countries: Individualism vs. Collectivism, Power Distance (PD), Uncertainty Avoidance (UA), Masculinity vs. Femininity, and Strategic Orientation (long-term vs. short-term). For example, Austria, Germany, Switzerland, Italy, Great Britain, and Ireland form one cluster that is medium-high on Individualism and high on Masculinity. These cultural characteristics signify the preference for "high performance" products and a "successful achiever" theme in advertising.

Geography. This is based upon the world region, economic stage of development, nation, city, city size and population density, climate, altitude, and sometimes, even the ZIP code. It is easy to form country segments using regional blocks such as NAFTA, European Union, MERCOSUR, or Asia-Pacific. However, the value of such segments may vary depending on the need. These groupings are viable for developing trade policies, but not for marketing products/ services given tremendous variation in other factors.

Environment. GMS is further complicated by different political, legal, and business environments in each country. Economic indicators such as Gross Domestic Product (GDP) may be used. However, it may not be relevant to refer to country segments based on this criterion because a country can move from one level of GDP to another, making this criterion obsolete.

Behavior-based segmentation includes three categories, which are shown in Exhibit 1.

EXHIBIT 1   Traditional segmentation basis (behavior-based)

Segmentation Basis	Brief Description	Example
Psychographics	This segment groups people in terms of their attitudes, values, and lifestyles and helps predict consumer preferences in products, services, and media.	Porsche AG divided its buyers into five distinct categories: Top Guns, Elitists, Proud Patrons, Bon Vivants, and Fantasists—each group having a particular characteristic.
Benefit	This approach focuses on the problem a product solves, regardless of location. It attempts to measure consumer value systems and perceptions of various brands in a product class.	Toothpaste consumers can be segmented into Sensory, Sociable, Worrier, and Independent segments. Sociable consumers seek bright teeth; Worriers seek healthy teeth. Aqua packaging could indicate fluoride for the Worrier segment, and white (for a white smile) for the Sociable segment.
Behavior	This examines whether or not people buy and use a product, as well as how often and how much. Consumers can be categorized in terms of usage rates (heavy, medium, and light).	ABB classifies customers according to their switchability criterion—oyal customers, those loyal to competitors, and those who can be lost to or won from the competition.

EMERGING SEGMENTATION BASES

Countries also can be segmented by means of product *diffusion patterns* and *response elasticities*. Some countries are fast adopters of the product, whereas some countries require a lag period to adopt the product. With this in mind, a firm could introduce its products in countries that are innovators (fast adopters) and later in those countries that are imitators (lag countries).

Rather than using macro-level variables to classify countries, a firm might consider segmenting markets on the basis of new-product diffusion patterns. As Exhibit 2 indicates, country segments formed on the basis of diffusion patterns may differ by product.

This type of segmentation allows the global marketer to segment countries on the basis of actual purchase patterns. Having knowledge of purchase patterns can help marketers make mode-of-entry decisions and help determine the sequence of countries in which the product should be introduced.

Consumers in lag countries can learn about the benefits of the product from the experience of adopters in the lead country, and this learning can result in a faster diffusion rate in the lag markets. Thus, countries can be grouped according to the degree of learning they exhibit for a given lead country. Lag countries that exhibit strong learning ties are potential candidates for sequential entry (using a waterfall strategy). Entry into countries that exhibit weak learning effect can be accelerated since there is not much to gain by waiting. Here, a sprinkler strategy (simultaneous entry into the relevant markets) would work well.

If a firm wants to introduce its innovation into a new country, it must be aware that the diffusion rate depends upon the kind of innovation. The diffusion pattern of a continuous innovation (one that has a majority of features in common with earlier products plus some new features that improve performance or add value) is very different from a discontinuous innovation (which is new or drastically different from earlier forms in several relevant features or attributes).

In the case of continuous innovations, such as home computers, the introduction of a successive generation will influence not only its diffusion but also the diffusion of the earlier generations. In such cases, diffusion will occur more quickly since consumers have some related knowledge. Hence, when a new generation of the product is introduced in the lead market while the lag markets are still adopting the existing (older) generation, information on the added benefits of the new generation travels faster from the lead market to potential adopters in the lag markets. The users in the lag markets will be familiar with the innovation and can easily absorb the benefits of the next generation.

Another interesting way to group countries is according to their response elasticities. Consumers across countries respond in different ways when the price of the product changes. Grocerystore scanner systems store a wealth of information that can then be used to find customer buying patterns. If the data shows the customers are price sensitive toward a particular product, couponing strategies can help target that segment, where legal.

IMPLEMENTING GMS

It is important to consider some of the conceptual and methodological issues so GMS can fulfill its high potential. Exhibit 3 gives a brief description of the four critical types of equivalencies that should be taken into account when implementing GMS.

Construct equivalence refers to whether the segmentation basis has the same meaning and is expressed similarly in different countries and cultures. Different countries under study must have the same perception or use for the product being researched. Otherwise, comparison of data becomes meaningless. If, for example, a firm is studying the bicycle market, it must realize that, in the United States, bicycles are classified under the recreational-sports industry, whereas in India and China they are considered a basic means of transportation.

EXHIBIT 2 — Segments based upon diffusion patterns

Product Categories

Segment	VCRs	Cellular phones	Home computers	Microwave ovens	CD players
1	Germany, UK, France, Sweden	Denmark, Norway	Belgium, UK, Netherlands	Germany, Italy, Denmark, Austria	Belgium, Netherlands, Sweden, Austria, Finland
2	Belgium, Denmark, Spain, Austria, Finland	Finland, France	France, Italy, Sweden, Norway, Austria, Germany	Belgium, UK, Netherlands, France, Spain	Spain, Denmark, Germany
3	Italy, Portugal	Germany, UK, Italy, Switzerland	Spain, Portugal	Norway	Switzerland, Italy

Source: Kumar, V., Jaishankar Ganesh, and Raj Echambadi, "Cross-National Diffusion Research: What Do We Know and How Certain Are We?" *Journal of Product Innovation Management*, 15, 1998.

Similar activities also may have different functions in different countries. For example, for many U.S. families, grocery shopping is a chore to be accomplished as efficiently as possible. However, in India and many other countries interaction with vendors and local shopkeepers plays a very important social function.

Construct equivalence is easier to establish for the general bases, such as geographic variables. However, for bases such as values and lifestyles, construct equivalence is much harder to achieve. VALS-2 identifies eight segments based on two main dimensions: self-orientation and resources. Another VALS system was developed for Japan, presumably because the U.S.-based VALS-2 system was not appropriate for that country. Instead it identifies 10 segments based on two key dimensions: life orientation and attitudes toward social change.

Scalar equivalence means that scores from different countries should have the same meaning and interpretation. The first aspect used to determine scalar equivalence concerns the specific scale or scoring procedure used to establish the measure. The standard format of scales used in survey research differs across countries. For example, in the United States a 5- or 7-point scale is most common. However, 20-point scales are used in France.

EXHIBIT 3 — Types of equivalence

Equivalence

Construct	Scalar	Measurement	Sampling
Are we studying the same phenomena in Brazil, India, and Britain?	Do the scores on consumers in the U.S., Argentina, and Japan have the same meaning?	Are the phenomena in France, Singapore and South Africa measured in the same way?	Are the samples used in Hong Kong, China, and Romania equivalent?

The second aspect concerns the response to a score obtained in a measure. Here the question arises as to whether a score obtained in one research context has the same

meaning and interpretation in another context. For example, on an intention-to-purchase scale, does the proportion of likely buyers indicate a similar likelihood of purchase from one country to another, or does a position on the Likert scale have the same meaning in all cultures?

Differences in response styles often result in a lack of scalar equivalence. Some of these response styles include "extreme" responding and "social desirability" responding. Research shows Chinese respondents show a "marked degree of agreeability," while Americans show a "marked willingness to dissent." These differences can cause problems in the data-collection process, which can lead to erroneous grouping of countries.

Measurement equivalence refers to whether the measures used to operationalize the segmentation basis are comparable across countries. For example, consider the level of education. The United States uses one educational scale while in Europe the educational system is quite different, and the term "college" is not appropriate. Also, household income is difficult to compare across countries owing to differences in the tax structure and purchasing power.

Some items of a segmentation basis have measurement equivalence, but the others do not. For example, research shows that in the U.S. consumer innovativeness is expressed both in terms of purchase of new products and in social communication about new products. In France, however, the latter does not apply. Hence, only items pertaining to the person's tendency to purchase new products have measurement equivalence across the two countries. The researcher thus faces the dilemma of either using the same set of items in each country (etic scale) or adapting the set of items to each country (emic-scale). A compromise would be a combined emic-etic scale with some core items common to all countries and some country-specific items.

Sampling equivalence deals with problems in identifying and operationalizing comparable populations and selecting samples that are simultaneously representative of other populations and comparable across countries. One aspect of sampling equivalence deals with the decision-making process, which varies across countries. For example, in the United States, office supplies are often purchased by the office secretary, whereas this decision is made by a middle-level manager or CEO in some countries.

It is also important to consider whether the sample is representative of the population. In most developed countries, information on potential markets and sampling frames is easily available. However, in Japan, the most popular residential list for sample studies was made inaccessible to researchers. Developing countries do not have extensive databases and so obtaining the sampling frame to suit the needs of the research could be difficult.

Equivalence presents a dilemma in the minds of managers. On one end, it would be wise to develop scales specifically for each culture; on the other, responses collected in this manner may not mean the same thing. This issue can be resolved to some extent by using a combination of items in the scale.

Think Globally, Act Locally

Used effectively, segmentation allows global marketers to take advantage of the benefits of standardization (such as economies of scale and consistency in positioning) while addressing the needs and expectations of a specific target group. This approach means looking at markets on a global or regional basis, thereby ignoring the political boundaries that define markets in many cases.

The greatest challenge for the global marketer is the choice of an appropriate base for segmentation. Pitfalls that handicap global marketing programs and contribute to their suboptimal performance include market-related reasons, such as insufficient research and overstandardization, as well as internal reasons, such as inflexibility in planning and implementation. If a product is launched on a broad scale without formally researching regional or local differences, it may fail.

The successful global marketers will be those who can achieve a balance between the local and the regional/global concerns. Procter and Gamble's Pampers brand suffered a major setback in the 1980s in Japan when customers favored the purchase of diapers of rival brands.

The diapers were made and sold according to a formula imposed by Cincinnati headquarters, and Japanese consumers found the company's hard-sell techniques alienating. Globalization by design requires a balance between sensitivity to local needs and global deployment of technologies and concepts.

GMS offers a solution to the standardization vs. adaptation issue because it creates the conceptual framework for offering standardized products and marketing programs in multiple countries by targeting the same consumer segments in different countries. The formulation of a global strategy by a firm may result in the choice of one particular segment across markets or multiple segments. However, in implementing the marketing mix for maximum effect, the principle "Think globally, act locally" becomes a critical rule for guiding marketing efforts.

Additional Reading

Ganesh, Jaishankar, V. Kumar, and Velavan Subramaniam (1997), "Learning Effect in Multinational Diffusion of Consumer Durables: An Exploratory Investigation," *Journal of the Academy of Marketing Science*, 25 (3), 214–228.

Hofstede, Geert (1984), *Culture's Consequences: International Differences in Work-Related Values*. California: Sage Publications.

Kotabe, Masaaki, and Kristiaan Helsen (1998), *Global Marketing Management*. New York: John Wiley & Sons Inc.

Kumar, V. (2000), *International Marketing Research*. New Jersey: Prentice Hall.

V. Kumar (VK) is Marvin Hurley Professor of Business Administration, Melcher Faculty Scholar, Director of Marketing Research Studies and Director of International Business Programs at the University of Houston, Bauer College of Business, Department of Marketing. He may be reached at vkumar@uh.edu.

Anish Nagpal is a doctoral student at the University of Houston, Bauer College of Business, Department of Marketing.

International marketing research: A management briefing

Many firms expand globally with little marketing research. But noteworthy business failures have occurred that could have been prevented with a minimal amount of study. Products and marketing campaigns usually need to be adapted overseas. The same is true for marketing research methods. Accepted approaches to conducting research are based on methods that were developed to study the U.S. market. Different conditions overseas, however, especially in emerging markets, make these methods difficult to apply. A look at typical problems in conducting research overseas can help in developing some guidelines for adapting methods in foreign countries.

Tim R. V. Davis
Professor of Management and International Business,
Cleveland State University, Cleveland, Ohio

Robert B. Young
Market Research Director, Stores Division,
ICI Paints/Glidden, Cleveland, Ohio

International marketing research is much more crucial than many managers think. With a burgeoning number of companies pursuing global strategies, managers are in great need of dependable information on foreign markets. Attempting to expand overseas without doing adequate research too often means having to face the crippling costs of business failure. Moreover, American market research techniques often don't work well abroad; managers must confront different challenges when conducting research overseas, especially in developing countries.

Corporate blunders in foreign markets frequently occur because of a lack of understanding of the Four Ps in the marketing mix—Product, Price, Place, and Promotion. Failure to investigate and, where necessary, reinterpret the Four P's abroad has proved costly.

Product and packaging problems

The failure of many products that lack acceptability overseas could have been predicted with minimal market research. Chase & Sanborn's attempt to introduce instant coffee in France failed because brewing real coffee is a cherished culinary delight for most French people. Instant coffee was considered a somewhat vulgar substitute.

In other cases, the problem may not be the product but the packaging. Snapple encountered difficulty marketing its bottled drinks through vending machines in Japan, where cans load more easily and are less fragile than glass. In China, Procter & Gamble marketed diapers in pink packaging that conveyed a preference for female babies. But many Chinese consumers shunned the product; under the country's one-child-per-family rule, the preference in many families is for a son. This type of product image problem could have been uncovered with prior research.

Pricing problems

Many companies do too little research on product or service pricing in overseas markets. In some cases, the price a company charges is simply the foreign currency equivalent of the domestic price, which may bear little relationship to what the customer is willing to pay. Ford recently tried to sell its economy model Escort car in India for more than $21,000. But in an emerging market like India, only a small percentage of the total population have incomes of $20,000 or more. So most Indians saw the Escort as a luxury automobile that very few could afford.

Even when managers are aware of acceptable pricing levels, they may still price products or services too high or too low. Exporters often set high prices to recover special labeling and packaging charges, overseas transportation, and import tariffs—costs that local competitors do not have to incur. These expenditures may prevent a company from pricing the product competitively. On the other hand, management may price products lower than the competition and be willing to take a loss early with a view to achieving profits later when more volume is achieved. Frequently, sufficient volume is never achieved and the foreign venture fails to break even. The lack of adequate cost analysis and pricing research is another major cause of business failure.

Place (distribution) problems

How products are placed or distributed in overseas markets can be the most important international business decision a company makes. Firms can try to break into established wholesale, retail, or direct sales networks, piggyback on other firms' distribution systems, or build their own channels, which can be costly and time-consuming. Neilson, Canada's largest manufacturer and marketer of confectioneries, has distributed its products successfully in such far-flung markets as Japan, China, and the Middle East. But success has eluded it in the market it would most like to succeed in: the United States. The reason for this is Neilson's choice of distributor. In the early 1990s, the company chose Pro Set, a collectible trading card producer, as its distributor. However, Pro Set's sales force lacked experience in selling confectionery and never achieved significant penetration in the US market. The firm was poorly managed and eventually filed Chapter 11 bankruptcy, leaving Neilson with a huge outstanding receivables balance and a severely damaged reputation with customers.

Promotional problems

Promotional methods and advertising media vary around the world. The lack of understanding of branding, selling, advertising, and promotion practices in different countries may also land companies in difficulty. Lincoln Electric, a US-based manufacturer of electric motors and welding equipment, acquired an arc welding firm in Germany and immediately slapped its own brand on the products that were made by the firm. Many customers

had a strong "Buy German" attitude and were contemptuous of American engineering, so they immediately switched to other German products. Although Lincoln's problems in Germany ran considerably deeper, the company never recovered from its poor start and eventually had to close its operation there. Royal Applicant, an American manufacturer of small, hand-held vacuum cleaners like the "Dirt Devil," suffered a similar disaster. The company assumed that its successful domestic promotional strategy would work equally well in Europe. In the United States, expenditures on television advertising were closely correlated with predictable increases in sales volume. But in the different European countries, the growth in TV ad spending did not produce the predicted increases. Even though sales had risen to over $20 million by 1993, they never produced a return on investment. The company eventually withdrew entirely from the European market.

It is critical for managers to investigate the Four Ps in every country in which they do business and make modifications when and where they are needed. As these and other examples illustrate (see the box on the next page), mistakes are often made by well-known corporations, not just small firms. The tendency to take market knowledge for granted is the most insidious problem in international business, and often a fatal one.

Difficulties in conducting global marketing research

Even if managers are convinced of the need for foreign market research, they may have little understanding of the differences involved in carrying it out. They must become acquainted with the challenges it will bring—challenges they may not encounter at home.

More diverse research projects

The main types of marketing research projects are basically the same whether they are conducted at home or abroad. Studies typically deal with market entry, customer satisfaction, buyer behavior, and aspects of the Four Ps, and focus mainly on differences across countries. This may involve straight comparisons between a single foreign country and the domestic market or comparisons among multiple countries. But international research studies must contend with wide-ranging cultural diversity, which may include marked differences in language, religion, race, and ethnic origin that affect the sale of products and services. Domestic studies often examine regional differences, but they generally do not approach the level of diversity that is encountered in country comparisons.

More unknowns

Most managers know considerably more about their own domestic market than they do about conditions overseas. International research must shed light on more unknowns, providing insight on issues that may be clearly understood in the domestic market. Considering the lack of published information on many foreign markets, researchers have a heavy burden to bear. There are limits to the type and amount of data they can collect. The scope of what is to be studied will be constrained by the amount of time and resources available. So choices must be made about the focus of market research and what issues can be investigated.

Longer completion time

Generally, each phase of international marketing research—planning, design, execution, and interpretation of findings—requires more time to complete than in domestic research. The studies take longer to plan because they tend to be more complex and more difficult to arrange. Research designs must take into account viable data collection methods. Execution of the study will take longer if multiple countries are involved because of the separation in time and distance. In vast countries like China and India, the distance between markets makes large-scale studies extremely difficult to conduct. Interpreting the findings also takes time because of the logistics of coordinating comparison studies across countries.

Higher costs

Because of such factors as the different data collection techniques, the need for translation, and long-distance travel, conducting international marketing research is usually much more expensive than at home. Consumer telephone surveys that are a bargain in the United States cost much more abroad. In Japan, studies are mainly conducted door-to-door. In many developing countries, telephone ownership is low and interviewers must often travel vast distances to contact a representative sample of respondents. The time and cost required to collect primary data may make the research prohibitively expensive.

Suspect samples

Census data are unreliable or unavailable in many developing countries. Street maps and phone directories may not exist. Unreliable population statistics often make surveys of the general population difficult to conduct. In planning studies, market researchers need to question the accuracy of available demographic information and the study subjects: Are there any inherent biases in the sample? What proportion of the universe is covered? How are the data verified to ensure proper market coverage? Does

Gaffes, twists, and trials abroad

Many managers view foreign markets as being no different from domestic ones. They assume that successful marketing strategies and tactics used at home will work equally well overseas. But when Gerber first marketed baby foods in Africa, consumers thought the pictures of babies on the bottles meant that the jars contained ground-up babies! Research can also uncover unexpected uses to which products are put, such as the use of Jolly Green Giant sweet corn as fishing bait in Italy.

Obtaining adequate distribution for products is a real challenge when entering emerging markets, particularly transporting them over vast distances. The well-developed air, rail, and highway systems of the US and Europe that offer a variety of transportation options are virtually nonexistent in many developing countries, so research needs to be conducted on how products can reach far-flung markets. Wrigley, which has long been attempting to introduce chewing gum in China, had to face this problem. It discovered from its own market research that only about 17% of the Chinese population could be reached by conventional transportation. Bicycles, tricycles, carts, and motorbikes are used to reach small towns and villages, where products are sold through street kiosks and plywood stands. Wrigley found that many consumer products took eight months to reach the marketplace. After lengthy negotiations with state agencies, the company decided to use a combination of its own representatives and state-owned distributors to get its product to market. The typical route covered by a shipment of chewing gum consists of traveling 1,000 miles by truck, an additional leg by freighter, and finally by bicycle to small street stands. The process requires two weeks to complete, but the product is still freshly soft and sugar dusted at the time it is sold. This distribution method helped Wrigley sell more than 400 million sticks of chewing gum in China during 1999.

Some famous examples of translation errors have occurred in print, poster, TV, and radio advertising. In the late 1980s, Hispanics in the US were encouraged to fly on Braniff Airlines. A radio commercial mentioned flying Braniff *en cuero*, which means "in leather." But a very similar Spanish expression, *en cueros*, means "naked," and the two phrases sound identical when spoken quickly. Clairol, a popular marketer of hair care products, introduced a curling iron in Germany called the "Mist Stick," then discovered that the word "mist" is German slang for "manure." All these problems could have been averted with prior market research.

the sample cover all regions or cities? Is the sample source updated regularly?

Representative sampling may be less of a problem in countries with more homogeneous populations like Japan and South Korea, but it may be a serious concern in places where the population is more diverse, such as Hong Kong and Indonesia. More culturally diverse populations will require larger research samples or more sub-samples. Researchers may also have to deal with population movement and migration. For instance, approximately two-fifths of the population of the gulf states of the Middle East consist of expatriate males working in the region for only four to five years. An unstable population is an additional headache when trying to establish a representative sample.

In one study, when asked to choose which of several brands of vodka she would buy, a Russian woman replied, "I would buy all of them because they won't be in the stores tomorrow."

Data collection difficulties

Few countries provide such open access and freely available information as the United States. In many countries, business, government, and the population at large may be less willing to discuss issues, share information, and open up to questioning. People may be unwilling to talk to strangers without formal introductions, referrals, or invitations. An interviewer arriving at a home unannounced may be seen as a threat and treated hostilely. Moreover, the usual data collection methods used at home may be inappropriate in other countries. High levels of illiteracy may rule out written surveys. Mail surveys may be hindered by unreliable postal delivery. Other methods of collecting data may be unavailable. The mall or shopping center interviews common in the US are rarely used in Asia because there are so few shopping malls. In India, electronic point-of-sale cash registers and scanners are virtually nonexistent, so retail checkout data must be collected manually. In most Middle Eastern countries, few women would consent to be interviewed by a man, so female interviewers must be recruited.

Gathering data on certain types of products can also be difficult. For instance, the idea of discussing grooming and personal care products with a stranger would be considered too personal and perhaps offensive in many countries. These data collection difficulties may result in the number of completed interviews and usable questionnaires being quite low.

Translation errors and unintended meanings

A common problem in international marketing research is the errors that occur in translation. The literal translation of brand names and terms from one language to another sometimes creates misunderstandings. Managers of Schweppes tonic water decided to shorten the name in Italy when they learned that the phonetic equivalent of the brand name translated to "bathroom water" in Italian. Questionnaires developed in one country may be difficult to translate because of differences in idioms, the vernacular, and phrasing. This can occur in the US as well, where a large section of the population are bilingual. But it is a much bigger problem in, say, India, where 13 major languages are spoken and salient cultural differences exist across regions. Questions may also take on an entirely different meaning in another country. In one study, when asked to choose which of several brands of vodka she would buy, a Russian woman replied, "I would buy all of them because they won't be in the stores tomorrow."

Measurement problems

Attitude measurement is not universal around the world. As the example of the Russian woman illustrates, participants' responses may be partly culturally determined. Skewed results on attitude scales are common. Products and services routinely achieve well above 60 or 70 percent approval ratings on five-point scales in Latin American countries. Indeed, a product has to be very poor to receive anything less. Latin Americans do not like to hurt others' feelings, including marketers. In contrast, a response of "not bad" in France would be almost the equivalent of "extraordinary." And a response of "somewhat interested" would represent a much stronger commitment than in England, where the term "somewhat" has a less enthusiastic connotation.

Respondent incentives and biased results

The use of incentives as a means to increase participation is another issue. A common criticism of paying respondents for their opinions is that it invites biased answers. But in many countries, incentives are necessary for getting respondents to participate at all. In some countries, such as Brazil, a drink and a willingness to socialize may be enough for an interview to be granted. In other countries, incentives may be considered somewhat insulting.

Reliance on outside research firms

MNCs must work closely with market research firms that collect data for them in different countries. Decisions must be made over how much autonomy will be given to these outside researchers and how closely their work will be supervised or monitored. MNCs with marketing research departments in foreign subsidiaries will be able to work more closely with local firms in different countries. But even large corporations do not have in-house marketing research staff in every country in which they do business. MNCs can send out their own staff to brief people in each country, but inevitably they must place considerable reliance on local researchers. Differences in data collection techniques and concerns about the comparability of findings across countries are significant issues when using various research firms in different countries.

Restrictive laws and disclosure of results

A more sinister threat may be the imposition of legal regulations that make it more difficult to keep research results confidential. For example, new laws enacted in the summer of 1999 control the conduct of market research in China, where government officials monitor questionnaire construction and insist on seeing survey results. Not only is this is in direct conflict with the required nondisclosure of proprietary research studies, in which the results are made known only to the clients commissioning the work, but the new disclosure requirements may unwittingly leak new product plans and marketing proposals to competitors. Managers need to be fully aware of such laws and regulations in various countries.

Inadequate use of findings

The real value of market research depends on how the findings are used. International research will add little value to management decision-making if the findings are not interpreted and acted upon appropriately. Reports from domestic market studies may languish on the shelf because management sees little relevance in the research, or disagrees with the findings. This tendency is greater in international research, where studies may be commissioned at the headquarters level but the findings may need to be implemented in foreign subsidiaries. When managers in the local subsidiaries conduct their own research, they will tend to have more ownership and belief in the findings. But corporate management at headquarters may want to control the questions that are investigated and compare the findings across countries or regions. In this case, local management may resent corporate interference and question the usefulness of the research.

Proposals for improving global marketing research

Given all these difficulties, what can marketers do to make their international research both efficient and effec-

tive? Most companies will need to adapt their approach to conducting research. Here are some guidelines for doing that.

Look for ways to cut costs

It is essential to stretch marketing research dollars so that the maximum benefit can be obtained from budgeted resources. Two excellent ways of doing this are by making the fullest use of published sources and tapping available government assistance.

Make extensive use of secondary sources

The United States and most of Western Europe have a wealth of secondary market data that can be accessed online at little or no cost. All market entry studies should begin by consulting published sources. Many international business texts urge managers to organize relevant macro region or country data (political stability, economic stability, currency strength, quality of infrastructure) and micro industry data (current sales by product, distribution access, raw material availability, labor costs, competitive activity) into a matrix where they can be weighed, ranked, and scored. Although the value of this assessment will depend on the availability of published sources, the objectivity of the data, and the accuracy of the rankings, it is generally a useful first pass for comparing countries, considering alternative selection criteria, and narrowing market entry choices. No attempt should be made to collect primary data before secondary sources have been thoroughly investigated and analyzed.

Seek help from government agencies

Most developed countries and many developing ones have state agencies that aid businesses. Virtually all governments try to promote the development of exports. The Export Market Information Center offers assistance to exporters in the UK. In the US, the International Trade Administration, a division of the Department of Commerce, provides a wide variety of market intelligence on different countries. It conducts low-cost market surveys and searches for sales agents and distributors for companies. Many export-driven emerging countries also provide assistance to help local businesses contribute to a balance-of-trade surplus.

Appoint a single market research coordinator for major studies

The use of a coordinating market research vendor with a network of affiliated offices around the world can improve the consistency and accuracy of results across countries and languages. One major vendor can organize and coordinate the work. With a single point of contact, special instructions and changes can be communicated and implemented simultaneously across multiple countries. Leading MNCs tend to appoint coordinating agencies that have offices in multiple countries. VeriFone uses a single vendor that has extensive experience in global market research and a network of branch offices throughout the world. The vendor's branch office personnel conduct most of the fieldwork. Project briefings, interviewer training, and pilot tests can be conducted and monitored much more easily. Other well-known MNCs like IBM, Compaq, Carrier, and Federal Express also use a single global vendor to manage large-scale research projects around the world.

Walker Information is a leading international research firm with more than 60 years of experience. Based in Indianapolis, it has a network of affiliate offices in more than 50 countries helping global clients conduct research studies that take into account cultural and language differences. Walker provides a diverse range of services, including studies of customer loyalty, employee commitment, corporate reputation, supplier relationships, and corporate philanthropy. Its clients include consumer packaged goods companies, heavy manufacturing firms, consumer and business services, trade associations, not-for-profits, and government agencies.

Pay close attention to the translation of questionnaires

The validity of market research can be improved by having strict, formalized guidelines governing questionnaire preparation and translation. Using a small number of translators can help reduce errors by lowering the potential for different interpretations of terms. Back translation—the process of translating questionnaires from one language to another, then back again with the aid of a second, independent translator—can reveal unintended losses of meaning. The back translator is usually a person whose native tongue is the language that will be used for the final questionnaire. Pilot tests can also help ensure better quality in the final study.

For many years, IBM has been conducting a strategic tracking study across its major markets in Europe, North and South America, and Asia. Conducted in 14 languages across 27 countries, this survey assesses IBM's products against competitors' offerings on such strategic issues as product demand, marketing channels, and preferred information sources. The study reveals broad information on trends rather than in-depth information on customer wants and needs. IBM uses only two translation firms to reduce inconsistency in terms, one for the various European languages and another for Asian languages. It also makes sure these firms use back translators to improve questionnaire accuracy. Local IBM employees in engineering, manufacturing, or sales may also be called upon

to double-check technical terms. All surveys are piloted in the field prior to conducting full-scale studies.

Develop a core set of questions to enhance comparability across countries

To compare countries and regions, many MNCs develop a core set of questions that will be used worldwide. At Carrier Corporation, a core set of 25 questions was used in a global study. Allowance was made for differences in each region by giving subsidiaries the opportunity to ask an additional five questions that were tailored to their area. Compaq uses a Customer Satisfaction Council to develop and maintain a consistent set of customer satisfaction measures across business units and geographic areas. Headed by the vice president of customer satisfaction and quality, this global, cross-divisional, interdisciplinary team meets regularly and invites representation from manufacturing and functions worldwide. Its goal is to establish internal metrics that are linked to customer satisfaction. Consistent validity and reliability among each customer segment across each country is a key strategic objective. Study results are used globally as well as locally. Some measures are customized and modified by market. The Council is responsible for integrating customer satisfaction information into product planning initiatives and process improvements.

In some countries, class, caste, or racial differences determine who speaks and who does not.

Use alternative data collection methods

The difficulties in collecting data overseas often mean that researchers need to adapt their approach to each country or region. Greater use may have to be made of qualitative methods in developing countries. The lack of accurate census and demographic information may sometimes rule out probability sampling. As a result, researchers may have to rely more on nonprobability sampling techniques such as convenience and quota sampling. Convenience sampling is often used for populations that are difficult to approach. The sample size gradually grows through introductions and referrals. Drawing quotas from different segments of society may help reduce sample bias (respondents with the same class, caste, or kinship ties, for example).

Methods will depend partly on the stage of the research, the market knowledge required, and the need for statistical precision. The lack of representative samples may be less of a handicap if the research is in the discovery stage and the objective is to obtain broad qualitative data. Indepth interviews and focus groups will often be the best method for exploring a broad range of issues.

Cultural differences may determine whether to use individual interviews or focus groups. American-style focus groups usually consist of eight to ten selected respondents who freely express their perceptions, attitudes, opinions, and feelings on pertinent research issues under the guidance of a moderator. Such discussion often provides rich qualitative data reflecting a diversity of opinions. Similar diverse results are often achieved in male focus groups carried out in the Middle East. The main problem there may be getting participants to show up on time and controlling the discussion when everybody starts talking at once. However, in collectivist cultures such as Japan and Southeast Asia, individuals may be reluctant to speak out, especially if their opinions are contrary to other group members. In some countries, class, caste, or racial differences may also determine who speaks and who does not. In these circumstance, individual interviews may encourage more openness and candor than focus groups.

Approaches to running focus groups may also partly reflect research traditions in different countries. American focus groups typically emphasize direct questioning, specific issues, and more direct interpretations. In Europe, discussions are more open-ended, with greater use of projective techniques and broader interpretations of the findings.

Recruit native language interviewers and moderators

Many consumers are reluctant to be interviewed for marketing research studies. Often, individual interviewers and group discussion moderators may have to build rapport with them. Companies can raise the comfort level of respondents by using native language interviewers and moderators who can converse in the local dialect. This is also a matter of courtesy. Native language interviewers and moderators can enhance the quality of interviews or focus groups when subtle nuances are important. Both telephone and personal interviews are influenced by country cultural norms. Local interviewers and moderators need to be able to interpret facial gestures and body language and to clarify respondent questions.

Select lead countries as a starting point

Lead countries should be chosen as a data collection point prior to conducting research elsewhere. These may be the wealthiest economies in the region or those with the best prospects. They can sometimes be used as proxies for other countries in the area. For instance, some broad cultural similarities have been found among Southeast Asian countries. Handled with care and prudence, this is another way firms can cut the costs of international mar-keting research. Selected lead countries can also be used to iron out problems before rolling the research out on a broader scale. Surveys may be vetted for consistency and accuracy. A thorough debriefing following the initial research allows new learning to be taken into neighboring countries.

Test market in smaller countries to maintain secrecy

Secrecy or confidentiality can be a problem in conducting marketing research. Regulations need to be investigated in each country. Given the recently announced disclosure requirements in China, that may not be the best place to test new products. Smaller countries may sometimes be used to keep new product plans more private. Carewell Industries test-marketed its Dentax toothbrush in Singapore before introducing it in the United States because of the country's remoteness from the American market. It is also a relatively self-contained, low-cost environment for testing new products.

Use start-up offices and stores as research labs

An alternative method of collecting intelligence overseas is to establish a branch office, small-scale assembly operation, or service store as a research lab. This may be especially helpful for introducing new products and services into different countries. Marketing research studies rely heavily on people's perceptions and opinions—views that may be suspect when respondents have little direct experience with a new product or service. By establishing an office, factory, or store, management may learn a great deal more from having a direct presence in a country than simply relying on others' opinions about a product's or service's acceptability. Setting up a small-scale test site on a joint venture basis with a local partner can also lower risk and expense.

Citibank maintained a branch office in Tokyo while researching the market before setting up a successful retailing operation throughout Japan. Outpost factories have been used widely in manufacturing. Small, experimental assembly plants are often set up in developing countries to test the feasibility of manufacturing there and establishing local supplier relationships. Outpost factories may also be set up close to major competitors to gather intelligence. McDonald's and Pizza Hut opened experimental stores in Moscow to test the feasibility of selling fast food in Russia. KFC did the same thing in China. These outpost stores were used to adapt the menu, adjust store policies and procedures to local requirements, and explore alternative supplier relationships. Having established a successful, experimental prototype, management could then roll out more stores with a considerable degree of confidence.

Encourage broad participation by those who must use the findings

When corporate managers coordinate marketing research studies around the world, they need to build ownership at the local level. A wide range of stakeholders should be involved if the findings are to be interpreted and used properly. This is especially important when international studies are first conceived and when the implications of the findings are explored. It may necessitate involving general management at the central, regional, and local levels as well as sales, R&D, manufacturing, and other affected functions. Outside entities such as advertising agencies and local distributors may also need to be closely involved. More participation at critical stages in the research can help eliminate resistance and lead to fuller use of the study findings.

Capture and share findings in corporate marketing information system

By capturing research findings in the corporate marketing information system and sharing them across countries, management can build an understanding of the differences and similarities among markets. Marketing research information is not widely shared across the subsidiaries of most MNC's. Country managers know very little about the findings from studies that have been carried out in other foreign subsidiaries, or of product, pricing, distribution and promotional differences, brand names, slogans, and value propositions in other countries. Sharing such information can promote better understanding and collaboration between foreign subsidiaries.

Keep a close watch on the Net

The recent emergence of Internet-based research is making international marketing research easier to conduct. As more people go online, the Net is helping to define global user communities for different products. Direct contact with subjects in different countries over the Web may shrink the time and cost of conducting the research. The main methods of gathering research data over the Net are (1) e-mail based surveys, (2) Web site surveys, (3) online discussion groups, and (4) computer-assisted interviewing. With only a small portion of the world's population online, these methods are largely untried and untested. But online market studies could eventually help replace onsite interviewing and mail surveys for certain types of studies. Innovations in Net-based research need to be closely monitored. They have the potential to create major advances in international marketing research.

Many US firms are latecomers to doing business globally. With the munificence of the US market, most have not had to venture into foreign markets. Thus, few American managers have extensive international business experience. Many are unaware of the differences overseas. They may be surprised by how little is known about many foreign markets and how little has been written about international marketing research. Managers need to be educated about these differences as well as the research methods that can be used to uncover them. Ultimately, global business success depends on a foundation of valid foreign market information.

References and selected bibliography

Axtell, R. E. 1993. *Do's and taboos around the world.* 3rd ed. New York: Wiley.

Bartlett, C. A., and S. Ghoshal. 1989. *Managing across borders: The transnational solution.* Boston: Harvard Business School Press.

Byfield, S., and L. Caller. 1997. Horses for courses: Stewarding brands across borders in times of rapid change. *Journal of the Market Research Society* 39/4: 589–601.

Ceteora, P. R., and J. L. Graham. 1999. *International Marketing.* 10th ed. New York: Irwin/McGraw-Hill.

Childs, R. 1996. Buying international research. *Journal of the Market Research Society* 38/1: 63–66.

Craig, C. S., and S. P. Douglas. 2000. *International Marketing Research.* 2nd ed. New York: Wiley.

Crampton, M. F. 1996. Where does your ad work? *Journal of the Market Research Society* 38/1: 35–53.

Frevert, B. 2000. Is global research different? *Marketing Research* 12/1: 49–51.

Goodwin, T. 1999. Measuring the effectiveness of online marketing. *Journal of the Market Research Society* 41/4: 403–406.

Iyer, R. 1997. A look at the Indian market research industry. *Quirk's Marketing Research Review* (November): 22–26.

Jeffries-Fox, B. C. 1995. Dance with me: US firms need good international partners to keep in step. *Marketing Research* 7/2: 15–18.

Keillor, B., D. Owens, and C. Pettijohn. 2001. A cross-cultural/cross-national study of influencing factors and socially desirable response biases. *International Journal of Market Research* 43/1: 63–84.

Kent, R., and M. Lee. 1999. Using the Internet for market research: A study of private trading on the Internet. *Journal of the Market Research Society* 41/4: 377–385.

Lee, B., and A. Wong. 1996. An introduction to marketing research in China. *Quirk's Marketing Research Review* (November): 18–19, 37–38.

Leonidou, L. C., and N. Rossides. 1995. Marketing research in the Gulf States: A practical appraisal. *Journal of the Marketing Research Society* 37/4: 455–467.

Lewis, S., and M. Hathaway. 1998. International focus groups: Embrace the unpredictable. *Quirk's Marketing Research Review* (November): 36–41.

McIntosh, A. R., and R. J. Davies. 1996. The sampling of nondomestic populations. *Journal of the Market Research Society* 38/4: 431–446.

McKie, A. 1996. International research in a relative world. *Journal of the Market Research Society* 38/1: 7–12.

Meier, G. M. 1998. *The international environment of business.* New York: Oxford University Press.

Moseley, D. 1996. Information needs for market entry. *Journal of the Market Research Society* 38/1: 13–18.

Mytton, G. 1996. Research in new fields. *Journal of the Market Research Society* 38/1: 19–33.

Pawle, J. 1999. Mining the international consumer. *Journal of the Market Research Society* 41/1: 19–32.

Prahalad, C. K., and K. Lieberthal. 1998. The end of corporate imperialism. *Harvard Business Review* 76/4 (July–August): 69–79.

Ricks, D. A. 1983. *Big business blunders: Mistakes in multinational marketing.* Homewood, IL: Dow Jones Irwin.

Robinson, C. 1996. Asian culture: The marketing consequences. *Journal of the Market Research Society* 38/1: 55–62.

Root, F. R. 1994. *Entry strategies for international markets.* Rev. ed. New York: Lexington.

Rydholm, J. 1996. Leaping the barriers of time and distance. *Quirk's Marketing Research Review* (November): 10–11, 42–45.

Soruco, G. R., and T. P. Meyer. 1993. The mobile Hispanic market: New challenges in the 90s. *Marketing Research* 5/1: 6–11.

Valentine, C. F. 1988. *The Arthur Young international business guide.* New York: Wiley.

Wilsden, M. 1996. Getting it done properly: The role of the coordinator in multicountry research. *Journal of the Market Research Society* 38/1: 67–71.

Zikmund, W. 2000. *Exploring marketing research.* 6th ed. Orlando, FL: Dryden Press.

The New Land of Opportunity

It's a global economy—so quit whining about outsourcing. India's booming middle class has $420 billion to spend. Here's how to grab your share.

By Om Malik

On a typical afternoon, 26-year-old Shruti Sharma heads with friends to Gurgaon, a New Delhi suburb that's also a shopper's paradise. The malls here are vertical versions of their U.S. counterparts: five-story high-tech bazaars with multiplex cinemas, ice cream parlors, escalators, parking lots, even Muzak (smarmy versions of Bollywood disco hits). Outside it's so hot the asphalt is melting—talk about Indian summer—but inside, shoppers stroll in air-conditioned bliss past a Pizza Hut, a Subway, a Benetton, and a TGI Friday's. Sharma volunteers that her favorite brands are, in no particular order, Nike, Nokia, McDonald's, and Levi's. "Buying habits are changing," she says with a shy smile. "Nothing less than a brand name like Nike or Adidas will do."

I'm not sure what's more amazing: Gurgaon or Sharma. When I was growing up not far from here, Gurgaon was little more than a tiny town built on a fly-blown cow pasture where my friends and I would go to buy cheap Kingfisher beer. In the past three years, it's sprouted six malls—with five more under construction—and a skyline of shiny new office buildings and call centers. Filling these new structures are people like Sharma, who answers phones in a South Delhi industrial park for a U.S. Internet service provider. She earns more than $9,000 a year, 19 times the average Indian wage.

To some in America, which I now call home, that makes her a job stealer. But in India, people like her are becoming so common that local newspapers have begun referring to them as "zippies"—young Indians who walk with a zip in their stride, oozing with attitude, ambition, and money. Zippies represent India's burgeoning middle class, which, by the way, outnumbers the entire U.S. population.

Instead of a threat, the zippies signify an unprecedented opportunity for American business. India is undergoing an eco-nomic boom the likes of which the world sees perhaps twice a century. In places like Gurgaon's Mall Mile, you can feel the explosion of commerce. Malls have sprung up in Bangalore, Calcutta, Mumbai, and scores of smaller cities. Thanks to low interest rates, deregulation, and an influx of 785,000 new jobs at call centers and programming houses, Indian consumers are buying up everything from imported computers and software to cell phones and clothes. According to some estimates, 487 million middle-class Indians will spend an additional $420 billion during the next four years.

There are other tantalizing hints that India will become even more attractive as an emerging market for U.S. businesses. The new prime minister, Manmohan Singh, is an Oxford-educated former finance minister whose 1990s fiscal reforms are credited with setting India on its remarkable trajectory. Indeed, India's economy is projected to grow 7.2 percent this year. Next January the World Trade Organization will eliminate trade restriction on industries such as textiles and pharmaceuticals, which should boost exports in these sectors and put even more disposable income in Indians' pockets. In turn, that will open the door wider to more imports from the United States.

Of course, nothing in business, especially global business, is without risk. A big wild card is India's notoriously unstable government. The communists and socialists who helped forge Prime Minister Singh's new ruling alliance could easily derail progress. They promote a populist agenda that includes using the country's precious resources to subsidize power and fuel for farmers and the poor. Investment banker friends of mine joke about India's "democracy discount," imposed by foreign investors afraid to do business in a country that has elected 10 new governments in the last 20 years.

Nevertheless, Rakesh Jhunjhunwala, a 44-year-old investor who's been called India's Warren Buffett, sees the nation's economic engine only getting stronger. Once an accountant who made just $100 a month, he's now India's largest private investor, with an estimated net worth of $250 million. Like the Sage of Omaha, he takes the long view and bets on fundamentals.

At the wood-paneled bar of Mumbai's white-shoe Cricket Club of India, Jhunjhunwala imparts the key to understanding India's future. "This is much like America in the 1950s," he says, his back to a veranda that looks out on the lush outfield, a reminder of India's colonial past. "It's a bottom-up kind of growth driven not by temporary circumstances." While he believes outsourcing is helping, he cites a more important demographic shift, in which spenders are replacing savers. By 2006, India's 20- to 34-year-old population will swell to 280 million. These zippies-to-be will marry, start families, and buy homes, appliances, automobiles, and consumer products. For India, Jhunjhunwala forecasts "long-term consumerism."

How Do You Capitalize?

BUT CLEARLY THE OPPORTUNITY IS ALREADY here. And plenty of big-name companies, from America and elsewhere, have started moving in. U.S. exports to India surged to $5 billion in 2003 from $4 billion a year earlier. Fiber-optic equipment maker Corning, ailing in the United States, has sold an estimated $50 million worth of cable to Indian telecom operators. Likewise, South Korean carmaker Hyundai has captured nearly 20 percent of India's auto market. Indians have bought $2 billion worth of cell phones and networking gear from Nokia alone. It doesn't hurt that Indians are exposed to global marketing messages through CNBC, HBO, and MTV. "The Indian middle class is easier to target because people understand English and have a Western orientation," says Rory Cowan, president of Lionbridge Technologies, which sells database translation software throughout Asia. "In China it's a longer slog."

Still, it's one thing to salivate over half a billion Indian mall rats, and another to start selling to them. Foreign companies that have made the attempt complain of ridiculously low margins, slow implementation of business-friendly laws, and bewildering cultural diversity: The residents of India's 28 states and seven union territories speak 17 major languages and practice seven religions. Such frustrations led scores of multinationals to pull out of India in the 1990s, according to Ingrid Belton, director of trade policy at the U.S. Chamber of Commerce's U.S.-India Business Council. "Those companies were the pioneers," she says, "and the pioneers tend to take the arrows."

Belton says India isn't yet an easy place to do business, "but it's better." And now that there's so much money to be made there, executives I interview in America routinely prod me for the key to cracking the Indian market. Having grown up in India and followed its rise for the past two decades, I usually tell them they need to think locally, offer value, and be patient. That last one is key: You can make an elephant dance. But it takes time

BOLLYWOOD BLOCKBUSTERS

SOME FOREIGN PRODUCTS THAT HAVE MADE IT BIG IN INDIA—AND SOME THAT HAVEN'T.

In a country that is mostly vegetarian, MCDONALD'S launched in 1996 with a menu built around the Maharaja Mac—a mutton burger. Recent introductions like the potato-based McAloo Tikki have fared better.

Handsets made especially for India—such as the 1100, which doubles as a flashlight—have helped NOKIA sell $2 billion worth of mobile-phone equipment to Indians.

COCA-COLA launched in India with 300-ml bottles priced at 24 cents, but saw higher profits when it shifted to selling 200-ml bottles for around 10 cents.

Having built a plant just outside Chennai, HYUNDAI can sell its wildly popular Santro for just $7,000. The South Korean carmaker now ranks second in the Indian market.

Ambani's Law

PERHAPS NO ONE UNDERSTOOD THE DYNAMICS of Indian marketing better than the late Dhirubhai Ambani, a self-made billionaire who started out as a gas station attendant in the 1950s. Expanding first to textile production, then to oil refineries, Ambani and his family built a business empire that today accounts for more than 3 percent of India's gross domestic product. Ten years ago, when India began deregulating communications, U.S. telecom executives approached Ambani to form a mobile-phone company.

Ambani refused, saying (according to Indian business folklore), "When it's possible to offer calls that cost about the same as a postcard, then we can think about setting up a mobile-phone business." At the time, postcards in India cost a penny, and per-minute phone charges averaged about 50 cents, among the highest in the world.

I like to call his philosophy Ambani's Law of Indian Marketing. If Ambani had coined such a law, it would have stated that you don't make money in India until your product or service makes sense for the masses, the hundreds of millions of people who earn as little as $3 a day. In 2002, Ambani's son Mukesh finally launched a phone company, Mumbai-based Reliance Infocomm. Reliance charges less than 2 cents a minute. (Postcards, meanwhile, are getting more expensive: They now cost 1.5 cents.) Reliance has already captured 22 percent of the Indian mobile-phone market—7.5 million users—and is profitable despite an average customer phone bill of about $11 per month.

Value Sells

YOU'RE MISSING THE POINT IF YOU BELIEVE that Ambani's Law simply equates cheapness with mass markets; if that were true, Chinese companies would be cleaning up in India. They aren't. Rather, the secret is a blend of price, utility, and cachet.

Cell phones are the perfect example; in fact, nothing symbolizes India's newfound consumerism better. As I walk through my old stomping grounds in a decidedly dowdy district of New Delhi, I notice that the *paan walaas*—street vendors who sell cigarettes, chewing gum, and betel nuts—now also hawk prepaid phone cards. Enrique Iglesias's latest album is being promoted here, not on MTV but through downloadable ringtones hosted by wireless service providers. Twenty years ago, when my parents got their first landline, friends came over to celebrate as if the whole neighborhood had won the lottery. Now I can't pray in temple without hearing beeps between chants.

Yet with cell phones, brand names matter. Otherwise, everyone in India would carry a $50 model from Chinese manufacturer Ningbo Bird or inexpensive offerings from the likes of Philips and Alcatel. But they've all lost out to higher-priced handsets from Nokia and Samsung. In fact, Samsung, the fastest-growing cell-phone maker, is on track to garner nearly 29 percent of India's handset sales, roughly 5 million units by the end of 2004. It positions its color-screen camera phones as lifestyle items. (In April, Samsung sponsored a cell-phone fashion show, with stylish models walking down runways making mock calls.) "Price is not the only criterion in the Indian market," agrees Kunal Ahooja, vice president for Samsung's telecom business in India. The proof: Samsung charges $80 to $550 per phone—up to twice as much as other brands.

India is filled with examples of foreign products that sell because they deliver value over outright cheapness. Hyundai has recently become the No. 2 car seller in India, thanks to its $7,000 Santro, which is gaining on the national favorite, the $5,700 model 800 from Maruti Suzuki. Both cars are made in India by foreign companies, but the Santro commands a higher price because air-conditioning comes standard and the car is considered more fuel efficient and better made. (Ford and General Motors are still marginal players, offering models starting at about $9,000.) South Korean consumer-products giant LG has trumped Whirlpool and China's Haier by making slightly more expensive refrigerators and air conditioners that are more resistant to the dust, extreme heat, and frequent power surges common in India's vast rural territory. Like compatriot Samsung, LG has gone from zero to roughly $1 billion in sales in India in less than 10 years. "The Koreans understand Indians' need for 'value-for-money' products," says R. Amarnath, head of research for ICICI Securities.

That said, any business wishing to truly thrive here has to do so on volume—making a small amount of profit on mass unit sales. On a per capita basis, Indians simply can't pay very much for the stuff they buy—yet.

Levi Strauss entered India in 1995 with a number of exclusive stores and premium-priced jeans, but the brand was not well-known to the Indian consumer. It cracked the zippie code by introducing lower-priced lines like Red Tabs, which go for about $25. Last year, sales grew by 20 percent over 2002. In 1996, McDonald's opened its first Indian outlet in New Delhi with a menu built around the $2 Maharaja Mac—a mutton burger designed for India's Hindu majority that doesn't eat beef. Yet sales only took off with the introduction of cheaper options like the McAloo Tikki (a potato-based patty) and McCurry Pan (chicken and vegetables baked onto a spiced bread), which go for about a dollar. The fast-food giant now has more than 50 restaurants in India.

A BEGINNER'S GUIDE TO INDIAN MARKETING

Cultural barriers, poor infrastructure, and government restrictions make even one of the world's fastest-growing economies a challenge. Here are the lessons of foreign pioneers that have positioned their companies to cash in on India's remarkable progress.
—BRIDGET FINN

- **SCALE DOWN**
  Americans snap up supersize containers at Costco, but Indians save cash by buying smaller quantities. Revlon reduced the size of its nail polish bottles and saw sales volume increase.

- **PRICE FOR MASS APPEAL**
  The average income for a middle-class Indian worker is just $1,200 a year. Phone equipment maker UTStarcom found that spending constraints trickle down: It had to design cheaper network switches to sell to local phone companies.

- **TAILOR PRODUCTS TO INDIAN TASTES**
  In most countries, Subway carries only one or two local-cuisine menu items, but in India, the franchise offers separate vegetarian counters and a specialized "Indian Delights" menu. It's opened 27 new stores since December 2001.

- **LOCALIZE YOUR MESSAGE**
  In the 1990s, Pepsi ran the same commercials in India that it aired elsewhere. But the brand didn't take off until it tapped local talent like Shahrukh Khan, India's biggest box-office star, and Sachin Tendulkar, a hugely popular cricket batsman.

- **FIND A GOOD PARTNER**
  India's fragmented distribution channels present a challenge to foreign companies. Tap into booming local chains like Foodworld, Pantaloon, and Shopper's Stop, which offer access to India's middle class.

The Lesson of the Shampoo Packet

How do you cut unit costs without sacrificing quality? Think outside the box—and in the tiny tube. While Americans buy half-gallon bottles of Pantene from Sam's Club, 70 percent of Indian shampoo is sold in 5-milliliter packets costing less than a nickel.

Likewise, Indian consumers buy 70 percent of cell-phone airtime through prepaid cards in increments as low as a few dollars. And a majority of the nearly 10 million DVD players purchased in India this year will be $45 do-it-yourself assembly kits sold at places like Old Delhi's Lajpat Rai Market, a centuries-old bazaar where rickshas and mangy dogs compete for space with salesmen spouting microcontroller specs. Buyers are really distributors: They purchase the kits for $45, assemble the players, and resell them in their own neighborhoods for a profit of about $11.

Some U.S. companies have already adopted "shampoo thinking." After introducing 300-ml bottles priced at 24 cents, Coca-Cola is finding it more profitable to shift production to 200-ml bottles sold for less than half that. Colgate toothpaste also comes in tiny packets.

Even tech companies are doing it. In 2001, Alameda, Calif., telecom equipment maker UTStarcom opened an office in New Delhi, betting that India's consumer boom would translate into greater demand for network gear. The move was prescient: India's "teledensity"—phones per million people—has jumped from 44,000 in 2000 to 77,000 today. Still, selling to Indian phone companies turned out to be more difficult than expected for Ruchir Godura, UTStarcom's India manager. He recalls the first time he walked into a potential customer's office: "The guy said, 'A dollar may be equal to 47 rupees on currency markets, but to us it's worth only 10.'" In other words, after converting UTStarcom's American prices at the going exchange rate, Godura was asked to divide by five.

Godura knew he couldn't do that and make money. One of UTStarcom's main offerings is a specialized telecom switch called a digital loop carrier (DLC), which lets phone companies deliver voice and Internet services to subscribers. The box was a hit in China, in part because it could handle as many as 480 customers. But for India's local carriers, it was overkill: Anxious to conserve cash, they only wanted to expand their networks in 100-user increments. To make matters worse, Godura found that customers preferred well-known European brands. "It seemed we couldn't sell anything in this country," he says.

UTStarcom went back to the drawing board, spending nearly a year designing a scaled-down DLC. It was just like selling good shampoo in tiny bottles: Starcom's box was small, scalable, and cheap enough for local markets. Today the company counts all major Indian phone companies as customers, and its 2004 sales in India are likely to top $50 million. Godura's advice to others tackling India: "First, figure out what your customer can charge his customers and still be profitable. If you can work within that, you can make money."

BETTING ON THE BOMBAY BORSE

PUTTING YOUR MONEY TO WORK IN INDIA ISN'T A CINCH, BUT THERE ARE WAYS TO REDUCE THE RISK.

So you missed the upside of Japan in the mid-1960s, South Korea in the 1980s, and China in the 1990s. Maybe you were too timid, or maybe your parents just didn't think a sixth-grader should be playing the international stock market. Either way, you could have made a killing.

Is now the time to invest in India? There's certainly plenty of risk, including volatile domestic politics, an uneasy peace with Pakistan, and an agricultural economy that depends on unpredictable monsoon rains. While the Indian stock market was up an incredible 101 percent in 2003, a recent sell-off has pushed values down 18 percent this year. No telling whether that's a buying opportunity or a fool's gambit.

If you do decide to take the plunge, there are only a few ways to play—the Indian government doesn't let foreigners buy local shares. The easiest route is through American depositary receipts of the 11 Indian companies trading on U.S. Exchanges, such as blue chips Wipro and HDFC Bank.

But unless you know a lot about a particular company and can follow it closely (www.indiainfoline.com is a good place to start), you'll want the reduced risk that funds offer. While there are only three that invest exclusively in India, you can also buy into the subcontinent through emerging-markets mutual funds that carry significant Indian exposure. –Michael V. Copeland

---

An Indian Investment Sampler

Name (Symbol)	Category	Recent Price[1]	YTD Return[1]	Largest Holding
India Fund (IFN)	Closed-end fund (traded on NYSE)	$20.42	-14.0%	Reliance Industries
Morgan Stanley India Investment (IIF)	Closed-end fund (traded on the NYSE)	$19.50	-14.0%	State Bank of India
Eaton Vance Greater India A (ETGIX)	Single-country mutual fund	$9.49	-18.3%	Punjab National Bank
Opperheimer Developing Markets A (ODMAX)	Emerging-markets mutual fund (19.6% Indian exposure)	$20.03	-2.8%	Bharat Petroleum[2]
Heritage International Equity A (HEIAX)	Emerging-markets mutual fund (18.4% Indian exposure)	$19.44	0.3%	ICICI Bank

1)Based on net asset values as of May 31. 2) Largest Indian holding.
Source: Morningstar

Find the Emerging Market

LOOK HARD ENOUGH, AND THERE EXIST enough profitable niches in India for virtually any American company—even one that makes software. In 1987, San Jose-based Cadence Design Systems, which sells applications used to design microchips, established a research and development branch in New Delhi to gain access to India's affordable but sophisticated programming talent. Cadence's sales in India were so meager that the company farmed them out to a local distributor.

But in 1996, Saugat Sen, Cadence's engineering director in India, predicted that the outsourcing trend would bring chip-design work to high-tech meccas like Bangalore and Hyderabad. So Cadence converted its Indian outpost into a freestanding subsidiary with sales capability. The company acted just in time: With Analog Devices, Intel, and Texas Instruments opening research facilities in India, Sen estimates that 10 percent of all chip-design software users reside here. And as young Indians abandon the old quest for "babudom"—cushy jobs in the government bureaucracy—to set up entrepreneurial ventures designing cutting-edge Bluetooth and other wireless chips, there's a long list of customers willing to pay hundreds of thousands of dollars for Cadence's high-end software. "As long as we offer value for money, people will buy it," Sen says. He estimates that within three years, as much as 15 percent of the world's chip design will happen in India, boosting demand for workstations and other development tools.

All the economic activity in my homeland makes me a little wistful. These zippies strut around with a confidence—yes, a zip—I never had growing up. When I was their age, I wanted to be a journalist, so I left India for the United States. Today, with 100 TV channels—14 of which offer news—and 39,000 newspapers, a reporter can find fame, even a little fortune, at home.

One of the last people I meet in India is my old friend J.J. Valaya, a fashion designer I once wrote about for an Indian newspaper. Seven years ago, when I last visited here, he drooled over the Armani jeans, Oliver Peoples eyeglasses, and Apple Power-Book I brought from the United States. This time, as he welcomes me into his spacious Gurgaon office (not far from Mall Mile), he shuts down his Apple eMac, puts his Sony Ericsson P800 smartphone on vibration mode, and tells me about the new Hugo Boss and Tommy Hilfiger boutiques. Freakin' Tommy Hilfiger is selling in India!

However, there are still some things my old friend can't get his hands on. As I sit down, I pull out a silvery treasure smaller than a pack of cigarettes and finger its touch-sensitive dial. Apple sells iPods in India, but not yet the iPod mini. My friend sits silently, but his eyes speak volumes.

Note to Steve Jobs, and everyone else: The elephant is putting on its tutu.

Om Malik (omalik@business2.com) is a senior writer at Business 2.0.

Made in India vs. Made in China

Multinationals See Big Upside To Subcontinent

Keith Bradsher

SHENZHEN, China—When Crystal Chen, a 28-year-old mechanical engineer, started designing microwave oven doors for Whirlpool in 2001 in this gleaming Chinese metropolis, one of her biggest surprises was the size of the ovens.

Built to be installed over ranges in spacious American kitchens, the ovens were twice the size of the countertop microwaves sold for Chinese kitchens. And as she has kept working on them, the Whirlpool models, nearly all of them made to be exported to the United States and Europe, have grown even larger, approaching three times the size of a typical Chinese microwave.

By contrast, at a Whirlpool complex more than 2,500 miles away in Thirubhuvanai, on the southeastern tip of India, the washing machines built in a hot low-tech factory are products the Indian workers easily recognize. Unlike the microwave ovens in Shenzhen, these washing machines are very much designed for local use, not for export.

They have rat guards to keep vermin from nibbling laundry or hoses. They have extra-strong parts to survive being bumped around in trucks on India's potholed roads. And they are built with heavy-duty wiring to cope with the powerful ebbs and surges in India's electrical grid.

The difference is telling. Whirlpool's emphasis on using China to make goods for export while locating in India to enter the local market reflects a broader trend that is becoming apparent for many household appliances, from television sets to refrigerators. And it highlights a division that could spread in the coming years to other industries.

For all the dreams of selling goods into a fast-growing market of 1.3 billion Chinese, the reality is often very different. While China still holds considerable allure, many multinationals have struggled to earn profits selling here.

Companies setting up shop in China face domestic manufacturers that consistently undercut them by building factories at practically no cost, borrowing the money cheaply from state-owned Chinese banks and using various strategies to avoid repayment. To make matters worse, many department stores are still owned by municipal or provincial governments that give floor space to local products and resist selling foreign brands.

A result has been a struggle among manufacturers to see who can discount wares more deeply—a struggle with little appeal for multinationals that need to make real profits.

"We're not interested in chasing a price-driven strategy," said Garrick D'Silva, the regional vice president for Asia at Whirlpool.

India's economy has been growing nearly as quickly as China's in recent years. By dismantling many barriers to foreign investment, the government in New Delhi has also made the country an increasingly attractive market for globalizing companies.

Marketing is easy through thousands of privately owned retailers, from department stores to corner shops. Risk-averse banks in India charge such steep interest rates to local manufacturers, and so strongly insist on repayment, that some economists worry they may even be slowing growth unnecessarily.

India's steep tariffs, although starting to decline, long insulated its markets from international competition and still keep prices somewhat higher for many manufactured goods.

And because India did not follow China's draconian "one child" policy, United Nations demographers forecast that India's population will surpass China's as soon as 2040.

With all those factors, Whirlpool—while still strongly interested in tapping the Chinese market — has found greater opportunity to lock in profits and expand its market share in India than in China, Mr. D'Silva said.

LG Electronics of Korea, Whirlpool's rival in Asia for many kinds of household appliances, shares that view.

"We couldn't make a profit in China," chiefly because of the free loans available to local competitors, said Kim Kwang Ro, the managing director of LG Electronics India. "The main focus of expansion for LG is India, not China."

China's effort recently to brake its economy, in response to rising inflation and a growing problem of nonperforming bank loans, is also starting to take the edge off some companies' interest. China's political prospects remain murky.

By contrast, India has just gone through a peaceful change of democratic government that produced a mere two-day drop in the stock market followed by an immediate recovery in share prices and corporate confidence.

"The Chinese economy is looking rather unstable," Mr. Kim said. "Meanwhile, in India, the political, economic situation is becoming more stable."

Despite rising costs for steel and many other commodities that go into factory goods, prices for manufactured products are still falling in China because companies keep building more and more facilities to take advantage of the nation's extraordinary investment boom. Refrigerator prices, for example, fell 2.2 percent in China in the 12 months through April 2004. In India, they rose 3.5 percent.

India's combination of duties on imports and complex regulations on manufacturing start-ups has tended to benefit companies with factories in the country. "The harder the obstacles, the bigger the advantage for the inside firm," Mr. Kim said.

Many companies, of course, remain bullish on the Chinese market. Automakers are racing each other to build more assembly plants in China, but have moved more cautiously in India, where incomes are still somewhat lower and roads are in much worse repair. **Anheuser-Busch** just beat out **SABMiller** in a costly battle to take over a low-margin beer business in China's northeastern corner.

Moreover, for all their differences, India and China share a growing popularity as places for companies from the United States and other countries with high labor costs to set up shop.

Like many of its counterparts, Whirlpool is moving quickly to tap Asia's huge supply of well-trained engineers. Its employment of engineers and technicians in India and China has grown from zero in 1999 to 240 currently, with plans for 700 by 2007, or more than a quarter of the company's engineering work force.

India's population is expected to surpass China's as soon as 2040.

"We're shifting quite a bit of our technology capacity to these countries from the higher-cost parts of the world, part of it from the United States and Europe," Mr. D'Silva said.

Like many companies, Whirlpool insists that it has been able to manage this without significant layoffs among its engineers and technicians in the United States. But it acknowledges that it has not been increasing the size of its American staff, either.

As it has expanded abroad, the company has increased the number of different models of everything from big Whirlpool refrigerators to KitchenAid coffee grinders. It has cut the time it takes to develop new models of the larger appliances to 12 to 14 months, from 30 to 36 months a few years ago.

Engineers in the United States now work in the day on new designs, using computer-aided design software, then send the project around the world in the evening so that engineers in India and China, earning less than $1,000 a month, can continue the work during their normal daytime hours.

The high cost of the necessary computer software is an important reason for the 24-hour programming, which allows different technical centers to take turns using a limited number of software licenses, said Herbert Fu, the company's product development director here in Shenzhen.

As the sun sets each evening in the United States and computer-design work is transferred across the Pacific, engineers in India and China operate very differently. The Chinese engineers tend to continue working on the same projects as their American colleagues: designing or improving products for the American market. The Indian engineers, who occupy a warren of cubicles upstairs from the factory in Thirubhuvanai, devote a lot more of their effort to revising designs for sale in the local market.

As with many outsourcing issues, the expansion of Whirlpool's engineering activities in Asia has been much more complicated than a simple transfer of American jobs.

The main job losses, in fact, have been in Sweden rather than the United States. Whirlpool cut employment in half at a microwave oven factory there in 2003, to 305 jobs, while expanding research and development here and increasing its output at a factory up the Pearl River in Shunde.

While the share of Whirlpool's work force overseas will continue to grow in the coming years, the increase will come from expanding the company's total employment; the overall number of jobs in the United States is not expected to decline, according to Stephen J. Duthie, a company spokesman.

In India, Whirlpool has catered to customers like Rupam Shekhar, a New Delhi housewife whose husband has a small export business selling bed linens and curtains. They live with their two children in a walk-up apartment on the outskirts of New Delhi.

The Whirlpool refrigerator they own is quite different from those sold to Americans. Milk in India is seldom pasteurized, for example, so consumers boil it in a very tall steel urn on a stove. Whirlpool made it possible to fold away part of the top shelf in the refrigerator, so that the urn, known as a patila, could rest on the shelf below.

At the same time, Whirlpool also uses a much smaller percentage of the refrigerator's space for the freezer than in other markets. Research showed that two-thirds of India's people are vegetarians who have little use for a freezer—except for storing a little ice cream and a few ice cubes.

Few Indian kitchens have room for refrigerators, and the appliances are also something of a status symbol: the cost is equal to nearly two months' salary for an engineer. So they are commonly displayed in living rooms or dining rooms. In response, Whirlpool now sells refrigerators in bright colors and curvy doors and sides.

Mrs. Shekhar, more traditional in her tastes, has bought a plain white Whirlpool refrigerator and put it in the bedroom, next to a small shrine to Hindu deities. She used to have to boil milk and chill it a pint at a time for her son and daughter.

"Now, I can boil it all," she said, showing off the inside full of steel pots and fresh vegetables.

Whirlpool has been able to overcome the typically fractious factory floor labor disputes and work stoppages in India by locating in the Pondicherry region, a former French colony that has a tradition of social peace described in Yann Martel's novel "The Life of Pi."

India also appeals to Whirlpool because it is easier to enforce contracts there than in China. A Whirlpool executive said that the company had a contract in 2002 with a Shenzhen company to supply many of the components for a new toaster oven, only to have the supplier raise the price sharply.

Whirlpool switched production to India. "We had a contract but we decided it wouldn't be prudent to enforce it," the executive said. "You never try to put a supplier too much in the corner because you get it back in quality."

But Whirlpool is not giving up on China, despite its difficulties here so far. In a workroom near Ms. Chen's cubicle, Cindy Wu, a 30-year-old engineer, was testing a new design for the fan blade that cools the microwave oven.

"Maybe someday," Ms. Wu said, "Chinese families will have microwaves like these."

Cracking China's Market

Adapting to Chinese Customs, Cultural Changes, Companies From U.S., Europe Find Profit

By LESLIE CHANG And PETER WONACOTT

Beijing

LONG-HELD perception: China is a perpetual market of tomorrow, sucking money from foreign companies tantalized by visions of a billion new consumers, even as hope of profit recedes year by year.

Dawning reality; China has turned into a profitable market for foreigners in relatively short order.

Capitalizing on dramatic changes that include the emergence of urban consumers, more open local governments, the spread of modern retail outlets and the entrepreneurialism of the Chinese, a critical mass of foreign companies are now making money in China. According to an August report by the American Chamber of Commerce, 64% of about 200 companies surveyed in China say they are profitable.

As multinational

consumer-products companies such as Coca-Cola, Eastman Kodak and Motorola make further inroads—and more money—in a rapidly changing China, their logos are becoming an integral part of the nation's landscape

China is now **Eastman Kodak** Co.'s second-biggest film market after the U.S., and sales here are growing faster than in any other major market, the film firm says. Food conglomerate **Groupe Danone** SA of France has in the past six years built a $1.2 billion business in China that is profitable in all its divisions. Germany's **Siemens** AG, selling everything from washing machines to high-speed railways, saw double-digit profit growth last year in China, now its No. 3 market after the U.S. and Germany. **Procter & Gamble** Co. has invested $1 billion in China and says its operation here is profitable. The KFC restaurant chain, owned by **Yum Brands** Inc., opens a new store every other day in China, all funded by its Chinese prof-

its, "China is an absolute gold mine for us," Yum's chief executive David Novak told analysts recently.

China continues to be one of the most challenging markets around owing to brutal price wars, backstabbing business partners, widespread counterfeiting and a slow-moving judicial system. But here is how some of the most successful players in China are turning a profit:

Kodak: Just $12,000 to Run an Outlet

Under a tropical evening sky in Xiamen, executives from Eastman Kodak pile out of a minibus to be greeted by hundreds of cheering workers. They climb to a stage festooned to red-and-gold Kodak colors, and a worker reads a poem commemorating production of the 20-millionth Kodak disposable camera in this seaside city. "Kodak, I love you," he gushes.

Kodak is loving China back. "There were a lot of people that were burned and hurt and called China a shattered dream," says one of the executives, Ying Yeh, a vice president for Kodak. "But I never had any doubt."

Kodak, which is based in Rochester, N.Y., has nearly 8,000 photo stores across China, one of the country's largest retail networks in any sector. The company taps the desire of many Chinese to run their own businesses while helping them negotiate the ins and outs of setting up shop on their own. Because of China's vast size, foreign companies seeking national reach must rely to an unusual extent on such a far-flung network of people, then find ways to tie their interests to the company's own.

One Kodak campaign, "99,000 Will Make You a Boss," offered all the necessary photo-development equipment, training, and a store license for the equivalent of a one-time fee of 99,000 yuan, less than $12,000. Kodak negotiated a deal with the Bank of China and other big banks to arrange financing for individual operators lacking capital. As its numbers of distributors and outlets boomed, Kodak factories have fed these "mini-bosses" with competitively priced cameras and film. That's thanks to a big

Opening Doors for Big Business

Multinational companies are expanding their operations in China and turning profits. Some examples:

COMPANY	SCALE OF OPERATIONS	EMPLOYEES	TOTAL INVESTMENT	PROFIT DETAILS
Coca-Cola	31 bottling plants with three joint-venture partners and two concentrate plants	20,000	$1.1 billion	Profitable for eight years
Danone	More than 50 manufacturing plants for biscuits, beverages and dairy products	25,000	NA	Operating profit margins higher than the company's global average, amounting to at least $140 million in 2001
Kodak	Five manufacturing plants for cameras, chemicals and film and more than 8,000 outlets	5,000	$1.2 billion	Company says it's profitable
Motorola	Two manufacturing plants for mobile-phone handsets, cellular networks and semiconductors	12,000	$3.4 billion at end of 2001	Company says it's profitable
Procter & Gamble	Five plants for food, personal care and household consumer goods	4,000	$1 billion	Company says it's profitable
Siemens	40 companies with businesses including telecommunications, machine automation, power, transport and home appliances	21,000	More than $610 million	Profit grew at double-digit rates in 2002
Yum Brands	Close to 800 KFC restaurants and 100 Pizza Hut restaurants	40,000 to 50,000	More than $400 million	China is expected to account for 29% of international profits for 2002

Source: The companies

bet Kodak made on manufacturing in China in 1998, when it picked up three debt-laden state firms and many of their workers for over $1 billion. In return, Beijing barred new foreign-invested film factories for four years.

The gamble helped Kodak, a distant fourth when it arrived in China in 1994, leapfrog rivals including Japan's **Fuji Photo Film** Co., which relies on imports to stock its stores. Today, Fuji's market share has shrunk to 25% compared with Kodak's 63%.

Kodak is now expanding in China's poorer west. In a country where fashion and new lifestyles spread at warp speed, many are buying cameras for a first time to record the change. Says Paul Walrath, a plant manager in Xiamen and a 26-year Kodak veteran, "We're counting on great performance in China to drive the company where we want to go."

Danone: Master of Piggybacking

Like Kodak, France's Danone was a relative latecomer when it started building its China business around 1996. It decided to piggyback off the successes of domestic brands rather than to build all its businesses from scratch, in 1996 buying a controlling stake in Hangzhou Wahaha Group Co., an enterprising maker of vitamin-enriched milk drinks targeted at children.

Danone embarked on a massive expansion for Wahaha—building multiple plants across the country, backed by a huge advertising campaign—that pushed annual sales from 800 million bottles when it bought the company to four billion bottles within two years. It then

quickly leveraged that scale, distribution network and brand-name recognition into a new business: bottled water, for China's increasingly health-conscious population. Through the same obsessive focus on scale and speed, Danone has built Wahaha into China's biggest water company—and made China into Danone's biggest water market, with $908 million in revenue in 2001.

In launching a new drink, Danone expects that prices will collapse by 50% within three years, thanks to local competition. Only through investing heavily up-front is it possible to achieve economies of scale and, hence, profitability. "You need to recover your investment before the price wars start," says Simon Israel, Danone's Asia-Pacific chairman. "I've never seen anything move so fast as it does in China."

Rare for multinationals, Danone acquires Chinese companies but continues to sell their products under their own brands. The strategy has smoothed the way for a steady diet of acquisitions and curried favor with Chinese executives and officials, who are loath to see national brands go under.

Today, 80% of Danone's sales here are under Chinese brands. The company has so played down its multinational origins that it was asked by the government to help Wahaha manufacture a "domestic" cola to take on Coke and Pepsi. Thus did Danone, which does not sell soft drinks anywhere else in the world, become the parent of Future Cola, which holds the No. 3 spot in China and is known as "the Chinese people's own cola."

The moves have handed Danone dominance despite its late start. The company had $1.2 billion in sales here in

2001 and is one of China's largest food and beverage concerns. Danone has more than 50 plants and 25,000 employees around the country, all built up in the past six years.

Coca-Cola Co. which has seen eight straight years of profit in China, says sales are growing faster here than anywhere in the world. The Atlanta-based company already reaches 600 million consumers in China's large and medium-size cities, but its latest drive focuses on reaching the other half.

A survey the company conducted in Yunnan, a largely rural province in the southwest, revealed that most consumer offerings, from ice cream to drinks, cost between six cents and 36 cents, which means a 30-cent can of Coke was too expensive for many. Coke's solution: ramp up its business in returnable bottles, in which a customer drinks a Coke on the premises of a shop or restaurant. The business, which drives down costs because bottles and crates can be reused many times, brings the price of a Coke servicing down to a single yuan—about 12 cents.

"We're looking for this to be a solution for our rural markets," says Nick Moore, region manager for the North and Southwest China Region.

Such minute price distinctions are crucial in China. At an Internet cafe in Tangshan, where customers can surf the Web for an hour for a mere 24 cents, 2,000 cases of Coke sold last year, compared with 300 cases in 2001, before Coke launched its cheaper drinks in returnable bottles. "Customers always want the cheapest thing to drink," says the cafe's owner. "Now, the Coke is the same price as the water."

Yum Brands: Localize, Localize

When KFC set up its first China store in 1987, the venture was seen as so politically sensitive that the site required the approval of the Beijing mayor, and foreign novelty was a big part of its appeal. Recently, it took Yum Brands only a day to get most of the approvals it needed to set up a new Pizza Hut restaurant in the central city of Zhengzhou.

Globalization is taking hold in China faster than anyone expected, and fast food has become part of the Chinese landscape. Catering to national tastes, KFC offers soup, rice and Chinese breakfast porridge. It does its own tests and product launches with minimal input from the home office in Louisville, Ky. "We're free to create our own products. Our company is not a company that micro-manages from a distance," says Sam Su, president of Greater China for Yum Restaurants China.

KFC now has about 800 restaurants here and plans to open 200 a year for some time to come, and China is the company's biggest source of profit after the U.S.

Glossary

This glossary of marketing terms is included to provide you with a convenient and ready reference as you encounter general terms in your study of marketing that are unfamiliar or require a review. It is not intended to be comprehensive, but taken together with the many definitions included in the articles themselves, it should prove to be quite useful.

acceptable price range
The range of prices that buyers are willing to pay for a product; prices that are above the range may be judged unfair, while prices below the range may generate concerns about quality.

adaptive selling
A salesperson's adjustment of his or her behavior between and during sales calls, to respond appropriately to issues that are important to the customer.

advertising
Marketing communication elements designed to stimulate sales through the use of mass media displays, direct individual appeals, public displays, give-aways, and the like.

advertorial
A special advertising section in magazines that includes some editorial (nonadvertising) content.

Americans with Disabilities Act (ADA)
Passed in 1990, this U.S. law prohibits discrimination against consumers with disabilities.

automatic number identification
A telephone system that identifies incoming phone numbers at the beginning of the call, without the caller's knowledge.

bait and switch
Advertising a product at an attractively low price to get customers into the store, but making the product unavailable so that the customers must trade up to a more expensive version.

bar coding
A computer-coded bar pattern that identifies a product. *See also* universal product code.

barter
The practice of exchanging goods and services without the use of money.

benefit segmentation
Organizing the market according to the attributes or benefits consumers need or desire, such as quality, service, or unique features.

brand
A name, term, sign, design, symbol, or combination used to differentiate the products of one company from those of its competition.

brand image
The quality and reliability of a product as perceived by consumers on the basis of its brand reputation or familiarity.

brand name
The element of a brand that can be vocalized.

break-even analysis
The calculation of the number of units that must be sold at a certain price to cover costs (break even); revenues earned past the break-even point contribute to profits.

bundling
Marketing two or more products in a single package at one price.

business analysis
The stage of new product development where initial marketing plans are prepared (including tentative marketing strategy and estimates of sales, costs, and profitability).

business strategic plan
A plan for how each business unit in a corporation intends to compete in the marketplace, based upon the vision, objectives, and growth strategies of the corporate strategic plan.

capital products
Expensive items that are used in business operations but do not become part of any finished product (such as office buildings, copy machines).

cash-and-carry wholesaler
A limited-function wholesaler that does not extend credit for or deliver the products it sells.

caveat emptor
A Latin term that means "let the buyer beware." A principle of law meaning that the purchase of a product is at the buyer's risk with regard to its quality, usefulness, and the like. The laws do, however, provide certain minimum protection against fraud and other schemes.

channel of distribution
See marketing channel.

Child Protection Act
U.S. law passed in 1990 to regulate advertising on children's TV programs.

Child Safety Act
Passed in 1966, this U.S. law prohibits the marketing of dangerous products to children.

Clayton Act
Anticompetitive activities are prohibited by this 1914 U.S. law.

co-branding
When two brand names appear on the same product (such as a credit card with a school's name).

comparative advertising
Advertising that compares one brand against a competitive brand on a least one product attribute.

competitive pricing strategies
Pricing strategies that are based on a organization's position in relation to its competition.

consignment
An arrangement in which a seller of goods does not take title to the goods until they are sold. The seller thus has the option of returning them to the supplier or principal if unable to execute the sale.

consolidated metropolitan statistical area (CMSA)
Based on census data, the largest designation of geographic areas. *See also* primary metropolitan statistical area.

consumer behavior
The way in which buyers, individually or collectively, react to marketplace stimuli.

Consumer Credit Protection Act
A 1968 U.S. law that requires full disclosure of the financial charges of loans.

consumer decision process
This four-step process includes recognizing a need or problem, searching for information, evaluating alternative products or brands, and purchasing a product.

Consumer Product Safety Commission (CPSC)
A U.S. government agency that protects consumers from unsafe products.

consumerism
A social movement in which consumers demand better information about the service, prices, dependability, and quality of the products they buy.

convenience products
Consumer goods that are purchased at frequent intervals with little regard for price. Such goods are relatively standard in nature and consumers tend to select the most convenient source when shopping for them.

cooperative advertising
Advertising of a product by a retailer, dealer, distributor, or the like, with part of the advertising cost paid by the product's manufacturer.

corporate strategic plan
A plan that addresses what a company is and wants to become, and then guides strategic planning at all organizational levels.

Glossary

countersegmentation
A concept that combines market segments to appeal to a broad range of consumers, assuming that there will be an increasing consumer willingness to accept fewer product and service choices for lower prices.

customer loyalty concept
To focus beyond customer satisfaction toward customer retention as a way to generate sales and profit growth.

demand curve
A relationship that shows how many units a market will purchase at a given price in a given period of time.

demographic environment
The study of human population densities, distributions, and movements that relate to buying behavior.

derived demand
The demand for business-to-business products that is dependent upon a demand for other products in the market.

differentiated strategy
Using innovation and points of difference in product offerings, advanced technology, superior service, or higher quality in wide areas of market segments.

direct mail promotion
Marketing goods to consumers by mailing unsolicited promotional material to them.

direct marketing
The sale of products to carefully targeted consumers who interact with various advertising media without salesperson contact.

discount
A reduction from list price that is given to a buyer as a reward for a favorable activity to the seller.

discretionary income
The money that remains after taxes and necessities have been paid for.

disposable income
That portion of income that remains after payment of taxes to use for food, clothing, and shelter.

dual distribution
The selling of products to two or more competing distribution networks, or the selling of two brands of nearly identical products through competing distribution networks.

dumping
The act of selling a product in a foreign country at a price lower than its domestic price.

durable goods
Products that continue in service for an appreciable length of time.

economy
The income, expenditures, and resources that affect business and household costs.

electronic data interchange (EDI)
A computerized system that links two different firms to allow transmittal of documents; a quick-response inventory control system.

entry strategy
An approach used to begin marketing products internationally.

environmental scanning
Obtaining information on relevant factors and trends outside a company and interpreting their potential impact on the company's markets and marketing activities.

European Union (EU)
The world's largest consumer market, consisting of 16 European nations: Austria, Belgium, Britain, Denmark, Finland, France, Germany, Greece, Italy, Ireland, Luxembourg, the Netherlands, Norway, Portugal, Spain, and Sweden.

exclusive distribution
Marketing a product or service in only one retail outlet in a specific geographic marketplace.

exporting
Selling goods to international markets.

Fair Packaging and Labeling Act of 1966
This law requires manufacturers to state ingredients, volume, and manufacturer's name on a package.

family life cycle
The progress of a family through a number of distinct phases, each of which is associated with identifiable purchasing behaviors.

Federal Trade Commission (FTC)
The U.S. government agency that regulates business practices; established in 1914.

five C's of pricing
Five influences on pricing decisions: customers, costs, channels of distribution, competition, and compatibility.

FOB (free on board)
The point at which the seller stops paying transportation costs.

four I's of service
Four elements to services: intangibility, inconsistency, inseparability, and inventory.

four P's
See marketing mix.

franchise
The right to distribute a company's products or render services under its name, and to retain the resulting profit in exchange for a fee or percentage of sales.

freight absorption
Payment of transportation costs by the manufacturer or seller, often resulting in a uniform pricing structure.

functional groupings
Groupings in an organization in which a unit is subdivided according to different business activities, such as manufacturing, finance, and marketing.

General Agreement on Tariffs and Trade (GATT)
An international agreement that is intended to limit trade barriers and to promote world trade through reduced tariffs; represents over 80 percent of global trade.

geodemographics
A combination of geographic data and demographic characteristics; used to segment and target specific markets.

green marketing
The implementation of an ecological perspective in marketing; the promotion of a product as environmentally safe.

gross domestic product (GDP)
The total monetary value of all goods and services produced within a country during one year.

growth stage
The second stage of a product life cycle that is characterized by a rapid increase in sales and profits.

hierarchy of effects
The stages a prospective buyer goes through when purchasing a product, including awareness, interest, evaluation, trial, and adoption.

idea generation
An initial stage of the new product development process; requires creativity and innovation to generate ideas for potential new products.

implied warranties
Warranties that assign responsibility for a product's deficiencies to a manufacturer, even though the product was sold by a retailer.

imports
Purchased goods or services that are manufactured or produced in some other country.

integrated marketing communications
A strategic integration of marketing communications programs that coordinate all promotional activities—advertising, personal selling, sales promotion, and public relations.

internal reference prices
The comparison price standards that consumers remember and use to judge the fairness of prices.

introduction stage
The first product life cycle stage; when a new product is launched into the marketplace.

ISO 9000
International Standards Organization's standards for registration and certification of manufacturer's quality management and quality assurance systems.

joint venture
An arrangement in which two or more organizations market products internationally.

just-in-time (JIT) inventory control system
An inventory supply system that operates with very low inventories and fast, on-time delivery.

Lanham Trademark Act
A 1946 U.S. law that was passed to protect trademarks and brand names.

late majority
The fourth group to adopt a new product; representing about 34 percent of a market.

lifestyle research
Research on a person's pattern of living, as displayed in activities, interests, and opinions.

limit pricing
This competitive pricing strategy involves setting prices low to discourage new competition.

limited-coverage warranty
The manufacturer's statement regarding the limits of coverage and noncoverage for any product deficiencies.

logistics management
The planning, implementing, and moving of raw materials and products from the point of origin to the point of consumption.

loss-leader pricing
The pricing of a product below its customary price in order to attract attention to it.

Magnuson-Moss Act
Passed in 1975, this U.S. law regulates warranties.

management by exception
Used by a marketing manager to identify results that deviate from plans, diagnose their cause, make appropriate new plans, and implement new actions.

manufacturers' agent
A merchant wholesaler that sells related but noncompeting product lines for a number of manufacturers; also called manufacturers' representatives.

market
The potential buyers for a company's product or service; or to sell a product or service to actual buyers. The place where goods and services are exchanged.

market penetration strategy
The goal of achieving corporate growth objectives with existing products within existing markets by persuading current customers to purchase more of the product or by capturing new customers.

marketing channel
Organizations and people that are involved in the process of making a product or service available for use by consumers or industrial users.

marketing communications planning
A seven-step process that includes marketing plan review; situation analysis; communications process analysis; budget development; program development integration and implementation of a plan; and monitoring, evaluating, and controlling the marketing communications program.

marketing concept
The idea that a company should seek to satisfy the needs of consumers while also trying to achieve the organization's goals.

marketing mix
The elements of marketing: product, brand, package, price, channels of distribution, advertising and promotion, personal selling, and the like.

marketing research
The process of identifying a marketing problem and opportunity, collecting and analyzing information systematically, and recommending actions to improve an organization's marketing activities.

marketing research process
A six-step sequence that includes problem definition, determination of research design, determination of data collection methods, development of data collection forms, sample design, and analysis and interpretation.

mission statement
A part of the strategic planning process that expresses the company's basic values and specifies the operation boundaries within marketing, business units, and other areas.

motivation research
A group of techniques developed by behavioral scientists that are used by marketing researchers to discover factors influencing marketing behavior.

nonprice competition
Competition between brands based on factors other than price, such as quality, service, or product features.

nondurable goods
Products that do not last or continue in service for any appreciable length of time.

North American Free Trade Agreement (NAFTA)
A trade agreement among the United States, Canada, and Mexico that essentially removes the vast majority of trade barriers between the countries.

North American Industry Classification System (NAICS)
A system used to classify organizations on the basis of major activity or the major good or service provided by the three NAFTA countries—Canada, Mexico, and the United States; replaced the Standard Industrial Classification (SIC) system in 1997.

observational data
Market research data obtained by watching, either mechanically or in person, how people actually behave.

odd-even pricing
Setting prices at just below an even number, such as $1.99 instead of $2.

opinion leaders
Individuals who influence consumer behavior based on their interest in or expertise with particular products.

organizational goals
The specific objectives used by a business or nonprofit unit to achieve and measure its performance.

outbound telemarketing
Using the telephone rather than personal visits to contact customers.

outsourcing
A company's decision to purchase products and services from other firms rather than using in-house employees.

parallel development
In new product development, an approach that involves the development of the product and production process simultaneously.

penetration pricing
Pricing a product low to discourage competition.

personal selling process
The six stages of sales activities that occur before and after the sale itself: prospecting, preapproach, approach, presentation, close, and follow-up.

point-of-purchase display
A sales promotion display located in high-traffic areas in retail stores.

posttesting
Tests that are conducted to determine if an advertisement has accomplished its intended purpose.

predatory pricing
The practice of selling products at low prices to drive competition from the market and then raising prices once a monopoly has been established.

prestige pricing
Maintaining high prices to create an image of product quality and appeal to buyers who associate premium prices with high quality.

pretesting
Evaluating consumer reactions to proposed advertisements through the use of focus groups and direct questions.

price elasticity of demand
An economic concept that attempts to measure the sensitivity of demand for any product to changes in its price.

price fixing
The illegal attempt by one or several companies to maintain the prices of their products above those that would result from open competition.

price promotion mix
The basic product price plus additional components such as sales prices, temporary discounts, coupons, favorable payment and credit terms.

price skimming
Setting prices high initially to appeal to consumers who are not price-sensitive and then lowering prices to appeal to the next market segments.

primary metropolitan statistical area (PMSA)
Major urban area, often located within a CMSA, that has at least one million inhabitants.

PRIZM
A potential rating index by ZIP code markets that divides every U.S. neighborhood into one of 40 distinct cluster types that reveal consumer data.

product
An idea, good, service, or any combination that is an element of exchange to satisfy a consumer.

product differentiation
The ability or tendency of manufacturers, marketers, or consumers to distinguish between seemingly similar products.

product expansion strategy
A plan to market new products to the same customer base.

Glossary

product life cycle (PLC)
A product's advancement through the introduction, growth, maturity, and decline stages.

product line pricing
Setting the prices for all product line items.

product marketing plans
Business units' plans to focus on specific target markets and marketing mixes for each product, which include both strategic and execution decisions.

product mix
The composite of products offered for sale by a firm or a business unit.

promotional mix
Combining one or more of the promotional elements that a firm uses to communicate with consumers.

proprietary secondary data
The data that is provided by commercial marketing research firms to other firms.

psychographic research
Measurable characteristics of given market segments in respect to lifestyles, interests, opinions, needs, values, attitudes, personality traits, and the like.

publicity
Nonpersonal presentation of a product, service, or business unit.

pull strategy
A marketing strategy whose main thrust is to strongly influence the final consumer, so that the demand for a product "pulls" it through the various channels of distribution.

push strategy
A marketing strategy whose main thrust is to provide sufficient economic incentives to members of the channels of distribution, so as to "push" the product through to the consumer.

qualitative data
The responses obtained from in-depth interviews, focus groups, and observation studies.

quality function deployment (QFD)
The data collected from structured response formats that can be easily analyzed and projected to larger populations.

quotas
In international marketing, they are restrictions placed on the amount of a product that is allowed to leave or enter a country; the total outcomes used to assess sales representatives' performance and effectiveness.

regional marketing
A form of geographical division that develops marketing plans that reflect differences in taste preferences, perceived needs, or interests in other areas.

relationship marketing
The development, maintenance, and enhancement of long-term, profitable customer relationships.

repositioning
The development of new marketing programs that will shift consumer beliefs and opinions about an existing brand.

resale price maintenance
Control by a supplier of the selling prices of his branded goods at subsequent stages of distribution, by means of contractual agreement under fair trade laws or other devices.

reservation price
The highest price a consumer will pay for a product; a form of internal reference price.

restraint of trade
In general, activities that interfere with competitive marketing. Restraint of trade usually refers to illegal activities.

retail strategy mix
Controllable variables that include location, products and services, pricing, and marketing communications.

return on investment (ROI)
A ratio of income before taxes to total operating assets associated with a product, such as inventory, plant, and equipment.

sales effectiveness evaluations
A test of advertising efficiency to determine if it resulted in increased sales.

sales forecast
An estimate of sales under controllable and uncontrollable conditions.

sales management
The planning, direction, and control of the personal selling activities of a business unit.

sales promotion
An element of the marketing communications mix that provides incentives or extra value to stimulate product interest.

samples
A small size of a product given to prospective purchasers to demonstrate a product's value or use and to encourage future purchase; some elements that are taken from the population or universe.

scanner data
Proprietary data that is derived from UPC bar codes.

scrambled merchandising
Offering several unrelated product lines within a single retail store.

selected controlled markets
Sites where market tests for a new product are conducted by an outside agency and retailers are paid to display that product; also referred to as forced distribution markets.

selective distribution
This involves selling a product in only some of the available outlets; commonly used when after-the-sale service is necessary, such as in the case of home appliances.

seller's market
A condition within any market in which the demand for an item is greater than its supply.

selling philosophy
An emphasis on an organization's selling function to the exclusion of other marketing activities.

selling strategy
A salesperson's overall plan of action, which is developed at three levels: sales territory, customer, and individual sales calls.

services
Nonphysical products that a company provides to consumers in exchange for money or something else of value.

share points
Percentage points of market share; often used as the common comparison basis to allocate marketing resources effectively.

Sherman Anti-Trust Act
Passed in 1890, this U.S. law prohibits contracts, combinations, or conspiracies in restraint of trade and actual monopolies or attempts to monopolize any part of trade or commerce.

shopping products
Consumer goods that are purchased only after comparisons are made concerning price, quality, style, suitability, and the like.

single-channel strategy
Marketing strategy using only one means to reach customers; providing one sales source for a product.

single-zone pricing
A pricing policy in which all buyers pay the same delivered product price, regardless of location; also known as uniform delivered pricing or postage stamp pricing.

slotting fees
High fees manufacturers pay to place a new product on a retailer's or wholesaler's shelf.

social responsibility
Reducing social costs, such as environmental damage, and increasing the positive impact of a marketing decision on society.

societal marketing concept
The use of marketing strategies to increase the acceptability of an idea (smoking causes cancer); cause (environmental protection); or practice (birth control) within a target market.

specialty products
Consumer goods, usually appealing only to a limited market, for which consumers will make a special purchasing effort. Such items include, for example, stereo components, fancy foods, and prestige brand clothes.

Standard Industrial Classification (SIC) system
Replaced by NAICS, this federal government numerical scheme categorized businesses.

standardized marketing
Enforcing similar product, price, distribution, and communications programs in all international markets.

stimulus-response presentation
A selling format that assumes that a customer will buy if given the appropriate stimulus by a salesperson.

strategic business unit (SBU)
A decentralized profit center of a company that operates as a separate, independent business.

strategic marketing process
Marketing activities in which a firm allocates its marketing mix resources to reach a target market.

strategy mix
A way for retailers to differentiate themselves from others through location, product, services, pricing, and marketing mixes.

subliminal perception
When a person hears or sees messages without being aware of them.

SWOT analysis
An acronym that describes a firm's appraisal of its internal strengths and weaknesses and its external opportunities and threats.

synergy
An increased customer value that is achieved through more efficient organizational function performances.

systems-designer strategy
A selling strategy that allows knowledgeable sales reps to determine solutions to a customer's problems or to anticipate opportunities to enhance a customer's business through new or modified business systems.

target market
A defined group of consumers or organizations toward which a firm directs its marketing program.

team selling
A sales strategy that assigns accounts to specialized sales teams according to a customers' purchase-information needs.

telemarketing
An interactive direct marketing approach that uses the telephone to develop relationships with customers.

test marketing
The process of testing a prototype of a new product to gain consumer reaction and to examine its commercial viability and marketing strategy.

TIGER (Topologically Integrated Geographic Encoding and Reference)
A minutely detailed U.S. Census Bureau computerized map of the U.S. that can be combined with a company's own database to analyze customer sales.

total quality management (TQM)
Programs that emphasize long-term relationships with selected suppliers instead of short-term transactions with many suppliers.

total revenue
The total of sales, or unit price, multiplied by the quantity of the product sold.

trade allowance
An amount a manufacturer contributes to a local dealer's or retailer's advertising expenses.

trade (functional) discounts
Price reductions that are granted to wholesalers or retailers that are based on future marketing functions that they will perform for a manufacturer.

trademark
The legal identification of a company's exclusive rights to use a brand name or trade name.

truck jobber
A small merchant wholesaler who delivers limited assortments of fast-moving or perishable items within a small geographic area.

two-way stretch strategy
Adding products at both the low and high end of a product line.

undifferentiated strategy
Using a single promotional mix to market a single product for the entire market; frequently used early in the life of a product.

uniform delivered price
The same average freight amount that is charged to all customers, no matter where they are located.

universal product code (UPC)
An assigned number to identify a product, which is represented by a series of bars of varying widths for optical scanning.

usage rate
The quantity consumed or patronage during a specific period, which can vary significantly among different customer groups.

utilitarian influence
To comply with the expectations of others to achieve rewards or avoid punishments.

value added
In retail strategy decisions, a dimension of the retail positioning matrix that refers to the service level and method of operation of the retailer.

vertical marketing systems
Centrally coordinated and professionally managed marketing channels that are designed to achieve channel economies and maximum marketing impact.

vertical price fixing
Requiring that sellers not sell products below a minimum retail price; sometimes called resale price maintenance.

weighted-point system
The method of establishing screening criteria, assigning them weights, and using them to evaluate new product lines.

wholesaler
One who makes quantity purchases from manufacturers (or other wholesalers) and sells in smaller quantities to retailers (or other wholesalers).

zone pricing
A form of geographical pricing whereby a seller divides its market into broad geographic zones and then sets a uniform delivered price for each zone.

Sources for the Glossary
Marketing: Principles and Perspectives by William O. Bearden, Thomas N. Ingram, and Raymond W. LaForge (Irwin/McGraw-Hill, 1998);
Marketing by Eric N. Berkowitz (Irwin/McGraw-Hill, 1997); and the *Annual Editions* **staff.**

Test Your Knowledge Form

We encourage you to photocopy and use this page as a tool to assess how the articles in *Annual Editions* expand on the information in your textbook. By reflecting on the articles you will gain enhanced text information. You can also access this useful form on a product's book support Web site at *http://www.dushkin.com/online/*.

NAME: DATE:

TITLE AND NUMBER OF ARTICLE:

BRIEFLY STATE THE MAIN IDEA OF THIS ARTICLE:

LIST THREE IMPORTANT FACTS THAT THE AUTHOR USES TO SUPPORT THE MAIN IDEA:

WHAT INFORMATION OR IDEAS DISCUSSED IN THIS ARTICLE ARE ALSO DISCUSSED IN YOUR TEXTBOOK OR OTHER READINGS THAT YOU HAVE DONE? LIST THE TEXTBOOK CHAPTERS AND PAGE NUMBERS:

LIST ANY EXAMPLES OF BIAS OR FAULTY REASONING THAT YOU FOUND IN THE ARTICLE:

LIST ANY NEW TERMS/CONCEPTS THAT WERE DISCUSSED IN THE ARTICLE, AND WRITE A SHORT DEFINITION:

We Want Your Advice

ANNUAL EDITIONS revisions depend on two major opinion sources: one is our Advisory Board, listed in the front of this volume, which works with us in scanning the thousands of articles published in the public press each year; the other is you—the person actually using the book. Please help us and the users of the next edition by completing the prepaid article rating form on this page and returning it to us. Thank you for your help!

ANNUAL EDITIONS: Marketing 05/06

ARTICLE RATING FORM

Here is an opportunity for you to have direct input into the next revision of this volume.
We would like you to rate each of the articles listed below, using the following scale:

1. **Excellent: should definitely be retained**
2. **Above average: should probably be retained**
3. **Below average: should probably be deleted**
4. **Poor: should definitely be deleted**

Your ratings will play a vital part in the next revision.
Please mail this prepaid form to us as soon as possible.
Thanks for your help!

RATING	ARTICLE		RATING	ARTICLE
	1. The Next 25 Years			35. Global Ads Aim for One Brand, Image
	2. High Performance Marketing			36. Web Plays Vital Role in Marketing Push
	3. Marketing High Technology: Preparation, Targeting, Positioning, Execution			37. Segmenting Global Markets: Look Before You Leap
	4. Brand Killers			38. International Marketing Research: A Management Briefing
	5. Pitching It to Kids			39. The New Land of Opportunity
	6. E-Biz Strikes Again!			40. Made in India vs. Made in China
	7. Marketing Myopia (With Retrospective Commentary)			41. Cracking China's Market
	8. Why Customer Satisfaction Starts With HR			
	9. Start With the Customer			
	10. Talking Shop			
	11. What Drives Customer Equity			
	12. Creating Growth with Services			
	13. Life Support: Hospitals Must Create Brand that Differentiates			
	14. Surviving in the Age of Rage			
	15. Trust in the Marketplace			
	16. Ethics Can Be Gauged by Three Key Rules			
	17. A Different Approach for Developing New Products or Services			
	18. Product by Design			
	19. Marketing Surprise: Older Consumers Buy Stuff, Too			
	20. What Women Want			
	21. Race, Ethnicity and the Way We Shop			
	22. Top Niche: Growth in Asian-Am. Spending Fuels Targeted Marketing			
	23. What Makes Customers Tick?			
	24. Tough Love			
	25. Defining Moments: Segmenting by Cohorts			
	26. The Very Model of a Modern Marketing Plan			
	27. The Power of Design			
	28. In Praise of the Purple Cow			
	29. Have It Your Way			
	30. Kamikaze Pricing			
	31. Mind Your Pricing Cues			
	32. Which Price is Right?			
	33. The Old Pillars of New Retailing			
	34. Got Advertising That Works?			

(Continued on next page)

BUSINESS REPLY MAIL
FIRST CLASS MAIL PERMIT NO. 551 DUBUQUE IA

POSTAGE WILL BE PAID BY ADDRESEE

McGraw-Hill/Dushkin
2460 KERPER BLVD
DUBUQUE, IA 52001-9902

NO POSTAGE
NECESSARY
IF MAILED
IN THE
UNITED STATES

ABOUT YOU

Name

Date

Are you a teacher? ❏   A student? ❏
Your school's name

Department

Address   City   State   Zip

School telephone #

YOUR COMMENTS ARE IMPORTANT TO US!

Please fill in the following information:
For which course did you use this book?

Did you use a text with this ANNUAL EDITION? ❏ yes ❏ no
What was the title of the text?

What are your general reactions to the *Annual Editions* concept?

Have you read any pertinent articles recently that you think should be included in the next edition? Explain.

Are there any articles that you feel should be replaced in the next edition? Why?

Are there any World Wide Web sites that you feel should be included in the next edition? Please annotate.

May we contact you for editorial input? ❏ yes ❏ no
May we quote your comments? ❏ yes ❏ no